WHY PRESIDENTS FAIL

WHY PRESIDENTS FAIL

Richard M. Pious

ROWMAN & LITTLEFIELD PUBLISHERS, INC.
Lanham • Boulder • New York • Toronto • Plymouth, UK

ROWMAN & LITTLEFIELD PUBLISHERS, INC.

Published in the United States of America
by Rowman & Littlefield Publishers, Inc.
A wholly owned subsidary of The Rowman & Littlefield Publishing Group, Inc.
4501 Forbes Boulevard, Suite 200, Lanham, Maryland 20706
www.rowmanlittlefield.com

Estover Road
Plymouth PL6 7PY
United Kingdom

British Library Cataloguing in Publication Information Available

Library of Congress Cataloging-in-Publication Data:

Pious, Richard M., 1944–
  Why presidents fail / Richard M. Pious.
    p. cm.
  Includes bibliographical references and index.
  ISBN-13: 978-0-7425-6284-4 (cloth : alk. paper)
  ISBN-13: 978-0-7425-6285-1 (pbk. : alk. paper)
  ISBN-10: 0-7425-6284-0 (cloth : alk. paper)
  ISBN-10: 0-7425-6285-9 (pbk. : alk. paper)
  e-ISBN-10: 0-7425-6339-1
  e-ISBN-13: 978-0-7425-6339-1
  1. Presidents—United States—History—20th century. 2. Presidents—United States—
History—21st century. 3. Leadership—United States—History—20th century. 4.
Leadership—United States—History—21st century. 5. United States—Politics and
government—20th century. 6. United States—Politics and government—2001– I. Title.
  JK511.P56 2008
  973.92092'2—dc22   2008008901

Printed in the United States of America

∞™ The paper used in this publication meets the minimum requirements of American
National Standard for Information Sciences—Permanence of Paper for Printed Library
Materials, ANSI/NISO Z39.48-1992.

To my students at Barnard College and Columbia University

The only man who never makes a mistake is the man who never does anything.—Theodore Roosevelt

My God, it's as bad as Eisenhower. The worse I do the more popular I get.
—John F. Kennedy

Contents

Acknowledgments   ix

Introduction: Presidential Fiascoes   1

1 Reputation: Eisenhower and the U-2 Flights   11
2 Power Stakes: Kennedy and the Bay of Pigs   29
3 Compellence: Johnson and the Vietnam Escalation   47
4 Command and Control: Ford and the *Mayaguez*   77
5 Rhetoric: Carter and the Malaise Speech   91
6 Prerogative Power: Reagan and the Iran-Contra Affair   115
7 Gamesmanship: Bush 41 and the Budget Summit   149
8 Program Innovation: Clinton and Health Care   183
9 Parallel Governance: Bush and Iraqi Weapons of
   Mass Destruction   217
10 Presidents Unbound: Crises of Authority and Legitimacy   245
11 Risk and Resilience: Toward a White House Learning Curve   279

For Further Reading   299

Index   303

About the Author   317

Acknowledgments

I THANK MY BARNARD COLLEGE and Columbia University students in my graduate-level courses on the presidency and the constitutional law of the presidency, to whom I first introduced the arguments in this book. I also thank my former and present colleagues in the Department of Political Science at Barnard College, many of whom have given me ideas about presidential power and performance, and all of whom have made my professional life so rewarding.

In this same vein I thank former graduate students, now colleagues teaching at other institutions, particularly Brigitte Nacos, Sally Cohen, Larry Jacobs, Nancy Kassop, Kelly Patterson, Judith Russell, and Tom Langston, all of whom have given me useful ideas, primary documents, or alerted me to new research I might find useful. Wynn Waller Pomeroy, a colleague and former graduate student at Columbia University, provided me with materials from the Carter Presidential Library. Jeffrey Helsing, a Columbia graduate student on whose dissertation I served as cosponsor, developed in his work many of the insights and research that I rely upon in my case study on Vietnam (as I acknowledge in the citations to the chapter). As always, the ideas of my friends and colleagues John Chambers, Caren Dubnoff, Louis Fisher, Michael Goldstein, Robert Lamb, Robert Mutch, John Prados, Allan Silver, and Robert Sommers inform my work. I am particularly indebted to David Yao, Thomas Alva Edison Professor of Engineering at Columbia University, for helping me clarify ideas about risk, uncertainty, "high risk" events, and "normal accidents" on our commute to the university. The late Jerome "Jerry" Davis also helped me gain an appreciation for risk and uncertainty in engineering in the defense industry.

I have clarified my thinking about the presidency by participating in several conferences or ongoing seminars, including a conference organized at Oxford by George Edwards III, at which I presented a paper on the war on terrorism; another in London in 2003 for the British Library, at which I presented a paper on prerogative power and the postmodern presidency; and a panel at the American Political Science Association in Boston in 2002, in which I presented a paper on the Iran-Contra affair (with special thanks to Louis Fisher for his insightful critique).

I have also benefited from four sessions that I chaired for students of the CMC Washington Program between 1994–1998: My thanks to Rep. Stephen Solarz, Terry Eastland, and my former students George Stephanopoulos and Abby Lowell for their participation and insights, particularly on questions of political values and ethics, and my thanks to the then director of the program, Michael Goldstein, for inviting me to moderate these sessions. I have gained a great deal of insight from the participants in the Bertelsmann Seminars for German financial commentators and reporters, who put me through the wringer for several years when I presented to them my analysis of the politics of American fiscal policy; and the participants in the Citicorp Foreign Journalists Program, to whom I have presented similar materials for fifteen years. Special thanks to George Edwards III of *Presidential Studies Quarterly* for pushing me hard to bring out the analytical points in my work on presidential budgeting and presidential failure.

My understanding of game simulations, gamesmanship, and spatial positioning, as well as some of the pathologies of rational choice, comes not only from the literature but also from semester-long game simulations I have run for undergraduates at Barnard College and Columbia University, who for more than two decades have enrolled in my colloquium on American political decision making. My deep appreciation goes to the students in that course who have educated me about the difference between decision theory and decision making in practice.

I wish to thank the diplomats I have worked with in the Consulate General of Japan in New York City for helping me place American decision making in comparative perspective.

The reference librarians at Barnard College and Columbia University were most helpful. Nell Dillon-Ermers, the Political Science Departmental Administrator, saved me time and effort with numerous tasks. Invaluable research assistance was provided by Barnard College students Amy Bromberg, Katherine Delaney, Sasha Soreff, and Chlöe Teasdale.

I am indebted to President Judith Shapiro of Barnard College, who appointed me to two five-year terms and then an indefinite term as Adolph and Effie Ochs Professor of American Studies. Attached to the chair was a research stipend, administered by Provost Elizabeth Boylan, that helped me enormously at just the right time. My own experience leads me to be skeptical of claims that you cannot solve problems by throwing money at them.

Finally, heartfelt thanks to my wife, Susan Delancey Weil, and to our children, Samantha and Benjamin, not only for their forbearance while I was writing but also for their faith that although presidents might fail, I would not.

Richard M. Pious
South Salem, New York, 2008

Introduction

Presidential Fiascoes

THIS BOOK IS ABOUT PRESIDENTIAL FIASCOES, about "deep doo-doo," about Mayday, Mayday blunders, about quagmires and swamps and risky business, about the kind of failure that led President John Kennedy to groan after the Bay of Pigs invasion, "How could I have been so stupid?" It is about what the military calls a *fubb* (sanitized as "fouled up beyond belief"), what the French call *une affaire*, the Spanish *un fracaso*, the Chinese *shihbai*, and the Japanese *shippai*. After a "What was I thinking?" blunder, the media pack takes off in hot pursuit, and White House spin artists try to contain the damage and presidential commissions and congressional committees investigate and issue reports. Inspectors general, special prosecutors, or independent counsels may be appointed to investigate illegal acts, while presidents try not to sweat on their upper lip as they proclaim "I am not a crook" or "I was sick at heart" at news conferences.

Learning Curves

"My God, Dean, don't we learn anything?" General Matthew Ridgeway, the commanding officer of U.S. forces during the Korean War, asked Secretary of State Dean Rusk after learning of President Lyndon Johnson's decision to escalate the war in Vietnam.[1] "It is maddening to see one set of White House officials after another, many of them lawyers," columnist David Broder remarked about the Clintons's Whitewater stonewalling, "come in and do the same dumb things, skirting the law and them covering it up, that got their

— 1 —

predecessors in trouble."[2] Why does the same kind of failure occur time and time again? Political strategists and White House counsel surround presidents: Presumably they all know enough to avoid making the mistakes their predecessors have made. Why do presidential failures follow similar scripts? Why is it always déjà vu all over again?

"Human beings have got to examine their failures," Robert McNamara observed about the Vietnam War. "We've got to acquaint people with how dangerous it is for political leaders to behave the way we did."[3] In that spirit I explore "if only I could take it back" decisions, in the same spirit (if not in the exact way) that crash investigators explore air disasters, hospital review committees examine treatment records, human factor analysts look at mishaps on the factory floor, high reliability theorists look at "normal accidents" (in which the interactions of equipment cause accidents even when each part functions according to specifications), telecommunication engineers analyze "rare events," scholars of business organizations examine failure rates, financial engineers analyze "black swans," and intelligence analysts "walk back the cat." I want to question the fundamental assumptions of existing theories about presidential performance and failure and use the conventional axioms, not as givens from which to deduce the probabilities of power, but as assumptions open to question.

In the chapters that follow I take a fresh look at cases that became defining events in presidencies from Dwight Eisenhower's through George W. Bush's. I recount the decisions (hopefully avoiding retrospective reasoning and the tendency toward ex post facto reconstructions that describe events with more intelligibility and structure in the situation than participants experienced at the time) and then draw generalizations about presidential power, authority, rationality, and legitimacy.[4] Throughout these case studies I focus on orthodox insights about the rational choice, cost-benefit analysis, risk management, gamesmanship, positioning, and power stakes and indicate how the use of these insights often creates or compounds failures.

I should add that I am less interested in assigning blame after the fact than in figuring out how presidents might avoid crash-and-burn events in the future. If the first rule for doctors is to do no harm and the first rule for pilots is to get the plane down in one piece, surely for occupants of the White House the first rule should be to avoid the avoidable blunders in decision making.[5]

Performance versus Failure

At the outset we should distinguish routine operations, in which failure rates should approach zero, from risky decisions in which failure is both inevitable and useful and in many instances is a prelude to subsequent successes. For the exceptional decisions—and most White House decision making falls into this category—we should remember that in engineering it is axiomatic that designers learn the most from failure and that one definition of technological progress is the development of new techniques in the aftermath of disasters.[6]

We need to distinguish at the outset between a poor performance and failure. An overloaded plane flying against the wind travels slower than a plane without cargo flying with tailwinds; the performance of the two planes can be quantified and correlated with various factors. Failure is qualitatively different: a plane spinning out of control, an emergency landing, or worse. Quantitatively oriented political scientists deal with performance when they measure public approval ratings, the number of seats the president's party holds in Congress, and the length of time the president has been in office, and correlate these numbers with budget appropriations, support for the president's legislative initiatives, sustaining of vetoes, and appointments and treaties consented to by the Senate. These correlations help us compare presidents and provide baseline measures within a presidency, but they don't tell us anything about the prospects of a presidential collapse. Consider the Clinton presidency: Bill Clinton won in 1992 with the smallest proportion of the voting age population since John Quincy Adams, but for two years his party enjoyed a comfortable margin of seats in the House and Senate. Political scientists correctly predicted that Clinton would enjoy a high "box score" of legislative successes, but they could not—and did not—predict his 1994 midterm electoral debacle. No one using quantitative indicators could have predicted that Clinton would be able to turn his political situation around by *failing* to get a budget compromise in 1995, rather than by making the budget process work. They also failed to predict the rise in his approval ratings during the impeachment crisis and were completely off base when they predicted a Republican gain in House seats in the 1998 midterm elections.[7] They were caught off base by both his failures *and* his successes, because neither had much to do with performance measures.

One way to begin to get a better handle on the relationship between performance and failure is to consider the routing strategy of airlines: By using computerized operation control centers, they can route planes to get the maximum mileage and maximum flight time for crews, subject to federal regulations. The goal is to keep less than 2 percent of fleets and crews idle. Yet this efficiency comes at a price: Any small disturbance (such as bad weather) plays havoc with scheduling, and delays may cascade, crews may remain in the air too long (in which case they must be grounded for legally mandated rest periods) or they may sit on the ground when they should be in the air. Airlines try to control—or as they put it to "truncate"—the cascade, but the paradox remains that high performance increases the odds of failure because there is no margin for error.[8] The White House is also subject to performance paradoxes: A poorly performing presidency sometimes avoids failure *because* of its low routine performance; a high-flying presidency may go into a tailspin.

Failure analysis studies performance factors at the moment they become qualitatively different (i.e., when headwinds turn into a storm and gusts turn into a downdraft), or when components supporting a system suddenly interact destructively. In studying presidential decision making we must look at these "crash-and-burn" spectaculars.[9] We must also look for what engineers call *signal events*: disasters that reveal previously unknown or underestimated dangers.[10] To make things right in the White House we first have to see what occurs when things go horribly wrong.

Personality and Leadership

Is it just a question of getting the right person into the Oval Office? There is a lesson recounted by military historians that goes something like this. The Prussian General Staff in the 1890s classified junior officers according to several traits: The intelligent and active were suitable for the highest levels; the intelligent and passive were shunted off to less important staff positions; the stupid and passive were suitable for line commands if they showed sufficient bravery. The final classification was of stupid and active officers, and these were marked down for dismissal lest they endanger their troops in combat. If only it were as easy to classify potential presidents and weed out the stupid and active who are prone to fail.

But there is no single kind of presidential personality or leadership style that causes presidential failure: Incumbents of different levels of intellect and energy, with different leadership styles and character, all make disastrous decisions. Presidents who love their job, enjoy life, and define their responsibilities expansively are no more likely to escape from fiascoes than energetic presidents with unresolved personality problems who rigidly adhere to a failing course of action in crises.[11] Clinton, for instance, was the antithesis of the rigidifying personality type: With his ebullience, his love for life, his gargantuan appetites, his zest for political maneuver, and his willingness to cut corners, he was the closest we have come in the postwar period to the two Roosevelts in pure political skill and the zest for playing it. Yet Clinton was *too* willing to maneuver and *too* willing to jettison principles. He didn't get into trouble because he rigidified; he got into trouble because he improvised and transgressed ethical boundaries. Clinton and Richard Nixon stand at opposite ends of the continuum in terms of personality traits, yet both wound up in impeachment crises. What one can say about the "rigidification" hypothesis can be said about any other generalization about the relationship between presidential personality and failure: Presidents with different personality traits often wind up in similar swamps. Dwight Eisenhower approved the Bay of Pigs concept and Kennedy authorized the operation, yet the personalities of the two presidents could hardly have been more dissimilar, and neither was able to understand the risks involved in approving the operation.

Supposedly amateurs in the White House, who think first of the public interest and then of strategy and tactics, will fail because they don't guard their reputation for effectiveness and they don't understand or protect their power stakes. They don't make decisions today that will provide them with influence tomorrow. They don't understand their vantage points and their leverage. Supposedly professionals, who define the public interest itself in terms of their own power stakes, will succeed because they know how to play all the political angles.[12] These distinctions are designed to help us understand the difference between a Franklin Roosevelt and an Eisenhower or a Kennedy and a Carter or a Bush and a Clinton, but they are problematic for two reasons. First, the extent to which so-called amateur presidents acted in the public interest rather than in their own political interests may be vastly overstated. Eisenhower, for example, seems to have played a "hidden hand," in which pretending to act in an amateurish and a nonpartisan and nonpolitical manner was a key element in his deception.[13] As a soldier and as a poker player, he knew that on some occasions it pays to be underestimated. Second, the "professional versus amateur" distinction cannot account for the spectacular failures of presidents such as Nixon, Johnson, or Clinton, all of whom understood and acted on their power stakes and showed no signs of sacrificing their political interests for any abstract conception of the public interest. If anything, being considered "professionals" by the Washington community and the electorate may have been counterproductive for them.

Do presidents conduct transactions with other politicians, negotiating with legislators, bargaining with governors, offering favors and benefits for constituencies and constituents? Or do they transform the political landscape by redefining the public interest and reshaping fundamental values? Some argue the case for presidents who act as transformational lions; others believe that transactional foxes do better.[14] There is no evidence that adopting either a bold or a cautious style makes a difference in avoiding catastrophic decisions. For every Wilson or Roosevelt who succeeds in gaining passage of a New Freedom or New Deal, there is a Carter or Clinton, washed up on the rocks early in their terms after attempting bold transformations in policy areas such as energy and health. Who today remembers Carter's "New Foundation" or Clinton's "New Covenant"? And for every Eisenhower whose modest steps and "middle of the road" course ensured him two terms and high approval ratings, there is a Ford or Bush 41, turned out of office after one term for similar centrist positioning and modest rhetoric and results.

Do good presidential advisers help presidents avoid failure? We might assume that a president who gets good advice will succeed, and conversely, that failure is due primarily to a poorly managed and dysfunctional advisory system. But when presidents have failed, often they and their advisers have thought clearly about issues and the politics surrounding these issues; when they have succeeded sometimes it is because they have bypassed or ignored their principal aides, as Kennedy did with the majority of the national security advisers on his "ExComm" committee during the Cuban Missile Crisis.[15]

Some political scientists believe that presidents such as Thomas Jefferson, Andrew Jackson, Abraham Lincoln, and Franklin Roosevelt created *regimes*: stable relationships for mutual advantage among the elected officials in Washington, voting blocs mobilized by party organizations, and interest groups. Their argument is that regime creators (such as FDR) will be more successful than presidents who inherit regimes and simply maintain them (such as Harry Truman), or those who get elected from the minority party in a deviating election (such as Eisenhower).[16] But Washington, Jefferson, Jackson, Lincoln, and Franklin Roosevelt all had their fiascoes: One need only recall Washington's failure to win diplomatic concessions from the British in the Jay Treaty, which was one of the catalysts for development of political parties that he had hoped to avoid; Jefferson's unsuccessful prosecution of Aaron Burr for treason and his failed embargo policy during the Napoleonic Wars; Jackson's Specie Circular that sparked a financial panic and depression; Lincoln's failures in prodding a succession of generals to fight in the early stages of the war; and Roosevelt's court-packing scheme that ended his chances to get Congress to pass additional New Deal legislation.

The Failure Machine

Would presidents fail less often if they adopted cost-benefit and other quantitative decision making techniques of rational choice? Traditionally the vocation of the democratic politician is to be a conciliator, a broker, or a fixer, who uses favors, side payments, compromises, logrolls, package deals, and other techniques to build temporary majority coalitions. A political decision always involves some shift from a prior position: the honoring or abandonment of a pledge; the granting or denial of an approval; the fixing of an unpleasant situation or a decision not to pull strings; the making or an appointment or the firing of an official; the willingness to change procedures or insistence that they be followed.

Presidents, like all politicians, *substitute* their own decisional rules for what would otherwise be "rational" economic payoffs. That is why we have politicians: If we didn't want these substitutions we could simply leave to nonpartisan professional managers the responsibility to make "rational choices" in running the country. There is, however, one similarity between political and rational decision making: The substitution occurs because presidents face uncertainty (where odds are not known), wish to convert uncertainty into risk (where odds are known), and then try to play the odds after doing all they can to minimize their risks. But political rationality should never be confused with the cost-benefit calculus of economic rationality: The politician's course of action must take into account not only distributions of tangible goods but also intellectual and moral authority, constitutional legitimacy, and democratic accountability.

There is a strategic approach to the presidency, developed by the dean of presidency scholars Richard Neustadt, that equates a president's own political stakes with the national interest. This precept, which has become a central axiom of presidential studies since the 1960s, argues that the president has more information, a better advisory system, and a wider vantage point from which to see and weigh the national interest than anyone else. What presidents see as good politics for themselves will come closer to viable public policy than any other definition of the national interest.

In the chapters to come I want to consider the validity of Neustadt's assumptions in the *hard* cases—in the risky business of the White House: covert operations, crisis diplomacy, military actions, and big-ticket domestic programs. Typically when a fiasco occurs, retrospective explanations (backward mapping) focus on dysfunctions in decision making. No one doubts that there is plenty of irrational decision making and therefore plenty of blame to go around. But I want to pose some heretical questions that have not been raised by presidency watchers: What happens when presidents *do* formulate policies to protect their political stakes? When *do* they control the implementation of their decisions? When *do* they make rational choices to maximize their preferences? Is it possible that they fail *because* they are able to implement their decisions, *because* they act in a politically astute manner, *because* they are adept at gamesmanship and positioning and rational choice? What if the White House *systematically* produces certain kinds of errors that are likely to lead to fiascoes? What if the presidency is *organized* to do so?[17]

Is it possible that presidents fail *because* they understand their power stakes and have taken rational decisions in accordance with them? Do their policies go awry when presidential command and control reign supreme and they can implement policy unilaterally? Is it the case that *because* the office has become "the presidency," equipped with a huge staff in the West Wing and agencies in the Executive Office Buildings, *because* presidents can "go public" and attempt to capture the national agenda, and *because* presidents have claimed vast formal powers through historical and case law precedents and by delegation from Congress—they have failed?

Raising these questions about the limits of decision making based on power stakes and rational choice flies in the face of much of the conventional wisdom about the modern presidency and much of the newer theoretical approaches to White House decision making. So be it. The presidency itself has always been a work in progress, and there is no reason to assume that the collected wisdom of presidency watchers is not a work in progress as well.

Notes

1. Quoted in Robert Buzzanco, *Masters of War: Military Dissent and Politics in the Vietnam Era* (Cambridge, UK: Cambridge University Press, 1996), 227.

2. David Broder, "An Aide's Higher Loyalty," *Washington Post National Weekly Edition* (July 7, 1997): 2.

3. David K. Shipler, "Robert McNamara and the Ghosts of Vietnam," *New York Times Magazine* (August 10, 1997): 30.

4. My focus is not on the form of government itself (macro), nor on a single case study of events (micro), but it is a "meso" level of analysis, dealing with the workings of an institution (in this case the presidency) in dealing with policy problems. For a discussion of this level of analysis see Mark Bovens and Paul 't Hart, *Understanding Policy Fiascoes* (New Brunswick, NJ: Transaction Publishers, 1996), 106–7. Also see Paul Ormerod, *Why Most Things Fail: Evolution, Extinction and Economics* (New York: Pantheon, 2007).

5. A brief methodological note for my political science colleagues: My method is problem-driven rather than theory-driven. I use selective, empirical, exploratory case studies of presidential decision making to develop inductive propositions about presidential failures. These case studies have not been randomly chosen (a prerequisite for any statistical generalization), but they are intended to cover many of the "defining moments" of recent presidencies. I am not interested in systematically generating or testing propositions, either logically through formal models or statistically with random case studies: What I come up with does not fall into the category of "social science" because it produces neither a general axiomatic theory nor statistical generalizations. What I am doing here is considerably more modest: illustrating phenomena that may occur, but without a specification of when or how often. This approach is similar to that used in operations research, particularly in "rare event" analysis, in which the purpose of investigation is not to assess probabilities through factor analysis but rather to discover the critical path that led to an event and devise a method to close off the path and prevent a reoccurrence. My ontological approach for the case studies involves "backward mapping," which begins with operations and traces decisions backward and upward toward the White House. The bias in this approach, well known to policy analysts, is that blame for failure also tends to shift up the chain of

command, at least when compared with a forward-mapping methodology. My own cultural orientation is egalitarian rather than individualist and market-oriented, and I focus on failure in the context of improving the authority, legitimacy, and just acts of government. As for my epistemological biases, my work lies more in the positivist rather than in the postmodern "interpretivist" tradition. I do not agree with those who see most failure and fiascoes as culturally or socially constructed, though I do agree that real-world failures become grist for politics and that there are politically driven definitions of failure. My research approach is eclectic, borrowing from risk analysis, rational choice, operations research, cultural anthropology, history, policy analysis, and social psychology as well as political science. In prescriptive terms, I am an institutional realist, who believes that some problems of the presidency can be resolved by changing the way the institution works, but I am also, as a presidency scholar, inclined to focus directly on the president, rather than on the institutionalized presidency as the prime causal agent for presidential failures.

6. On the positive effects of failure in promoting technological innovation, see Edward Tenner, *Why Things Bite Back: Technology and the Revenge of Unintended Consequences* (New York: Alfred A. Knopf, 1996), especially 18–20, 256, 273–77; also Henry Petroski, *To Engineer Is Human: The Role of Failure in Successful Design* (New York: Vintage, 1982).

7. On the need for public opinion researchers to consider new variables see Samuel Kernell, "The Challenge Ahead for Explaining President Clinton's Public Support," *PRG Report* vol. XXI, no. 3 (Spring 1999): 1–3.

8. James Gleick, "Flight Control," *New York Times Magazine* (April 20, 1997): 24.

9. See the Failure Database Project of the Japanese government at shippai.jst.go.jp; also the Association for the Study of Failure, www.shippai.org.

10. Paul Slovic, "Perception of Risk," *Science* vol. 236, no. 4799 (April 17, 1987): 280–85.

11. James David Barber, *The Presidential Character: Predicting Presidential Performance in the White House*, Fourth Edition (Englewood Cliffs, NJ: Prentice-Hall, 1992).

12. Richard Neustadt, *Presidential Power and the Modern Presidents: The Politics of Leadership from Roosevelt to Reagan* (New York: John Wiley, 1960).

13. Fred Greenstein, *The Hidden-Hand Presidency: Eisenhower as Leader* (New York: Basic Books, 1982).

14. James MacGregor Burns, *Leadership* (New York: Harper & Row, 1978).

15. Richard M. Pious, "The Cuban Missile Crisis and the Limits of Crisis Management," *Political Science Quarterly* (Winter 2001): 81–106.

16. Stephen Skowronek, *The Politics Presidents Make: Leadership from John Adams to Bill Clinton* (Cambridge, MA: Belknap Press of Harvard University, 1993).

17. These questions are well known to organizational theorists. See Diane Vaughan, *The Challenger Launch Decision: Risky Technology, Culture, and Deviance at NASA* (Chicago: University of Chicago Press, 1996), xiv.

1

Reputation

Eisenhower and the U-2 Flights

T HE POINT OF LYING FOR A POLITICIAN—of making statements with the intent to mislead—is to change power relationships, to block others from attaining their objectives, to obscure their choices, to distort their estimates of costs and benefits, to interfere with others' calculations about their options. The benefits of lying may well be outweighed by the costs: the strain of keeping the story going, the coarsening of character that affects the liar as well as those lied to, and eventually, the loss of reputation.[1]

In foreign affairs, lies may involve "reasons of state" that cushion diplomatic relations. While the philosopher Kant argues that "truthfulness is a duty no circumstances may abrogate," and others suggest that lying requires a reason, a justification for the act, while truth-telling does not and is self-evidently good—this is not how diplomats see it.[2] They would argue that candor can be brutal, that truth can be an act of aggression, and that lying at times is the right thing to do. As Grotius did, they claim that a misstatement is a lie only if it conflicts with the rights of the person to whom it is addressed. To stop a crime, to hinder an evildoer, to prevent the loss of innocent life, to advance the public good, to smooth roiled relations among nations—a lie might well be justified.

What of lying and deception in crisis situations? The Greeks used the word *krisis* in a double sense: It not only meant dangerous times in which actions were required but also referred to the internal "action," the moral choices that the leader faces. In this sense its double meaning parallels the double sense of a lie, both as a misstatement of fact and as a decision to deceive. The choice of whether to lie or to tell the truth becomes apparent to the leader and to others, affecting his or her moral authority and legitimacy.

President Dwight Eisenhower found this out the hard way just before a four-power summit meeting in Paris: He hoped to gain the Soviet Union's assent to a comprehensive test-ban treaty as a prelude to a broader détente. As part of his presummit preparations, Eisenhower ordered a reconnaissance flight of "The Deuce," the U-2 plane he believed to be invulnerable to Soviet antiaircraft missiles.[3] On May 1, 1960, a plane piloted by Francis Gary Powers took off for a flight across Russia, triggering the biggest foreign policy blunder of the Eisenhower presidency—one that would force the president to confront the dilemmas of deceit, at a huge cost to his reputation at home and abroad.

Operational Failure

Power's flight, designed to monitor the Soviet installation of ballistic missiles, was troubled from the start: The weather was poor and at times the autopilot didn't work, requiring him to fly the plane manually. Because his maps and bearings were inaccurate, he often drifted off course and had to use dead reckoning and bearings from radio stations. At Sverdlovsk, 1,200 miles into the flight, Powers heard an explosion near the tail of the plane; the U-2 was damaged and began spinning downward out of control, and he decided to bail out at 15,000 feet.[4] A destruct mechanism, 2.5 pounds of cyclonite, was attached to the aft bulkhead, but Powers was unable (or unwilling) to activate it before he jumped.[5] His U-2 was the first plane shot down by the new Soviet surface-to-air missile, the SA-2. In spite of his James Bond equipment—six currencies, two gold watches, gold coins, gold rings, pistol with silencer, flares, and an American flag poster (saying in fourteen languages, "I am an American and do not speak your language. I need food, shelter and assistance. I will not harm you. I bear no malice toward your people. If you help me, you will be rewarded"), Powers was captured and brought to Moscow. On him were two identification cards, two driver's licenses, two flying licenses, a Selective Service card, a Social Security Card, and other identification, all in his name.[6]

President Eisenhower was informed that the plane was missing, and the CIA confirmed that the plane had been downed. A preapproved cover story was activated: NASA announced that a weather plane on a joint NASA–air force flight was missing. The pilot, identified as a Lockheed Corporation employee under contract to NASA, had "reported over the emergency frequency that he was experiencing oxygen difficulties" and a search of the area in Turkey was under way. The Russians countered with their own version: Soviet Premier Nikita Khrushchev announced at a presummit meeting of the Central

Committee, with world media in attendance, that a spy plane had been shot down by Soviet air defenses. But he did not reveal anything about the fate of the pilot, leaving the impression that the pilot had not been taken alive. "The question then arises," he asked the delegates, "who sent this aircraft across the Soviet frontier? Was it the American Commander in Chief who, as everyone knows, is the President? Or was this aggressive act performed by the Pentagon without the President's knowledge?" He offered Eisenhower a diplomatic way out: "I do not doubt President Eisenhower's sincere desire for peace."

Risk Assessment

Before considering Eisenhower's options and his reaction to Khrushchev's gambit, we need to backtrack to consider the decisions he had already made. Why had he sent the U-2 over the Soviet Union just prior to a summit?

The U-2 had been the brainchild of the intelligence community. In 1954, Edwin Land (inventor of the Polaroid instant developing film camera), a member of a subpanel of Eisenhower's scientific advisory panel, proposed a high-altitude plane to fly over the Soviet Union. Eisenhower assigned the operation to the CIA since military overflights could be construed as an act of war. The CIA ordered twenty planes (at a cost of $20 million) to be designed by the "Skunk Works" at Lockheed Aircraft. Land developed a "type B" camera with thirty-six inch focal length lenses fitted for the plane. "Well boys, I believe the country needs this information, and I'm going to approve it. But I tell you one thing. Some day one of these machines is going to be caught and we're going to have a storm," Eisenhower told his advisers in 1955.[7] The National Aeronautics and Space Council announced that it had procured weather research aircraft that would make high altitude flights from Turkey, Norway, West Germany, Pakistan, Japan, and Alaska.

Every U-2 flight was approved personally by the president (sometimes with modifications of flight plans) after consulting with his top civilian advisers: the secretaries of state and defense, the chair of the Joint Chiefs of Staff, the director of central intelligence, and his military assistant Andrew Goodpastor. After Eisenhower approved a flight, Goodpastor would give the orders to CIA deputy director Richard Bissell, in charge of the operation.[8] CIA director Allen Dulles would brief the president and provide him with reconnaissance photos.

The system was designed to offer the president plausible deniability: He could feign ignorance about the program and about specific flights if they were discovered. Eisenhower's advisers understated the risks involved: They told him there was a good chance Soviet radar would not even pick them up.

Yet the first two U-2 flights across the Soviet border in 1956 showed up on radar, including one that passed right over Moscow. The Soviets made a diplomatic protest five days later, and the State Department, in its response, claimed that no *military* plane had violated Soviet airspace (technically true, since the program was run by the CIA). The CIA also told Eisenhower that the flimsy U-2 would disintegrate if it were ever shot down and that no pilot could survive a crash at high altitude. But it seemed to have never occurred to the CIA that the film might survive; evidence of intelligence activity.[9] The CIA told Eisenhower that the U-2s were fitted with a device that would destroy the plane; in fact, the two and one-half pounds of explosive charge could do no such thing and had to be activated by the pilots, who were told that they should throw a "destruct" switch before ejecting from the plane, and then they would have seventy seconds to get clear (which was not true). They were also provided with a parachute, a survival pack, and a needle dipped with curare to commit suicide. But they were not ordered to do so—the CIA indicated to them that they were expected to survive ejection, an impression the agency fostered because it boosted pilot morale—which was inconsistent with the curare. The CIA's approach almost guaranteed that if a plane went down over Soviet territory, the pilot *would* try to survive.

The flights pushed the envelope of existing technology. Several crashed or made forced landings, although none over hostile territory. When U-2s crashed, most of the wreckage fell to the ground intact and the pilots lived. In 1958, a "worst-case scenario" occurred: The CIA was engaged in a covert program to destabilize the Indonesian government, and Allen Pope, the pilot of a U-2 flying over one of the islands, was shot down and captured and was to be put on trial. The price set by President Achmed Sukarno for releasing Pope was for the CIA to disengage from its Indonesian activities.

Eisenhower now recognized the risks of continuing the program. He asked his Board of Consultants on Foreign Intelligence Activities to reevaluate the usefulness of the U-2 flights. With the board remaining enthusiastic, Eisenhower continued the program against his better judgment.[10] Eventually spy satellites could replace the U-2, but as of May 1960, there had been thirteen unsuccessful launches of reconnaissance satellites, either because the launcher or the camera on board had malfunctioned.[11] U-2 flights would continue until the satellites were up and cameras working.

Presummit Calculations

For their own presummit "one-upmanship," the Soviets were planning to launch either a space mission or test a new ICBM (intercontinental ballistic missile). The CIA wanted authorization for several flights over Soviet territory to find out what was to occur. The CIA conducted one (and the Soviets made no protest), then the CIA asked for another: Officials wanted a look at a new missile base at Plesetsk (which might be equipped with the first operational SS-6 ICBMs); they also wanted to see the military industrial complex at Sverdlovsk and the space center of Tyuratam. Eisenhower authorized the flight, provided it took place prior to April 25, 1960, but when bad weather delayed the mission, he agreed it could take place as late as May 1—after that it would be too close to the summit.

Why was the flight so important? The CIA wanted to find out, prior to summit negotiations, whether the Soviets had deployed their first operational ICBMs so that the administration would know whether a "missile gap" existed. The agency argued that in northern latitudes there was only a small window of opportunity for photos, between April and September (because of the angle of the sun), and in that time frame, there would be only a few days without clouds. It was also essential to fly at the earliest opportunity, before roofing was put over key facilities under construction. The CIA wanted as many flights as possible, before the Soviets deployed new SAMs (surface-to-air missiles).

Eisenhower approved an extremely risky flight plan. The plane, *Article 360*, was one of the worst in the fleet; it had almost crashed a year before at Atsugi, Japan, due to problems with its fuel feed line. Powers would have his flying skills taxed to the limit: He would be close to running out of fuel if he went too high but would be vulnerable to the new SAM-2 Guideline missiles if he flew below 60,000 feet. Since the U-2 was expected to fly at 68,000 feet, there was a small margin. The flight was to be the longest ever attempted: 3,800 statute miles (of which 2,920 would be over the Soviet Union) from Peshawar, Pakistan, to Bodo, Norway (on a difficult landing field), and it was the first flight that would transverse Soviet territory from South to North.

The CIA followed the assumption of former Secretary of State John Foster Dulles, who reassured the president that the Soviets would never admit if they shot down a plane because it "would make it necessary for them to admit also that for years we had been carrying on flights over their territory while the Soviets had been helpless to do anything about the matter."[12] The cover story concocted in 1956 had assumed that any U-2 shot down would be destroyed, and the pilot would not survive. It was not revised even after Pope's Indonesian experience.

Crisis Containment

Those who believed that the Russians would never reveal a downed plane were wrong: Khrushchev's statement indicated that the Soviets intended to make the U-2 an international issue. Khrushchev genuinely was enraged at Eisenhower for complicating his position in the Presidium and the Central Committee. Eisenhower, "his friend," had played him for a fool and shown him a complete lack of respect with this intrusion so close to the summit.

This was a summit Khrushchev had wanted: After meeting President Eisenhower at Camp David in September 1959, he had dropped his November 1958 threat that he would sign a treaty with East Germany (opposed by NATO). His negotiating team at Geneva had agreed in February 1960 to allow Western inspection teams into the Soviet Union to investigate suspect earth tremors if a nuclear test-ban treaty were signed. Khrushchev believed that in return for progress on the test-ban treaty, he could negotiate agreements that would enable him to gain new Western concessions on Berlin. Moreover, a summit would ratify his status as an equal with the other leaders of the great powers. Just before the summit Semyon Tsarapkin, his chief negotiator at the Geneva arms talks, had made fresh concessions on verification. But Khrushchev's political position was shaky: Just before the summit some of his supporters had been replaced on the Presidium and the Central Committee. Field Marshall Rodion Malinovsky was to go with Khrushchev to the summit to see that he followed Presidium policy. Now the failed U-2 flight would play right into the hands of the hard-liners who saw little or no use for his policy of détente. In the aftermath of the U-2 flight Khrushchev would have to hit back hard at the Americans to bolster his own position.

Initially Eisenhower's cover story held. On May 6, the *New York Times* ran a banner headline, "Soviet Downs American Plane; U.S. Says It Was Weather Flight," and in the story (five columns from the right) the headline read: "Capital Explains: Reports Unarmed U-2 Vanished at Border after Difficulty." The plane was unarmed, on a scientific mission, and was clearly marked with NASA insignia and could fly up to 55,000 feet, according to the administration. Eisenhower was said to have ordered an immediate inquiry, and the State Department was to take up the fate of the pilot with Soviets: A U.S. note asked for information about the pilot, reiterating that it was an unarmed weather plane. The State Department questioned why the weaponless plane was not just forced down. On May 6 the Soviets released photographs of a plane purported to be the downed U-2, but it showed a different model, leading U.S. intelligence analysts to assume that Power's U-2 had disintegrated when it was shot down, that he had died, and that the Soviets had neither the pilot nor the plane. The following day NASA announced that "all U-2 weather observation planes" based in foreign countries would be grounded to check their oxygen systems, while State Department spokesperson Lincoln White told reporters at a department news briefing, "There was absolutely no—N-O—no deliberate attempt to violate Soviet airspace. There never has been."

Up until this point Eisenhower and his spokespersons had used the cover story. In doing so, they disobeyed some of the maxims Eisenhower had laid down for himself, first as a military tactician and then as president. His "hidden hand" approach to the presidency required that he never make decisions in a contest with others until two conditions were satisfied: First, that he had a good grasp of the motivation and capabilities of the other side; second, that his opponents were deceived about his motivations and capabilities.[13] As it turned out, in the U-2 crisis the Soviets played the hidden hand against Eisenhower. On May 7 Khrushchev showed photographs of the U-2 to the Supreme Soviet, and added, "We also have the pilot, who is quite alive and kicking." He presented Powers to a group of Western journalists, which destroyed the American cover story. Now he offered Eisenhower what looked like a face-saving diplomatic way out: "I am quite willing to grant that the President knew nothing about the fact that such a plane was sent into the Soviet Union. . . . But this should put us even more on guard."[14] He blamed the "militarists" in the United States who "run the show." Eisenhower now faced a dilemma: He could take full responsibility for authorizing the flights, which would put him on a collision course with the Soviet leaders; or he could use his "plausible deniability," which would minimize the confrontation with the Soviets but would also confirm the Soviet claim that "militarists" controlled the American government.

Lincoln White briefed reporters and released a statement after clearing it with the president: "As a result of the inquiry ordered by the President," White told reporters, "it has been established that insofar as the authorities are concerned, there was no authorization for any such flights as described by Mr. Khrushchev." There was, however, a qualification, inconsistent with the first statement: "Nevertheless, it appears that in endeavoring to obtain information now concealed behind the Iron Curtain, a flight over Soviet territory was probably taken by an unarmed civilian U-2 plane." Finally, White attempted to justify the flights: "It is in relation to the danger of surprise attack that planes of the type of unarmed civilian U-2 aircraft have made flights along the frontiers of the Free World for the past four years." The statement raised more questions than it answered. If there were no authorization, then did the pilot just decide on his own to fly over the Soviet Union? If the flight were a violation of U.S. policy, then why the attempt to justify surveillance behind the Iron Curtain by raising the specter of surprise attack?

White House press secretary Jim Haggerty announced that the administration had ordered the resumption of underground nuclear testing to improve the American ability to monitor underground tests through seismic instruments—hardly an announcement to calm the roiled waters. Meanwhile the State Department retracted the original NASA cover story, claiming NASA had issued it "in good faith," a qualifier that made no sense at all, since an agency that issues a cover story knows full well that the flight in question, if not its own, must be covering up something. Newspaper columnists James Reston and Walter Lippmann both asked the same question: Who, then, is running the U.S. government? Lippmann observed, "In denying that it authorized the flight, the Administration has entered a plea of incompetence." The criticisms hit home: Eisenhower had smarted for years when critics called him disengaged, amateurish, and unable to run his government. Now he had to face up to the consequences of a misplayed hand: a bluff that the Soviets had successfully called.

As a former military leader, Eisenhower was uncomfortable with the idea that a top commander could evade accountability for the performance of his subordinates. He felt that he had to reassure other world leaders that he was in control in key national security matters; otherwise, they might believe that rogue officials could start a crisis on their own. Eisenhower now told Secretary of State Christian Herter that he intended to take full responsibility.[15] "We're going to take a beating on this," he told the National Security Council on May 9. "And I'm the one, rightly, who is going to have to take the brunt."[16]

Abandoning the option of "plausible denial" was the worst possible approach the president could take in dealing with the Soviets. "This U-2 thing has put me in a terrible spot," Khrushchev told U.S. ambassador Llewellyn Thompson in Moscow, adding, "You have got to get me off it."[17] But immediately thereafter, at the State Department briefing on May 9, Secretary Herter admitted in a two-page statement read to reporters by Lincoln White that flights had been conducted under a presidential directive, which contradicted the original cover story.[18] Eisenhower was trying to have it both ways: He did not assume the responsibility for Power's flight, but he was in control of his administration and not the "militarists":

> In accordance with the National Security Act of 1947, the President has put into effect . . . directives to gather by every possible means the information required to protect . . . against surprise attack. . . . Programs have been developed and put into operation which have included extensive aerial surveillance by unarmed civilian aircraft, normally of a peripheral character but on occasion by penetration. Specific missions . . . have not been subject to Presidential authorization.

The statement was misleading on three counts: There was *no* evidence that the president in ordering these flights was worried about surprise attack by the Soviets; specific missions *were* subject to presidential authorization; and Powers's flight *had* been authorized by the president. From a diplomatic standpoint, the statement would not make Khrushchev's position any easier in the Kremlin because it left open the possibility that Eisenhower might order U-2 surveillance in the future. The Soviet leader saw it as a deliberate rebuff of his request to Thompson that Eisenhower help him out and as a calculated insult.[19]

Up to that time American newspapers had accepted the government's version of events and had put quotation marks around Khrushchev's accounts to undercut them. After Herter's statement was released, all subsequent statements by U.S. officials were dissected and analyzed for inconsistencies and evasions, while the Soviet version of the facts was accepted. However, American reporting now developed new criteria to fault the Soviets: If Khrushchev *in this instance* was not lying, nevertheless he was ill-mannered, hostile, aggressive, and deceptive. He had not, after all, initially told the truth about the pilot—just the sort of trick one would expect from the Soviets.[20] Khrushchev accommodated himself all too well to the media characterization of him as an aggressive bully: On May 9 he threatened to bomb bases in any country that permitted U-2 flights over the Soviet Union. On May 10 the United States pledged to defend its allies if their bases were attacked (as Lincoln White stated that other nations didn't know of these flights, which was another falsehood); on May 11 Khrushchev said he "was horrified to learn that the President had endorsed the acts."

That same day Eisenhower held a news conference and reiterated that he was taking responsibility: "Ever since the beginning of my administration," Eisenhower said, "I have issued directives to gather, in every feasible way, the information required to protect the United States and the free world against surprise attack and to enable them to make effective preparations for defense." He added that "No one wants another Pearl Harbor," so the United States must know the probability of a surprise attack. The flights were "a vital necessity" because the Soviets "make a fetish of secrecy and concealment." Again, the implication was that the flights might continue, adding insult to injury by justifying them on the basis of avoiding a sneak attack. As to Soviet objections that we might be preparing for war, Eisenhower indignantly replied, "This is just—it's absolutely ridiculous and they know it is."[21]

Eisenhower decided on May 12 to suspend future U-2 flights, but he did not make a public announcement, nor did he communicate the decision to the Soviets. He wanted to make it in Paris on May 16 as part of a new Open Skies proposal. Washington sent out mixed signals: After officials dropped hints that the flights would not be renewed, Eisenhower's press secretary Jim Haggerty denied they would be canceled, and Eisenhower echoed Haggerty in his pre-Paris press conference. Meanwhile, Khrushchev was left to stew.

The Paris Summit

Khrushchev arrived in Paris and went to see French President Charles de Gaulle prior to the first meeting. He told de Gaulle that Eisenhower must apologize for the flights, order their termination, and punish those involved. "I hope that no one is under the assumption that I am going to crawl on my knees to Khrushchev," Eisenhower told de Gaulle at their first meeting when the French leader relayed these demands.[22] Eisenhower took no initiative to meet privately with Khrushchev to smooth things over. Khrushchev, acting as the aggrieved party, felt that in failing to do so, Eisenhower deliberately had snubbed him. For his part Eisenhower was prepared to follow diplomatic protocol, but he was not prepared to take extraordinary actions to save a summit he had now come to believe was doomed.

At the first "presummit" session convened by de Gaulle, Khrushchev insisted on making the opening remarks, and he bluntly reiterated his demands directly to Eisenhower, whom he claimed had acted like "a thief caught red-handed in his theft." Khrushchev demanded that Eisenhower "apologize for his wrong and punish his responsible confederates, if a meeting would proceed."[23] He insisted on a promise that there would be no further U-2 overflights. In response, Eisenhower told Khrushchev that the U-2 flights had been suspended and "are not to be resumed" for the remainder of his term, but he could not offer assurances that the next American president would not resume them. He offered Khrushchev bilateral discussions about this issue while the general conference was under way, but he didn't give Khrushchev an apology. De Gaulle, who in private had referred to the U-2 incident as "this absurdly ill-timed violation of Soviet airspace," for once closed ranks with the United States and Britain in a public show of solidarity. Khrushchev stalked out, and within thirty-six hours the summit was over before it even officially had begun.[24] On May 14 the Defense Department announced that the armed forces had been put on worldwide alert as a "sound precautionary measure," and the Joint Chiefs promptly instituted a Def Con 3 nuclear alert.[25] The following day Vice President Richard Nixon told a nationwide television audience that U-2 flights were necessary to protect the United States against a Soviet surprise attack, and "such activities may have to continue in the future."[26]

The Aftermath

Khrushchev was later to suggest that the entire U-2 affair might have been a conspiracy hatched by military and intelligence officials at the top levels of the U.S. government to scuttle a summit for which it was unenthusiastic and unprepared. (American conspiracy theorists likewise claimed that the U-2 was downed by the CIA, using the explosive charge attached to the rear of the plane.) "It was as though the Americans had deliberately tried to place a time bomb under the meeting, set to go off just as we were about to sit down with them at the negotiation table."[27] Such a conspiracy is highly unlikely and certainly did not involve the president, as Khrushchev also recalled that his interpreter heard Eisenhower ask Secretary of State Herter, "Well why not? Why don't we go ahead a make a statement of apology?"[28] It seems far more likely that operational bungling rather than a conspiracy explains the downing of the U-2 and that the reassertion of Cold War hostilities was a reflexive result rather than a conspiratorial maneuver.

Khrushchev put the United States on the defensive for the U-2 flights; caught the president in a lie that diminished his stature and allowed the Soviets to reiterate their claims that the West had no moral superiority over the Soviet Union; and won Eisenhower's pledge that the U-2 flights would be suspended, an implicit admission that the Soviets had legitimate complaints. From Khrushchev's perspective, summit negotiations would not be nearly as useful as the propaganda coup Eisenhower had handed him, which could help him shore up his position in the Kremlin. And if the U-2 incident put Republicans on the defensive and eventually led to the election of a Democrat to the White House, so much the better—negotiations could then resume with a more amenable administration.

Some 200,000 people lined the airport at Andrews Air Force Base when Eisenhower returned from a hastily arranged postsummit meeting in Lisbon with Portuguese officials, designed to demonstrate that he was still "leader of the Free World." In a May 25 nationwide address, Eisenhower claimed that the initial statement about the flight "was issued to protect the pilot, his mission, and our intelligence processes, at a time when the true facts were still undetermined. . . . Our first information about the failure of this mission did not disclose whether the pilot was still alive, was trying to escape, was avoiding interrogation, or whether both plane and pilot had been destroyed. Protection of our intelligence system and the pilot, and concealment of the plane's mission, seemed imperative." Even at that late date Eisenhower was averse to telling the truth: The initial cover-up actually had been concocted not on the premise that the pilot was still alive, but rather on the assumption that the pilot was dead.

The Soviets played their propaganda cards over the summer for all they were worth, and the administration remained on the defensive. Khrushchev canceled Eisenhower's invitation to visit the Soviet Union. The Turkish government was overthrown, calling into question the future of U.S. bases, although soon the new government affirmed the alliance. U-2s were withdrawn from Japan, but even so, the government fell after riots by left-wing students, and Premier Nobusuke Kishi was forced to cancel an invitation for Eisenhower to visit Japan, a humiliation that marred the president's last months in office. Negotiations with the Soviets on arms control went into the deep freeze. In a conversation with his science adviser, George Kistiakowski, in July, a despairing Eisenhower said, "He saw nothing worthwhile left for him to do now until the end of his presidency."[29]

The Legitimacy Problem

The U-2 flights were a violation of international law, and after the cover story collapsed the United States tried to downplay the legal issues. At the United Nations Security Council the Soviets pressed the offensive, calling the flights "aggression." With the exception of Poland, most others on the Council thought that the U.S. declaration that there would not be any more flights made discussion moot. The Soviet proposal to condemn the United States was rejected. Instead, a resolution passed calling on superpowers to resume talks, refrain from force or threat of force, and "respect each others sovereignty, territorial independence, and political independence."[30]

In spite of the U.S. success at the United Nations, on the legal merits the United States had no case. It is customary international law that "every state has complete and exclusive sovereignty over the air space above its territory." In the Air Commerce Act of 1926 and the Civil Aeronautics Act of 1938, the United States had taken "complete and exclusive sovereignty" over its airspace, as had the Soviet Union in its Air Code of 1935.[31] The United States had signed various conventions recognizing the sovereignty of the subjacent airspace of each nation. The first article of the Paris International Convention for the Regulation of Aerial Navigation gives "complete and exclusive sovereignty over the airspace above [national] territory and the territorial waters adjacent thereto." The Chicago Convention on International Civil Aviation prohibits "state aircraft" of a contracting state from flying over the territory of any other state (whether contracting to the convention or not) "without authorization" from that state. Even though the Soviet Union was not a signatory, the United States was bound by the convention to respect its borders, and that it had not done.[32] The United States never challenged the claim that it had intruded into Soviet airspace, nor did it ever make a formal protest against the destruction of the U-2.

Noted international jurists such as Quincy Wright, a member of the board of editors of the *American Journal of International Law,* called the intrusion a violation of international law, not justified by doctrines of self-defense or reprisal. The United States could not use the *tu quoque* ("you're another" or "you do it too") defense usually employed in justifying intrusive surveillance, because this form of espionage is not the same as spying. As former Nuremberg prosecutor Telford Taylor pointed out, "The U-2 flights were not espionage in the conventional sense."[33] The distinction is that overflights violate sovereignty and might be mistaken for an act of war, while the spy usually enters a nation legally and then engages in unlawful conduct. International lawyers did agree with Eisenhower that the Soviet argument that the flights were themselves a form of aggression, or a prelude to aggression, was nonsense. But the bottom line for the international lawyers was the same as for the diplomats: Violation of a state's sovereignty ordinarily leads to a demand for an apology, and there was nothing out of line in Khrushchev's demand in Paris, although his crude approach could be faulted.[34] Quincy Wright concluded with some exasperation: "Apart from the importance of promoting by example a law-abiding world, it seems clear that calculation of immediate national interest would have counseled observance of law in this instance."[35]

The United States defended the flights on the grounds that Article 51 on the UN Charter allowed it to prepare to defend itself against potential Soviet aggression. But Article 51 refers to armed aggression and assumes that aggressive acts have already occurred. It requires a nation to notify the Security Council of measures it is taking to meet aggression. Obviously the United States had no intention of notifying the Security Council of the flights. Then there was the argument that sovereign nations have an inherent right of self-defense. This is a truism, but nations are expected to consider the *likelihood* of aggression rather than its *possibility* when determining behavior toward other nations.

Every nation has the right to prepare for such an attack, especially a nation that had suffered such an attack less than two decades before. But U-2 surveillance was not designed to catch the Soviets in preparations for war: It was designed to assess Soviet military strength. Even if targets were then chosen to establish a "balance of terror" that was designed to deter a surprise Soviet nuclear attack (Herter's justification), at the time of the summit there was no likelihood of a Soviet first strike. On May 3, just two days after the U-2 flight, the U.S. Army issued a report concluding that there was a low probability of a Soviet first strike on the United States because Soviet military doctrines cautioned against general war.[36] Stripped to its essentials, the ultimate U.S. justification for the flights was that the Soviets were the "bad guys," they had engaged in extensive espionage, and we were merely reciprocating by other means.

Conclusion: Guarding Reputation

The media sharply criticized Eisenhower's performance. *Time* took the administration to task for handing the Soviets "high cards" before the summit with a poorly planned cover story followed by a presidential decision to take personal responsibility.[37] Yet *Time* argued that Russians had lost more. "Nikita Khrushchev has lost stature. His ranting has lost him respect around the world." In contrast, "There was widespread admiration through the free world for Dwight Eisenhower's dignified rebuff of Khrushchev's wild demands, but a concern—not confined to the U.S.—that Washington's handling of the affair had been clumsy and inept."[38] The U-2 affair had a silver lining, according to *Time*: It revealed the real Soviet intentions. "The summit conference and the dream of peaceful coexistence smashed against the rock of Nikita Khrushchev's intransigent belligerence."[39] Ernest K. Lindley, the Washington columnist for *Newsweek*, commended Eisenhower and Herter for bringing aerial surveillance "into the open and examining it in honest perspective."[40] In contrast, the liberal *New Republic* likened the overflights and subsequent deceptions to the 1950s quiz show scandals and the fraud perpetrated on the viewing public by quiz contestant (and Columbia English professor) Mark Van Doren: ". . . the Government of the United States has itself been deeply corrupted; it too has assumed that 'anything goes'; it too has practiced Van Dorenism, only telling the truth when caught with the boodle."[41] Columnist Walter Lippmann argued, "To avow that we intend to violate Soviet sovereignty is to put everybody on the spot. . . . The cardinal rule, which makes spying tolerable in international relations, is that it is never avowed."[42] But Telford Taylor pointed out in *New York Times Magazine* that "the explosion of a cover story may reduce official credibility to the point where nothing but avowal can survive ridicule."[43] The *Economist* concluded that "the blame, in an immediate sense, rests squarely on the shoulders of the Russians; nothing can excuse Mr. Khrushchev's insolence in actually bringing Mr. Eisenhower to Paris for a meeting that he did not intend to allow to happen."[44]

In the aftermath of the botched summit, Harry Truman pronounced, "I feel that the integrity of the United States is one of its greatest assets. When we tarnish that, we've made a mistake."[45] But at least publicly Democratic congressional leaders made a show of closing ranks behind the president: Senate Majority Leader Lyndon Johnson (D-TX) and Speaker of the House Sam Rayburn (D-TX) greeted Eisenhower on his return at Andrews Air Force Base and emphasized the bipartisan unity of the American people. Congress then settled down to the business of making the U-2 affair a partisan issue. Chair of the Senate Foreign Relations Committee James William Fulbright (D-AR) led the Democratic charge: "The prestige of our country among nations has reached a new low."[46] He cast doubt on the importance of the flight itself. The cover story was inept, because "cover statements made about the flight were far too specific, and made us look ridiculous when the full extent of Soviet knowledge was revealed." Fulbright faulted Eisenhower for admitting to his own involvement: "The gravest mistake was made when the President assumed responsibility for the flight." The president embodied the sovereignty of the nation, and "it is totally unacceptable for one chief of state because of this personal embodiment [of sovereignty] to impinge upon the sovereignty of another, and much less so for him to assert the right to do so." The statements by the administration were provocative and only inflamed the situation, Fulbright observed, when the United States argued "that if the Soviets had not been so secretive, we would not have had to spy on them. This attitude of smug self-righteousness must have been unbearably provocative to the Soviet government and contributed substantially to the violence and intemperate bad manners of their representative, Mr. Khrushchev, at Paris." Fulbright concluded, "It is difficult to see how anyone could have been expected to act substantially different from the way Chairman Khrushchev acted under the circumstances that confronted him in Paris." The Senate Foreign Relations Committee did not question the operational aspects of the flight: "The committee has no reason to believe that the technical preparations for the flight were faulty or that the pilot was unreliable in any respect. From the technical point of view—that is, the preparation and equipment of plane and pilot—what befell the U-2 on May 1 was just plain bad luck."[47] The cover stories, the lies, the lack of coordination among agencies, particularly the State Department and NASA, led the committee to conclude that "the U.S. reaction to the failure of the U-2 complicated the problems that resulted from that failure."[48]

Administration officials were less than forthcoming in testifying before the committee. Gates and Herter did not reveal to the committee that Eisenhower had approved specific flights. They testified that there had been no decision to terminate the planned series of U-2 flights prior to the summit, leaving the impression that no decision of any kind was taken on the May 1 flight, even though Eisenhower had expressly approved it.[49] The administration invoked executive privilege and refused to tell the committee what the U-2 flight was after—the information needed to make a judgment about whether the risk was worth the flameout.[50] The committee pointed out that Khrushchev, "at least before the U-2 incident, was identified with the Soviet advocates of a less aggressive, more cooperative course . . . it would have been in our interest to have done what we could . . . to strengthen Khrushchev's position vis-à-vis the Soviet military and the Chinese communists." It concluded that the U-2 flight "should not have gone," but given the incomplete and misleading testimony by the secretaries, it did not pin the blame on the president.[51]

The U-2 flight was no isolated incident of failure, an exceptional case involving unusual circumstances. Rather, most aspects of the operation are typical of risky business that fails. An operation is poorly conceived and executed. Risks and opportunities are not accurately assessed. Past failures are not remembered and play no role in the assessment of risk. Authorization does not go through a formal staffing and briefing process that would allow the president to consider all risks and benefits and all objections raised by knowledgeable officials, but rather involves one or two close confidantes who press their own point of view. The president often expresses a sense of foreboding about the risks of proceedings, yet against his better judgment allows himself to be convinced by these officials to authorize the operation. When the mission fails, the president and his top officials implicate themselves with cover stories and deceptive accounts (sometimes required because the operation skirts or violates the law). Sometimes plausible denial holds, which means that the American people learn the wrong lessons. Other times the truth comes out, in which case presidents squander the moral authority of their office in futile attempts to legitimize activities that violate international and (sometimes) domestic law.

Notes

1. Sissela Bok, *Lying: Moral Choice in Public and Private Life* (New York: Vintage Books, 1979), 28.

2. Bok, *Lying*, 24.

3. By 1956 the United States had lost a dozen air force and navy planes and eighty air force soldiers in flights near or just within Soviet borders. The U-2 obtained much more intelligence, and in the next four years none were shot down. Soviet SA-2 missiles had a ceiling of 60,000 feet, and the U-2 had a ceiling of at least 82,000 feet. *Aviation Week* (May 11, 1960): 26.

4. Powers was either flying over 70,000 feet according to plan and had been hit by a high-altitude missile or else he had descended to a much lower altitude due either to negligence or an engine flameout. Powers told the Soviets he had been hit at 68,000 feet.

5. U.S. Senate, Committee on the Armed Services, *Hearings: Francis G. Powers, U-2 Pilot* (Washington, DC: U.S. Government Printing Office, 1962).

6. James Nathan, "A Fragile Detente: The U-2 Incident Re-examined," *Military Affairs* vol. 38 (October 1974): 97–104; for a critique of Nathan see Michael Beschloss, *Mayday: Eisenhower, Khrushchev and the U-2 Affair* (New York: Harper & Row, 1986), 358.

7. Robert A. Divine, *Eisenhower and the Cold War* (New York: Oxford University Press, 1981), 147–48.

8. Beschloss, *Mayday*, 140.

9. Lyman Kirkpatrick, *The Real CIA* (New York: Macmillan, 1968), 97.

10. Beschloss, *Mayday*, 161.

11. Stephen E. Ambrose, *Ike's Spies: Eisenhower and the Espionage Establishment* (Garden City, NY: Doubleday, 1981), 291.

12. Dwight Eisenhower, *Waging Peace* (Garden City, NY: Doubleday, 1965), 546.

13. For a full discussion of Eisenhower's style see Fred Greenstein, *The Hidden-Hand Presidency: Eisenhower as Leader* (New York: Basic Books, 1982).

14. Beschloss, *Mayday*, 61.

15. Beschloss, *Mayday*, 253.

16. Divine, *Eisenhower*, 149.

17. Beschloss, *Mayday*, 257.

18. "Department of State Bulletin," vol. 42 (May 23, 1960): 816.

19. Vernon Walters, *Silent Missions* (Garden City, NY: Doubleday, 1978), 341.

20. Jef Verschueren, *International News Reporting: Metapragmatic Metaphors and the U-2* (Philadelphia: John Benjamins Publishing Company, 1985).

21. Felix Belair, Jr. "President Asserts Secrecy of Soviet Justifies Spying," *New York Times*, May 12, 1960, 1.

22. Divine, *Eisenhower*, 150.

23. Charles E. Bohlen, *Witness to History, 1929–1969* (New York: Norton, 1973), 470.

24. Khrushchev told Kennedy he did not believe Eisenhower had approved the flight. Theodore Sorensen, *Kennedy* (New York: Harper & Row, 1965), 544.

25. "Def Con" refers to the readiness condition of U.S. military forces. Def Con 5 is a peaceful condition; Def Con 1 is imminent or actual hostilities.

26. David Wise and Thomas Ross, *The U-2 Affair* (New York: Random House, 1962), 149.

27. Nikita Khrushchev, *Khrushchev Remembers: The Last Testament*, trans. Strobe Talbott (Boston: Little, Brown, 1974), 450–51.

28. Khrushchev, *Khrushchev Remembers*, 450–51.

29. Divine, *Eisenhower*, 152.

30. Quincy Wright, "Legal Aspects of the U-2 Incident," *American Journal of International Law* vol. 54, no. 4 (October 1960): 836–54.

31. "Note: Legal Aspects of Reconnaissance in Airspace and Outer Space," *Columbia Law Review* vol. 61, no. 2 (June 1961): 1074–1102.

32. John Cobb Cooper, "Legal Problems of Upper Space," *Proceedings of the American Society of International Law* (1956).

33. Telford Taylor, "Long-Run Lessons of the U-2 Affair," *New York Times Magazine* (July 24, 1960): 20.

34. Wright, "Legal Aspects," 851.

35. Wright, "Legal Aspects," 854.

36. Jack Raymond, " Army Analysis Discounts Nuclear Attack by Soviet," *New York Times*, May 5, 1960, 1, 18.

37. "High Cards," *Time*, May 30, 1960, 8–9.

38. "High Cards," 7.

39. "Confrontation in Paris," *Time*, May 23, 1960, 18.

40. Ernest K. Lindley, "Cheers for Candor," *Newsweek*, May 23, 1960, 59.

41. *The New Republic* (May 16, 1960): 1. Mark Van Doren had been a contestant on a quiz show, and it was alleged that the producers had fed him correct answers in advance.

42. *New York Herald Tribune* (May 13, 1960): 4.

43. Taylor, "Long-Run Lessons," 32.

44. *Economist* (May 21, 1960): 725.

45. *New York Times* (May 12, 1960): 4.

46. *Congressional Record,* 86th Cong., 2nd sess., CVI, Part II, 14733–37.

47. U.S. Senate, Foreign Relations Committee, "Events Relating to the Summit Conference," 86th Cong., 2nd sess., Report No. 1761 (June 28, 1960): 22 (hereafter Senate Report).

48. Senate Report, 25.

49. U.S. Senate, Foreign Relations Committee, "Hearings on Events Incident to the Summit Conference," 86th Cong., 2nd sess. (1960): 25, 63–76.

50. Senate Report, 7.

51. Senate Report, 4–7.

2

Power Stakes

Kennedy and the Bay of Pigs

THE U-2 CASE IN THE PREVIOUS CHAPTER demonstrates the pitfalls of presidential inattention and delegation. Yet when presidents micromanage operations, failure may result as well: They make too many decisions about timing, resources, scale, scope, and methods. The White House requires too much feedback and insists on too much adherence to predetermined plans; it gives short shrift to the local knowledge of operatives on the ground, and its own reporting requirements overload them. Micromanagement occurs for a very good reason: Presidents want their political uncertainties converted to minimal risk; They want to obtain benefits and off-load costs to others.

Presidents are supposed to protect their *power stakes*, which political scientists have defined as the decision maker's ability to gain mastery in future situations by the way he or she makes decisions about current issues.[1] Just as a chess master thinks many moves ahead and plays out lines of move and countermove before settling on the most advantageous line, so too presidents must make decisions today that provide them options and lower their risks for the situations they will face tomorrow. This is the conventional wisdom about presidential power; as it turns out, there are times when attempting to preserve power stakes leads to a failure of the initial operation—and narrows future options rather than expands them. The Bay of Pigs is such a case.

A Perfect Failure

President John Kennedy's decision shortly after he became president to support a CIA-planned invasion of Cuba by exile forces was a case of micromanagement gone awry.[2] On April 15, 1961, two days prior to a planned exile invasion, eight B-26 bombers conducted an air strike from bases in Nicaragua. The strike was not intended to neutralize Cuban air power but was part of a CIA cover story that Cuban air force pilots had defected. The B-26 pilots, Americans and Cubans recruited by the DoubleChek Corporation (a CIA proprietary), claimed in their debriefing that they had inflicted great damage on Castro's air force. This was not so: The exiles had lost one plane and two others had to make forced landings after the strike, but Castro still had three B-26s, two T-33 trainers, and three Sea Furies. The air strikes did give Castro advance warning about exile attacks so he could mobilize his 200,000-member militia and arrest 100,000 potential dissidents, ending any possibility of an uprising in support of the exiles. Because of this mobilization, a diversionary landing in Oriente Province of 164 exile troops was aborted when they spotted militias patrolling the beach. Counseled by Secretary of State Dean Rusk and the U.S. Ambassador to the UN, Adlai Stevenson, both of whom were worried about reaction in Latin America, Kennedy canceled a second air strike aimed at airfields and communications towers just hours before the main landing was scheduled to start.

The plan for landing the exile Brigade 2506 was designed to move troops and equipment onto the beaches quickly and shuttle them to the coastal road heading toward Cienfuegos. The landing would have to be tightly coupled (each step timed perfectly in a prescribed sequence) and performed correctly to avoid a WOW (worst on worst): a situation in which one error would cascade into another, and the effect of each error would be amplified.[3] Although Kennedy had insisted that the invasion take place at night, logistical difficulties postponed it to the morning of the 17th because the landing craft and small boats were slowed offshore by coral reefs off Playa Larga that CIA planners did not account for (in spite of cautions from Cubans who knew the conditions at the bay). The off-loading started to go behind schedule because night-lights and heavy equipment didn't arrive on the first boats. Two of the supply ships were sunk by Fidel Castro's remaining T-33s: the *Houston*, hit by a rocket below the waterline, had carried the exile's reserve ammunition (and if it had been hit higher the exploding ammunition would have killed the crew), and the *Río Escondido*, which had carried their communications equipment. Other communications gear carried by the *Atlántico* couldn't be off-loaded because the ship was driven away by heavy fire. Two cargo ships and several other smaller vessels pulled out to sea to get away from enemy fire.

From the first moments ashore the exiles faced stiff resistance from the local militia and from a regular Cuban army infantry battalion as well as strafing from T-33s. They ended their advance after they had briefly gained a beachhead forty-two miles in length and twenty miles deep. They tried to cut a main road to Jaguey Grande and failed, enabling Castro to bring in reinforcements and tanks. Exercising poor fire control, the exiles soon ran low on ammunition, and they had no naval supporting fire or the air cover that their CIA handlers had promised. Late in the evening on April 17 Castro's forces counterattacked with tanks and infantry supported by artillery fire.[4]

The U.S. cover story at the United Nations (that the exiles had organized the first bombing by themselves using Cuban air force defectors) quickly fell apart. Latin American nations could hardly defend a U.S. violation of Cuban sovereignty, and nonaligned nations and Communist countries condemned the attack. To avoid further diplomatic costs, Secretary of State Dean Rusk and National Security Adviser McGeorge Bundy recommended that a second proposed air strike set for April 18 on behalf of the exiles' force be canceled. Kennedy agreed and scrubbed the mission even as the planes on the aircraft carrier *Essex* were warming up.[5] Admiral Arleigh Burke, chief of naval operations, asked Kennedy for permission to use the 1,500 marines on the *Essex* to rescue the exile force. Instead, Kennedy approved a final bombing strike, supported by jets from the *Essex*, to help extricate the force. The time difference between Guatemala (where exile bombers had taken off) and Cuba (where the *Essex* and its jets were located) led to a final snafu: The bombers showed up an hour before the jets and two bombers were promptly shot down by Cuban T-33s, ending the possibility of any air cover for an evacuation. Meanwhile, in an exchange of warnings, Soviet leader Nikita Khrushchev called on Kennedy to end the "aggression" and warned he would provide Cuba with "all necessary help"; Kennedy in his response denied any American involvement.[6]

With no CIA contingency plans for infiltration to the Escambray Mountains, with the navy and the rebels using different communications equipment and unable to contact each other, and with no plans for evacuation, the exile force had no choice but to surrender. A few men were picked up by two U.S. destroyers that ventured close to the shore. One hundred of the exiles were killed and close to 1,200 surrendered, paraded as prisoners by the triumphant Castro regime in Havana.

Standard Explanations

Standard accounts of the Bay of Pigs focus on both people and procedures: The president was poorly served by the professional military and got taken in by the intelligence community.[7] The CIA itself conducted a report by its In-spector General Lyman Kirkpatrick, who had been skeptical through the late 1950s of covert operations conducted by the agency's Clandestine Services. The report confined itself to agency performance and made "no evaluation of or judgment on any decision or action taken by any official not employed by the agency." It concluded, "The fundamental cause of the disaster was the Agency's failure to give the project, notwithstanding its importance and its immense potentiality for damage to the United States, the top-flight handling that it required—appropriate organization, staffing throughout by qualified personnel, and full-time direction and control of the highest quality."[8] The beach landings were disorganized and poorly coordinated because CIA agents in the field had misled their superiors, and these superiors, in turn, had not properly assessed the operational or political risks of an operation that could not be plausibly denied because of its size and scope.[9] The CIA did not cor-rectly evaluate the depth of support for Castro, and it had no contingency plans if the operation ran into trouble.[10] The report focused on changes to CIA procedures and recommended the transfer to the Defense Department (DOD) of large-scale operations, supervised by a board of senior CIA, DOD, and State officers, "to make cold, hard appraisals." The CIA should not under-take activities "until clearly defined policy has been received."[11] Kirkpatrick's report was viewed within the CIA as an attack by an in-house skeptic against the covert operations planners. Copies of the report were confiscated, and only a single copy remained in the safe of the CIA director until 1996.

Presidential historians later focused on "groupthink" (the tendency for peo-ple in small groups to come to a consensus rather than disagree) and other dysfunctions of the presidential advisory system. Kennedy admitted that he was overconfident and inexperienced, and he observed that he didn't get skeptical-enough advice from the Joint Chiefs.[12] After the Bay of Pigs Kennedy modified his decision making methods, dropped the people who had led him into the Cuban swamps, remained suspicious of advice from the intelligence community, and developed better procedures for crisis decision making.

Shortcomings of the Standard Explanations

Not one of the statements in the standard accounts bears up. We can start by posing some obvious questions: Why was the CIA so confident in its ability to overthrow Castro with an exile force? To argue for the invasion, the CIA claimed to have "learned" lessons from past efforts to overthrow unfriendly governments. In fact, the agency deliberately distorted its own performance, particularly in describing the 1954 Guatemala operation. Supposedly a handful of exiles (supported by U.S. pilots in unmarked "rebel" aircraft) had over-thrown the leftist government of Jacobo Arbenz y Guzmán in 1954. But the CIA's account was misleading: The invasion force it sponsored had run into trouble, and just as the operation had been about to fall apart, top generals of the Guatemalan military had mounted their own coup d'état against Arbenz and had installed the CIA choice, Colonel Castillo Armas, as the head of a mil-itary junta.[13] Agency lore had it that Arbenz and his supporters had panicked and been defeated by the "psywar" efforts of the agency at the start of the in-vasion, especially its clandestine radio broadcasts. But had the Guatemalan military not intervened against Arbenz, the invasion force would have been defeated. President Eisenhower was given false information by the CIA—that only one soldier of the invasion force had been killed—and he had been mis-led about the performance of the exile force. What the CIA *had* learned from this intervention—and an earlier one in Iran in which street thugs managed to paralyze army officers and keep them from defending a leftist regime that the CIA managed to topple—was this: Covert operations relying on psywar disinformation could panic the leaders or turn the officers of unfriendly regimes.

Richard Bissell, the man in charge of the Bay of Pigs operation, had run the U-2 program and was being groomed to take over the CIA. He was inexperi-enced in covert operations, but he had been in on the meetings of the top de-cision makers during the Guatemalan invasion, had bought into the psywar myth, and shared the "can do" culture of CIA covert operatives.[14] After Bissell made his case, Eisenhower did not ask the CIA's Board of National Estimates to evaluate the depth of Castro's support or the likelihood of military defec-tions and a popular uprising, estimates that would be crucial in assessing whether or not Cuba could be a replay of the Guatemalan experience. The Board had concluded on March 10, 1960, in a study done for a separate pur-pose, that there was no internal threat to the Castro regime, "which by now has established a formidable structure of control over the daily lives of the Cuban people."[15] The Intelligence Directorate had reached similar conclu-sions. The fate of agents sent into Cuba—usually caught by Castro's security forces within a day or two—should have forewarned the CIA that Castro had a popular base.

Why did the invasion land in such an unpromising location? Kennedy was poorly served as well by his military advisers. After receiving his first CIA briefing Kennedy requested the Joint Chiefs to study the feasibility of the plan. The chiefs never obtained written briefing documents from the CIA, and they were not inclined to criticize the agency. Their report to Kennedy delicately concluded that the plan had a "fair chance"—which in military parlance might mean about 30 percent—though they pointed out that "personnel and logistic support are marginal at best" and that the Cuban army could eventually reduce the beachhead.[16] Individual chiefs were skeptical: Army Chief Lyman Lemnitzer told Kennedy that an invasion "would have very little chance of success," and shortly before the invasion, Naval Chief Arleigh Burke told him that the landing had at best "about 50 percent" chance of success. But the chiefs as a group merely responded to infrequent requests from the CIA for logistical advice and gave a cautious but not condemning evaluation of the initial Trinidad landing site, preferring it to other possibilities. When that site was rejected by the president, the chiefs then gave their "preference" for the Zapata (Bay of Pigs) site, not mentioning that it was merely the least objectionable, not a site they favored—their wording left the impression with Secretary of State Dean Rusk and Secretary of Defense Robert McNamara that the chiefs *did* favor it. Neither McNamara nor Lemnitzer told Kennedy of their doubts about the location. By that time the chiefs believed they should hold their fire since they thought Kennedy had given the CIA his backing—but they had already protected themselves with a paper trail. Their February 3 memo pointed out: "Since the success of this operation is dependent on the degree of local Cuban support this factor should be a matter of continuous evaluation until a decision to execute the operation is made."[17]

Kennedy was inexperienced in national security decision making: He failed to understand that the Joint Chiefs of Staff's (JCS) acquiescence was not the same as an endorsement, and he didn't appreciate its understated form of bureaucratic communication. He misinterpreted weak or mixed signals from the military as signals to proceed. Kennedy made no effort to probe the chiefs' attitudes, just as he had not probed for differences of opinion within the CIA. Doubts at the lower levels of the military never reached the president: The logistics experts who evaluated an invasion at the Trinidad site—a town supposedly rife with anti-Castro sentiment, according to the CIA—had said that odds against surprise were 85 to 15 and that without surprise the invasion would fail if even a single Cuban plane with a machine gun could attack the landing craft. If Castro could put up effective resistance with his 40,000 troops and 200,000 reserves, the exiles' logistical capabilities would be impossible to sustain.[18] Kennedy was unaware of most of the objections raised by JCS analysts, especially about the poor state of readiness and training of the exile force. Agency turf rivalry didn't help: The CIA Director of Plans rejected a JCS offer of military advice on the landing.

The State Department's Bureau of Intelligence and Research was not given information about the plan, and its Cuban specialists were not consulted. Secretary of State Rusk chose prudence over candor and did not confide the doubts of Undersecretary Chester Bowles nor of Assistant Secretary Thomas Mann (who had long experience in Latin American affairs) to the president, nor those of Roger Hilsman, director of the Department of State's intelligence bureau. But Rusk did warn Kennedy of problems with Latin American nations that would oppose the invasion.[19] A memo from Mann to Rusk was routed to the president late in February. Mann predicted that there would be no uprising or disaffections in the Cuban army, that the invasion brigade would fail to maintain a lodgment, and that Kennedy's choice at that point would be to abandon it or help it get to the Escambray Mountains with an overt U.S. intervention. Mann also pointed out that an invasion would violate the UN Charter, the Organization of American States (OAS) Charter, and the Rio Treaty, impairing our moral position in the hemisphere and resulting in a catastrophic impact on our leadership in Latin America.[20] So Kennedy had ample warning of the risks and the costs involved if he approved the plan.

Presidential Choice

The advisory system failed, in part because the information about conditions in Cuba were inaccurate, in part because theories about what might happen during an invasion used a false learning curve based on Guatemala, in part because of slippage between the JCS and CIA and between the JCS and the president's National Security Adviser, and in part because of systemic distortions by officials trying to make their best case. But there was no strong consensus to proceed, no "groupthink" that convinced officials to act; more than a few top officials, such as Mann, raised doubts to the president personally or through memos. Kennedy himself excluded skeptical advisers such as Stevenson (who was kept in the dark) and Bowles, discounted the opposition of Senator J. William Fulbright (D-AR) and White House aides Arthur Schlesinger and Richard Goodwin, and ignored the prescient memo from Mann. Had Kennedy wished to encourage dissenting voices, he could have done so. Had he paid attention to skeptics, there was plenty of intelligent analysis of his risks and options available to him.

The president *chose* not to listen, in what seems to have been an exercise of *willful* self-deception, utilizing what organization theorists call a disqualification heuristic: a mindset that downplays or neglects information that would contradict an existing conviction to act. Recognizing his reluctance to change course, advisers were diffident, reluctant to challenge a president uninterested in a real debate. Kennedy wanted to proceed with some action on behalf of the Cubans, and most of his advisers, still trying to gain his confidence at the beginning of the administration, were reluctant to advise him to the contrary or to pursue matters once they had stated their case. The question is: Why did Kennedy ignore the informed advice and advisers? Why did he decide to go ahead? Why did *he* fail his advisory system?

Presidential Risk Management and Gamesmanship

Presidents do not make decisions in small groups: They make decisions alone. Kennedy's own decisions were faulty, and for predictable and understandable reasons, having little to do with his inexperience or his arrogance or the dysfunctions of the advisory system. It had much to do with his own attempts at *gamesmanship* (structuring a situation to outwit an opponent by retaining one's own options and limiting the options of others), and the negotiation of risk (structuring a situation to lower one's own risks while increasing risks of others), based on his power stakes as he understood them.[21]

Start with gamesmanship, some of which was carried on by the CIA, some by the president. The CIA acted disingenuously with the president. It gave Kennedy three options, two of which (disband the exile force or wait and do nothing), were phony spreading of alternatives (a ploy in which only the middle alternative offers a real option). Bissell assured Kennedy, even after he changed the invasion site to the Bay of Pigs, that if all else failed and no uprising occurred, the invading force could get to the Escambray Mountains to mount guerrilla operations—assurances it gave in spite of the fact that two of the original planners of the operation threatened to resign when the site was changed.[22] No one told Kennedy that when he approved the landing at the Bay of Pigs he was giving up the guerrilla option, since there were swamps and poor roads and the mountains were eighty miles away, on the other side of the town of Cienfuegos.

The CIA attempted to structure the operation so that the president would use the U.S. armed forces in defense of the exile force. If Castro were to be overthrown, supposedly the main brunt of the effort would be borne by the invaders, yet the CIA did not expect this small force of exiles to defeat a large Cuban army on the field of battle. Bissell's Clandestine Services seemed to think that the invasion would serve as a psychological shock, triggering urban uprisings and disaffection among Cuban troops that would eventually lead to overthrow of the regime. Castro and his government would assume the invasion was the prelude to a much larger American effort. The CIA's Branch 4 planners wanted the landing force "to survive and maintain its integrity on Cuban soil" in order to spark a general uprising: "The way will then be paved for United States military intervention aimed at pacification of Cuba, and this will result in the prompt overthrow of the Castro Government."[23]

Although Eisenhower had approved the invasion plan and even called for a more ambitious plan, saying, "We should be prepared to take more chances and be more aggressive," he nevertheless had cautioned "the main thing was not to let the U.S.' hand show."[24] Yet the CIA, as Director Allan Dulles observed, had organized many operations that had begun with prohibitions set by the president against direct U.S. involvement but that had eventually involved U.S. forces.[25] "We felt that when the chips were down—when the crisis arose in reality, any action required for success would be authorized rather than permit the enterprise to fail," he recalled.[26] Even McGeorge Bundy had weighed in with a memo to Kennedy outlining a scenario in which a civil war would justify U.S. intervention.[27] Kennedy had already signaled confidence in the CIA by approving the operation, letting it be the advocate and the judge of its viability, and downplaying advice from those who opposed it. Dulles and Bissell assumed that once Kennedy had approved the invasion, he would be drawn into a situation in which he would have to back up the exiles with American forces.

Kennedy was fully aware of this CIA ploy to limit his options and force him to support the exiles with American forces. As early as February 8 Bundy had sent him a memo summarizing agency positions on the invasion: "Defense and CIA now feel quite enthusiastic about the invasion from Guatemala," he wrote the president, adding, "At worst they think the invaders would get into the mountains, and at best they think they might get a full-fledged civil war in which we could then back the anti-Castro forces openly."[28] But Kennedy assumed that the CIA had accepted his decision that the exiles, after the initial bombing raid, would be on their own, at least until they secured a beachhead and captured the nearest airfield at Girón. The airfield was crucial, because if rebels took it, then any American air cover could plausibly be claimed to come from inside Cuba, involving rebel forces or defecting pilots—a cover story the White House felt was essential to conceal the U.S. role. So the CIA misjudged the president as much as the president misjudged the CIA. The CIA thought Kennedy had given it a blank check, but Kennedy had actually given it a limited hunting permit, at least until its force demonstrated it could take and hold the airfield.

Kennedy was playing his own game: because the CIA misinformed him about the landing site, he believed that the exile force could get to the mountains if an uprising in Cuba did not follow the landing. Invasion seemed to him to be an operation with considerable gain no matter which way it turned out. Whether the exiles succeeded or failed, Kennedy observed, he would be able to "get rid" of the exile Brigade and "dump" its members in Cuba, "especially if that is where they want to go."[29] In his worst-case scenario, they would wind up fighting a guerrilla war from the mountains. He would have proven his bona fides with the exile community in Florida and protected himself against right-wing Republican charges that he was doing nothing to "liberate" Cuba.

It is possible that Kennedy may have been playing a deeper game. Bissell later suggested that a CIA operation just prior to the landings was supposed to eliminate Castro, and his final willingness to proceed occurred just after poison was transferred from the CIA to a Cuban agent who was supposed to slip it to Castro at a restaurant. The Church Committee (which held hearings on CIA assassination plots against foreign leaders) provided evidence in 1975 of several plots against Castro. Conceivably Kennedy might have made his key decisions about going ahead with a limited operation at the very time he had reason to believe that a CIA assassination attempt was going forward.[30] But by the time the invasion took place, Castro remained alive and well, and this might have accounted for Kennedy's unwillingness to commit U.S. forces or make good the promise of air support for the exile brigade. The assassination plotting might also explain why the CIA had been willing to acquiesce when Kennedy cut back the scope of the operation. The CIA (with or without Kennedy's knowledge) might have planned the Bay of Pigs Operation as a cover for the real operation—the assassination of Castro.

This line of reasoning remains speculative: Until we have more evidence, it is more likely that President Kennedy did *not* know about these CIA activities until after Attorney General Bobby Kennedy had been briefed by the CIA's General Counsel Lawrence Houston in May 1961, after the failed invasion attempt.

Irrationalities of Rational Choice

Presidential gamesmanship involves choice, but not completely *rational* choice, because often presidents set limiting conditions that constrain the operation's viability. Consider Eisenhower's early caution that "our hand should not show in anything that is done."[31] This "hidden hand" style of leadership, used successfully in the Guatemala and Iran operations and disastrously in the U-2 affair, constrained CIA planning, because in the Cuban operation the planners put all their chips on a bluff—on an *open* hand designed to spook Castro. The CIA ploy would only work if the American involvement were known to Castro and other Cubans. But Eisenhower would have none of it: By August 18, 1960, he had approved a $13 million budget to establish training bases in Guatemala for 300 exiles, but shortly thereafter he cautioned that no U.S. military personnel could be involved in combat.[32] Thus two key parameters were set, but in contradiction to each other: The operation must be covert (which would make the odds of sparking an uprising very low), but the exiles could not be assisted if the mission stalled or failed (because U.S. forces would then be in combat). The mission could not accomplish its psywar objectives without American involvement. Worse, the exiles could not be extricated if their mission failed.

On March 17, 1960, Eisenhower had allowed the CIA to go ahead with planning for Operation Pluto, which involved creation of "a responsible, appealing and unified Cuban Opposition" and an invasion by "an adequate paramilitary force outside of Cuba."[33] When Eisenhower approved the training plan he decided not to give a final approval to the invasion until the CIA came up with a government in exile led by a leader that might win popular support.[34] Subsequently Kennedy pressed for a reorganization of the exile group, to move it toward progressive positions that would give it political legitimacy. Yet no Cuban government-in-exile—no matter how progressive its program—could be considered legitimate if it were sponsored, financed, and militarily protected by the United States. By the time the invasion had begun, the United States was backing Manuel Artime y Buesa (an obscure politician supported by the conservative wing of the exiles' Revolutionary Council) whom it set up in the Democratic Revolutionary Front, a political movement that would form the nucleus of a new Cuban regime. Even in the unlikely event that Artime could have been installed in Havana at the head of an exile regime, he could only have remained in power with substantial U.S. support.

Were there any alternatives? The CIA rejected the idea of supporting the underground movement in Cuba itself, headed by Manuel Ray (former minister of public works under Castro), whose Revolutionary Movement of the People (MRP) was too radical for the CIA, which thought of it as "Fidelismo without Fidel." Ray and the MRP not only had some popular support in Cuba but also had demonstrated their ability to engage in sabotage. But Ray left Cuba in October 1960, undercutting his own stance as a resistance leader, and his movement then lost CIA financial and logistical backing. Ray's supporters in Cuba were given no advance word by either the CIA or the exile commanders about the invasion, reducing any chance for an internal uprising that had supposedly been a key part of the plan.

Kennedy made rational trade-offs with the CIA along two dimensions: One involved the covert versus overt issue; the other involved the legitimacy that could be achieved with the proper cover story. The larger the force, the more viable in battle, but the more likely the U.S. role would become obvious. If the landing involved a set battle, the U.S. role would be difficult to hide; if it involved an infiltration of a guerrilla force into the mountains, the U.S. role could be disavowed. Whatever was planned, if the U.S. military helped the exile force if it ran into trouble, the cover story would likely be blown, and Kennedy intended to give almost no help until the rebels had gained an airfield (so that the cover story could be maintained). But Kennedy's own positioning ran completely counter to the whole rationale of the CIA plan, which would rely for its maximum effect on the Cuban understanding that the United States was supporting a large-scale invasion force. In fact, the CIA was putting all its eggs in the psywar basket: Its plans only covered the landing of the exile force, and there was no planning either for infiltration or for actions to exploit urban uprisings or defections in the Cuban armed forces. "We had no plan on how to end the war," Bissell later recalled.[35] The idea was simply to land an invasion force, see if it created the psychological shock, and then hope for a presidential decision to intervene with the 1,500 marines aboard ships near the Cuban coast.

International Legitimacy

American intervention was precisely what Kennedy intended to avoid. In the United States an invasion of Cuba would be a popular move. But governments in the Western Hemisphere would view an invasion by an exile force assisted by the United States as a violation of a large body of hemispheric international law, such as the Havana Convention of 1928, that requires signatory nations to use all means at their disposal to "prevent the inhabitants of their territory, nationals or aliens, from participating in, gathering elements, crossing the boundary or sailing from their territory for the purpose of starting or promoting civil strife."[36] The invasion would violate the Anti-War Treaty of 1933, which forbids "intervention either diplomatic or armed,[37] and the Montevideo Convention of 1933, the Buenos Aires Protocol of 1936, and the Act of Chapúltepec of 1945, all of which uphold the principle of nonintervention. A unilateral American intervention would be on a collision course with hemispheric international law.[38]

Latin American governments would assume that the United States had violated the United Nations Charter, which recognizes principles of sovereign equality, respect for the "territorial integrity and political independence" of member states, upholds the principle of nonintervention in domestic jurisdictions, and the right of "self determination" of all peoples. Article 2, paragraph 4 of the Charter requires that all members "settle their international disputes by peaceful means in such a manner that international peace and security, and justice are not endangered." They would also take the invasion as a violation of the Rio Treaty of 1947, particularly Article 2, requiring states to submit disputes "to methods of peaceful settlement," and Article 6, respecting the inviolability and integrity of territory and sovereignty of states. They would believe that the United States had violated Article 5 of the OAS Charter that specifies that "international Law is the standard of conduct of States in their reciprocal relations," that "good faith shall govern the relations between states," and that "controversies of an international character arising between two or more American states shall be settled by peaceful procedures."

They would also assume that it violated the OAS Article 15 ban against intervention "for any reason whatever, in the internal or external affairs of any other State," a ban not only against using armed force, "but also any other form of interference or attempted threat against the personality of the State or against its political, economic and cultural elements." A landing designed to create a "lodgment" within Cuba that would spark an uprising would violate OAS Article 17, which declares "the territory of a State inviolable," and "prohibits military occupation or other measures of force taken by another State, directly or indirectly, on any grounds whatever."

These prohibitory provisions admitted no exceptions: It would not matter that the Castro regime might be subverting other nations and itself violating these provisions. If there were evidence of such Cuban wrongdoing, the Rio Treaty (as well as the Caracas Declaration of 1954 specifying that communism was a threat to the Western Hemisphere) was clear about the procedures the United States would be required to follow: Only collective security measures by the OAS could be invoked. Article 6 of the OAS Charter refers to "aggression which is not an armed attack or by an extra-continental or intra-continental conflict, or by any other fact or situation that might endanger the peace of America." Arguably the military buildups in Cuba and the subversion sponsored by the Castro regime might fit this category, in which case the United States could call for the convening of the OAS Organ of Consultation, which could "agree on the measures which must be taken in case of aggression to assist the victim of aggression or, in any case, the measures which should be taken for the common defense and for the maintenance of the peace and security of the Continent." These measures (provided the United States could obtain the concurrence of the OAS) comprised diplomatic and economic sanctions as well as "use of armed force." The rub, of course, was that the OAS would not approve severe measures: The only way for the United States to remove Castro was to act unilaterally. To avoid legal complications, any such actions had to be covert.

Negotiating Presidential Risk

Maintaining the covert nature of American involvement would raise operational risks, as McGeorge Bundy indicated to Kennedy in National Security Memorandum 31, while lowering operational risk with some level of American military assistance would increase the political and diplomatic risks. On March 11 Kennedy told the CIA to chart a middle course.[39] "They have done a remarkable job of reframing the landing plan so as to make it unspectacular and quiet, and plausibly Cuban in its essentials," Bundy reported to the president with satisfaction on March 15 about CIA changes.[40] Kennedy continued to try to minimize his exposure. As Bundy reported, "The President did not like the idea of the dawn landing and felt in order to make this appear as an inside guerilla-type operation, the ships should be clear of the area by dawn."[41]

Kennedy kept coming back to the idea of *infiltration* rather than *invasion*. Let a small 250- to 300-member rebel force get to the mountains and then launch attacks, so that the fighting would seem to have originated in Cuba.[42] The CIA demurred, suggesting that the exile force, having been trained for an invasion (and believing that it would spark an uprising to end the regime), would not accept the idea. When infiltration was discarded because of its political unacceptability to the Cubans, Kennedy split the difference between a full-scale U.S.-backed invasion and a Cuban initiative. He rejected the ambitious "Trinidad" plan, a large, daylight invasion with U.S. air support, in favor of a smaller night operation. He wanted something small in large measure to forestall a Soviet response, particularly over Berlin, and because of State Department concerns about international law. Kennedy opted for Eisenhower's "hidden hand" to limit the damage to U.S. diplomatic leadership in the hemisphere, but there was an element of wishful thinking in Kennedy's image of a force of 1,500 troops equipped with tanks and artillery quietly infiltrating into Cuba. "Kennedy thought he had ordered a large but quiet infiltration of freedom fighters," one researcher later concluded, but "meanwhile, the CIA was staging a miniature Normandy landing."[43]

To minimize his own diplomatic risks Kennedy had approved a hybrid concoction that had the disadvantages rather than the advantages of both the maximalist and the minimalist approaches, so as he put it, "to do everything possible to make it appear to be a Cuban operation partly from within Cuba but supported from without Cuba, the objective being to make it more plausible for U.S. denial of association with the operation. . . ."[44] But the president had dodged the key operational questions: Would he use air power to support the invasion? If so, how much and under what circumstances? The CIA did not press him, preferring to leave matters ambiguous. It assumed Kennedy would use whatever military force it would take to protect the invasion force. If the CIA had neglected to plan for anything more than phase I of an invasion, Kennedy had matched their neglect by failing to insist that it plan for phase II or for plans for disengagement.

Presidential Power Stakes

Could Kennedy have refused to authorize the invasion? Exiles would have attacked his administration and tarnished his anti-Communist reputation.

Presidents Eisenhower and Nixon, with their own scores to settle, would have come after him: During the election Kennedy had attacked them for failing to support Cuban "freedom fighters." Before the fourth presidential debate Kennedy had charged that anti-Castro forces "have had virtually no support from our government." He had called for direct U.S. involvement in over-throwing Castro, charging the Eisenhower administration with failing to act, a charge he knew at the time was false since he had been briefed on the planning for the exile invasion by Alabama Governor John Patterson (D), who had sent the national guard from his state to help with training and logistics at the CIA camps.[45] Allen Dulles, the CIA director, might have resigned in protest if Kennedy had scuttled the plans, and the president would have lost support from many southern Democrats, who would have had to distance themselves from him. "If he hadn't gone ahead with it," Robert Kennedy later observed, "everybody would have said it showed he had no courage." He paraphrased the line of attack: "Eisenhower trained these people, it was Eisenhower's plan; Eisenhower's people all said it would succeed—and we turned it down."[46]

Could Kennedy have delayed the decision? The exiles were eager to get started and might have objected if it were postponed (there had already been one mutiny in the camps); the Guatemalan government was shaky and wanted the exiles out; the rainy season was about to begin, making air cover difficult; Soviet advanced weaponry was due to arrive within a month, in-cluding eight MiG fighter jets that would be manned by Czech pilot trainers and fifty-five tanks. Worst of all, journalists had learned about the camps and were asking questions: The *Nation* already had run an article about CIA train-ing of exiles, and so had the *New York Times*.[47] In early April the editor of *New Republic* showed Kennedy the draft of an article about invasion plans but killed the story at the president's request; a different version counseling that an invasion should not take place was to be published the third week of April. The *New York Times* was prepared to print a story about the invasion on April 7, but Kennedy persuaded publisher Orville Dryfoos to edit the story back, omitting mention of the CIA role or of an "imminent" invasion.

All the ingredients for crisis decision making were now at work: high stakes, uncertainty about future events, narrowing options, dubious legality, and a closing window of opportunity. The CIA told Kennedy he would have to agree to an April invasion or cancel it altogether. Had Kennedy had the time to re-view the final version of the plan carefully its irrationalities, operational prob-lems, and high risks for him might have been apparent. But Kennedy did not engage in a full-scale review before giving his final approval. He thought he had protected his power stakes and resolved his diplomatic vulnerabilities.

Why did Kennedy fail? The fault was more his own than the CIA's, more a result of his own desire to protect his power stakes and preserve a cover story fashioned to conceal American involvement than because of a lack of information, errors in facts, or even errors in the premises of the plan, though clearly all these factors were present and contributed to the failure.[48] Every decision Kennedy took made matters worse by increasing the operational risks even as they were intended to minimize political and diplomatic risks. This operation was supposed to demonstrate the kind of hard-nosed, realistic, vigorous foreign decision making Kennedy would bring to the Oval Office; it failed *because* of its hard-nosed realism, *because* of the gamesmanship the president played with the CIA, *because* of the compromises in the operation Kennedy forced on the Cubans, and above all, *because* of the president's approach that placed his own power stakes front and center. Kennedy ignored and discounted the views of the skeptics. They lacked a crucial piece of male anatomy, Kennedy remarked to his aides, not stopping to consider that in planning covert operations, it is just as important to be well endowed between the ears as anywhere else.

Notes

1. On power stakes see Richard M. Neustadt, *Presidential Power and the Modern Presidents: The Politics of Leadership from Roosevelt to Reagan* (New York: John Wiley and Sons, 1960), passim.

2. Lucien S. Vandenbroucke, "Anatomy of a Failure: The Decision to Land at the Bay of Pigs," *Political Science Quarterly* vol. 99, no. 3 (Fall 1984): 471–91; Edward R. Drachman and Alan Shank, "Kennedy: Bay of Pigs Invasion," *Presidents and Foreign Policy: Countdown to 10 Controversial Decisions* (New York: SUNY Press, 1997), 85–112. Also James G. Blight and Peter Kornbluh, eds., *Politics of Illusion: The Bay of Pigs Invasion Reexamined* (Boulder, CO: Lynne Rienner Publishers, 1998). Primary documents are contained in *Foreign Relations of the United States, Vol. 10: Cuba 1961–1962* (Washington, DC: U.S. State Department, 1997). A detailed history of the paramilitary operations conducted by exiles with assistance from the United States is contained in Colonel J. Hawkins, "Record of Paramilitary Action against the Castro Government of Cuba, 17 March 1960–May 1961," Clandestine Services History, *CS Historical Paper No. 105* (May 5, 1961).

3. Charles Perrow, *Normal Accidents: Living with High-Risk Technologies* (New York: Basic Books, 1984).

4. Victor Andres Triay, *Bay of Pigs: An Oral History of Brigade 2506* (Gainesville: University Press of Florida, 2001), 68–130.

5. Peter Wyden, *Bay of Pigs: The Untold Story* (New York: Simon & Schuster, 1979), 197.

6. Mark J. White, "Letter from Chairman Khrushchev to President Kennedy" and "Letter from President Kennedy to Chairman Khrushchev," in *The Kennedys and Cuba: The Declassified Documentary History* (Chicago: Ivan Dee, 1999), 32, 34.

7. Neustadt, *Presidential Power*, 247–49.

8. "Inspector General's Survey of the Cuban Operation and Associated Documents, February 16, 1962," CIA Historical Review Program 1997, 34.

9. "Inspector General," 143.

10. "Inspector General," 144.

11. "Inspector General,"149.

12. Mark J. White, "Memorandum for the Record Prepared by Chief of Naval Operations Admiral Arleigh A. Burke," in *The Kennedys and Cuba* (Chicago: Ivan Dee, 1999), 30–31.

13. Nicholas Cullather, *Operation PBSUCCESS: The United States and Guatemala, 1952–1954* (Washington, DC: National Archives, 1994).

14. Thomas Powers, *The Man Who Kept the Secrets: Richard Helms and the CIA* (New York: Alfred A. Knopf, 1979), 97–104.

15. Wyden, *Bay of Pigs*, 99.

16. Mark J. White, "Memorandum for the Secretary of Defense: Military Evaluation of the CIA Para-Military Plan, Cuba, February 3, 1961," in *The Kennedys and Cuba* (Chicago: Ivan Dee, 1999), 17–18.

17. White, *The Kennedys and Cuba*, 18.

18. Luis Aguilar, ed., *Operation ZAPATA: The "Ultrasensitive" Report and Testimony of the Board of Inquiry on the Bay of Pigs* (Frederick, MD: University Publications of America, 1981), 108–10, 154–55.

19. Mark J. White, "Memorandum of Meeting with President Kennedy, February 8, 1961," in *The Kennedys and Cuba* (Chicago: Ivan Dee, 1999), 19. Rusk stated that he "deeply regretted" not telling Kennedy his opposition to the operation. Richard Rusk, *As I Saw It* (New York: W. W. Norton, 1993), 212.

20. "Memo from Thomas Mann to Dean Rusk, February 15, 1961," in Piero Gleijeses, "Ships in the Night: The CIA, the White House and the Bay of Pigs," *Journal of Latin American Studies* vol. 27, part 1 (February 1995): 23–24.

21. Richard Bissell's response to the Inspector General's report focused on "political compromises" that Kennedy had ordered, which in Bissell's view caused the failure of the operation. See "An Analysis of the Cuban Operation" attachment to the Inspector General's report.

22. Bissell claimed that the change of location was "the most clearly identifiable single error that we can be accused of." Richard M. Bissell Jr., *Reflections of a Cold Warrior: From Yalta to the Bay of Pigs* (New Haven, CT: Yale University Press, 1996), 172.

23. Internal CIA memorandum, January 4, 1961, cited in Gleijeses, "Ships," 17–18.

24. "Memorandum of Meeting with the President, Tues., Nov. 29, 1960." Eisenhower Library. Quoted in "Bay of Pigs, 40 Years After, Chronology," at www.gwu.edu/~nsarchiv/bayofpigs/chron.html.

25. Vandenbroucke, "Anatomy of a Failure," 479.

26. Trumbull Higgins, *The Perfect Failure: Kennedy, Eisenhower, and the CIA at the Bay of Pigs* (New York: W. W. Norton, 1987), 103.

27. Higgins, *The Perfect Failure*, 88–99.

28. McGeorge Bundy, "Memorandum for the President, February 8, 1961," in Wyden, *Bay of Pigs*.

29. Wyden, *Bay of Pigs*, 159.

30. H. Bradford Westerfield letter to the editor, *New York Review of Books* (October 23, 1997): 76.

31. "Memorandum of Meeting with the President, Tues., Nov. 29, 1960." Eisenhower Library. Quoted in National Security Archives "Bay of Pigs, 40 Years After, Chronology," posted at www.gwu.edu/~nsarchiv/bayofpigs/chron.html.

32. "Memorandum of Meeting with the President, August 22, 1960," Eisenhower Library.

33. "A Program of Covert Action against the Castro Regime," discussed in Gleijeses, "Ships," 3–4.

34. Stephen Ambrose, *Eisenhower: Soldier and President* (New York: Simon & Schuster, 1984), 557.

35. Quoted in Gleijeses, "Ships," 28.

36. *American Journal of International Law* 22, supp. 159 (1928).

37. *American Journal of International Law* 28, supp. 79 (1934).

38. C. Neale Ronning, "Intervention, International Law, and the Inter-American System," *Journal of Inter-American Studies* vol. 3, no. 2 (April 1961): 249–71.

39. Mark J. White, "Notes on White House Meeting," in *The Kennedys and Cuba* (Chicago: Ivan Dee, 1999), 30–31.

40. Quoted in Gleijeses, "Ships," 35.

41. White, "Notes on a White House Meeting," 21.

42. Mark J. White, "Notes on a Meeting between President Kennedy and Advisers, April 4, 1961," in *The Kennedys and Cuba* (Chicago: Ivan Dee, 1999), 25.

43. Vandenbroucke, "Anatomy of a Failure," 487.

44. White, "Notes on a White House Meeting," 26.

45. Gerald S. and Deborah H. Strober, *"Let Us Begin Anew": An Oral History of the Kennedy Presidency* (New York: Harper Collins, 1993), 325.

46. Edwin O. Guthman and Jeffrey Shulman, eds., *Robert Kennedy: In His Own Words: The Unpublished Recollections of the Kennedy Years* (New York: Bantam, 1988), 247.

47. Paul Kennedy, "U.S. Helps Train an Anti-Castro Force at Secret Guatemalan Air-Ground Base," *New York Times* (January 10, 1961): 1; Carleton Beals, "Cuba's Invasion Jitters," *Nation* vol. 191, no. 16 (November 12, 1960): 360.

48. Irving Janis, *Groupthink*, 2nd ed. (Boston: Houghton Mifflin, 1982), 19–27.

3

Compellence

Johnson and the Vietnam Escalation

" I WAS DETERMINED TO BE A LEADER OF WAR *and* a leader of peace," President Lyndon Johnson said about his decision to fight a war in Vietnam. "I refused to let my critics push me into choosing one or the other. I believed in both, and I believed America had the resources to provide for both."[1] In 1964 there was a training mission in South Vietnam and several thousand military personnel; by 1968 the United States had 548,000 combat troops in Vietnam, and 30,000 troops had been killed and many more wounded. Johnson's approval ratings had dropped from 70 percent in mid-1965 to below 40 percent by 1967. "I can't get out, I can't finish it with what I have got. So what the hell do I do?" Johnson complained to his wife, Lady Bird.[2]

Was Vietnam a quagmire, as journalist David Halberstam argued, in which Johnson became committed in a series of small steps, none of which taken alone established an American commitment but cumulatively if inadvertently added up to a massive commitment and a failed policy?[3] Was it a folly, as Defense Secretary Robert McNamara concluded, because top policymakers in the State Department or Pentagon lacked knowledge of Southeast Asia?[4] Was it an example of groupthink, in which a small group of poorly informed advisers deliberated in a situation in which group solidarity took precedence over individual searches for the most viable decision?[5]

The quagmire, ignorance, and groupthink explanations all shift the focus away from the president and toward the advisory system and lead to the conclusion that better advice and advisers would have made a difference. But what if the escalation had *not* been incremental? What if Johnson and his advisers had known from the very beginning how costly and dangerous the escalation might be? What might then explain why Johnson made a decision that divided the nation, split his party, unbalanced the economy, weakened the American position in the world, and destroyed his presidency?[6]

Decisions to Escalate

Johnson did not escalate because of the promise of victory—he escalated because of a fear of defeat. Early in 1964, McNamara noted that 40 percent of the countryside was controlled by the Vietcong, the local population was apathetic and indifferent, the South Vietnamese military's desertion rates were high and increasing, draft dodging was endemic, and the morale of hamlet militia and self-defense corps was poor. Yet he concluded that if the government of Prime Minister Nguyen Khanh remained in power, "the situation in South Vietnam can be significantly improved in the next four to six months."[7]

This combination of a realistic appraisal of deteriorating current conditions and optimism about efforts to stabilize the situation shows up in many memos and discussions. After Ambassador Maxwell Taylor reported back in December 1964 that "it is impossible to foresee a stable and effective government under any name in anything like the near future," Johnson instructed him to insist on tangible measures from the Saigon government, including increasing the workforce of the military and police, replacing incompetent officials, strengthening the interrogation of Vietcong suspects, and (based on a visit Johnson had made while vice president) implementing "a sanitary clean-up of Saigon."[8] The following month Assistant Secretary of State William Bundy was warning officials in Washington that "the situation in Vietnam is now likely to come apart more rapidly than we had anticipated in November." He warned of the possibility that Saigon might start secret negotiations with Hanoi. National Security Adviser McGeorge Bundy and McNamara then sent a memo to Johnson telling him that "both of us are now pretty well convinced that our current policy can lead only to disastrous defeat." By early February 1965 William Bundy warned the president that "the situation in Vietnam is deteriorating, and without new U.S. action defeat appears inevitable—probably not in a matter of weeks or perhaps even months, but within the next year or so."[9] These memos were followed by recommendations as to how the situation could be turned around. After each round of apocalyptic memos warning of defeat, the president ordered an escalation to stave it off.

Choosing Advisers and Advice

Johnson listened to advisers who got things wrong and ignored those who had a track record for correctly predicting developments in Vietnam and those with knowledge of conditions in Southeast Asia. He got rid of diplomats and counterinsurgency experts who urged him to limit his commitments (Roger Hilsman, Averell Harriman, Michael Forrestal, and John Kenneth Galbraith), all of whom had emphasized political reform in Saigon. They were eclipsed by national security advisers who counseled escalation in order to stabilize the situation. Johnson also distanced himself from elected politicians who gave him cautious advice, such as Vice President Hubert Humphrey and Senator Mike Mansfield (D-MT), and old political friends such as Washington lawyer Clark Clifford.

At the lower levels of the State Department there were China and Southeast Asia hands (Allen Whiting, Edward Rice, Marshall Green, Louis Sarris, Paul Kattenburg, and Dorothy Avery), whose memos were ignored by the higher-ups.[10] Kattenburg, a State Department official, recounted that after attending meetings to discuss the Diem regime in August 1963: "I grew increasingly appalled as I listened to speaker after speaker, men at the top of our government like Rusk, McNamara, Taylor, and Robert Kennedy who simply did not know Vietnam, its recent history, or the personalities and forces in contention."[11]

One "higher-up" who did have deep misgivings about escalation was Undersecretary of State George Ball. On October 5, 1964, he presented his views in a 67-page memorandum to Rusk, McNamara, and McGeorge Bundy: The gist of his argument was that the government in Saigon was deteriorating and there was no possibility it would be able to rally the South Vietnamese. No one had shown that action against the North could create political cohesiveness and popular support in the South. Bombing the North would not get it to desist, the political impact worldwide would be negative, and it would only lead the North to step up infiltration or even invade in the South. Escalation would pass the options over to the other side. "Once on the Tiger's back," he argued, "we cannot be sure of picking the place to dismount."[12] Ball then concluded with an outline for a negotiated settlement: North Vietnam would end its insurgency in the South, which would allow the establishment of an independent government in Saigon that would have a free hand to deal with the insurgency; Saigon could call on the United States for assistance in dealing with the Vietcong and there would be guarantees of the independence of the Saigon government.

But why would North Vietnam end its assistance to the Vietcong when the Vietcong were defeating the Saigon regime? Ball had no answer and did not even pose the question. McNamara later admitted that he and the other advisers all erred in not exploring the possibilities that Ball's memo had raised. More to the point, they erred in not understanding the risks of escalation, which Ball *had* understood. Even as Ball's objections were being brushed aside, the field commander General William Westmoreland was offering his own gloomy assessment: "Unless there are reasonable prospects of a fairly effective government in South Vietnam in the immediate offing, then no amount of offensive action by the U.S. either in or outside Vietnam has any chance by itself of reversing the deterioration now underway."[13]

Vice President Humphrey sent a lengthy memo to Johnson early in 1965 outlining the political costs of escalation. He reminded Johnson, "We have never stood for military solutions alone, or for victory through air power. We have always stressed the political, economic and social dimensions." He warned, "American wars have to be politically understandable by the American public. There has to be a cogent, convincing case if we are to enjoy sustained public support." He observed, "Politically, in Washington, beneath the surface, the opposition is more Democratic than Republican. This may be even more true at the grassroots around the country." He counseled, "It is always hard to cut losses. But the Johnson administration is in a stronger position to do so now than any Administration in this century." Although he concluded, "I intend to support the Administration whatever the President's decisions," Johnson froze him out of the war councils.[14] Johnson stopped holding formal meetings of the National Security Council (NSC) and instead, as Humphrey later recalled, "began to discuss Vietnam in the informal sessions he preferred—meetings staffed with his own, selected advisors."[15]

With Ball he took a different tack, using him as the designated devil's advocate—a position Ball was willing to take as a loyal careerist perhaps hoping eventually to ascend to the top position at the State Department. By allowing Ball to argue his case, Johnson could keep a line out to skeptics in the Senate, particularly J. William Fulbright (D-AR), chair of the Foreign Relations Committee. Johnson urged Ball to solicit Fulbright's views, cautioning, "There will be trouble if we don't take him with us."[16] And so, because of his connection with the skeptics in the Senate, Ball had a privileged position at Johnson's table. Although Johnson invited Ball to debate supporters of escalation, he kept the burden of argument on those seeking a way out of war, a burden that no one, not even Ball or Johnson's closest political advisers, could overcome.[17] "My hope to force a systematic reexamination of our total situation had manifestly failed," Ball later recalled.[18]

The National Security Managers

The president listened to his national security managers. They were used to taking risks and managing crises, and they were comfortable with strategies of *compellence*: the threat or use of limited amounts of force to induce changes in an adversary's behavior based on its own rational choice to end the threat or stop the pain. When McNamara met with his top military officials in Honolulu on April 19 and 20, 1965, to assess the war's progress, they unanimously recommended a major increase in U.S. forces.[19] From the 33,500 then in Vietnam, none organized as combat units and most involved in training or military delivery of equipment, they recommended an increase to 82,000 troops in thirteen maneuver battalions. They also anticipated getting three battalions from Korea and one each from Australia and New Zealand for an additional 7,250 troops. Even though the United States was then engaged in a sustained bombing campaign, they believed that ground forces were needed to stave off defeat.[20] No one thought the introduction of combat forces would lead to victory, however. General Earl Wheeler reported to McNamara in late April that air strikes between February and April "have not reduced in any major way the over-all military capabilities" of the North Vietnamese.[21] Publicly the administration remained optimistic: "There is no evidence that the Vietcong has any significant popular following in South Vietnam," Rusk claimed at a news briefing on April 23.[22]

Ball recommended against the military requests coming from Honolulu. He sent a new memo calling for a diplomatic settlement instead of escalation, but his attempt to get Johnson to turn to diplomacy failed, even though Johnson's advisers had predicted some success with air power and had been incorrect while Ball had predicted that the North Vietnamese would step up infiltration with regular army units and had been correct. The fact that Ball had been correct and his other advisers mistaken about the impact of bombing the North seemed to make no difference to the president.[23] The United States had violated the "tacit understanding" with the North that so long as the United States did not bomb, Hanoi would not send troops into the South, just as the area specialists in the State Department such as Roger Hilsman had warned. Now enemy troops infiltrated down the trail at an increasing rate. On April 30 the CIA reported that "the general outlook remains dreary and in some respects the dangers of the situation have increased."[24]

Some national security advisers, such as Walt Rostow, maintained an optimistic front. Hanoi, Rostow told Rusk on May 20, "is now staring at quite clear-cut defeat, with the rising U.S. strength and GVN morale in the South and rising costs in the North." But in Vietnam, Ambassador Taylor saw things differently. On June 3 he cabled Rusk that no amount of bombing would get the North to give up its actions: "Our strategy must be based on a patient and steady increase of pressure following an escalating pattern while making maximum effort to turn the tide here in the South."[25] Taylor also admitted, "It will probably be necessary to commit U.S. ground forces to action."[26] By June a new escalatory step was necessary: B-52s from Guam started carpet bombing the large Vietcong concentrations operating in the South.

The military called for more troops. On June 7 Westmoreland asked for thirty-four U.S. battalions (175,000 troops) and ten battalions from other nations or from the United States. "I see no course of action open to us except to reinforce our efforts in SVN with additional U.S. or third country forces as rapidly as is practical during the critical weeks ahead. . . . The basic purpose of the additional deployments recommended . . . is to give us a substantial and hard hitting offensive capability on the ground to convince the VC that they cannot win."[27] As McNamara later recalled: "Of the thousands of cables I received during my seven years in the Defense Department, this one disturbed me the most. We were forced to make a decision. We could no longer postpone a choice about which path to take."[28] The following day the top advisers met to consider Westmoreland's request. McNamara, Rusk, McGeorge Bundy, and Taylor agreed that they would have to give Westmoreland 100,000 troops.

On June 10 the CIA issued another pessimistic evaluation about the impact of new U.S. forces: "The arrival of U.S. forces in these numbers [150,000] would not change the Communists' basic calculation that their staying power is inherently superior to that of Saigon and Washington."[29] The situation was rife with uncertainty: No one could tell how well the U.S. forces would do in the jungles (the previous day fourteen U.S. soldiers had been killed in a Vietcong attack on a special forces camp) and so no one could tell in advance how many troops would be needed.

Even as Johnson was pondering his choices, one in a series of military coups was occurring in Saigon. The civilian government resigned, and the military set up a National Leadership Committee. Nguyen Cao Ky would serve as prime minister and General Nguyễn Văn Thiêu as president—a duo whom William Bundy characterized as "the bottom of the barrel, absolutely the bottom of the barrel!"[30] In the aftermath of the coup, the South Vietnamese army was in full retreat. By June 14 Westmoreland characterized his forty-four battalion request as "no force for victory but as a stop-gap measure to save the ARVN from defeat."[31]

The Stalemate Option

Johnson was left with no options: He either would escalate or the South Vietnamese regime would be eliminated. On June 15 he approved deployment of the 1st Air Cavalry Division, with 28,000 troops and support personnel. "Before we commit an endless flow of forces to South Vietnam," Ball cautioned in dissent, "we must have more evidence than we now have that our troops will not bog down in the jungles and rice paddies—while we slowly blow the country to bits."[32] Ball advised exploring a political solution with the Vietcong. Meanwhile the United States could keep the force level at 100,000 and see what happened over the summer. It could test the political performance of the South Vietnamese government and the field performance of U.S. forces and link future commitments to the results. Johnson took the memo to Camp David for the weekend and discussed it with Bill Moyers. "I don't think I should go over one hundred thousand but I think I should go to that number and explain it," he told Moyers, adding, "I told McNamara that I would not make a decision on this and not to assume that I am willing to go overboard on this. I ain't."[33]

"We think that if we can accomplish that stalemate, accompanied by the limited bombing program in the North, we can force them to negotiations, and negotiations that will lead to a settlement that will preserve the independence of South Vietnam," McNamara told the cabinet.[34] He was uncertain about the number of troops that might be needed to bring a stalemate, adding that 100,000 troops would not be enough. He cautioned that the United States could not go too far without the possibility of a "spasm response" by the Chinese. The cabinet response was skeptical. "Is that all we are going to tell the American people, that all we are getting is a stalemate?" Health, Education, and Welfare Secretary Anthony Celebrezze asked. McNamara responded, "I didn't tell that to the American people."[35]

"In the summer of 1965," General Wheeler later recalled, "it became amply clear that it wasn't a matter of whether the North Vietnamese were going to win the war; it was just a question of when they were going to win it."[36] Johnson himself was increasingly fretful. "The President mentioned to me yesterday his desire that we find more dramatic and effective actions in South Vietnam," McGeorge Bundy told McNamara on June 18.[37] In the last week of June, the Vietcong engaged in terror bombing in Saigon, executed a U.S. military adviser it had held prisoner, and announced a "death list" of top U.S. officials in Saigon, including Taylor and Westmoreland. In response, Johnson approved the deployment of three more marine battalions and gave Westmoreland authority to commit U.S. forces to combat "independently of" South Vietnamese operations.

McNamara now set out three options: cut U.S. losses and withdraw; continue at the present level of about 75,000; or escalate to 44 battalions (doubling the troop level) in the hope that such a commitment would get peace talks started. He recommended the third option, which included a quarantine on war supplies to North Vietnam; mining of harbors; destruction of rail and bridges to China; destruction of military depots, airfields, and SAM (surface-to-air missile) sites. "Since troops once committed as a practical matter cannot be removed, since U.S. casualties will rise, since we should take call-up activities to support the additional forces in Vietnam, the test of endurance may be as much in the U.S. as it Vietnam," he concluded.[38]

McGeorge Bundy, who had been closely allied with McNamara through prior escalations, was sharply critical of this memorandum. He observed that "our troops are entirely untested in the kind of warfare projected." McNamara had proposed more bombing when the value of the bombing was in dispute; he had proposed a naval quarantine by mining Haiphong in the North when the war was occurring in the South. "My first reaction is that this program is rash to the point of folly," Bundy concluded.[39] There seemed to be no upper limit on the number of troops that would be required: "If we need 200 thousand men now for these quite limited missions, may we not need 400 thousand later? Is this a rational course of action? Is there any real prospect that U.S. regular forces can conduct the anti-guerrilla operations that would probably remain the central problem in South Vietnam?" Bundy also faulted the memo for lacking negotiation or exit possibilities. "If U.S. casualties go up sharply, what further actions do we propose to take or not to take? More broadly still, what is the real object of the exercise? If it is to get to the conference table, what results do we seek there? Still more brutally, do we want to invest 200,000 men to cover an eventual retreat? Can we not do that just as well where we are?" But Bundy was no closet dove. He suggested to McNamara additional "big stick" actions.[40] McNamara later recalled a Bundy memo asking that the United States "at least consider what realistic threat of larger action is available to us for communication to Hanoi," a veiled reference to Eisenhower's threat to use nuclear weapons in Korea in 1953 unless the enemy agreed to negotiate an armistice.[41]

George Ball's premise was that the United States was losing the war and that the burden of proof should be on those who wanted to escalate: "Any prudent military commander carefully selects the terrain on which to stand and fight, and no great captain has ever been blamed for a successful tactical withdrawal." The terrain here was bad: "Politically, South Vietnam is a lost cause. . . . The 'government' in Saigon is a travesty." Ball advised Johnson to insist that South Vietnam establish a representative and democratic government that could demonstrate popular support: "South Vietnam is a country with an army and no government. Even if we were to commit five hundred thousand men to South Vietnam we would still lose."[42] His case was strengthened by a June 29 State Department report indicating that the bombing had strengthened the North Vietnamese regime with its own population and reinforced its determination to win and concluding that the Rolling Thunder bombing campaign had been a colossal miscalculation.[43]

Ball proposed to hold U.S. forces at 72,000, primarily as a reserve and for base security. The United States should enter negotiations based on the premise that we were losing the war and that we needed to "find a way out with minimal long-term costs." He foresaw the dynamic of escalation: "Once we suffer large casualties, we will have started a well-nigh irreversible process. Our involvement will be so great that we cannot—without national humiliation—stop short of achieving our national objectives. Of the two possibilities I think humiliation would be more likely than the achievement of our objectives—even after we had paid terrible costs."[44] In contrast, McNamara again suggested that the United States increase the pressure on the Vietcong and North Vietnamese by bombing military targets in North Vietnam and in Hanoi in order to get negotiations started when the United States had the advantage. He believed that forty-four battalions would establish a military balance by the end of the year and would convince the Communists they could not win. McNamara also called for a reserve call-up of 100,000 troops.[45]

Johnson dispatched McNamara, Lodge, Wheeler, and Andrew Goodpastor to Saigon for fact-finding. He sent Ambassador Taylor two main questions, along with twenty-five subsidiary questions, the gist of which were "Could we force Vietcong to settle on our terms? Would a large increase in U.S. forces cause the South Vietnamese to let up and result in an adverse popular reaction?" McNamara arrived in Saigon on July 16 and the next day had dinner with the flamboyant Prime Minister Nguyen Cao Ky and the more dignified President Thiêu. "Ky made a spectacular entrance," the diplomat Chester Cooper recalled. "He walked in breezily, wearing a tight, white dinner jacket, tapered formal trousers, pointed, patented leather shoes, and brilliant red socks. A Hollywood central casting bureau would have grabbed him for a role as a sax player in a second-rate Manila night club."[46] Ky requested 44 American battalions and an additional infantry division, for a total of 200,000 soldiers. General Westmoreland recommended 175,000 troops by year's end and then another 100,000 the following year.

While McNamara was in Saigon, Undersecretary of State Cyrus Vance sent him a memo, relaying Johnson's inclination to proceed with Westmoreland's forty-four battalion request.[47] Vance's cable to McNamara stated that it was the president's "current intention" to approve troop levels he anticipated that McNamara was going to recommend. Johnson may have been jumping the gun, but more likely he was sending a signal to McNamara to come back with a strong recommendation while putting the onus on McNamara and the military. McNamara returned on July 20 to give a bleak report to the president. The situation in Vietnam was continuing to deteriorate. The economy was near collapse. The South Vietnamese Army (ARVN) was being defeated, especially in the Central Highlands. The Communists had a large workforce pool and were finding it easy to replace their losses. The North Vietnamese were infiltrating large units into the South. Bombing had not stopped the flow of war materiel to the South, nor had it "produced tangible evidence of willingness on the part of Hanoi to come to the conference table in a reasonable mood." Yet McNamara optimistically concluded that "early commitment of additional U.S./Third Country forces in sufficient quantity, for general reserve and offensive roles, should stave off GVN defeat" and would "offer a good chance of producing a favorable settlement in the longer run."[48]

What would constitute a favorable outcome? McNamara specified nine elements: the Vietcong would end attacks, there would be less terror or sabotage, the North would reduce its infiltration, the North would withdraw its forces from the South, the South Vietnam government would control most of the South Vietnamese territory, the Vietcong and National Liberation Front (NLF) would become a political rather than military organization, the Communists would be quiescent in Laos and Thailand, South Vietnam would become neutral or pro-Western, and U.S. combat forces could withdraw. He pointed out that once negotiations began, the outcomes would probably be less favorable than these desired results.

To get North Vietnam to the negotiating table, McNamara recommended 175,000 to 200,000 troops, with another 100,000 possibly added by January 1966. He also called for extending tours of duty and calling up 235,000 troops from the Reserves and National Guard, all of which would increase the armed forces by 375,000. He warned Johnson that "it would imply a commitment to see a fighting war clear through at considerable cost in casualties and materiel and would make any later decision to withdraw even more difficult and even more costly than would be the case today."[49] He forecast five hundred American deaths a month by the end of 1965. The same day a CIA memo argued that an increase in U.S. troops would *not* deter Communists or alter their belief that they would ultimately win.[50]

As Johnson was mulling over his options, the military situation in Vietnam worsened badly. Regiments of the North Vietnamese regular army infiltrated into the South. ARVN battalions were destroyed in set piece battles. The Vietcong took over many district headquarters and made new gains in the Central Highlands. Intelligence reports warned that they were on the verge of cutting South Vietnam in half and establishing an NLF government in areas of their control.

Dysfunctions of the Advisory System

"No one was prepared to discuss why we persisted in a war that, in my view, we could not win, in pursuit of an objective that seemed every day to have less reality," George Ball later recalled.[51] Johnson structured the final discussions with the presumption that some action was essential: He kept the burden of proof on those who would reduce or end U.S. involvement, not on those who would continue or escalate. The predictive and analytical performance of the advisers Johnson retained was poor. Secretary Rusk and his top officials, advised by the embassy in Saigon, were wrong about the ability of generals such as Khanh, Ky, and Thiêu to gain political legitimacy and rally the South Vietnamese. Taylor at the embassy argued that escalation was necessary to improve morale and strengthen whatever leader was then in power, but with each escalatory step, those in power were weakened and soon removed in a revolving-door series of coups and countercoups. McNamara later concluded, "If we had had more Asia experts around us perhaps we would not have been so simpleminded about China and Vietnam. We had that expertise available during the Cuban Missile Crisis; in general, we had it available when we dealt with Soviet affairs, but we lacked it when dealing with Southeast Asia."[52] That is a weak excuse: There were plenty of experts around, but neither McNamara nor the president took their advice.[53]

Role of the Military

Was Johnson deceived into an escalation by military officers intent on escalation?[54] Some in Johnson's circle believed so. "In none of the discussions leading up to Rolling Thunder," presidential counselor Clark Clifford later recounted, "was the President told, either by the Joint Chiefs of Staff or his Secretary of Defense, that once bombing of the North began, the military would require, and demand, American combat troops, first to protect the American air bases from which the bombing was launched, and then, inevitably, to begin offensive operations against the enemy."[55] The military gave the president poor intelligence, covered up its failures, and projected enough optimism about the progress of operations so that Johnson was suckered into raising the stakes, according to this argument.[56]

Yet there is little evidence that the military played a decisive role in the decisions to escalate.[57] When the Pentagon's Joint War Games Agency held Sigma I-64 in March 1964, a war game with top NSC participants, the results gave no indication that U.S. escalation would make the Vietcong capitulate. If the United States escalated, they predicted "moral and legal questions" about bombing the North and hitting innocent populations. Westmoreland recalled that when he took command in Saigon "the thinking in Washington on increasing the American commitment in South Vietnam, possibly to include bombing North Vietnam, and even introducing American combat troops, [was] far more advanced than anything we were considering in Saigon."[58] Marine Corps commandant Wallace Greene wanted to keep his service's commitment at five hundred advisers and opposed sending in ground troops. For the navy, Admirals Sharp and Moorer opposed the "panhandle" strategy of ground troops. The air force favored reliance on bombing and not ground troops. Even so, many officers were skeptical about bombing. In September 1964 the Joint War Games Agency held a second round of war games, Sigma II-64. The participants predicted mounting political unrest and morale problems for the United States at home if there were a bombing escalation, and they predicted improved morale in North Vietnam. The United States would be vulnerable in other theaters if it made a greater commitment in Vietnam. If it escalated, other nations would brand the United States as the aggressor. Most career officers gave cautious advice and protected their own stakes from other services, from their superiors in the Pentagon, and from an impatient president.[59]

Johnson wasn't pressured or manipulated by the military; if anything, the reverse was the case. Johnson, according to Maxwell Taylor, "was the fellow with the black snake whip behind [the chiefs] saying, 'Let's get going—now!' He did all this behind my back. . . . Once he made his decision he couldn't get going fast enough."[60] Johnson was an intimidating presence, towering over his generals and admirals, peremptorily ordering them to "get things bubbling" on the battlefields or to present him with new ideas and new options. On March 5, 1965, just before sending a hapless general (also named Johnson) out to Vietnam for an inspection, the president berated him for not doing more: "You're not giving me any ideas and any solutions for this damn little pissant country. Now, I don't need ten generals to come in here ten times and tell me to bomb. I want some solutions. I want some answers."[61] General Johnson came back from his tour recommending more ground troops.

Another meeting, in November 1965, is illustrative of Johnson's treatment of his military advisers. General Wheeler asked Johnson to approve naval mining of Haiphong, blockading the North Vietnamese coastline, and bombing of Hanoi with B-52s. Johnson polled the chiefs, asking if they agreed, and they all concurred. Then, according to Lieutenant General Charles G. Cooper, a military aide present at the meeting, Johnson exploded: "He screamed obscenities, he cursed them personally, he ridiculed them for coming to his office with their 'military advice.' Noting that it was he who was carrying the weight of the free world on his shoulders, he called them filthy names— sh__heads, dumsh__s, pompous assh__s, and used 'the F-word' as an adjective more freely than a Marine at boot camp. He then accused them of trying to pass the buck for World War III to him. It was unnerving. It was degrading." Later in the meeting, according to Cooper, Johnson told the chiefs "that he was not going to let some military idiots talk him into World War III. He ordered them to 'get the hell out of my office.'"[62]

"Presidential advisers too often simply try to anticipate the president's decisions," George Ball pointed out, "telling him not what he ought to hear, but what they think he wants to hear. As the war went on, there was a clear tendency on the part of the men around Johnson to do that—all of them weary, frustrated with the duration of the struggle and the obvious lack of success."[63] The president was willing to drop advisers, shift generals' commands, and intimidate his military advisers into giving him what they thought he wanted to hear. He staged discussions so that he could legitimate decisions he had already made.[64] Johnson made the key decisions about military strategy (particularly escalation with "search and destroy" ground forces) and about the resources needed to carry it out and manipulated the Chiefs of Staff to obtain their concurrence. As with the Bay of Pigs incident, the chiefs individually and collectively were not in a position to challenge a president's assumptions. In any event, they were more interested in resolving their own interservice rivalries than in considering strategic issues about the use of American force.[65]

Perhaps it is just as well that Johnson did not listen to the advice of the chiefs. The army generals, after agreeing to escalate with ground troops in 1965, were wrong about the kind of war that was being fought: They expected that their troops would face main-force enemy units immediately and that they would get to fight and win a conventional war. They made this analysis just as the Vietcong were increasing terrorist attacks against South Vietnamese police and politicians and decreasing their conventional attacks. When the United States escalated, the Vietnamese Communists refused to fall into the trap of beginning what they called the "Third Phase" conventional war.

A culture of deception emerged within the U.S. Army in response to Vietcong tactics so that bad information flowed from the bottom to the top of the chain of command, from there to the Pentagon, and thence to the president.[66] Colin Powell, then a junior military adviser in 1962 with a Vietnamese army unit in the A Shau Valley, later described a system of "phony readiness reports, rampant careerism, old-boy assignments, phony body counts—the whole facade of illusion and delusion."[67] General Bruce Palmer, who served in Vietnam as a corps commander and deputy COMUSMACV (Commander, U.S. Military Assistance Command, Vietnam) admitted that although career officers were skeptical, "Not once during the war did the JCS advise the Commander-in-Chief or the Secretary of Defense that the strategy being pursued most probably would fail and that the U.S. would be unable to achieve its objectives."[68] McNamara added that Pentagon civilians "erred equally by not forcing such an appraisal."[69] But even career officers couldn't be expected to carry out that assignment in the face of Johnson's determination to proceed.

Corrupting the Advisory System

At every stage of decision making, Johnson had officials available to him who knew about the history of Western colonialism in Asia and who knew about North Vietnamese government and its intentions and capabilities. Most were buried in second- and third-echelon positions in the State or Defense Departments, but George Ball, Hubert Humphrey, Clark Clifford, and a number of Democratic senators were close enough to the president to press their cases. As time went on, they, and the experts in the bureaucracy, were marginalized, isolated, humiliated, ignored, patronized, deceived, or intimidated. If Johnson did not have confidence in this group, he could have concentrated harder on the CIA intelligence assessments, none of which painted a picture of a war that could be won with conventional arms.

Johnson's "disqualification heuristic" included all advisers with contrary opinions. Johnson allowed Ball to remain on board just so that Johnson would leave a documentary record of a president listening to all sides of the issue until he had made up his mind—thus Ball inadvertently was playing a role in a script that Johnson had created to provide his decisions with authority and legitimacy. At that point Johnson had not only created an advisory system that was fundamentally flawed but also he had deliberately corrupted it as well. This is clear when one looks at the meetings Johnson held with his top advisers as he made his final decision to escalate.

The President Decides

At the final meetings in July, Johnson's advisers formed into three camps: a "negotiate and withdraw" group consisting of George Ball and Clark Clifford (along with Vice President Humphrey); an "escalate and then negotiate" group led by McNamara and Rusk; and a "seek victory" group centered on the Joint Chiefs. On July 21, at a morning meeting of the NSC, Johnson framed the alternatives by paraphrasing from McNamara's memo of the prior day: "1. Leave the country—with as little loss as possible—the 'bugging out' approach. 2. Maintain present force and lose slowly. 3. Add 100,000 men—recognizing that may not be enough—and adding more next year."[70] The price tag, according to McNamara, would be $12 billion to meet Westmoreland's requests. Near the end of the discussion, the president asked, "Is there anyone here of the opinion we should not do what the memorandum says? If so, I want to hear from him now, in detail." On cue Ball responded: "Mr. President, I can foresee a perilous voyage, very dangerous. I have great and grave apprehensions that we can win under these conditions. But let me be clear. If the decision is to go ahead, I am committed." Johnson asked Ball, "Can you discuss it fully?" Ball responded, "We have discussed it. I have had my day in court." But Johnson wanted more discussion: "I think it's desirable to hear you out, truly hear you out, then I can determine if your suggestions are sound and ready to be followed, which I am prepared to do if I am convinced."

That afternoon Ball presented a chart showing a correlation between public opinion in the United States and casualties in the Korean War. We would lose support of the country, and allies would desert us. "No great captain in history ever hesitated to make a tactical withdrawal if conditions were unfavorable to him," Ball concluded.[71] "But George," Johnson asked, "wouldn't all these countries say that Uncle Sam was a paper tiger, wouldn't we lose all credibility breaking the word of three presidents, if we did as you have proposed? It would seem to be an irresponsible blow. But I gather you don't think so?" Ball responded: "No sir. The worse blow would be that the mightiest power on earth is unable to defeat a handful of guerrillas." The next morning Johnson followed the same pattern with the military as with Ball: He heard them out and challenged their arguments. He began by throwing the chiefs off balance: He asked McGeorge Bundy to summarize Ball's case. Bundy observed that all we had done thus far in Vietnam was fail. Now we were about to fight a land war in Asia. "How long—how much? Can we take casualties over five years— or are we talking about a military solution when the solution is political? Why can't we interdict better—why are our bombings so fruitless—why can't we blockade the coast—why can't we improve our intelligence—why can't we find the VC?" Bundy asked the chiefs.[72] Johnson played devil's advocate with the chiefs: "Are we starting something that in two to three years we simply can't finish?"[73] He posed the Ball question: Shouldn't we "be out of there and make our stand somewhere else?"

The chiefs replied that withdrawal was the worst possible alternative. Johnson pressed his attack: "Doesn't it really mean if we follow Westmoreland's request we are in a new war—this is going off the diving board?"[74] Then he asked the key question: "What will happen if we put in 100,000 more men and then two, three years later you tell me you need 500,000 more? . . . And what makes you think if we put in 100,000 men, Ho Chi Minh won't put in another 100,000, and match us every bit of the way?"[75] The chiefs' response was that if the North sent regular units to the South, these units could be destroyed without risking Chinese intervention. They would be fighting on our terms. The greater our troop strength, the smaller our losses, proportionately. When Johnson asked Wheeler what it would take "to do the job," the response was 700,000 to one million troops and seven years.[76] General Wallace M. Greene Jr. of the Marine Corps wanted to put 72,000 marines into Vietnam over and above McNamara's requests. He would bomb the North's industrial complex and oil facilities and blockade Cambodia. "How long would it take?" he asked rhetorically: "Five years, plus 500,000 troops. I think the American people would back you."[77] Johnson was skeptical: "Do all of you think the Congress and the people will go along with 600,000 people and billions of dollars 10,000 miles away?"[78]

In the afternoon, Johnson once again met with his civilian advisers, now broadened to include his key White House aides. Clark Clifford, who had heard the chiefs, still counseled against escalation, scoffing at the arguments of the military: "Some of what General Wheeler said today was ridiculous. . . . I am bearish about this whole exercise. I know what pressure you're under from McNamara and the military, but if you handle it carefully, you don't have to commit yourself and the nation."[79] Clifford and Ball urged negotiations. But most of the discussion dealt with how escalation should be managed. McGeorge Bundy and Dean Rusk counseled that they should downplay the decision to escalate and should avoid calling it a change of policy. In contrast, McNamara wanted full disclosure to the public.

In the midst of the debates on escalation and disclosure, the National Intelligence Board issued an intelligence estimate entitled "Communist and Free World Reactions to a Possible U.S. Course of Action." If the United States sent 175,000 troops to South Vietnam, the Communists would probably build up their own strength with more regular forces from the North. The North Vietnamese would get a Soviet air defense system. The Chinese "would believe that the U.S. measures were sufficient only to postpone defeat while magnifying its eventual effect." But the Board also recommended that any announcements about the U.S. buildup "be made piecemeal with no more high level emphasis than necessary."[80]

Near the end of July, Johnson went off for the weekend to Camp David to talk with his key adviser Clark Clifford. "A failure to engage in an all-out war will not lower our international prestige," Clifford told him. "This is not the last inning in the struggle against communism. We must pick those spots where the stakes are highest for us and we have the greatest ability to prevail." He added, "Five years, 50,000 men killed, hundreds of billions of dollars—it is just not for us."[81] But Johnson was not persuaded.

At a NSC meeting on July 27, Johnson announced a massive escalation. "We have chosen to do what is necessary to meet the present situation, but not to be unnecessarily provocative to either the Russians or the communist Chinese. We will give the commanders the men they say they need and, out of existing materiel in the U.S. we will get them the materiel they say they need. We will get the necessary money in the new budget and we will use our transfer authority until January. We will neither brag about what we are doing or thunder at the Chinese communists and the Russians."[82] The president's formulation of his policy offered him political cover. He was co-opting the military with the phrase "the men they say they need," and he calculated that the military would be willing to accept the accountability to get the troops. It was a brilliant stroke, and it produced the desired results. Johnson polled everyone in the room. No one objected. Even Earl Wheeler, head of Joint Chiefs of Staff

(JCS), nodded agreement, even though Johnson had rejected the wartime footing, expanded bombing, and call-up of reserves, which the chiefs had urged.

Johnson called in the cabinet and briefed congressional leaders.[83] He told them his decision to send a limited number of troops, but he didn't tell them that it meant 175,000 troops by November and an additional 100,000 by 1966.[84] When Senator George Smathers (D-FL) asked if there was a change in policy, Johnson responded, "As aid to the VC increases, our need to increase our forces goes up. There is no change in policy."[85] He told congressional leaders (and his own Council of Economic Advisers and Office of Management and Budget) that it would cost only "a few billion dollars," though the original McNamara estimate was $12 billion and a revised estimate had come in at $6 billion. Among those present, only Senator Mike Mansfield (D-MT) voiced his objections. The next morning Johnson briefed thirty-three senior members of Congress. He described his steps as moderate and incremental, and warned that "there are military men who'd like to go a lot further."[86] Several dovish senators tried to pressure Johnson to steer a moderate course. Russell, Mansfield, Fulbright, John Sparkman (D-AL), George Aiken (R-VT), and John Cooper (R-KY) sent the president a memo in which they noted "that your objective was not to get in deeply and that you intended to do only what was essential in the military line until January, while Rusk and [UN ambassador] Goldberg were concentrating on attempting to get us out."[87] The doves used the ploy of taking Johnson at his word (probably knowing he was not being completely candid) to lay down a marker for the limits of their support.

Johnson was no more candid with the American people than he had been with Congress. At his July 28, 1965, news conference the president referred to a "low-key strategy" that would involve an increase in troops from 75,000 to 125,000. "I have asked the Commanding General, General Westmoreland, what more he needs to meet this mounting aggression. He has told me. We will meet his needs."[88] Johnson did not mention that he had authorized a total of 175,000 troops for 1965 and 100,000 more troops for 1966. He talked about victory but did not explain the McNamara strategy of stalemate followed by negotiations.

In the question-and-answer session with the media Johnson continued to provide incomplete or disingenuous answers:

Q. Mr. President, does the fact that you are sending additional forces to Viet-Nam imply any change in the existing policy of relying mainly on the South Vietnamese to carry out offensive operations and using American forces to guard American installations and to act as an emergency backup?

A: It does not imply any change in policy whatever. It does not imply any change of objective.[89]

Technically Johnson was not lying, since the military policy already had been changed on April 1, prior to the recent announcements. The American people rallied round the flag: By early fall, Gallup polls indicated that 64 percent supported greater involvement as necessary, while opposition and "no opinion" responses sharply declined.[90] White House news management kept precise details of escalation under wraps: Its pressure forced the Pentagon to scrap a speech drafted by McNamara's aide Daniel Ellsberg that described the buildup to 175,000.[91]

In response to this buildup, at the twelfth Plenum of the Central Committee of the Communist Party in North Vietnam in December 1965, the leadership called upon the nation to resist the U.S. escalation, and "to foil the war of aggression of the U.S. imperialists in any circumstances, so as to defend the North, liberate the South, complete the national people's democratic revolution in the whole country, advancing toward the peaceful reunification of the country."[92] The cycle of escalation and counterescalation was now set in place. By December 1965 General Westmoreland would be back for a request for 440,000 troops.

Johnson had committed the nation to politically and economically unsustainable levels: 30,000 dead, more than 100,000 wounded, curtailment of the Great Society, and by 1968 the largest run on gold in history, a currency speculation that threatened not only the stability of the dollar but also of the world monetary system. Not only could higher military expenditures in Vietnam not be sustained but also it was clear that the existing level of expenditures, because they affected the U.S. balance of payments, could not be sustained either.[93] By spring 1968 Johnson was looking for ways to cap the U.S. commitment and reduce it. His successor, Richard Nixon, would eventually "Vietnamize" the war and then end the U.S. ground combat participation in it with the Paris Peace Accords in January 1973. Two years later North Vietnam defeated the South and reunified Vietnam on its own terms. Within one decade of the escalation the failure of Johnson's compellence strategy was complete.

The Compellence Game

In the early stages of the escalation in June 1964, Rusk, McNamara, McGeorge Bundy, George Ball, and William Bundy met at the White House West Wing to discuss a pessimistic report from Ambassador Taylor. A restless Lyndon Johnson dropped in on them and asked, "How do we get what we want?" The advisers responded, as they had done in the past, that with enough pain Hanoi would feel compelled to call its infiltration off.[94]

The Vietnam escalation was a variation of the "compellence" game. Just as President John Kennedy's advisers initially expected the Soviets during the missile crisis of 1962 to withdraw from Cuba on American terms because of its overwhelming local and strategic superiority, Johnson assumed that the Vietnamese Communists would end their attempt to topple the South Vietnamese regime because of American military superiority. He and McNamara thought the North Vietnamese would make a rational choice to submit to American pressure.

Johnson's decision to project an equivalence of military power with North Vietnam and the Vietcong was beside the point. If anyone were likely to withdraw when the use of force proved too punishing, it would be the American side. Johnson might have been playing a game of compellence, but unfortunately, American decision makers never seemed to have understood the game the Vietnamese were playing or the limits of game-playing analogies.[95] The United States had three related strategies: stabilization of the political situation in Saigon; military escalation to punish Communist forces in the North and South; and eventually, negotiations that would lead to an agreement preventing a Communist takeover in Saigon. Its strategy was based on three flawed assumptions: that there was a war between two separate states, North and South Vietnam; that it was facing a threat from the "Sino-Soviet bloc" that it would have to repel; and that if the Communists took power in Indochina they would have designs on neighboring non-Communist states. Each of these assumptions was incorrect: The fighting was a civil war between Communist and non-Communist forces in a single country that had been temporarily divided pending national elections into northern and southern "military regroupment" zones as an interim measure in 1954 under the Geneva Accords. The Communists were nationalists with broad popular support in the North and significant support in the South. The North Vietnamese were not puppets of China or the Soviet Union and remained suspicious of both powers. The Hanoi regime limited ambitions to influence Laos and Cambodia within Indochina, and none that went beyond the peninsula.

McNamara was wrong about the impact the escalation would have on the North Vietnamese. He assumed their will to resist would be broken with sufficient application of force against them while the morale of the South Vietnamese would rise. The JCS overestimated the impact of bombing as a tool of compellence, according to McNamara, because they did not "fully assess the probability of achieving these objectives, how long it might take, or what it would cost in lives lost, resources expended, and risks incurred."[96] There was a disparity of commitment; an asymmetry in the game each side played. For the North Vietnamese and Vietcong, fighting would go on for as long as it took, with whatever it took, no matter what the losses, because in their view they were fighting a Western colonial power. As Chester Cooper concluded three decades later at a conference in Hanoi whose participants included the key decision makers on both sides, "I am sure now that Hanoi had decided early on that, regardless of the sacrifices involved, they would continue to fight until they could confront the Americans with the kind of dramatic, demoralizing defeat they had inflicted on the French in 1954 at the battle of Dien Bien Phu."[97]

"The trouble with our policy in Vietnam," McNamara later admitted, "has been that we guessed wrong with respect to what the North Vietnamese reaction would be. We anticipated that they would respond like reasonable people."[98] McNamara and other advisers thought the Communists would use their own cost-benefit calculus and that hurting them would modify their behavior. He simply could not fathom the psychology of his adversaries or their willingness to endure and desire to prevail.[99] But for the North Vietnamese, reunification was an ultimate value, which could never be negotiated away. The Communists would pay any price to reunify the country under their rule.

For American officials Vietnam always remained a marginal war of containment along the Asian rim. It was a limited war, no matter how much the president might argue that U.S. prestige and commitments were on the line. The bloodier the war became, the more the asymmetry would favor the Communists, not the Americans. In both Korea and Vietnam, the "limited war" approach proved unsustainable politically, as casualties mounted while Americans believed that no victory was in sight.[100]

Rusk and McNamara were wrong about the ultimate implications of working for a "stalemate" in Vietnam. The idea that we could compel a negotiated solution through "graduated escalation" became the ultimate folly. Whenever the United States began to bomb or introduced more advisers, more perimeter guards, or more "search and destroy" battalions, it was not doing so to tighten the screws on North Vietnam. Instead, it was demonstrating its own desperation. Just prior to each American escalation the North Vietnamese were on the verge of gaining decisive advantage; each escalation merely allowed the United States to salvage the situation. Each American escalation was taken in Hanoi as an indication that victory was getting closer; each led to an increase in Hanoi's resolve and morale. Why would they not continue their course when each round of escalation by the United States would increase the political and economic costs to their adversaries? The Vietnamese Communists understood the cost-benefit calculation all too well: They understood that ultimately it would constrain the United States, not themselves. If anyone were making rational choices, it was the regime in Hanoi.

Advisers such as the Pentagon's John McNaughton were wrong about the need to "get bloody" in Vietnam as a test of our credibility and as a demonstration of American commitment to our adversaries and allies. Paying costs in real lives to establish an abstract "credibility" with allies makes no sense unless a nation achieves some stated aims. Fighting and dying is not an end in itself, nor does it establish the credibility of a great power. As George Ball neatly put it, "What we might gain by establishing the steadfastness of our commitments we could lose by an erosion of confidence in our judgment."[101] American officials erred in assuming their credibility was on the line: Other nations seemed not to have considered Vietnam a test of American strength or resolve, just as they did not consider the "fall" of China to signal an end to American power in Asia.

Why didn't the compellence game work in Vietnam? Because the Vietnamese had their own game, which was to draw in American forces to reduce the authority and legitimacy of the South Vietnamese regime. A government that needed to be propped up by outside forces that depended on American approval and support for its very existence would never be considered legitimate by most Vietnamese. Johnson's strategy in the winter of 1964 (secure a base in Saigon, then ratchet up the pressure on Hanoi) was superseded by a revised strategy in the summer of 1965: The United States would send up to 200,000 troops to fight the Vietcong in the countryside and hold terrain, while the South Vietnamese military would handle political security and pacification and "reorganize the rear."[102] This made it an American war, under conditions that guaranteed that no government in Saigon could gain popular support.

Decisional Rules

According to the conventional wisdom of small-group decision theorists, the president should be skeptical about his advisers and their information. He should avoid being pushed into decisions by a coalition of advisers "negotiating from below" and those who would narrow his options. He should guard his "power stakes"—his power to gain mastery of situations tomorrow by what he does today. Faced with a difficult choice, he should convert a large decision into sequential smaller steps to buy time and see how events turn out, especially since something may turn up before the most consequential decisions must be made. A president who acts this way should succeed, or at least not fail. Conversely, a president who fails must not have done these things. And so we get explanations of advisory system malfunctions, groupthink, and quagmires.

But Johnson did all the things the conventional wisdom prescribes, and he did them in correct textbook fashion. He pretty much wrote the book on these techniques. This is not surprising: Johnson was both an instinctive and practiced politician, and he could operate to preserve his options and his power better than anyone else. But if the record shows that Johnson acted at all times the way a "professional" in the Oval Office is supposed to act, the conventional wisdom about presidential decision making cannot explain why he failed.[103]

Gaining Cover

What did Johnson hope to accomplish with escalation? What did he ultimately expect to happen? The answer lies in his political position: His maneuvering was based on his analysis of his power stakes and on his need to convert uncertainty of outcome into manageable political risk. Johnson did not believe that he could take the political heat if Vietnam "fell" to the Communists. "If we walked away from Vietnam and let Southeast Asia fall," he argued, "there would follow a divisive and destructive debate in our country." Johnson echoed Kennedy's fears in the Cuban Missile Crisis about the congressional reaction if he didn't stand tall. "They'd impeach a President, though, that would run out, wouldn't they?" Johnson had asked his old Senate mentor Richard Russell (D-GA) in May 1964, just as he was making the initial decisions.[104] Even without an impeachment threat (which was somewhat farfetched), Johnson had more immediate problems: He was afraid that the Kennedy wing of the party would blame him, laying the groundwork for a challenge by Senator Robert Kennedy (D-NY) in the 1968 Democratic primaries. If he defeated Kennedy for the nomination, his Republican opponent would raise a new refrain: "Who lost Vietnam?" echoing their "Who Lost China?" card of the 1950s.

Johnson sought support from Eisenhower. By February 17, 1965, when Johnson met with the ex-president in the Cabinet Room, Eisenhower told Johnson that he should "use whatever force needed" and that he would support Johnson if he provided the troop levels the military believed necessary—a formulation Johnson later seized upon.[105] Eisenhower cautioned that the United States could not win the war with ground troops and took a dim view of sending twelve divisions or so to carry on the fight, but he suggested that we could "play a major role in destroying the will of the enemy to continue the war" (similar to McNamara's thinking) and advised using only six to eight divisions. If he did not raise the ante Johnson could foresee a new era of McCarthyite politics and perhaps a return to an isolationist foreign policy.[106] And Eisenhower would then criticize him.

Shortly before Johnson made the decision to escalate, Eisenhower told him that we have now "appealed to force" in Vietnam and therefore, with our credibility on the line, "we have got to win." That meant offensive action by ground forces, not just static defense of our airfields and Saigon.[107] He counseled

Johnson that Westmoreland's request for a massive increase in troops should be approved. Once Johnson had decided in his own mind to send ground forces, he called Eisenhower to secure his right flank. Johnson told Eisenhower of his decision, then said that he guessed the ex-president would support him, "conforming to the advice you gave me on Wednesday." Eisenhower responded, "Do what you have to do." Johnson then asked, "Do you really think we can beat the Vietcong?" Eisenhower responded, "We are not going to be run out of a free country that we helped establish," which conformed to the "don't lose" strategy of the Pentagon.[108] After the decision to escalate, Eisenhower sent back word via his aide Andrew Goodpastor, who briefed Johnson that "General Eisenhower stressed strongly that there is no question in any of this about his support for what the President is doing. He supports it strongly."[109]

Managing Risk

Johnson pursued several stratagems simultaneously to manage risk. By escalating, he could solidify a coalition of national security advisers, reinforce his reputation as an effective national security manager, and inoculate himself against attacks by the hawks. By offering to negotiate, he thought he could retain the support of doves dubious about a large and extended commitment. As of June 30, 1965, just before the decision to escalate, McGeorge Bundy summarized the political situation as follows: "At home we remain politically strong and, in general, politically united. Options, both political and military, remain available to us. . . ."[110] There was some wishful thinking in that analysis: Bundy himself cited a Gallup poll of June 9 indicating only 21 percent of the public wanted to escalate. In any event, Johnson felt he could adopt the McNamara formulation: Escalate now in order to negotiate from strength. In his July 21 meeting with top advisers in the Cabinet Room, he told them, "We have got to keep peace proposals going. It's like a prizefight. Our right is our military power, but our left must be our peace proposals. Every time you move troops forward, you move diplomats forward. I want this done. The generals want more and more—and go farther and farther. But State has to supply me with some too."[111]

In a nutshell, these instructions embody a policy that former Defense Department analyst (and marine officer) Daniel Ellsberg later described as a "stalemate machine."[112] As Ellsberg saw it, there were two decisional rules that would guide presidents in making policy for Vietnam. The first rule was that it was never politically acceptable to be the first president to lose a country to Communists during the Cold War. Therefore, it would not be acceptable to permit the Communists to win control of South Vietnam—defined operationally as raising the red flag over Saigon. The second rule was that a president would generally do as little as possible militarily consistent with the first rule. "The objective of our policy is to do all possible to accomplish purpose without use of U.S. combat forces," President Kennedy had cabled Ambassador Frederick Nolting in Saigon.[113]

Johnson would try not to disrupt U.S. life by major military commitments; he would commit as few troops as possible to prevent high U.S. casualties, he would minimize the impact on the economy. But the president would take whatever actions were necessary to keep the Communists from winning, to maintain the policy of "not losing." At the NSC meeting on June 11, 1965, Johnson cautioned, "We must delay and deter the North Vietnamese and VietCong as much as we can, and as simply as we can, without going all out. . . . We must determine which course gives us the maximum protection at the least cost."[114] The White House bought renewed stalemates by escalating every time the entire enterprise was put into doubt by fresh military disasters or political failures in the South, but each stalemate cost more than the one before.[115]

The politics of containment against Communist regimes supposedly bent on world conquest constrained the president and his advisers. They could not admit publicly that the Communists might also be nationalists with popular support whose claim to rule with popular support might be legitimate. They could not accept publicly the possibility of a coalition government. They could not threaten to walk away if the South Vietnamese did not introduce governing reforms. They could not question the domino theory, and therefore they could not base any policy on the possibility of a Communist victory in Vietnam.[116] For Johnson and his advisers it never made sense to propose publicly an exit strategy.

By choosing the stalemate option, Johnson overreacted to his risks, and it is this miscalculation of risk that defines his failure. President Harry Truman supposedly had "lost" much of Eastern Europe to the Soviets by 1948 according to the Republicans, but it didn't stop him from winning the 1948 elections. President Dwight Eisenhower in 1954 had not aided the French in Indochina, and the red flag flew over Hanoi during his watch. That did not hurt him in the 1956 presidential election, which he won in a landslide (Indochina was not even an issue). Eisenhower could have won a third term in 1960, even though in the interim Fidel Castro had taken control of Cuba and aligned its foreign policy with the Soviet Union. Johnson raised the stakes on himself. He had come up with cost-benefit calculations about his vulnerability and that of his party that made no sense at all, especially given the fact that he had won the 1964 election by a huge landslide as the "dovish" candidate.

Johnson defined his policy according to his miscalculations about his power stakes and the utility of the compellence option against Hanoi. His positioning was designed always to let him choose a middle option from those presented by his advisers, but it was the middle of a muddle of unrealistic military options and projections. The tragic dimension of Vietnam for the nation lay in the dissonance between Johnson's escalation and the actual stakes for the United States in the "loss" of Vietnam and between Johnson's unrealistic game of compellence and Hanoi's far more realistic game of exhaustion.

Notes

1. Lyndon Johnson, *The Vantage Point: Perspectives of the Presidency, 1963–1969* (New York: Holt, Rinehart & Winston, 1970), 324.

2. Lady Bird Johnson, *A White House Diary* (New York: Holt, Rinehart & Winston, 1970), 248.

3. David Halberstam, *The Best and the Brightest* (New York: Random House, 1972).

4. Robert McNamara, *In Retrospect: The Tragedy and Lessons of Vietnam* (New York: Times Books, 1995), 32.

5. Irving Janis, *Groupthink* (Boston: Houghton Mifflin, 1982).

6. Documents are cited to their locations in Johnson's presidential library. My understanding of these documents is based on the following works that have made use of them: David Barrett, *Lyndon B. Johnson's Vietnam Papers: A Documentary Collection* (College Station: Texas A&M Press, 1997); Senator Gravel Edition, *The Pentagon Papers: The Defense Department History of United States Decisionmaking on Vietnam*, Vols. I–IV (Boston: Beacon Press, 1971); David Barrett, *Uncertain Warriors: Lyndon Johnson and his Vietnam Advisers* (Lawrence: University Press of Kansas, 1993); Larry Berman, *Planning a Tragedy: The Americanization of the War in Vietnam* (New York: W. W. Norton, 1982); William J. Duiker, *The Communist Road to Power in Vietnam* (Boulder, CO: Westview, 1981); Daniel Ellsberg, *Papers on the War* (New York: Simon & Schuster, 1972); William C. Gibbons, *The U.S. Government and the Vietnam War: Executive and Legislative Roles and Relationships*, Parts I–III (Washington, DC: U.S. Government Printing Office, 1994); Jeffrey Helsing, *Johnson's War/Johnson's Great Society: The Guns and Butter Trap* (New York: Doctoral Dissertation, Columbia University, 1991).

7. McNamara to Johnson, March 16, 1964, NSC History, Box 38, LBJ Library.

8. Johnson to Taylor, December 3, 1964, NS File, Bundy Files, Box 2, LBJ Library.

9. William Bundy to Rusk, January 6, 1965, NS File, Bromley Smith Files, Box 1, LBJ Library; McGeorge Bundy to Johnson, January 27, 1965, NS File, Bundy Files, Box 2, LBJ Library; McGeorge Bundy to Johnson, February 7, 1965, NS File, Bundy Files, Box 2, LBJ Library.

10. Roger Hilsman, "McNamara's War—Against the Truth: A Review Essay," *Political Science Quarterly* vol. 111, no. 1 (1996): 153–54.

11. Paul Kattenburg, *The Vietnam Trauma in American Foreign Policy, 1945–1975* (New Brunswick, NJ: Transaction Books, 1980), 120.

12. George Ball, *The Past Has Another Pattern: Memoirs* (New York: W. W. Norton, 1982), 41.

13. McNamara, *In Retrospect*, 159.

14. Hubert Humphrey, *The Education of a Public Man: My Life and Politics* (Garden City, NY: Doubleday, 1976), 321–24.

15. Humphrey, *The Education of a Public Man*, 325.

16. Johnson to Ball, Telephone Conversation, June 14, 1965, Ball Files, Box 7, LBJ Library.

17. George Ball, "How Valid Are the Assumptions Underlying Our Vietnam Policies?" Johnson Library, National Security File, Memos to the President, Vol. XI, McGeorge Bundy, Attachment, "Memorandum from Under Secretary of State (Ball) to President Johnson," 1965.

18. Berman, *Planning a Tragedy*, 51; Ball, *The Past Has Another Pattern*, 392.

19. McNamara to Johnson, April 21, 1965, *The Pentagon Papers* vol. III, 706.

20. McNamara, *In Retrospect*, 183.

21. Wheeler to McNamara, April 6, 1965, "Overall Appraisal of Air Strikes against North Vietnam, February 7 to April 4, 1965," NSC History—Troop Deployment, quoted in Berman, *Planning a Tragedy*, 52.

22. "Department of State Bulletin," vol. 52, no. 1350 (May 10, 1965): 694–701, 699.

23. Roger Hilsman had also predicted that if the United States bombed in the North, Hanoi would send regular divisions south. Roger Hilsman, *To Move a Nation* (New York: Harper & Row, 1979), 526.

24. CIA, Office of National Estimates, Special Memo #12–65, April 30, 1965, "Current Trends in Vietnam," NSC History vol. III, tab 211, LBJ Library.

25. Cable from Taylor to Rusk, No. 4073, June 3, 1965, NS File Vietnam Box 46, LBJ Library.

26. Cable from Taylor No. 4074, June 5, 1965, NS File, Vietnam, Box 46, LBJ Library; McNamara, *In Retrospect*, 187.

27. McNamara, *In Retrospect*, 188.

28. McNamara, *In Retrospect*, 188.

29. CIA Memorandum, "US Options and Objectives in Vietnam," Raborn to McGeorge Bundy, June 10, 1965, NSC History vol. V, NS File, LBJ Library.

30. William Bundy Oral History, May 29, 1969, 30.

31. William Westmoreland cable to Joint Chiefs of Staff, "Concept of Operations—Force Requirements and Deployments, South Vietnam," June 14, 1965, NSC History vol. V, NS File, LBJ Library.

32. George Ball to Johnson, "Keeping the Power of Decision in the South Vietnam Crisis," June 18, 1965, NSC History vol. V, tab 317, NS File, Box 42, LBJ Library.

33. Ball, *The Past Has Another Pattern*, 396.

34. Cabinet Minutes, June 18, 1965, Cabinet Papers File, Box III, LBJ Library, 43; quoted in Helsing, *Johnson's War*, 190.

35. Cabinet Minutes, June 18, 1965, 52–53; quoted in Helsing, *Johnson's War*, 191.

36. Quoted in Barrett, *Uncertain Warriors*, 24.

37. Senator Gravel Edition, *The Pentagon Papers* vol. III, 476.

38. McNamara to Johnson, June 26, 1965, "Program of Expanded Military and Political Moves with Respect to Vietnam," Top Secret, NSC History—Troop Deployment.

39. McGeorge Bundy to McNamara, June 30, 1965, NSC History vol. V, NS File, LBJ Library.

40. Berman, *Planning a Tragedy*, 83.

41. McNamara, *In Retrospect*, 194.

42. George Ball, "Cutting Our Losses in Vietnam," in *Foreign Relations of the United States, 1964–1968*, vol. III. Vietnam, June–December 1965 (Washington, DC: U.S. Department of State).

43. Berman, *Planning a Tragedy*, 51.

44. George Ball, "A Compromise Solution for Viet-Nam," in *Foreign Relations of the United States, 1964–1968*.

45. "Program of Expanded Military and Political Moves with Respect to Vietnam," NSC History vol. V, NS File, LBJ Library.

46. Chester Cooper, *The Lost Crusade: America in Vietnam* (New York: Dodd, Mead and Co., 1970), 281.

47. Gibbons, *The U.S. Government and the Vietnam War*, 381.

48. Robert McNamara to Johnson, "Recommendations of Additional Deployments to Vietnam," July 20, 1965, NSC History—Troop Deployment, NS File, Vietnam, Box 2, LBJ Library, 3.

49. Robert McNamara to Johnson, "Recommendations of Additional Deployments to Vietnam," 4.

50. CIA, "Communist and Free World Reactions to a Possible U.S. Course of Action," July 20, 1965, NSC History vol. VI, tab 398, NS File, LBJ Library.

51. Ball, *The Past Has Another Pattern*, 376.

52. McNamara, *In Retrospect*, 117.

53. David Halberstam, "Vietnam: Why We Missed the Story," *Washington Post National Weekly Edition* (May 22–28, 1995): 8–10.

54. Doris Kearns Goodwin, *Lyndon Johnson and the American Dream* (New York: Harper & Row, 1976), 275.

55. Clark Clifford, *Counsel to the President: A Memoir* (New York: Random House, 1991), 406–7.

56. Sam Adams, "Vietnam Coverup: Playing War with Numbers," *Harper's* vol. 250, no. 1500 (May 1975): 41–46.

57. Robert Buzzanco, *Masters of War: Military Dissent and Politics in the Vietnam Era* (New York: Cambridge University Press, 1996).

58. William Westmoreland, *A Soldier Reports* (Garden City, NY: Doubleday, 1976), 71.

59. Buzzanco, *Masters of War*, 179.

60. Andrew Krepinevich Jr., *The Army and Vietnam* (Baltimore: Johns Hopkins Press, 1986), 148–49.

61. Halberstam, *The Best and the Brightest*, 564.

62. Charles G. Cooper, "The Day It Became the Longest War," *U.S. Naval Institute Proceedings* vol. 122, no. 5 (May 1996): 80.

63. Humphrey, *The Education of a Public Man*, 319.

64. Berman, *Planning a Tragedy*, 6–7.

65. H. R. McMaster, *Dereliction of Duty: Lyndon Johnson, Robert McNamara, The Joint Chiefs of Staff, and the Lies That Led to Vietnam* (New York: HarperCollins, 1997).

66. James William Gibson, *The Perfect War: Technowar in Vietnam* (New York: Vintage, 1986), 93–154.

67. Colin Powell, *My American Journey* (New York: Random House, 1995), 149.

68. McNamara, *In Retrospect*, 108.

69. McNamara, *In Retrospect*, 108.

70. Jack Valenti notes, July 22, 1965, in Helsing, *Johnson's War*, 219.

71. Ball, *The Past Has Another Pattern*, 400.

72. Jack Valenti notes, July 22, 1965, in Helsing, *Johnson's War*, 228

73. Jack Valenti notes, July 22, 1965, in Helsing, *Johnson's War*, 223.

74. Jack Valenti notes, July 22, 1965, in Helsing, *Johnson's War*, 228

75. Jack Valenti notes, July 21, 1965, in Helsing, *Johnson's War*, 221.

76. Leslie H. Gelb and Richard K. Betts, *The Irony of Vietnam: The System Worked* (Washington, DC: Brookings Institution, 1979), 126.

77. Quoted in Berman, *Planning a Tragedy*, 117.

78. Jack Valenti notes, July 22, 1965, in Helsing, *Johnson's War*, 225

79. Clifford, *Counsel to the President*, 415.

80. Senator Gravel Edition, *The Pentagon Papers* vol. III, 485.

81. Clifford, *Counsel to the President*, 420.

82. "Subject: Deployment of Additional U.S. Troops to Vietnam," NSC Meetings File vol. III, tab 35, Bromley Smith Notes, Box 1, LBJ Library; Helsing, *Johnson's War*, 234.

83. Present were Mansfield, Dirksen, Hickenlooper, Kuckel, Long, Smathers, McCormack, Albert, Arends, Boggs, and Ford.

84. Helsing, *Johnson's War*, 236.

85. Jack Valenti notes, July 27, 1965 meeting, in Helsing, *Johnson's War*, 236.

86. McGeorge Bundy notes, July 28 meeting, in Gibbons, *The U.S. Government and the Vietnam War*, Part III, 437.

87. Cited in George Kahin, *Intervention: How America Became Involved in Vietnam* (New York: Alfred A. Knopf, 1986), 391.

88. *The Johnson Presidential Press Conferences*, introd. by Doris Kearns Goodwin (New York: E. M. Coleman Enterprises, 1978), 349.

89. *The Johnson Presidential Press Conferences*, 355.

90. George Gallup, *The Gallup Poll, 1971–1972* vol. 3 (New York: Random House, 1972).

91. Ellsberg, *Papers on the War*, 113.

92. Duiker, *The Communist Road to Power in Vietnam*, 243.

93. Robert M. Collins, "The Economic Crisis of 1968 and the Waning of the 'American Century,'" *American Historical Review* (April 1996).

94. Bundy manuscript, 26; quoted in Helsing, *Johnson's War*, 180.

95. Jon Elster argues that the failure of game theory in Vietnam "only shows that the decision theorists were bad theorists and not that they used a bad theory." The ar-

gument would be more convincing if game theorists could point to successes using good theory. Jon Elster, *Ulysses and the Sirens: Studies in Rationality and Irrationality* (Cambridge, UK: Cambridge University Press, 1979), 133.

96. McNamara, *In Retrospect*, 152.

97. Chester Cooper, "A Lost Opportunity to Revisit Vietnam," *Washington Post National Weekly Edition* (July 7, 1997): 22.

98. Paul C. Warnke, Oral History Interview, LBJ Library.

99. David K. Shipler, "Robert McNamara and the Ghosts of Vietnam," *New York Times Magazine* (August 10, 1997): 42.

100. Larry Elowitz and John W. Spanier, "Korea and Vietnam: Limited War and the American Political System," *Orbis* vol. 28, no. 2 (Summer 1974): 510–34.

101. George Ball, "A Light That Failed," *Atlantic Monthly* (July 1972): 43.

102. "July 16 Meeting, Ky, Thiêu and McNamara," Gibbons Files, Box 1, LBJ Library.

103. Gelb and Betts, *The Irony of Vietnam*, 121.

104. Johnson Library, Recording and Transcripts, Telephone Conversation between the President and Russell, Tape F64.27, Side B PNO 121 and F64.28, Side A PNO 1.

105. Henry William Brands Jr., "Johnson and Eisenhower: The President, the Former President, and the War in Vietnam," *Presidential Studies Quarterly* vol. 15, no. 3 (Summer 1985): 589–601.

106. Johnson, *Vantage Point*, 152.

107. Goodpastor to Johnson, June 16, 1965, NS File, Eisenhower, Box 3, LBJ Library.

108. Johnson and Eisenhower, Telephone Conversation, July 2, 1965. Reproduced in Barrett, ed., *Lyndon Johnson's Vietnam Papers*, 202.

109. Goodpastor to Johnson, August 20, 1965. NS File Eisenhower, Box 3, LBT Library.

110. McGeorge Bundy to Lyndon Johnson, June 30, 1965, NS File, Bundy Files, Box 3, LBJ Library.

111. Meeting Notes File, "Memos to the President," Box 1, July 21, 1965. LBJ Library.

112. Ellsberg, *Papers on the War*, 26, 74–75.

113. *The Pentagon Papers* vol. II, 119.

114. NSC Meetings File vol. III, tab 34, Bromley Smith notes, Box 1, LBJ Library, 2; Helsing, *Johnson's War*, 185.

115. Ellsberg, *Papers on the War*, 73.

116. Ellsberg, *Papers on the War*, 89.

4

Command and Control

Ford and the Mayaguez

PRESIDENT GERALD FORD and his Secretary of State Henry Kissinger considered the May 1975 rescue of the American merchant ship SS *Mayaguez* to be one of their greatest foreign policy successes. They trumpeted it as a decisive moment in American foreign policy, a time when the country badly needed to reassure allies and adversaries alike of its determination to continue to play the role of a major power in Asia in the aftermath of the Vietnam War. "I would not be sitting here today if not for the military actions taken on May 13th and May 14th," a grateful *Mayaguez* Captain Charles T. Miller later told the subcommittee on International Political and Military Affairs of the House International Relations Committee. But the Seventh Fleet's Vice Admiral George P. Steele had a different view: "I just feel those men died in vain," he said of the marine casualties in the operation. "It was just a terrible rush to get it done."[1] It was also a case study in the pitfalls of direct presidential command and control of military operations; although the crisis turned into a public relations success for the White House, for those who participated in the operation, it turned into a disaster.

Defining a Crisis

On May 12, 1975, at 3:15 a.m. Washington time and 2:15 p.m. local time (all subsequent times are Washington unless otherwise noted) the *Mayaguez*, sailing from Hong Kong to Sattahip, Thailand, was fired upon by Cambodian PT boats seven miles off the Poulo Wai archipelago (itself fifty miles from the

Cambodian mainland), in sea-lanes the United States considered to be international waters. The Cambodians had recently extended their waters out to ninety miles and were seizing vessels that in their view were trespassing. The *Mayaguez* radioed for help, and its message reached the National Military Command Center at 5:12 a.m. A few minutes later Cambodian sailors boarded the ship and captured its crew.[2]

Ford and Kissinger viewed the seizure as a crisis requiring White House management rather than as an incident that might be handled by the State Department through low-level diplomatic channels. Ford wanted a speedy resolution: His fear, fanned by national security adviser Brent Scowcroft, was that he would be drawn into a prolonged negotiation with Cambodia, similar to the negotiations conducted by President Lyndon Johnson's administration with North Korea after that country seized the naval vessel USS *Pueblo* on January 23, 1968. The *Pueblo* crew had been badly mistreated, and it had taken thirteen months of negotiations to get the eighty-two crew members and naval vessel returned. Although Johnson had sent three aircraft carriers, eighteen destroyers, and twenty-six B-52s to the region, and had called up fifteen thousand reservists (and to placate the South Koreans he approved an additional $100 million in military aid), he could hardly afford to open up a second military front in Asia, and diplomatic negotiations dragged on for months. The *Pueblo* became an issue in the 1968 elections, and the crew was finally released only after the Nixon administration assumed office and allowed an apology to be read to the North Koreans that had been drafted by the outgoing Johnson administration. At the first National Security Council (NSC) meeting convened to deal with the *Mayaguez*, Kissinger warned that a repeat of the *Pueblo* must be avoided at all costs and insisted that only a forceful response could restore U.S. credibility with its allies in the aftermath of Communist guerrilla movements seizing power throughout Indochina in the preceding month.

The new Cambodian Khmer Rouge regime had not been looking to create a crisis. It had tried to seize several other ships on the same day its forces had taken the *Mayaguez*, and a few days earlier it had captured and then released a Panamanian ship and several Thai fishing vessels. Rather than seeking a confrontation with the United States, local commanders had been under standing orders to capture, warn, and then release all vessels that intruded in its newly proclaimed ninety-mile zone. With the Cambodian government preoccupied with consolidating its power and fomenting disturbances in the western parts of Vietnam's Mekong Delta to gain control of what it considered to be lost territories, it was not likely the new regime had any interest in a confrontation with the United States. But no one could be sure what the Khmer Rouge would do once a U.S. ship and crew was in its hands. Ford felt he could not take the risk of a drawn out situation: In the aftermath of the U.S. pullout

from South Vietnam, Laos, and Cambodia, completed just weeks before, Ford
had little international standing as a world leader, and public opinion polls
put him at the lowest point of his presidency.

The White House issued a public statement threatening military measures
if the ship and crew were not released. Since the United States had no diplomatic relations with the new Cambodian government, the State Department's
note to the Khmer Rouge was routed through its Liaison Office in Beijing. It
demanded an immediate release of crew and ship, adding, "Failure to do so
would have the most serious consequences." (The diplomatic activity produced no results: Chinese diplomats in Beijing returned the U.S. note a few
days later, reporting that the Cambodians had refused to accept it.) Ford ordered the aircraft carrier USS *Coral Sea* to the area and directed a buildup of
ground troops in the Philippines. At the conclusion of the first NSC crisis
meeting the president gave instructions to the Joint Chiefs of Staff (JCS) to
present a military plan later in the afternoon, but the chair of the JCS was not
under the impression that there was a deadline for operational plans, nor did
the JCS believe it could produce a plan quickly.[3] The military did not yet know
the precise location of the captured ship, the whereabouts of the crew, if Thailand would permit its facilities to be used for staging operations, and did not
know the military capability of the Khmer Rouge in the area. The JCS did not
present a plan in the afternoon meeting, a sign that managing the crisis might
prove more difficult than the president was anticipating. Another caution sign
was the problem of obtaining accurate intelligence: Contradictory reports
began to filter in during the evening. By 9:12 p.m. navy fliers had spotted the
Mayaguez anchored near the islands of Poulo Wai; by 10:15 p.m. NSC aide
Robert "Bud" McFarlane relayed reports to Scowcroft that the ship was headed
toward Kompong Som. By 2:30 a.m. information came in that the ship was
anchored off the island of Koh Tang.

A third NSC meeting was held on Tuesday morning, May 13. Director of
Central Intelligence William Colby thought that the ship's crew might soon be
transferred to the interior; therefore, time was of the essence. There was a
hitch: Thailand had refused the U.S. permission to use its bases for actions
against Cambodia, and the United States's chargé d'affaires had promised the
Thais that U.S. planes would not be used without permission. In spite of this
pledge, Ford ordered aircraft from Thailand to head off any Cambodian ships
going to or from Koh Tang. The military began assembling a task force, which
included a contingent of air force military police, twenty-three of whom
crashed and died (along with its helicopter crew) en route from their Philip-
pine base to Thailand. Units from the Third Marine Amphibious Force in
Okinawa were sent to U-Tapao; the troops had the least combat experience of
the marine forces in the area.

The staff officers in charge of planning the mission in Thailand were over-whelmed: The headquarters was being dismantled, and its functions were being transferred out of the country when the crisis erupted. Now the reduced staff, in the midst of coordinating a major pullout, was burdened with de-mands for information from CINCPAC (Commander-in-Chief, Pacific Com-mand) in Hawaii and from the Pentagon and the White House—demands that distracted staffers from thinking through their mission requirements and coordinating a complicated combined arms operation that required new forces to move into the area just as other forces were leaving.

White House command and control almost led to a tragedy at the outset. Navy reconnaissance planes spotted Cambodian boats going from the *Mayaguez* to Koh Tang. The White House ordered attacks on these ships: One boat was sunk, a second turned back, then a third was sunk. A fourth boat headed for the mainland. Ford gave the order to disable the boat but not sink it since the *Mayaguez* crew might be aboard. Pentagon officials delayed trans-mission of this order, fearing that crew members might be injured or killed. CIA director William Colby told the president that several "possible Cau-casians" had been spotted en route to the mainland in the boat that had been allowed to pass. The Pentagon's delay in implementing Ford's order saved the lives of the crew.[4]

At the next morning's NSC meeting Ford ordered a morning attack within two days. Air force helicopters would land marines at Koh Tang Island to res-cue the crew. Marines boarding it from the USS *Holt* would retake the Mayaguez. Naval and air attacks on Cambodia would prevent the Khmer Rouge from bringing in reinforcements. Joint Chiefs Chair General George S. Brown asked for a delay of twenty-four hours in the landing so that more ships would be in the area and helicopters would have a fifteen minute turn-around time rather than the two hour flight to U-Tapao (190 nautical miles away) to bring in reinforcements. Ford overruled his military advisers and gave the go-ahead for the Thursday morning (Cambodian time) operation. Ford refused to consider any delay, fearing that it would give the Cambodians one more day to disperse the crew on the mainland, but he did accede to the military about the choice of weapons: Kissinger and Vice President Nelson Rockefeller had urged punitive strikes with B-52s, but Secretary of Defense James Schlesinger and JCS Chair Brown called the idea an overreaction. The B-52s were put on hold.

The military's plans made risky assumptions and required difficult maneu-vers. Eight helicopters were to take a marine assault force into two landing zones on the East and West beaches of Koh Tang—five helicopter landings in the first wave and three landings to reinforce an hour later. There would be no preassault bombardments because of the danger to the ship's crew. After the first landing a company of marines would broadcast an ultimatum demanding the release of the crew and then storm Cambodian positions through the length and breadth of the island, a field of operations three miles long and a mile wide. The operation required combined arms, with marines landing from air force helicopters, but the air force and marines did not have time to train together. The assault force had no intelligence about conditions on the island: It had no maps and no reconnaissance. The marines would land unaware that there were up to 250 well-armed Khmer Kraham (infantry) on the island, although the Defense Intelligence Agency had come up with that estimate on May 12, because none of the overworked and harassed staff officers at operational headquarters had remembered to share it with them.[5] The 175 marines in the first wave of the assault force would not have the necessary 3 to 1 superiority over the defenders, nor would they know what they were up against. The element of surprise would belong to the defenders. The H-53 helicopters had precious little fuel and would be unable to remain in the area for long; if their external fuel tanks were hit they would have to return to U-Tapao immediately. The navy, air force, and marines had not developed a plan for coordinated air and naval suppressive fire support. The odds against successful extrication of the crew were long. If they were on the island, it was likely they would be hit by friendly fire air strikes or ground fire. The marines would not know the location of the crew or their captors, who could not immediately be neutralized and therefore would have time to kill the crew. To take back the *Mayaguez*, the plan was to spray it with tear gas, followed by a marine assault over the gunwales from the USS *Holt*. If the crew members were on board the ship, they would be in danger from Cambodian captors when the *Holt* moved alongside.

Claims of Success

On the evening of May 16 (Washington time), in a statement to the nation, President Ford triumphantly reported that "the vessel has been recovered intact and the entire crew has been rescued," adding that "the forces that have successfully accomplished this mission are still under hostile fire but are preparing to disengage."[6] The Senate Foreign Relations Committee passed a resolution in support of the president's actions. Senator Harry Byrd (D-VA) called it "a red-letter day in the official life of President Ford." Senator Jesse Helms (R-NC) said, "He will be remembered in history for his conduct in this difficult episode. I, for one, am very proud of him today."[7]

The media reported the military triumph: "U.S. Frees Cambodian-Held Ship and Crew" trumpeted the *New York Times.* Its story added that marines had stormed Koh Tang Island as part of the operation and had suffered what were described as "light casualties." A photograph accompanying the article showed the *Mayaguez* with the caption "recaptured last night by U.S. marines." The story reported that at 10:30 a.m. a Cambodian vessel with a white flag put thirty crew members on the USS *Wilson*, with the implication that it was under a flag of surrender.[8] A *New York Times* editorial commended Ford for his "great success" and for not acting precipitously or irresponsibly. *Newsweek* had on its May 26 issue a cover picture of marines boarding the ship to rescue the crew. Inside, a photo accompanying the article showed Ford in the White House receiving a phone call from the naval officers who ran the operation. "They're all safe," he was reported saying to his aides. "We got them all out, thank God. It went just perfectly, it went just great." *Newsweek* rhapsodized about the clockwork precision of the operation: "It was swift and tough—and it worked. It liberated the ship and its crew of 39, and it enveloped the Ford presidency in an almost euphoric afterglow."[9] *Time* drew the larger strategic implications of such a resolute show of force in its cover story, "Ford Draws the Line." The United States was putting "potential adversaries on notice."

None of the White House or media reports were accurate. The military action began at Thursday morning at 7:00 a.m. (all operations are in Cambodian time unless otherwise specified) when a flight of A-7s saturated the *Mayaguez* with tear gas. The *Holt* then maneuvered next to the *Mayaguez* and grappled. At 7:25 a.m. marines from the *Holt* went over the gunnels in a maneuver not used previously by American forces in the twentieth century, without opposition, as the Cambodian crew was not on the vessel. By 8:25 a.m. they declared the ship secured. The *Holt* began to tow the *Mayaguez*, while Military Sealift Command personnel readied it to sail under its own power, which was achieved by midafternoon. None of these activities involved any combat since no Cambodian troops had been aboard.

At Koh Tang it was a different story.[10] At 6:02 a.m. four helicopters tried to land on the island. One was shot down at sea; another crash-landed on East Beach; a third unloaded troops at West Beach, then was hit and ditched in the sea; and a fourth did not disgorge marines due to hostile fire. The landings left fourteen marines dead with fifty-four survivors pinned down on two separated beaches. All the radios for the command and fire groups had been on one of the downed helicopters. At 6:30 a.m. fighter bombers began pounding enemy positions. An hour later four helicopters landed more marines on West Beach, though three of them were heavily damaged. Ninety minutes into the mission, eight of the eleven helicopters that had started the operation were out of action, and marines were pinned down in three pockets: twenty-five on East Beach, sixty on West Beach, and another twenty-nine outside the West

Beach landing zone in an isolated area. They faced a larger veteran Khmer Rouge force fighting on its home ground.

Throughout the day air cover kept the situation from getting worse, but the A-7 fighter bombers could not do much damage to the Khmer Rouge because their loiter time on station was low, they could not identify any targets, and they had not rehearsed the necessary tactics or coordinated their efforts with the ground forces. Marines and Khmer troops exchanged grenades and small arms fire, at times from distances less than fifty yards. A Spectre-61 gunship arrived and alleviated the pressure with heavy fire suppression, but it had to leave by 10 a.m., and inexplicably, no AC-130 gunships were dispatched until the late afternoon. Helicopters used their miniguns as they improvised tactics to help the beleaguered troops; low-level commanders had sent these helicopters to the scene without waiting for orders from higher-ups.

At 6:07 a.m., just as the Koh Tang assault was getting under way, Cambodian Minister of Information and Propaganda Hu Nim, located somewhere in the interior, was beginning a radio address in which he offered to release the "CIA spy ship." President Ford was informed of this message at 8:29 p.m. Washington time (8:29 a.m. Cambodian time), but he decided to continue the U.S. military operations because the Cambodian minister had not mentioned the crew. The explanation was disingenuous: The minister had said that the ship would be permitted to continue on its way, and it could hardly do so without its personnel. Ford ordered three waves of planes from the *Coral Sea* to conduct further punitive bombings on Cambodia. Since there were no targets of any military or economic value in the war torn country, it was difficult to engage in a punitive mission, but the U.S. planes did their best, hitting unusable airfields and rusting inoperable oil refineries.

The crew of the *Mayaguez* was neither on the mainland nor on Koh Tang. Crew members had been on Rong Som Lem Island in Kompong Sam harbor and were released from custody at 6:20 a.m.—just as the marines were landing on Koh Tang Island. After posing for photographs with their Cambodian guards, they were put aboard a Thai fishing boat and headed back to the *Mayaguez.* They were picked up by 9:49 a.m. by the crew of the destroyer USS *Henry B. Wilson,* which had held its fire to make a positive identification of the vessel rather than blow up what it suspected was another hostile Cambodian PT boat. The Cambodians had made arrangements with the Thai fishing boat the evening before the U.S. operation, and it is highly unlikely that the timing of the release was made in response either to the landings at Koh Tang or the boarding of the *Mayaguez,* since the jailors would not have known about either action. The timing had been coordinated with the speech of the Information Minister and represented a decision to end the affair *before* the United States took military action. The Cambodian minister, deep in the jungle with the Khmer Rouge political leadership, could not have known of the U.S. decision to use force—had the government known, the crew's release might have been aborted.

With the ship and crew in U.S. hands, there was no need to continue the operation, though Kissinger and Ford agreed on one more set of punitive bombing strikes. By 10:45 a.m. Cambodian time, President Ford directed the JCS to order a disengagement. Local commanders had to spend some time getting the president's order modified so more troops could land before they could plan extrication. By 12:30 p.m. five helicopters put one hundred more marines on West Beach to create a secure perimeter and prevent the position from being overrun. The first attempt to get the twenty-five marines at East Beach out failed when the helicopters were driven off; eventually three helicopters took them off at 6:00 p.m. Shortly thereafter, without any warning for the marines on West Beach, a fifteen thousand pound BLU-82 pallet bomb, the largest in the U.S. arsenal, was dropped on the Cambodian positions by a circling C-130, which disrupted Khmer plans to assault marine lines. Then H-53s appeared (also a surprise to the marines) to take marines and the downed helicopter crew members off the beach under heavy enemy fire. By 8:15 p.m. all marines—including the dead and wounded—were out.

The United States had suffered a total of fifteen marines killed and three missing in action (and presumed dead) and fifty wounded. (To these casualties should be added the twenty-three pilots and members of the helicopter crew who lost their lives in the deployments to U-Tapao.) According to Cambodian radio transmissions, the Khmer Rouge suffered fifty-five killed and seventy wounded.

Prerogative Power

If cutting corners increases risk and reduces the viability of an operation, as we have seen in both the U-2 and Bay of Pigs fiascoes, then perhaps the converse proposition might also be the case. Ford made the decision to use force unilaterally, relying on his constitutional prerogatives as commander in chief. What would have happened had he followed the procedures of the War Powers Resolution of 1973 (hereafter WPR), a law passed by Congress to provide for consultation before the president engaged in military actions and policy codetermination thereafter?

The WPR requires that in all possible instances the president is to consult with Congress before introducing U.S. Armed Forces into hostilities or situations in which hostilities are imminent. At the second meeting of the NSC (on May 13) Ford had ordered his advisers to consider how to handle this requirement. Instead of presidential consultation with members of Congress required by the law, his advisers recommended briefings by relatively low-level national security staffers. NSC staff officers contacted ten representatives and eleven senators to relay information about the military measures taken to that point. On May 14 they briefed the same legislators about the sinking of three Cambodian patrol craft. A deputy assistant secretary for international security affairs provided a briefing to the House International Relations Committee and the House Armed Services Committee; the legal adviser to the Joint Chiefs gave a briefing to the Senate Foreign Relations Committee; and the House Appropriations Defense Subcommittee was briefed by a CIA intelligence officer.[11] Later the Assistant Secretary of State for Congressional Relations informed members of Congress that the administration had satisfied the requirements of WPR through these staff briefings.[12] An hour after the mission had begun, and a few minutes before the marines were to lift off from their bases, President Ford briefed seventeen congressional leaders and asked for their support. Once again there had been no consultation prior to the go-ahead for the operation. Senate Majority Leader Mike Mansfield (D-MT) later explained, "I was notified after the fact about what the Administration had already decided to do."[13] Nevertheless, the Senate Foreign Relations Committee, after receiving a briefing from a Deputy Assistant Secretary of State, issued a statement supporting the president "in the exercise of his constitutional powers within the framework of the War Powers Resolution to secure the release of the ship and its men."[14]

Once hostilities had started, Ford sent a report to Congress "consistent with" but *not* "pursuant to" the WPR. He ignored seven laws that Congress had recently passed prohibiting military actions in Indochinese (including Cambodian) waters, airspace, or territory. His report failed to mention the military buildup in Thailand, nor did it mention that the retaliatory actions (especially the bombings) went beyond measures necessary to safeguard American lives and property (assuming members of the crew were in danger), nor did it mention that the actions had gone far beyond the limited measures recommended by the JCS. Ford's report claimed that he had "previously advised" Congress, although as Senator Jacob Javits (R-NY) pointed out, "Consultations with the Congress prior to the *Mayaguez* incident resembled the old, discredited practice of informing selected members of Congress in advance of the implementation of decisions already taken within the executive branch."[15]

Had the president followed the procedures of the WPR and consulted with members of Congress, it is likely that the military action would have been delayed at least for the additional day that the Joint Chiefs had requested, which would have improved its operational viability. It is almost certain that legislators would not have approved the bombings of the mainland. The delay might even have aborted the mission, since members of Congress would have been informed of the early morning announcement by the Cambodians that they intended to release the ship.[16] At that point, legislators probably would have advised a delay in the operation to see if the Cambodians followed through, and that advice would have been supported by the Joint Chiefs. The lives of American and Cambodian soldiers would have been spared because a needless confrontation would have been avoided.

Protecting Power Stakes

Why rush into a poorly planned operation, without adequate intelligence or preparation? Ships and crews are seized all the time, all over the world, without immediate hostilities ensuing. Why did Ford and Kissinger treat this incident as a crisis, requiring immediate presidential consideration, especially since there was no evidence that the crew was in danger? Several observers of the *Mayaguez* incident have concluded that the president did not act with regard to his personal political fortunes.[17] But the evidence points in the other direction. South Vietnam, Laos, and Cambodia had fallen to Communist movements only weeks before. The United States not only had failed to honor its commitment to President Nguyên Văn Thiêu in South Vietnam to provide military assistance in the event of a threatened Communist takeover but also it had just pulled out all its military forces and civilians in a humiliating rout. Presidential advisers, especially Secretary of State Henry Kissinger, worried that allies and adversaries might draw the wrong conclusions. The United States, Kissinger had concluded even before the crisis, "must carry out some act somewhere in the world which shows its determination to continue to be a world power."[18] The operation itself was planned primarily as a demonstration of presidential commitment, especially the air strikes against Cambodia, which had nothing to do with recovering the crew. Ford later argued that 2,400 Khmer Rouge troops at Kompong Som and Ream had to be pinned down and prevented from reinforcing their compatriots fighting against U.S. Marines. But any reinforcement was improbable, given U.S. local naval and air superiority. "It was a demonstration—a punitive strike," observed Brent Scowcroft.[19] A demonstration, one might add, not necessarily directed at the Cambodians, who were used to displays of U.S. air power, but rather aimed at American allies. In his memoirs Ford claimed that he and Kissinger had agreed that it had been necessary to "signal" Cambodia and the rest of the world about U.S. resolve as a great power by instituting punishing air strikes. Of the dead and wounded, Ford said, "This was a high toll, and I felt terrible about it." But nevertheless, the president concluded, "We had recovered the ship, we had rescued the crew, and the psychological boost the incident had given us as a people was significant."[20]

The claim that *Mayaguez* was a successful display of "resolve" is ludicrous. Viewed from the Khmer Rouge perspective, the United States had blundered by sending a reconnaissance ship into their waters, and the Americans had learned a thing or two about Khmer Rouge resolve: The rescue mission had been trapped and then forced to withdraw under fire. It is also difficult to believe that U.S. bombing would have impressed the Khmer Rouge, who had just endured years of B-52 carpet-bombing raids. Since the United States had completed its final pullout from Indochina, and Congress had already passed several statutes prohibiting military strikes using air power in Indochina, why would the Khmer Rouge believe that the United States was now in a position to project power in the area? More likely the Cambodians and other observers in Asia would draw a different conclusion: The U.S. military action was a spasmodic and ill-conceived response by the White House to the frustration of liquidating a failed two-decade commitment in Indochina, not a signal of American intentions to project force in Indochina. Only in the imagination of U.S. national security managers could a botched rescue mission be considered a successful show of force.

American allies were not impressed. The Thai government was furious at American use of U-Tapao Air Base. The Thais had expected a negotiated resolution of the issue and saw no need for the use of force, believing that the Cambodians were more interested in marking out their newly enlarged territorial waters than in creating a major incident with the United States. The Thais formally protested American use of its territory without prior notification and approval. Eventually the United States expressed regret over the "misunderstanding" in a formal note, and both sides dropped the issue. Other allies also voiced regret at precipitous U.S. actions. Shortly thereafter the Thais began negotiations with Washington on ending its military presence.

It was inevitable, no matter how the rescue mission went, that it would be portrayed as a military and diplomatic success. It was, after all, an attempt to rescue an unarmed merchant ship and crew; a mission that would resonate with public opinion as a continuation of the naval exploits of the nineteenth century ("not one cent for tribute"), rather than a divisive chapter in the Vietnam War. At worst, it was likely to put Ford in the same position as Eisenhower after the U-2 crisis and Kennedy after the Bay of Pigs: The country rallies around a president after a debacle. Ford's actions, after all, reflected public and congressional sentiment: After the *Mayaguez* was seized, Democratic House Majority Leader Tip O'Neill (D-MA) exploded: "Those bastards, we can't let them get away with this. They'll harass us forever."[21] Conservative

Democratic senator James Eastland (MS) had this advice for the president: "Blow the hell out of them."[22]

The *Mayaguez* rescue was a political success. Ford's approval rating went up 12 points in the Gallup polls, from 39 to 51 percent, and his disapproval rating dropped from 46 to 33 percent.[23] Given the need of the United States to stand tall after Vietnam, almost any military action off the coast of Cambodia would have been portrayed in the same manner, while any nonmilitary negotiation would likely have been portrayed negatively. The congruence between a presidential decision and the deeply held values of the public may sometimes be strong enough to "frame" the operational results in a positive manner, irrespective of the results.

Learning Curves

National security managers claimed that the *Mayaguez* was a success on all counts. A study by three military officers, one of them an NSC staffer at the time of the crisis, prepared in cooperation with the National Defense University, concluded that "for the first time in several years, the utility of force was demonstrated in a successful U.S. military operation. That success generated a moral uplift for the American people, restored a belief in American credibility, and demonstrated a strategic resolve worthy of a great power."[24] John Guilmartin, who at the time was an air force officer handling helicopter maintenance for the mission, concluded. "It showed that American soldiers, sailors, and airmen could and would fight in the wake of humiliating defeat in Vietnam."[25] *It takes nothing away from the valor of the American marines involved in the operation, or the memory of those who were killed in action serving their country, to argue that these assertions are incorrect.* How was the utility of force demonstrated in a failed military operation on Koh Tang Beach that the Khmer Rouge could consider a victory?[26]

More than a year after the resolution of the crisis, a General Accounting Office (GAO) study suggested that the decision to use force rather than seek a diplomatic solution had not been warranted.[27] Before release of the final version of the report, Lawrence Eagleburger, then Deputy Undersecretary of State, in a letter to the GAO Comptroller General on March 15, 1976, complained that the authors of the report "went out of their way to develop wholly fictional diplomatic scenarios which bore no resemblance to fact or reality, and then criticized the Administration for its 'failure' to pursue their fantasies."[28] Yet it was difficult to argue with the GAO's pointed observation that the crew of the *Mayaguez* had already been released prior to the landing of the rescuers at Koh Tang. If anyone had developed fictional scenarios and indulged in fantasies it had been Ford and Kissinger. The close command and control of the operation from the White House and by CINCPAC almost led to two disasters—the bombing of the crew and the obliteration of the rescue mission. The rescue of the rescuers succeeded in spite of, rather than because of, White House operational controls. What successes there were involved theater improvisation by the warriors and their commanders, who had to deal with White House and Pentagon micromanagement.[29]

Inefficient command and control would have produced better results. Any delay, whether for reasons given by the JCS or to comply with the procedural consultation requirements of the War Powers Resolution, would have resulted in a better outcome. Even had the Cambodians not decided to release the crew, a day's delay still would have made sense, because a delay in getting organized would have resulted in greater operational performance later: The rescuers could have had time to train for the mission; intelligence data from the 307th Wing of the air force might have reached the marines; the *Coral Sea* would have arrived on station and provided quick reinforcement; and the *Hancock* would have been close enough to provide attack helicopters.

The irony of the *Mayaguez* crisis is that the White House communications success increased the *authority* of President Ford and those around him: the public's sense that the White House was in capable hands, that the president and his advisers knew what they were doing when they managed crises. In spite of the operational failure, Ford's use of force resonated with American *values*, one of the most paramount being the belief that the government stands ready to protect American lives and property from marauders abroad. Marines boarding a ship (even an abandoned one) certainly provide better images for the White House than desperate evacuees grabbing hold of the skids of helicopters on the roof of the American embassy in Saigon. The *Mayaguez* incident shows that if the goals of a presidential mission are consistent with deeply held values, and if the White House micromanages the news coverage, there is considerable opportunity for the president to turn operational failure into political success.

Notes

1. Quoted in Lucien S. Vandenbroucke, *Perilous Options: Special Operations as an Instrument of U.S. Foreign Policy* (New York: Oxford University Press, 1993), 113.

2. Richard G. Head, Frisco W. Short, and Robert C. McFarlane, *Crisis Resolution: Presidential Decision Making in the Mayaguez and Korean Confrontations* (Boulder, CO: Westview Press, 1978), 104–7.

3. Head et al., *Crisis Resolution*, 111.

4. Vandenbroucke, *Perilous Options*, 81.

5. Head et al., *Crisis Resolution*, 120.

6. *New York Times* (April 15, 1975): A-18. Ford reported to Congress that the military incursion at Koh Tang resulted in the recovery of ship and crew, followed by a disengagement and withdrawal from the island.

7. *Congressional Quarterly Almanac* (1975): 310–11.

8. *New York Times* (May 15, 1975): 1.

9. *Newsweek* (May 26, 1975): 16.

10. John F. Guilmartin Jr., *A Very Short War: The Mayaguez and the Battle of Koh Tang* (College Station: Texas A&M University Press, 1995).

11. Head et al., *Crisis Resolution*, 122.

12. House Resolutions 536 and 537 directed the secretary of state to provide information on the *Mayaguez* crisis and actions taken to resolve it short of the use of force.

13. U.S. Senate, "Hearings before the Committee on Foreign Relations, War Powers Resolution," 95th Cong., 1st sess. (Washington, DC: U.S. Government Printing Office, 1977): 67; Robert Zutz, "The Recapture of the S.S. *Mayaguez*: Failure of the Consultation Clause of the War Powers Resolution," *International Law and Politics* vol. 8 (1976): 457–78.

14. Pat Holt, *The War Powers Resolution* (Washington, DC: American Enterprise Institute, 1978), 17.

15. U.S. House, Committee on International Relations, "Hearings before the Subcommittee on International Security and Scientific Affairs," *War Powers: A Test of Compliance*, 94th Cong., 1st sess. (Washington, DC: U.S. Government Printing Office, 1975), 45.

16. U.S. House, Committee on International Relations, "Seizure of the *Mayaguez*, Hearings before the Committee on International Relations and the Subcommittee on International Political and Military Affairs," 94th Cong., 1st sess. (Washington, DC: U.S. Government Printing Office, 1975).

17. Christopher Jon Lamb, *Belief Systems and Decision Making in the Mayaguez Crisis*, 167 (Gainesville: University of Florida Press, 1989), 167.

18. Vandenbroucke, *Perilous Options*, 74.

19. Vandenbroucke, *Perilous Options*, 85.

20. Gerald Ford, *A Time to Heal* (New York: Harper & Row, 1979), 284.

21. Quoted in Vandenbroucke, *Perilous Options*, 79

22. Quoted in Vandenbroucke, *Perilous Options*, 79.

23. *Gallup Opinion Index: Political, Social and Economic Trends*, report no. 120 (Princeton, NJ: American Institute of Public Opinion, 1975).

24. Head et al., *Crisis Resolution*, 148.

25. Guilmartin, *A Very Short War*, 28.

26. Guilmartin, *A Very Short War*, 152.

27. U.S. House of Representatives, Report of the Comptroller General of the United States, "Executive Legislative Communications and the Role of the Congress during International Crises" (Washington, DC: U.S. General Accounting Office, 1976).

28. Quoted in Head et al., *Crisis Resolution*, 145.

29. Guilmartin, *A Very Short War*, 29–30.

5

Rhetoric

Carter and the Malaise Speech

"**W**HILE I WAS IN JAPAN," President Jimmy Carter recalled in his memoirs, "the news from home was all bad. Public opinion polls indicated that my popularity had dropped to a new low." In 1979 OPEC had raised its prices for crude oil by 15 percent. There were gas lines throughout the Northeast and Midwest, and stations were threatening a nationwide strike unless the Department of Energy allowed greater profit margins, although gas prices were up 55 percent for the year. The refiners' target of 240 million barrels of distillate would not be reached by October, leading to shortages of oil in the Northeast and higher energy prices, which was fuelling inflation—even as energy shortages threatened economic growth. "I don't need to detail for you the political damage we are suffering from all of this," his policy counselor Stuart Eizenstat noted. "The polls are lower than they have ever been. (The latest Harris poll shows something never before seen—a Republican opponent, Reagan, leading you by several points.) Kennedy's popularity appears at a peak. And the Congress seems completely beyond anyone's control."[1] Eizenstat counseled Carter to cut short his visit to the Far East, go to Camp David and meet with advisers, and make a nationwide address on the energy crisis.[2]

Carter did make a speech designed to restore his authority. He reorganized his presidency and reshaped energy policy as part of a new "transformational politics." By the time his term was up, Carter had compiled one the most effective records on energy policy of any other president, yet conventional wisdom is that his "malaise" speech was a failure. In what sense did he fail when his policies succeeded?

A Time of Troubles

By early 1979 Carter had gone down sharply in the polls. Gallup had him at 47 in mid-March, then at 40 in early April, a slide that would not end until early June when it bottomed at 29 percent. His decline was especially great among Democrats, particularly union members and voters over fifty, the bedrock of the New Deal coalition. In pollster Patrick Caddell's view, Carter's slide was symptomatic of a problem he had outlined in a January 1979 "State of America" memo to the president. Caddell had talked about "social and political disintegration in America." His surveys showed that cynicism about the government was at an all-time high.[3] Half of the American people were pessimistic about the future compared with only 30 percent in 1975, and optimistic views had declined from 47 to 21 percent. A plurality thought it made no difference who got elected to office. Most people felt that the government was not paying attention to them.[4] Caddell told Carter that "all the legislative initiatives, programs, foreign policy efforts, while being good and important governmental actions, are essentially irrelevant to solving this deeper, more fundamental, and more demanding problem."[5] Yet Caddell saw in these bleak numbers an opportunity for Carter to develop a thematic presidency, to move from transactional politics to transformational leadership. "You were elected to restore trust, restore values, make the government responsive and closer to the people, to first and foremost deal with the spiritual malaise in America."[6]

In April Caddell sent the president a lengthy memo, "Of Crisis and Opportunity," describing a "crisis of confidence marked by a dwindling faith in the future."[7] It was not Carter's fault, Caddell hastened to point out, but was due to "the natural result of historical forces and events that have been in motion for twenty years." Yet Carter's political position was precarious. In the polling samples, "More people believe you to be ineffective than effective, wishy washy than decisive, not in control than in control. Concern for people has declined, as has the belief that you take on tough issues, even if they are unpopular. The half leg of competence is gone entirely."[8] The news got worse: "By two to one margins, the electorate believes you unable to take charge of the government and unable to reorganize the government."[9]

Caddell's memo focused on the immediate political danger to the president. Although he was running ahead of all potential Republican challengers in trial heats, the polls showed "you are slaughtered by [Senator] Ted Kennedy [D-MA]."[10] Carter already viewed Kennedy as a rival for the 1980 Democratic presidential nomination. "Kennedy, by definition, stands as a symbol of Hope," Caddell noted, "of a past which was America's high water mark; a period most remembered and cherished."[11] But Caddell saw an opportunity for Carter "to become a great President on the order of a Lincoln, a Wilson, and a Franklin Roosevelt." Carter could seize the moment and reshape "the structure, nature and purpose of the United States in ways which your predecessors could only dream."[12] How could this be done? ". . . [I]t demands a movement away from *solution* politics to a more difficult question of *process* politics. Rather than budgets, programs, etc., the emphasis must be directed toward larger needs such as purpose, individual value, individual responsibility, meaningful participation, consensus tradeoffs, as well as small intangible issues like productivity, excellence in work, education, etc., spiritual and moral value regeneration, worker satisfaction, volunteerism, long range planning, national service, and many others."[13]

Carter showed Caddell's memo to Vice President Walter Mondale, who reportedly thought it was "crazy."[14] But the Carters were impressed with Caddell's ideas as well as with a memo provided by White House communications director Gerald Rafshoon, who proposed that Carter restore confidence in his presidency by reorganizing his staff and cabinet.[15] The president had been getting similar advice from Eizenstat, who wanted Carter to create a White House chief of staff so that presidential priorities could be imposed on the cabinet. But first Carter would have to tackle the energy crisis again; he had already won a series of legislative victories to develop new energy policy in 1977, but it had not succeeded in providing for adequate supplies at reasonable prices.

Carter's 1977–1978 Energy Program

American dependence on foreign oil had been an economic and national security issue since the 1973 Arab oil embargo. In spite of the lip service paid by American presidents to reducing energy dependence, a year into Carter's presidency the nation was consuming more than one-quarter of OPEC's production, with consumption per capita 2.3 times the average for nations in the European Economic Community and 2.6 times Japan's.[16] Although Carter had not made energy policy an issue in his campaign, it pressed on him from the start: On his Inauguration Day plants and schools in the Northeast closed because of natural gas shortages, and within the week there were 200,000 workers laid off and an equal number of schoolchildren sent home. At a news conference just after his inauguration Carter announced he was sending emergency legislation to deal with the natural gas crisis, but he warned of "future sacrifices" and told everyone to set their thermometers at 65 degrees and put on sweaters.[17]

Carter introduced an Emergency Natural Gas Act, which would authorize the federal government to allocate interstate natural gas. It passed within two weeks, though not without some grumbling that he had not consulted the party leaders. Flush with his first accomplishment, Carter gave a "fireside chat" dressed in a tan cardigan sweater and seated by a roaring fireplace in the White House, announcing that he would propose a Department of Energy, a bill that Congress approved by August. Congress agreed to fund accelerated stockpiling of 500 million barrels of crude oil in a national security reserve.

The larger issues of conservation, deregulation of markets, and taxing energy production and consumption were dealt with by a special task force organized by former defense secretary James Schlesinger, who did not ask for congressional input nor consult Carter's economic advisers or cabinet secretaries (who didn't even know Schlesinger was working on an energy plan until the president briefly mentioned it at a cabinet meeting). The task force plan was reviewed by the Office of Management and Budget only after it had been drafted in March, and the Treasury and Council of Economic Advisers got only snippets.[18] The result of all this secrecy was predictable. Schlesinger had been fired by President Gerald Ford as Secretary of Defense because he had proven too overbearing in dealing with colleagues and the president, and his current maneuvering as "energy czar" left him with few allies and many enemies. He had to defend his proposals from Council of Economic Advisers Chair Charles Schultze and Treasury Secretary Michael Blumenthal, both of whom thought his proposals would contribute to inflation and retard growth. Carter backed his energy chief but insisted on pressing ahead to meet his deadline.[19]

Carter made another televised speech on energy policy on April 19. "This difficult effort will be the 'moral equivalent of war'—except that we will be uniting our efforts to build and not to destroy." (The "moral equivalent of war" became known by its acronym MEOW, courtesy of *New York Times* columnist Russell Baker.) Addressing the widespread public belief that the energy crisis was contrived, Carter promised "oil and natural gas companies must be honest with all of us about their reserves and profits. We will find out the differences between real shortages and artificial ones."[20] He then raised the stakes: "I have equated the energy policy legislation with either success or failure of my first year in office as leader of our country in domestic affairs."[21] MEOW rhetoric fit Carter's general approach to public policy: focus on comprehensive solutions that would require a recognition of limits; insist that a self-sacrificing citizenry summoned by an honest government act in the national interest; make the effort a test of character and morality for leaders and citizens alike. In Carter's world there would be plenty of opportunity for politicians, energy companies, and the American people to rise to the occasion—or to expose their own moral failings.

Rhetoric aside, Carter's proposals would require bills to reduce energy demand with conservation measures, increase supply by deregulating prices, recapture most of the profits that would accrue to energy companies, and redistribute them to the American people to alleviate the hardship caused by rising prices. Existing price controls would be modified, price ceilings for previously discovered oil ($5.25 a barrel for existing production and $11.28 for new oil) would be adjusted for inflation, and prices for domestic oil discovered since 1975 would be allowed to rise over a three-year period to the world price. The extra profits would be subject to new taxes on the difference between its prior controlled price and the new world market price. These revenues would then be returned to the American people through income tax rebates. The higher price for oil (as well as newly discovered gas by eliminating price controls on new fields) would encourage conservation rather than the overconsumption of cheap domestic oil and gas. The higher prices also would encourage exploration and production.[22]

The administration proposed conservation measures to keep the increase in energy consumption at less than 2 percent annually; reduce gasoline consumption by 10 percent below the 1976 level; reduce oil imports to less than six million barrels a day; require a gas tax of between five to fifty cents per gallon every year that gas consumption rose above annual targets, with revenues rebated through income tax credits; increase fuel economy by imposing a gas-guzzler tax on low-mileage vehicles; establish fuel-efficiency standards for new construction and for household appliances; enforce 55 mph speeds on highways and reduce highway funds for states not doing so; speed up nuclear energy licensing of light-water reactors; and provide for cogeneration of steam and electricity by requiring utilities to purchase surplus power and transmit it over their lines. There were also some sweeteners: tax credits of 10 percent for conversion to coal; tax credits for solar energy and residential conservation measures; funding for low-income weatherization; grants for schools and hospitals to insulate buildings; and provision of off-peak rates for residential customers.

These proposals, embodied in 113 separate provisions of a proposed energy bill, were so complex even Carter had trouble with them. "I am not satisfied with your approach," Carter wrote Schlesinger. "It is extremely complicated (I can't understand it)."[23] Carter had not given congressional leaders any advance notice. He would introduce the program without having created a constituency for it and before an Energy Department had been created to lobby for it.[24] Schlesinger and Eizenstat proposed an "outsider" strategy of White House briefings and speeches by the cabinet and the president in efforts to win over public opinion, even at the risk of "congressional sensitivity to 'going over their heads.'"[25] Congressional liaison staffers called for an "insider strategy" relying on closed-door negotiations with Congress.

Speaker Tip O'Neill (D-MA), who predicted "the toughest fight this Congress has ever had," convinced Carter he could carry the House with the insider approach. O'Neill created a special Ad Hoc Energy Committee that was dominated by party leaders and that lessened the influence of the energy lobbies. In spite of inexperienced and arrogant White House aides, technical flaws in the program (Schlesinger's numbers often didn't add up or were contradictory), and Carter's own aloofness, the energy package progressed. The administration dropped its insistence that the Secretary of Energy have power to set producer prices and accepted the House decision to remove the gasoline tax. Carter was angry when Congress modified his program, but O'Neill prevailed on him not to go public, and the House passed most of it.

In the Senate it was tougher going, particularly among Democratic leaders with little or no confidence in Carter's judgment. Kennedy was concerned about tax loopholes that producers might exploit. Henry Jackson (D-WA), heading the Energy and Natural Resources Committee, didn't want tax and other disincentives for consumption. Russell Long (D-LA), chair of the Senate Finance Committee, wanted more incentives for oil and gas producers. Alan Cranston (D-CA) and other westerners didn't want conservation measures that would hurt long-distance commuters. Carter went on television, calling on the Senate "to act responsibly" and "reject narrow, special interest attacks on all segments of the national energy plan." Robert Byrd (D-WV) responded by advising Carter to "cool it just a bit at this stage and let the process work."[26] Carter did not cool it: At a June 13 news conference, he warned that the public must get involved or "the special interest groups will prevail." But the public wasn't concerned: The weather was warmer, and the natural gas shortage was over. A June 2 Gallup poll reported that only half of the public realized that the United States had to import oil to meet its energy requirements, and a majority did not support Carter's program. By the spring of 1977 Carter's popularity dropped about ten points after he put the energy crisis on the national agenda. His drop in the polls stiffened Senate resolve to write the bill its own way.

Carter again addressed the nation on September 8, exhorting Congress to pass his bills. His party remained deeply divided on sectional and ideological lines: Democratic liberals filibustered the proposals to deregulate energy prices, a move that enraged conservatives. Carter sided with the oil-producing states, and Vice President Mondale used questionable rulings while presiding over the Senate to break the filibuster, and with it Democratic unity. Carter now attacked the oil companies: In his October 13 televised news conference he warned ominously of "the biggest rip-off in American history." He claimed that oil companies were following the OPEC cartel on price hikes and that natural gas producers were manipulating their levels of production to raise prices. He said that his plan was fair, but "the oil companies apparently want it all. . . . Our proposal, if adopted, would give the oil companies, the producers themselves, the highest prices for oil in all the world. But they still want more." Energy producers and other big businesses responded negatively. Nevertheless, Carter was willing to compromise. His staffers held meetings with Senator Long on the timetable for deregulation of natural gas prices. The White House blocked Senator Kennedy's amendment that would have prevented oil companies from acquiring other energy sources. In October the Senate finally passed a bill, but the White House found it unacceptable. In his January 1978 State of the Union address Carter proclaimed that both the president and Congress had "failed the American people," adding, "We still do not have a national energy program. Not much longer can we tolerate this stalemate."[27] In a CBS/*New York Times* poll only 43 percent of the public believed the energy crisis was real, while 47 percent believed it was a pretext for oil companies to raise prices.

For much of his second year Carter fought it out with Congress. In April, with the House and Senate still deadlocked in the conference committee over the pricing of natural gas, Carter made yet another appeal to Congress to "fulfill its duty to the American people." The administration changed its approach to deregulating energy prices, proposing a phaseout of controls but an extension of overall price ceilings into the mid-1980s—a concession to liberals and energy consumers. By the summer of 1978 Carter himself was actively lobbying interest groups, governors, and legislators for his natural gas deregulation package, and his aides were horse-trading for votes in the Senate. The final compromises eliminated the standby gasoline tax, the tax on domestic crude oil to raise prices to world levels, and the tax on industrial users of oil and natural gas, all measures to win over conservatives and senators from oil-producing states. The projected energy savings was reduced in half, from 4.5 billion barrels to 2.25 barrels. Carter signed this modified energy package on November 9, 1978.

Because Carter had gone public with his insistence on a "pure" bill and was always so negative about any compromises, when the final compromise was forged it seemed to him flawed, even though he had accomplished a great deal: creation of the Department of Energy, accelerated stockpiling for the Energy Reserves, abolition of the powerful Joint Committee on Atomic Energy (a step that would make it easier to block breeder reactors and move toward light-water reactors of the kind favored by the administration); a shutdown of the Clinch River Breeder Reactor; regulation of strip mining under the Surface Mining Control and Reclamation Act (a victory for environmentalists); and his preferred route for an oil pipeline in Alaska.

For any other president, these successes would have translated into a powerful boost in governing authority; for Carter they translated into a loss of confidence in his leadership. It was *how* Carter accomplished things, rather than *what* he accomplished, that seemed to be the problem. In an influential article that shaped public perceptions of the president, Carter's former speechwriter James Fallows wrote that the president's "skin crawled at the thought of the time consuming consultation and persuasion that might be required to bring a legislator around. He did not know how congressmen talked, worked, and thought, how to pressure them without being a bully or flatter them without seeming a fool."[28] Carter's reputation as an amateur, a moralist, and a reluctant compromiser was now set among the Washington pundits, and there was little he could do to change it.

Carter's 1979 Energy Proposals

No one in the White House assumed that energy would be a big issue for the remainder of Carter's first term. But by the end of 1978 the OPEC oil cartel posted price hikes of 14.5 percent. By the Christmas season, after the fall of the Shah of Iran, there was a slowdown of Iranian oil exports and then a complete halt. Prices began to rise above $13 a barrel as oil production plummeted by two million barrels a day in the first quarter of 1979. By June OPEC would raise prices again per barrel to $23.50 and then to $28, and finally to $34.

Carter directed Schlesinger to prepare a plan for standby rationing. When he submitted the plan, Congress under the law had the right to use a legislative veto to block it within sixty days. The House Commerce Committee did so, and Carter made a statement appealing to Congress to consider the national interest. Behind the scenes White House aides Eizenstat and Frank Moore brokered a deal with the Commerce Committee, which reported a modified version to the House for a vote. But then the Senate rescinded *its* approval, making the situation worse, and after Carter sent a letter reassuring the Senate about the proposed changes, it approved the plan (with a large majority of Democrats and some Republican support). The Senate resolution specified conditions under which the plan could go into effect without a later Senate veto.

Just as the White House was congratulating itself, urban states rallied a majority in the House to kill a bill giving the president standby gasoline rationing authority, 159–246.[29] On May 11 an enraged president slammed the House: "I am not willing to accept the judgment of a majority of the House of Representatives, whose Members have apparently put their heads in the sand and refused to take action, refused to acknowledge the threat, and refused to deal with what is acknowledged to be a very difficult issue. . . . This question indicates—and I hate to say this—that a majority of the House of Representatives have . . . local or parochial interests and let political timidity prevent their taking action in the interest of our Nation."[30] By mid-May a Gallup poll showed a plurality opposed standby rationing, 47–41. Carter dug in his heels and in spite of Senator Byrd's entreaties, he refused to send up a new plan. Because of the gasoline lines, public opinion eventually changed, and by the first week of August a 51 percent majority favored giving Carter standby rationing authority. The final version of the Emergency Energy Conservation Act passed at the end of October, with unified Democratic support, in part based on a provision that both houses of Congress could disapprove any rationing plan by joint resolution within thirty days.

Progress on other energy initiatives was slow. Price controls on domestic oil were scheduled to be lifted in June 1, 1979. The president had authority under existing law to modify price controls. He requested the windfall profits tax from Congress of 50 percent on old oil, with proceeds to go into an Energy Security Trust Fund for synthetic fuel development, low-income households to pay energy bills, and for mass transit. Congress delayed. Although the White House aides were functioning much more smoothly and effectively this time around in a task force led by Eizenstat, the magnitude of the energy crisis overwhelmed them. It was at this moment, with Carter's latest energy initiatives stalled and his poll ratings in free fall, that he returned from the Far East and went to Camp David to prepare a new effort to rally the American people behind his program.

Meetings at Camp David

Caddell was waiting for Carter with a 107-page memo calling for a speech about trust and leadership. Powell and Gerald Rafshoon urged him to concentrate on energy policy, but Carter had no new energy plan to propose, only those bills already working their way slowly through Congress. The president and White House aides had no confidence that Schlesinger would come up with any big new initiatives, and in fact were considering whether or not Schlesinger should continue as secretary of energy.

By July 4 Carter and his wife were at Camp David looking over speechwriter Gordon Stewart's draft of a speech on "Energy and National Goals." It didn't address what they took to be the central problem: the preoccupation Americans had with private interests rather than the public interest. Stewart himself had appended a note to his draft: "This is the best I can do going down the old road. I don't think there is any point to it."[31] The Carters agreed and turned to Caddell's latest memo. His data indicated that "the American people had become completely inured to warnings about future energy shortages, convinced that both the government and the oil companies were either incompetent or dishonest—or both."[32] Caddell advised Carter not to give an energy speech but rather talk about faith, hope, and trust, because "Americans were rapidly losing faith in themselves and in their country."[33]

Caddell wanted Carter to give a bold and creative "breakthrough" speech. His memo crystallized for Carter all the problems and frustrations of his presidency. Carter decided to cancel the July 5 energy speech and prepare a speech to be delivered later that would address larger issues. Rick Hertzberg and Gordon Stewart set to work on an address about healing the wounds of Vietnam and Watergate, changing the American mood and restoring confidence. Carter had nothing to lose by abandoning plans for a fifth speech on energy because he had already lost his audience: 80 million had watched his first energy speech but only 30 million had watched his fourth. But he did not explain why he was canceling, which created concern across the country about a crisis in Washington. The dollar declined on world markets while gold went up. Belatedly the White House issued a statement of reassurance that did little to reassure.

Carter convened his political advisers. Mondale wanted the president to deliver an energy speech and deal with substantive issues of energy, inflation, and unemployment. He was highly critical of Caddell's memo. He urged Carter to speak about real issues—not the public mood. His criticisms were echoed by Eizenstat. Caddell, Rafshoon, and Powell responded that Carter should deal with the national malaise.[34]

Carter intended to deal with Caddell's malaise but also understood that the problems with his presidency also involved the nuts and bolts of governance. The public was losing confidence in his abilities as chief executive. Rafshoon, who had been appointed communications director to straighten out his media operation, had written Carter a memo about this: "The American people want to see the government—and particularly the President—get control of the forces that affect their lives." He counseled that "each appearance should reinforce the fact that you are taking, or have successfully taken, action to bring these forces under control. The theme should run *explicitly* throughout our communication."[35] Carter intended to stress the theme by instituting presidential control of his cabinet, and not coincidentally, by cutting down on cabinet meetings. On July 6, White House aides met with Carter to talk about the cabinet's performance. By the second week at Camp David, Rafshoon, Powell, and Caddell all supported the idea of cabinet firings as a dramatic way to bring focus to the administration.

A new speech was set for July 15, and in the days before it the White House prepped commentators. "The President has made malaise a household word," the *Washington Post* wrote in an editorial on July 15, pointing out "some part of the disaffection may be not so much more than impatience and frustration growing out of his own performance in office."[36]

The Malaise Speech

Senator Eugene McCarthy (D-MN) once referred to Carter as "an oratorical mortician" who "inters his words and ideas beneath piles of syntactical mush."[37] The president mumbled, elided sentences, and jumbled words. He didn't speak well extemporaneously, was awkward in acknowledging the feelings of his audience, raised his voice at the end of sentences until he seemed to squeak, and was prone to non sequiturs. He refused entreaties from staffers that he worked with a voice coach.

Carter delivered his half-hour speech from the White House on July 15, and for once he didn't need a coach: His speech was from the heart, and he delivered it well. "I promised you a President who is not isolated from the people, who feels your pain and shares your dreams and who draws his strength and wisdom from you." This ad populum appeal would flatter his audience and gain its acceptance. Carter admitted that the more he had spoken about programs and policies, "the talks and the press conferences have become increasingly narrow, focused more and more on what the isolated world of Washington thinks is important." He went back to his anti-Washington theme, to the rejection of government that had characterized his 1976 "outsider" campaign. Then came the rhetorical question: "Why have we not been able to get together as a nation to resolve our serious energy problems?"

Carter segued into the Caddell theme: "It's clear that the true problems of our nation are much deeper—deeper than gasoline lines or energy shortages. Deeper, even than inflation or recession." Carter continued: "And I realize more than ever that as President I need your help." He defined a fundamental threat to American democracy: "It is a crisis of confidence. It is a crisis that strikes at the very heart and soul and spirit of our national will." Carter spoke of "the growing doubt about the meaning of our own lives and in the loss of unity of purpose for our nation." People were losing confidence in the future, and they were losing faith, "not only in the Government itself, but in their ability as citizens to serve as the ultimate rulers and shapers of our democracy." He talked of the assassinations of John Kennedy, Robert Kennedy, and Martin Luther King, and he talked of Vietnam and Watergate, of inflation and the decline of the dollar. Carter quoted one of his guests at Camp David, who told him, "The strength we need will not come from the White House, but from every house in America." The people over the years have been hearing "more and more about what government thinks or what the government should be doing, and less and less about our nation's hopes, our dreams, and our vision of the future."

But Carter didn't offer any vision of the future. At the very moment that he might have brought his audience into his hopes and dreams for America, he turned on his viewers: "Too many of us now tend to worship self-indulgence

and consumption." Owning and consuming things "does not satisfy our long-
ing for meaning." Carter ran through Caddell's findings on the crisis of the
American spirit: Two-thirds of the public didn't vote; a majority had no confidence in the future; worker productivity was dropping; family savings were
declining; there was growing disrespect for government, churches, schools,
news media, and other institutions. The gap between citizens and government
had never been so wide. "This is not a message of happiness or reassurance,
but it is the truth and it is a warning," a dour Carter told the nation.

"What can we do?" he asked. "First of all, we must face the truth and then
we can change our course. We simply must have faith in each other. Faith in
our ability to govern ourselves and faith in the future of this nation. Restoring
that faith and that confidence is now the most important task we face." But instead of talking about how to restore faith, Carter made an awkward transition into his energy program: He began by referring to "the path of common
purpose and the restoration of American values. That path leads to true freedom for our nation and ourselves." Then he continued: "We can take the first
steps down that path as we begin to solve our energy problem. Energy will be
the immediate test of our ability to unite this nation." He offered specific proposals: a goal of cutting 4.5 million barrels a day from what the United States
would otherwise import by 1990; establishment of a new energy corporation;
an energy mobilization unit to cut red tape; a 50 percent tax on windfall profits when oil prices were decontrolled to raise $220 billion in revenue in the
1980s. His energy program was anticlimactic and induced MEGO ("my eyes
glaze over") in his audience.

Carter had prophesied doom and called for repentance. He had begun with
a litany of his own shortcomings but had quickly moved to the shortcomings
of his audience. Joseph Califano, a member of his cabinet, was later to recall
that it was "a banal address, written . . . for Pat Caddell's polls and to manipulate the emotions of the people exposed in them."[38] True enough, yet it was
also the best speech Carter had made since his nomination acceptance speech:
It was well rehearsed and well delivered, and most importantly, well watched.
Mail and telephone responses, as monitored by the White House Staff Offices
Administration, supported his message by 3 to 1.[39]

The speech was favorably received by the major columnists and editorial
writers. *U.S. News and World Report* called it "an extraordinary effort by a
U.S. Chief Executive to rally a nation—and save a Presidency," an opinion
shared by the *New York Times*'s Hedrick Smith. Martin Schram of the *Washington Post* saw it as "a rebirth of the Carter presidency" and a "turnaround";
his colleague David Broder claimed that Carter had "found his voice again."
For Peter Goldman of *Newsweek,* it was a speech delivered "with an urgency,
a passion and an eloquence rare in his or in any other recent Presidency."

There was considerable negative commentary from conservative columnists George Will, William Safire, and Joseph Kraft. They argued that the speech was a public relations ploy to direct attention away from Carter's leadership failures; scoffed that his energy proposals would not work; and pointed out that Carter was blaming Congress and the American people for his own failures.[40] NBC's *Prime Time Sunday* had negative commentary from observers, but viewers had given a positive feedback on cable from Columbus, Ohio, where a new technological innovation, a QUBE two-way cable system, allowed viewers to "vote" their approval or disapproval by pushing a button on their remote controls.

The speech itself was a watershed in presidential rhetoric. Carter had begun by recounting his problems in the White House and disclosing his limitations as a leader. This was not only new for Carter, such a speech was also something new in presidential rhetoric, which up to that point had never been introspective or confessional.[41] The masculine "presidential" language of conquest and conflict had given way to a more intimate, conciliatory, "feminine" style.[42] As communications expert Kathleen Hall Jamieson pointed out, "Only a person whose credibility is firm can risk adopting a style traditionally considered weak."[43] For Carter, whose credibility was at stake, it was a risk.

Carter had not worked through the speech's rhetorical contradictions: He was confessing limitations but claiming expertise; he was speaking intimately about his own failures but preaching about the shortcomings of his listeners; he claimed to be talking about the public's concerns but devoted a lot of time discussing his own leadership failings. He was dealing with national problems but was focusing on the workings of the White House and the burdens of his office. His narrative of personal shortcomings, however self-effacing he might have portrayed himself, had the feel of a twelve-step confessional. Carter lacked the ability to take a foible, hold it up to ridicule, and by so doing, rob it of its force. Presidents Abraham Lincoln and Ronald Reagan could do this naturally, but Carter seemed to delight in magnifying his own limitations rather than defusing anxiety about them. (In religious terms his action could be considered mortification.) A deft self-deprecating phrase from Reagan would put an audience at ease; an earnest discussion of personal failings by Carter set an audience on edge.

Carter did not offer the panegyric rhetoric that would retell the American story of heroic triumphs and renew American faith. Carter's epideictic rhetoric, with its parceling out of blame, was puzzling, because he wasn't clear about who deserved the blame—the White House or the people.[44] His was a hectoring and nagging exercise, whose very delivery was negating: It expressed a lack of confidence in the American people while calling on the people to act on their own confidence in America. What one commentator had said about

President Lyndon Johnson could serve as well for Carter: His "sermonizing told people what they should feel without uttering sentiments capable of summoning those feelings."[45] Carter *asserted* rather than *evoked* confidence in the future, assertions that rang hollow after his own contradictory confessions of failed leadership and his criticisms of the public's loss of faith in God and Country. Carter could no more will the people's confidence in America than he could will their confidence in him.

When he came to the policy segment, Carter could not help trying to conquer his audience by force of argument, by an impersonal, data-based, and rational policy formulation, by an appeal to expertise and the public interest. Yet his speech was too short to narrate the history of the energy crisis, lay out the alternative policies, weigh the pros and cons, and persuade the country of the wisdom of his policies. He moralized, proclaiming that his approach was in the national interest and that anything else proposed was not. The policy section did not invite the audience to think anew about energy policy, or for that matter, to think at all.[46]

Carter was never able to master the "televisual" approach to presidential speechmaking. He made no attempt to substitute his own visual imagery for the images on the evening news of gas lines and pump prices, factory closings, and trucker strikes. He failed to personalize the speech by narrating the stories of average Americans who exemplified his ideas. He failed to provide drama, instead using Chicken Little assertions of a national emergency. By the time the speech was over, there were no new and positive images to substitute for the images in the news. Carter's worst mistake was his failure to provide a synoptic or digestive phrase that could summarize his speech.[47] There would be nothing that the media could pull from his speech as a shorthand for his ideas, nothing that would etch this speech into the national consciousness. But commentators abhor a rhetorical vacuum, and if there were no synecdoche (a figure of speech standing for the whole) that the American people could hold onto in the speech, they would provide one. Carter's effort became known as the "malaise" speech, though the president had never used the word in his address. "Malaise" became a foil for Carter's opponents, all of whom would vie with each other in claiming a confidence in the American people that they claimed Carter lacked.

Yet even with all the rhetorical shortcomings in Carter's style, content, and delivery, the public seemed to agree with the main premise of Carter's address. One day after the speech, a CBS/*New York Times* poll asked respondents if there was "a moral and spiritual crisis, that is, a crisis of confidence, in this country today." By a large majority, 86 percent of the public agreed. Within the next week Carter began moving up in the polls. The opinion of media commentators and students of presidential rhetoric to the contrary, it seemed as if

Carter had, by finally speaking his mind, transformed his presidency by regaining some moral authority. How then, did the president fail?

Controlling the Cabinet

"Most of my advisers," Carter later recalled, "told me that if I was determined to reassess my administration, then I also had to be prepared to make some major changes in my Cabinet." But Carter was reluctant: "I did not think that this was necessary and argued against the idea."[48] In his meetings with senior political advisers at Camp David he was finally convinced to bring in mature staffers, appoint a chief of staff to bring order into the White House, and remove disloyal or ineffective cabinet secretaries. Two days after his speech Carter met with his senior White House staffers and members of the cabinet. "I have deliberately excluded most of you from my life for the past couple of weeks," Carter began coolly, because he had "wanted to get away from you and from Washington."[49] He summarized the problem as he saw it: "My government is not leading the country. The people have lost confidence in me, in the Congress, in themselves, and in this nation." He talked about the disloyalty of some cabinet members, claiming that they were working for themselves and not the White House. "I intend to run for office and I intend to be re-elected." He told the astonished secretaries that there would be changes in the cabinet as he geared up for his re-election campaign, because "some Cabinet officers do not have support among their constituents."[50]

The comment was directed at Joseph Califano, who had stood up to the National Education Association on school reform, senior citizens on restraining health care costs, and the tobacco lobby on television advertising. Califano had made decisions as a "trustee" of the public interest rather than as a champion of interest groups—which ironically was Carter's own style of governance. Other secretaries were on Carter's hit list, though they did not know it from his general comments. Michael Blumenthal had remained out of the political arena, believing that a treasury secretary should not engage in politics, though Carter had told him to get involved. James Schlesinger did not have the confidence of energy producers, because, like Califano, he tried to act in the public interest. Brock Adams had made appointments in Transportation of people who might back Senator Kennedy rather than Carter in the 1980 nominating contest. Although Carter had talked the talk of the public interest in his Camp David address, his decisions to fire cabinet secretaries were designed to improve his political position.

According to Califano, Carter asked for letters of resignation at the meeting.[51] Secretary of State Cyrus Vance and Secretary of Defense Harold Brown replied that letters were not necessary and not a good idea, and Carter backed off. The matter was not resolved at the meeting, but Hamilton Jordan, the new chief of staff, placed a conference call that evening to members of the cabinet and told them that they would not have to submit letters but that the White House was announcing their offers to resign.[52] Press secretary Jody Powell then announced that all cabinet secretaries and senior staff, thirty-three officials in all, had offered their resignations. By July 27, five secretaries had been fired or had decided to resign (Schlesinger at Energy, W. Michael Blumenthal at Treasury, Califano at Health and Human Services, Griffin Bell at Justice, Brock Adams at Transportation), and fifty subcabinet officials had been fired. In addition, Patricia Harris was switched from Housing and Urban Development to Health and Human Services. Carter had done more than just reshuffle the cabinet; he had downgraded the cabinet and centralized command in a chief of staff. After the announcements gold went up, the dollar went down, and the markets were convulsed. Carter had once again exacerbated the very crisis of confidence that his actions were designed to alleviate.

The attempt to establish White House control over the cabinet was sensible in principle, though his appointment of Hamilton Jordan would not help him because Jordan was young and did not project authority on Capitol Hill or with the media. His appointment would dismay the party's congressional wing. What would help Carter politically would be the new cabinet appointees, who came with their own constituencies. Charles Duncan, the new Secretary of Energy, was a former Coca Cola executive and had close ties to oil companies, both important in securing his southern base and its crucial financial support during the renomination effort. For HUD, Carter appointed Moon Landrieu, who would give him support in Catholic Louisiana to counter Senator Kennedy. Neil Goldschmidt was put into Transportation, which would help solidify Carter in Oregon and would help him retain Jewish support. These appointments were made to win renomination and reelection.[53] Carter had gotten rid of the strongest policy players, each of whom had acted as a trustee in the public interest. He had placed political loyalty over policy competence and constituency politics over public goods.

Media coverage of the "resignations" was negative.[54] NBC aired an interview with Adams, and another with Califano, and continued with a story on the power struggle between the White House staff (the "band of Georgians") and the cabinet secretaries who had been dismissed. ABC led off with a question to press secretary Jody Powell, "Let me ask you about the things people are saying on Capitol Hill and elsewhere. They are actually questioning, you know, whether the president has taken leave of his senses."[55] CBS aired a discussion of a "loyalty form" that had been distributed to cabinet secretaries by Hamilton Jordan. *U.S. News and World Report* called the reshuffle a "desperate gamble to save his beleaguered Presidency." *Time* characterized it as "the most thoroughgoing and puzzling purge in the history of the U.S. presidency." Meg Greenfield of *Newsweek* thought it "mad."[56] Elizabeth Drew of the *New Yorker* wrote that "the action was so far outside the range of predictable behavior that people were bewildered; to many it seemed that things had gone out of control." She added that "the manner in which they were executed and the clear signals they gave off that he had capitulated to his own aides—young men without much national stature—made him appear to many people not strong but weak."[57]

The public was equally negative. Pollster Lou Harris reported to his clients that "President Carter's overall rating with Americans has dropped again to 74–25, the lowest he has yet been accorded and the worst standing for any president in modern times." Harris continued: "He is back where he began— essentially a chief executive who is rejected by his ultimate constituency, the American people. . . . In his specific task of rebuilding confidence in himself as the national leader, he has struck out."[58] By early September, a *Time* poll indicated that the public preferred Kennedy to Carter by a 62–24 percent margin, and that 58 percent of the public felt Kennedy was strong compared with 12 percent for Carter. Within a week, with all Washington astir, Carter made a brief and bizarre appearance lasting a little over a minute in the press room: He made an announcement that the changes in the cabinet would be for the better and expressed his thanks to those who had served him. It was a humorless, passionless performance, which only underscored his continuing political difficulties. The theme of a failing and passionless presidency dominated Carter's press coverage for months.[59]

Carter's Way

"Truth is the enemy of anyone presiding over a nation in decline," Pat Caddell once observed. "Anyone who acknowledges the truth is out, because it is an acknowledgment of failure. The only other option is denial. And that can only be carried off by offering a counter-reality that is further and further removed from the actual reality facing the country."[60] Is that why Carter failed? Because he told the truth, and a president cannot do that? Or was it something else, something about the *way* Carter told the truth?

Carter failed because he played his own peculiar political game—a game that was not understood by Washington hands, and one that would not have been appreciated even had it been understood. The way Carter handled Camp David and its aftermath mirrored the general problems of his presidency: He always sent mixed messages, always trampled on his successes, always found fault with himself and with others. Although Carter spent time and effort putting a positive media spin on events, he always subverted himself with his own negative approach toward politics.

Carter trumped his "malaise" speech with a reorganization that made a mockery of its premises. Having waited thirty months to shake up his presidency, he expected the American people to regain confidence in his leadership. For weeks afterward he continued to trample on his message (a pattern after major speeches), treating shabbily many people who had served him loyally. This only reinforced the judgment of the Washington community that he was a cold fish and an unfeeling boss who in dismissing loyal subordinates had lacked class. All of this, including subsequent spats with Califano and others, could have been foreseen in advance by a president who thought ahead and by White House staffers who thought more of the president's own stakes and less of their own desire to gain control and to get even. Camp David became a symbol of chaos and not of control.

Carter did not fail because he was an *amateur* (a politician who places the public interest above his own power stakes). Carter *was* a practiced politician, who had used effective campaign techniques to position himself as a conservative candidate in Georgia elections and then who had shifted adroitly to win the presidential nomination in 1976 by developing three different positions—liberal, centrist, and conservative—in different primary states. Carter knew his way around campaign finance, had hired a sophisticated campaign staff and taken his top political aides into the White House and then built up a sophisticated polling and communications operation run by savvy professionals who believed that governance was an extension of campaigning.

Yet Carter was a different breed of politician. In 1976 he had campaigned as an outsider: "The insiders have had their chance and they have not delivered. And their time has run out. The time has come for a great majority of Americans—those who for too long have been on the outside looking in—to have a President who will turn the government of this country inside out."[61] He had called for honesty and morality in government, and had asked, "Why Not the Best?" Once in office, however, he had relied on the Washington insiders, and then just after Camp David, seemingly without any reason, he had given many of them the axe. These were confusing developments—to the participants, to the media, and to the public at large. How could Carter rail against the government when he was running it?

Carter had always preferred an outside strategy: Go over the heads of Congress and put pressure on the president rather than working on policy from the inside. But he made no attempt to get the cabinet secretaries to reinforce his overall themes or speak with one voice. He had never had a "line of the day" meeting for the White House staff.[62] Not until May 1978 did he organize a communications office. Disregard for image management is not quite what one would expect from this president, and eventually he brought in two communications professionals: Gerald Rafshoon to run his media operation as assistant to the president for communications and Anne Wexler to run his group liaison.

Carter was an amateur only in the sense that he believed that he and his administration could develop policy proposals based on the public interest, and *then* if necessary modify them—minimally and grudgingly—to accommodate his political interests. Left to his own devices, he would implement "pure" policies, in the public interest. He would do the honest thing and the right thing. Carter tried to create a Trusteeship Presidency, appealing to national interest. He wanted as little bargaining, coalition-building, negotiating, and compromise as possible.[63] This is still politics, but it is the politics of public goods, not private interests. It is based on the southern progressive and reform tradition, emphasizing good government, recoiling from racist and populist demagoguery (Carter's race-baiting gubernatorial campaign excepted), and valuing above all expertise and technical proficiency. In Carter's administration, this translated into an aloofness from traditional southern "old boy" politicians. As an engineer governor, Carter admitted, "I was more inclined to move rapidly and without equivocation and without the . . . interminable consultations . . . that are inherent, I think, in someone who has a more legislative attitude, or psyche, or training or experience."[64]

Carter's impressive substantive accomplishments were eclipsed by his style. Yet his four-year record of "success scores" on congressional votes for his program was 76.4 percent (with a low of 75.1 and a high of 78.3), a rate much higher than that enjoyed by presidents Nixon, Ford, Eisenhower, Reagan, and Bush—which one would expect, since Carter had party control of Congress and they had not. But it was also close to Johnson's 78 percent and higher than Kennedy's scores. Based on the party margins he enjoyed in Congress, some political scientists believe he should have done better, especially in his first year in the House.[65] Even so, he clearly had more than respectable legislative accomplishments. For a president who didn't want to bargain, who found politicking distasteful in the extreme, Carter turned out to be willing to engage in it.

The Camp David fiasco did not torpedo Carter's substantive accomplishments. The president won a huge tax on the oil and gas industry. "Overall it was a good compromise," he concluded.[66] Passage of this measure, as well as Carter's prior energy bills, shows a president capable of effective positioning and compromise. Carter also won passage of a bill creating the U.S. Synthetic Fuels Corporation, which would provide $20 billion in joint ventures with private industry. He may have intended a "trusteeship" presidency, but in energy policy some of his compromises favored corporate interests he might bring into the Democratic coalition.[67]

Carter was more successful than any other Democrat or than Nixon and Ford in getting significant energy legislation through Congress, even though it often modified his program and twice rejected his policies. Congress even overrode a presidential veto of a bill that Congress had passed repealing an oil import fee—the first time in twenty-eight years that Congress had overridden a veto by a president from the majority party. It defeated the creation of an Energy Mobilization Board intended to cut through "red tape" in developing new sources of energy. Nevertheless, Carter got most of his energy legislation passed, and most of his energy policy was successful in the long run. Consumption of foreign oil went down, from 48 percent when Carter took office to 40 percent in 1980, with a reduction of 1.8 million barrels a day. As he left office there were high inventories of oil and a surplus of natural gas. There was more oil exploration than before, leading to an oil glut and a drop in prices in the 1980s (Carter's Department of Energy had predicted big increases in price). Carter's initiatives began a conservation process that reduced the amount of energy needed to produce an equivalent amount of goods and services by 40 percent. As a result, the cost of oil to business and consumers declined from 8 percent of GNP in 1980 to only 3 percent by 1997, all of which helped break the power of the OPEC cartel.

None of these policy successes helped Carter with his own political prospects. Carter's governing style led him to minimize his successes. He remained too negative about both his victories and his defeats. If he defined his initial program proposals in the public interest, then by definition any compromise would be flawed and sullied and would be less than honest—and so would he for engaging in it. He would communicate his disgust to the American people, since no compromise could meet his standards, even one to which he himself had been a party. The public responded negatively to his negativity. Carter was a taskmaster, a schoolmaster, an "eat your peas" president. His hectoring tone alienated followers rather than invited support from them.

Carter possessed a bizarre combination of humbleness (wearing a cardigan for a major policy address on energy) and arrogance, a combination of Jacksonian contempt for Washington with Jeffersonian intellect. Put another way, Carter's humility was inextricably connected with his arrogance, because posturing with the one, he could indulge himself in the other.[68] Because his motives were pure, he had a corner on truth, and therefore his opponents must be ill-motivated or ill-informed. Carter might have to descend into the arena, but for him it would be just that, a descent from a loftier moral plane. The media responded to these confusing and off-putting messages by portraying the president as a well-meaning honest amateur, a policy wonk, and a moralistic crusader. They got none of it right, but that would be small comfort to the beleaguered president.

There is irony in Carter's struggle to define himself at Camp David. During his presidency Carter was called "the passionless president," faulted for being a technocrat, for being programmatic rather than political. His two rounds of energy policy legislation succeeded in resolving the energy crisis for more than a decade. Yet for his overt political acts—putting politicians in the cabinet and taking out the technocrats, becoming thematic and political rather than programmatic and technical—Carter put his presidency at risk. He went down precisely when he was most courageous and most passionate about his relationship with the American people and when he attempted an intimacy with the people that he had always found difficult to express. It was a brave and honorable—if flawed—attempt at communication as communion. For presidents there are worse and much less honorable ways to fail.

Notes

1. The Eisenstadt memo is quoted in "Carter was Speechless," *Time*, July 16, 1979, 13.

2. The Gallup poll had Carter at 29 percent, a 17-point decline in three months. ABC/Harris had it at 25 percent, one point lower than Nixon's lowest rating. A CBS/*New York Times* poll said Democrats favored Kennedy over Carter, 53–13. *New York Times* (July 13, 1979): 1.

3. Caddell to Carter, Memo, "The State of America," January 17, 1979, White House Central Files, Box 1, o/a#743, Carter Presidential Library.

4. Elizabeth Drew, "A Reporter at Large," *New Yorker* (August 27, 1979): 45–73.

5. Caddell to Carter, "The State of America," 4.

6. Caddell to Carter, "The State of America," 19.

7. Patrick Caddell, "Of Crisis and Opportunity," April 23, 1979, Jody Powell Files, Box 40, Carter Presidential Library, 1.

8. Caddell, "Of Crisis and Opportunity," 17.

9. Caddell, "Of Crisis and Opportunity," 18.

10. Caddell, "Of Crisis and Opportunity," 19.

11. Caddell, "Of Crisis and Opportunity," 16.

12. Caddell, "Of Crisis and Opportunity," 64–65.

13. Caddell, "Of Crisis and Opportunity" 65.

14. Drew, "A Reporter at Large," 50.

15. Gerald Rafshoon to President Carter, "Leadership Memorandum," February 29, 1979, Rafshoon Files, Box 27, Carter Presidential Library.

16. Marilu Hunt McCarty, "Economic Aspects of the Carter Energy Program," in Herbert D. Rosenbaum and Alexej Ugrinsky, *The Presidency and Domestic Policies of Jimmy Carter* (Westport, CT: Greenwood Press, 1994), 555.

17. Russell D. Motter, "Seeking Limits: The Passage of the National Energy Act as a Microcosm of the Carter Presidency," in Rosenbaum and Ugrinsky, *Presidency and Domestic Policies*, 574.

18. Barbara Kellerman, *The Political Presidency: Practice of Leadership from Kennedy through Reagan* (New York: Oxford University Press, 1988), 187–88, 211.

19. Erwin C. Hargrove, *Jimmy Carter as President: Leadership and the Politics of the Public Good* (Baton Rouge: Louisiana State University Press, 1988), 50.

20. *Public Papers of the President, Jimmy Carter* vol. I (Washington, DC: U.S. Government Printing Office, 1979), 70.

21. Kellerman, *The Political Presidency*, 200.

22. Anthony S. Campagna, "Economic Policy in the Carter Administration," in Rosenbaum and Ugrinsky, *Presidency and Domestic Policies*, 137–40.

23. Jimmy Carter, *Keeping Faith: Memoirs of a President* (Toronto: Bantam Books, 1982), 96.

24. Charles O. Jones, *The Trusteeship Presidency: Jimmy Carter and the United States Congress* (Baton Rouge: Louisiana State University Press, 1988), 138.

25. McCarty, "Economic Aspects of the Carter Energy Program," 564.

26. *Washington Post* (June 12, 1977): 1.

27. Kellerman, *The Political Presidency*, 204.

28. James Fallows, "The Passionless Presidency," *Atlantic* (May 1979).

29. Christopher Caplinger, "The Politics of Trusteeship Governance: Jimmy Carter's Fight for a Standby Gasoline Rationing Plan," *Presidential Studies Quarterly* vol. 26, no. 3 (Summer 1996): 778–94.

30. *Public Papers of the President, Jimmy Carter* vol. 1, 840.

31. Carol Gelderman, *All the Presidents' Words: The Bully Pulpit and the Creation of the Virtual Presidency* (New York: Walker and Company, 1997), 139.

32. Carter, *Keeping Faith*, 114.

33. Carter, *Keeping Faith*, 115.

34. Rosalynn Carter, *First Lady from Plains* (Boston: Houghton Mifflin, 1984), 302.

35. John Anthony Maltese, *Spin Control: The White House Office of Communications and the Management of Presidential News* (Chapel Hill: University of North Carolina Press, 1992), 164.

36. "Changing the Way Things Are," *Washington Post* (July 15, 1979): E6.

37. Kathleen Hall Jamieson, *Eloquence in an Electronic Age: The Transformation of Political Speechmaking* (New York: Oxford University Press, 1988), 173.

38. Joseph Califano, *Governing America: An Insider's Report from the White House and the Cabinet* (New York: Simon & Schuster, 1981), 428.

39. Dan Chew to Dan Malachuk, Memo, September 13, 1979, Staff Offices Administration, Box 2, Carter Presidential Library.

40. Mark Rozell, *The Press and the Carter Presidency* (Boulder, CO: Westview Press, 1989), 133–36.

41. Jamieson, *Eloquence*, 66, 81.

42. Jamieson, *Eloquence*, 50–55, 66.

43. Jamieson, *Eloquence*, 87.

44. George Kennedy, *The Art of Persuasion in Greece* (Princeton, NJ: Princeton University Press, 1963), 152–53.

45. Jamieson, *Eloquence*, 142.

46. Jamieson, *Eloquence*, 5.

47. Jamieson, *Eloquence*, 119.

48. Carter, *Keeping Faith*, 116.

49. Califano, *Governing America*, 429.

50. Califano, *Governing America*, 430.

51. Califano, *Governing America*, 430.

52. Drew, "A Reporter at Large," 66.

53. Betty Glad, *Jimmy Carter: In Search of the Great White House* (New York: Norton, 1980), 448.

54. George Edwards III, *The Public Presidency* (New York: St. Martin's Press, 1983), 175.

55. Quoted in Edwards, *Public Presidency*, 173.

56. "Behind the White House Purge," *U.S. News and World Report* (July 30, 1979); "Carter's Great Purge," *Time* (July 30, 1979): 10; Meg Greenfield, "Post-Surgical Care," *Newsweek* (July 30, 1979): 84.

57. Drew, "A Reporter at Large," 66, 70.

58. Haynes Johnson, *Absence of Power* (New York: Viking Adult, 1980), 315.

59. Rozell, *The Press and the Carter Presidency*, 142–44.

60. Maltese, *Spin Control*, 169.

61. Motter, "Seeking Limits," 67.

62. Maltese, *Spin Control*, 150.

63. Jones, *Trusteeship Presidency*, 210–11, 213.

64. Erwin Hargrove, "Jimmy Carter: The Politics of Public Goods," in Fred Greenstein, ed., *Leadership in the Modern Presidency* (Cambridge, MA: Harvard University Press, 1988), 230.

65. Richard Fleisher and Jon Bond, "Assessing Presidential Support in the House: Lessons from Reagan and Carter," *Journal of Politics* vol. 45 (August 1983): 745–58.

66. Carter, *Keeping Faith*, 123.

67. McCarty, "Economic Aspects of the Carter Energy Program," 566.

68. Mary Stuckey, *The President as Interpreter-in-Chief* (Chatham, NJ: Chatham House Press, 1991), 104.

6

Prerogative Power

Reagan and the Iran-Contra Affair

PRESIDENTS ARGUE THAT THERE IS A TRADE-OFF between restraining executive prerogative and success in foreign affairs. They warn against congressional micromanaging through passage of framework laws that require interbranch policy codetermination and argue that "unity in the executive," as John Jay put it in *The Federalist Papers*, leads to successful policymaking. The Iran-Contra affair offers a test of that proposition. It involved two covert operations ordered by President Ronald Reagan. One involved secret sales of arms to the Islamist regime in Iran; the other involved the transfer of some of the profits from those arms sales to the Contras, a rightist group of guerrillas attempting to overthrow the leftist Sandinista regime in Nicaragua. The Iran-Contra affair had three characteristics. First, policymaking was inverted: The president set events in motion, either explicitly or with a wink and a nod, but he sacrificed White House command and control to preserve plausible deniability, which meant that high-level officials became facilitators for policies determined and implemented by low-level operators. Second, the operation was *privatized*: Arms dealers and syndicates funded it, and crucial negotiations were conducted not by professional diplomats but by arms dealers with financial investments at stake. Third, it involved prerogative governance: Reagan bypassed framework laws passed by Congress that required notifications to congressional committees, and Reagan dispensed with the laws governing covert and intelligence operations.

Intervening in Nicaragua

Covert operations against the Sandinista regime were first authorized on December 1, 1981, when President Reagan signed an Intelligence Finding and reported to Congress that he was authorizing the CIA to "support and conduct paramilitary operations against . . . Nicaragua," in order to interdict arms being sent by the Sandinista regime to leftist rebels in El Salvador. At a cost of $20 million, the CIA would arm and train 500 Nicaraguan exiles, most of whom had been members of the right-wing Somoza regime's Guardia. The CIA created the Nicaraguan Democratic Force based in Honduras and also opened a second front in Costa Rica. The Democratic-controlled Congress, opposed to CIA support of the Contras, responded with restrictions: The Boland II Amendment, passed on October 10, 1984, prohibited the CIA, the Department of Defense, or "any other agency or entity of the United States involved in intelligence activities" from supporting the Contras.[1]

Faced with a congressional funding cutoff, Reagan passed off the operation to Marine Lieutenant Colonel Oliver North (then detailed to the National Security Council [NSC]), who was assigned to "Project Democracy" in an attempt to find funds for the Contras in contravention of Boland II. Alternative funding had been used even before Boland II: After negotiations conducted in 1983 by Deputy Assistant Secretary of Defense (and retired air force general) Richard Secord, the Israelis, in two operations (Tipped Kettle I and II) had transferred to the Contras over $10 million in arms they had captured from the Palestine Liberation Organization in Lebanon. Beginning in May 1984, the Contras had begun receiving $1 million each month from the Saudis (at the behest of the United States), and the amount doubled as of February 1985.

The Contras received at least $32 million in third-country assistance *after* the Boland Amendment banned Contra aid. These funds were controlled by North, who mounted a resupply operation for Contra forces under the supervision of Secord. Using Udall Research Corporation as his cutout (i.e., an organization engaged in activities as a cover for intelligence agencies), Secord bought two C-123 and two C-7 military cargo planes, gained landing rights at airfields in Aguacate in Honduras and Ilopango in El Salvador, and bought an airstrip at Santa Elena in Costa Rica. Secord's partner, expatriate Iranian Albert Hakim, set up dummy corporations, known collectively as "The Enterprise," to disguise the sources of funding used to buy supplies for the Contras.

By 1986 North and Secord had twenty full-time employees in the resupply operation, on a payroll of more than $60,000 per month. They also provided military intelligence, weapons drops, and political guidance. The Enterprise had its own secure communications system, apart from the CIA, with its own KL-43 encryption devices supplied by the NSC. North may have kept the existence of The Enterprise from national security adviser Colonel Robert "Bud" McFarlane, in what McFarlane later referred to as "the worst act of betrayal I have ever experienced in my life."[2]

The congressional cutoff was modified on August 8, 1985, when Congress passed the International Security and Development Cooperation Act of 1985 and authorized $27 million in humanitarian aid to the Contras for fiscal year 1986 but prohibited weapons, ammunition, or other equipment inflicting serious bodily harm or death.[3] It allowed officials to solicit third parties for humanitarian aid and the exchange of "information with the Nicaraguan democratic resistance," but it prohibited the conditioning of any foreign aid to any other nation or that nation's giving assistance "to persons or groups engaging in an insurgency or other act of rebellion against the government of Nicaragua."[4] Congress in a related measure authorized the CIA to provide communications equipment and intelligence information to the Contras and did not explicitly prohibit the State Department from soliciting humanitarian assistance for them from third parties, provided there was no quid pro quo or threat to withhold foreign aid if they did not comply with U.S. wishes.[5] Congress then authorized creation of the Nicaraguan Humanitarian Assistance Office (NHOA). The NHOA could not lawfully resupply the Contras with lethal aid, but on nine resupply flights in the spring of 1986 The Enterprise commingled its own lethal weapons with NHOA humanitarian assistance.[6]

The Enterprise resupply operation was plagued with problems. Robert Owen, North's liaison with the Contras, reported that the Contra leaders based in Miami were "not first rate people; in fact they are liars and greed and power motivated. They are not the people to build a new Nicaragua," adding that "this war has become a business to many of them."[7] Some people supporting the Contra program were alleged to be drug traffickers; one key Honduran general supporting them had been convicted for selling cocaine to finance a murder plot.[8]

Members of The Enterprise treated the operation as a chance for large profits: CIA operative Felix Rodriguez briefed Vice President George H. W. Bush's chief of staff Donald Gregg, and on August 12, 1985, Gregg told a group of resupply officials that Rodriguez was concerned that the arms dealers were ripping off Contras and were not to be trusted.[9] Between April 1985 and September 1986, The Enterprise partners withdrew $4.579 million in profit distributions.[10] Although everyone was making money, the resupply operation cut corners: Pilots constantly complained about the quality of their planes, their maintenance, and the flying conditions. In spite of North's efforts, the Contras never managed to foment a popular uprising or establish a base in an urban area. In the summer of 1985, in spite of North's resupply operation, the Sandinistas took the offensive in the northern provinces near

Honduras. Contras and their families were forced to flee back into their original bases in Honduras.

McFarlane and North kept reassuring Congress that they were complying with the Boland Amendment. North told the House Intelligence Committee at a meeting at the White House Situation Room on August 6, 1986, that he "did not in any way, nor at any time violate the spirit, principles or legal requirements of the Boland Amendment."[11] Based on these assurances, Congress provided the Contras in September 1986 with military assistance, appropriating $70 million for military and paramilitary operations by Contras as well as $30 million for humanitarian assistance. In Boland IV, Congress provided in the Intelligence Authorization Act for FY 1987 that support for Contras could only be "pursuant to any provision of law specifically providing such funds, material or assistance."

Trading Arms with Iran

North and The Enterprise were involved in a second risky operation—trading arms with Iran. By offering to sell arms, the United States also hoped Iran would lean on its surrogates in Lebanon, the Hezbollah, to release seven American hostages taken in Lebanon between 1982–1985, including CIA Middle East Station Chief William Buckley, who was being tortured for information. Reagan for several years had considered overtures to Iran to build up the "moderates" in Tehran, but any overt attempt to do so would violate the executive agreement signed between Iran and the United States on January 19, 1981. The agreement had ended a crisis involving American diplomats held hostage in Tehran, but its first article had provided that the United States would not interfere in the internal affairs of Iran. Whatever overtures would be made would have to be covert, and not only because of that agreement: The State Department had put Iran on its list of "terrorist" nations in January 1984, which would prohibit assistance to the regime, and Reagan had campaigned in 1980 vowing never to do business with terrorists.

Israeli Arms Transfers

In the 1980s Iran was locked in a war with Iraq and desperately needed anti-tank and surface-to-air weapons. NSC consultant Michael Ledeen met with Israeli prime minister Shimon Peres, who offered to sell American-made arms to Iran (which would require U.S. approval), arguing that it would facilitate Buckley's release.[12] Similarly, CIA analyst Graham Fuller recommended arms sales to Iran by friendly nations as a way of regaining some influence over a "faltering" Khomeini regime and to prevent Iran from moving toward the Soviet Union. By June 11, 1985, a draft National Security Decision Directive from McFarlane recommended that U.S. allies help Iran meet "import requirements"—meaning military equipment.[13] Secretary of State George Shultz and Secretary of Defense Caspar Weinberger opposed the Israeli plan. Shultz argued that Iran's weakness in arms was in our interest and that reviving its military capacity would only lead to greater anti-Americanism in the region. But Ledeen had gotten McFarlane on board, and McFarlane briefed Reagan and chief of staff Donald Regan on July 18, followed by a full review at the White House on August 6. Shultz warned, "We were just falling into the arms-for-hostages business and we shouldn't do it."[14] But Reagan approved the Israeli sales at a final briefing on August 8. The United States agreed to replenish Israeli stocks with more advanced weapons.

Why did Reagan decide on the transfers? Partly because of a need to improve the strategic relationship with Iran, but partly because of his anguish at having done nothing for the hostages and their families. And there were also domestic politics, with a midterm election coming up the next year in which Republicans were not expected to do well. As Thomas Twetten of CIA Near East Division recalled in a reference to President Jimmy Carter and the American diplomats held hostage by Iran near the end of his term: "There was a lot of fear about the yellow ribbons going back up and that this President would have the same problems that the last president had with the Iranian hostages."[15]

At the end of August Israel sent ninety-six U.S.-made TOW missiles to Tehran in exchange for Buckley. Members of the Revolutionary Guard commandeered the cargo at the airport, and Iranian officials who had made the deal with the Israelis claimed not to have received any weapons and gave up no hostages. Israel sent an additional 408 TOWs on September 14. The Iranians then revealed that Buckley had died early in June, but in a "bait and switch" they released Benjamin Weir, a Presbyterian minister. On November 22, Israel was to ship eighty HAWK antiaircraft missiles in exchange for more hostages as part of an overall exchange involving about five hundred missiles for the six remaining hostages. Shultz objected and Weinberger commented, "We shouldn't pay Iranian[s] anything," but their views were ignored.[16] To disguise the mission, the plane was to be routed through Lisbon, but Portugal denied landing permission to the Israeli charter flight. After frantic attempts by North and McFarlane to get the mission on track, Dewey Clarridge (CIA deputy for European covert operations) stepped in to salvage matters. On November 25, a St. Lucia 707 airplane (a CIA proprietary airline) went to Israel, loaded on eighteen HAWKs to Iran (as many as could fit in its hold), flew to

Cyprus, then overflew Turkey (after CIA intervention to secure permission) and landed in Tehran.

Even with CIA assistance, the transaction could not be completed. Low altitude I-HAWKS had been delivered (with Star of David markings), which were unable to shoot down the Iraqi planes at high altitudes that were bombing Tehran and were useless to the Iranians. The Iranians refused to take delivery or release hostages. The day after the aborted mission, Reagan indicated to Admiral John Poindexter that high-altitude missiles should be furnished on the next mission. Because of the direct CIA involvement in running interference for the Israelis on this flight, CIA deputy director John McMahon insisted on a retroactive written presidential Finding for this operation in order to comply with the Intelligence Oversight Act. Reagan signed such a Finding, dated December 5, 1985, which indicated that the shipment had been for a hostage swap.

On December 7, continuing the arms trades was discussed at the White House. Weinberger pointed out that there was an arms embargo on Iran and washing transactions through Israel wouldn't make it legal. Shultz and Regan agreed. Reagan responded that "the American people would never understand if four hostages died because I wouldn't break the law."[17]

American Arms Sales

Reagan shortly thereafter decided that the United States would conduct the trades itself. At a January 16 meeting Weinberger offered legal objections (pointing out that arms sales to terrorist nations were prohibited), but Meese presented a 1981 opinion of then Attorney General William French Smith that a president could approve an arms transfer using the Economy Act and the National Security Act to "achieve a significant intelligence objective." Smith's opinion specified that under the Intelligence Oversight Act the congressional intelligence committees would have to be informed, but Meese advised that the National Security Act and "the President's broad and independent constitutional authority to conduct foreign policy" authorized the president to withhold prior or contemporaneous notice to Congress in a delicate operation in which secrecy was essential, at least until the operation had concluded. He argued that the hostages might be killed if there were leaks to Congress.[18] The following day Reagan signed an Intelligence Finding in the presence of Vice President Bush, chief of staff Regan, and NSC adviser Poindexter. It authorized the sale of arms to the CIA from Pentagon stocks and the use of third parties to transfer the weapons to Iran—a way to disguise the role of the CIA and of the U.S. government by using The Enterprise. The Finding also authorized the United States to "assist selected friendly liaison services, third countries, and third parties sympathetic to U.S. government interests . . . for the purpose of (1) establishing a more moderate government in Iran, (2) obtaining from them significant intelligence not otherwise unobtainable to determine the current Iranian government's intentions with respect to its neighbors and with respect to terrorist acts, and (3) furthering the release of the American hostages held in Beirut and preventing additional terrorist acts by these groups."[19] The Finding instructed "the Director of Central Intelligence to refrain from reporting this Finding to the Congress . . . until I otherwise direct."[20] The cover memorandum prepared by Attorney General Edwin A. Meese III developed the legal rationale for the operation, indicating that laws requiring congressional notification of arms sales would not apply to an intelligence operation.[21]

After the Finding was signed, Weinberger, through his aide Major General Colin Powell, authorized the Defense Logistics Agency to transfer arms to the CIA, but he prohibited the department from doing anything else to facilitate the shipments to Iran.[22] Weinberger later received intelligence reports on the arms sales, but for the most part, he and Shultz (who was also briefed as the sales continued) were cut out of the operations.

Go-Between Negotiations

On February 18, 1986, the United States sent five hundred TOW missiles to Iran and took back seventeen of the unsatisfactory missiles from the November Israeli shipment, but no hostages were released. Between February 24 and 26, Iranian representatives met with North and Secord, and they demanded intelligence and Phoenix missiles before they would consider giving up hostages. On February 27, the United States sent five hundred more TOW missiles, and again, no hostages were released. The new NSC adviser, Poindexter, gave North a conditional go-ahead for further negotiations on April 16, 1986, with the following instructions: "There are not to be any parts delivered until all the hostages are free in accordance with the plan that you layed (sic) out for me before. None of this half shipment before any are released crap. It is either all or nothing." He suggested that the Iranians be told that "if they really want to save their asses from the Soviets, they should get on board."[23]

To move the negotiations forward, on May 25, 1986, McFarlane (now a consultant for the NSC) and North flew to Tehran to meet with Iranian officials. They took a pallet of HAWK missile parts, a Bible inscribed with a message from Reagan, and a kosher chocolate cake as peace offerings. No high or even midlevel Iranian official received them, and they were taken from Mehrabad Airport to the fifteenth floor of the Istaqlal Hotel, where they remained out of sight. The Iranians demanded that all the HAWK parts be flown in before any hostages would be released, while the United States insisted on hostages before it would deliver the parts.

McFarlane broke off discussions, incensed at his treatment, leaving North to conduct the talks. Without experience as a negotiator North was taken to the cleaners: He agreed to seek the release of Da'Wa terrorists (who had bombed a U.S. embassy) from Kuwaiti prisons and to exchange two shipments of arms for two hostages. McFarlane overruled him, and the negotiations fell through. After several days they departed without accomplishing anything, and on May 29 McFarlane recommended to Reagan that the initiative end. But North disagreed: He advised a strategy of "sequentialism" rather than an "all or nothing" approach. North was optimistic because he had found what he thought was a second channel to finally make contact with the elusive "moderates" in Tehran. He was now dealing with Ali Hashemi Bahramani, a nephew of the Iranian Parliament's Speaker Hojatolislam Hashemi Rafsanjani. Unbeknownst to North, Bahramani was part of the same group of radicals with whom North had already been dealing. Rafsanjani had all the important Iranian factions involved in the trade, so that none could make political capital by publicizing the deals; he used his nephew to deliver some bait for North—Rev. Lawrence Jenco was freed on July 26. On July 30, Reagan approved the sequential approach, and on August 3 he approved transfer of the remaining HAWK spare parts. After delivery of a new shipment of five hundred TOWs to Iran, hostage David Jacobsen was released on November 2. As of that date, a total of 2,004 TOW missiles, 18 HAWK missiles, and 240 HAWK spare parts had been sent, and 3 hostages had been released. Reagan had not strengthened any "moderates" in Tehran because he had to deal with the most extreme group, but at least he had gotten some hostages home and had successfully blunted the issue for the upcoming midterm elections.

Failed Negotiations

"Our guys . . . got taken to the cleaners," Secretary of State Shultz later observed.[24] At first the United States relied far too much on Israel, which had its own hostages to consider as well as the plight of thousands of Jews it was trying to get out of Iran. For its own national interests Israel would try to keep negotiations going, whether or not that would be helpful to its American allies. But once the United States took direct control, North relied on a set of new intermediaries and continued to cede operational control to those with their own interests, not the American national interest.

North's main go-between, Manucher Ghorbanifar, was unreliable. The CIA viewed him as a fraud because he had failed several lie detector tests, and it issued a "burn" (avoid) notice on him in mid-1984. McFarlane reported to Reagan that he was a "borderline moron" and "the most despicable character I've ever met."[25] Ghorbanifar offered North all sorts of inducements to continue dealing with Iran, including funding for the Contras: "We do everything. We do hostages free of charge; we do all terrorist[s] free of charge; Central America for you free of charge."[26] But Ghorbanifar had his own interests at stake. He owed money to people in Iran who might try to kill him if he didn't repay, and his only way of repaying was to earn commissions on the arms deals. The arms dealers Secord and Hakim negotiated with the Iranians in Europe for release of hostages, at one point making a nine-point agreement that included a promise of help to release the seventeen Da'Wa terrorists from Kuwaiti jails, help in toppling Saddam Hussein, and the exchange of five hundred TOW missiles in return for hostage David Jacobsen. Arms dealers talked about the possibility of dealing with "moderates," but no one in the United States even knew the names of any Iranian moderates—assuming there were any. "The only moderates in Iran are in the cemetery," defense secretary Weinberger noted.[27] The two top Iranian go-betweens were as radical as anyone in Iran: Hassan Karrubi had close ties with the Ayatollah; Mohsen Kangerlou was close to the prime minister and had helped plan the attack on the U.S. embassy in Kuwait.[28] The extremists proved to be hard bargainers. They had no interest in improving relations with the United States or maintaining an ongoing relationship. Their only concern was to obtain maximum value for the hostages. In contrast, U.S. negotiators always kept their positions on the table, even when Iran breached agreements, because the United States remained the suitor, hoping for a relationship and making advances, which Iran could accept or spurn as it suited.

When the Americans realized they were dealing with the most extreme elements, it weakened their hand even further. Ghorbanifar began to plant the idea that if negotiations went badly, the Iranians might get angry enough to harm hostages. The United States sent all of the HAWK missile spare parts to Iran in exchange for Jenco as a gesture to keep negotiations moving forward— this after McFarlane two months earlier in Tehran had spurned an Iranian offer of the release of two hostages for the missiles as inadequate. The Iranians realized that it made sense to take more hostages for future deals. In the midst of negotiations they took two new hostages in Beirut: Frank Reed on September 9 and Joseph Cicippio on September 12. By that time two hostages had been released and two taken in exchange for thousands of missiles and spare parts. In January 1987 they took three more hostages. This was a game the Iranians could play indefinitely.

Nevertheless, North was under the delusion that he was getting the best of the Iranians. He overcharged them for the missiles (they paid $10,000 per TOW missile, while The Enterprise had obtained each from Defense Department stocks for $3,700). In total The Enterprise paid $12.2 million to the CIA for the arms and shipping costs and received $30 million from Iran in a complicated series of wire transfers to confidential bank accounts. The Enterprise wound up with more than $16 million in funds that by law should have been deposited in the U.S. Treasury.[29] By June 1986, the Iranians had gotten Defense's pricing schedule and realized they had been overcharged for TOWs and the HAWK spare parts, which put the entire operation in jeopardy and may have threatened the lives of the hostages.

Because the president approved of this covert operation, the United States was now subject to blackmail. McFarlane initially argued that the Iranians would never disclose the operation because of the danger to their own positions in Iran if it were known they had dealings with the "Great Satan." Prime Minister Mehdi Bazargan had been forced to resign when his dealings with Zbigniew Brzezinski, President Jimmy Carter's National Security Adviser, had become known, and presumably no Iranian wanted to follow in his footsteps. But this analysis looked only at the Iranians; others had no similar inhibitions.

To understand the motives for revealing the operation, it is important to look at the financing for the deals. Funds had been raised by Saudi financier Adnan Khashoggi and his syndicates of Canadians and Arabs. They were loaned to Ghorbanifar as bridge financing (after Kashoggi took out 20 percent for his commission), then transferred to Swiss bank accounts controlled by Lake Resources (the financial instrument of the arms dealers), which then transferred funds (at the prices fixed by Defense Department for the arms) to a CIA account. The CIA then paid the Defense Department for the weapons. Once weapons were delivered, the Iranians would authorize their banks to make good on checks they had previously deposited upon delivery of acceptable arms shipments. The Enterprise would then reimburse Ghorbanifar, who would repay the bridge loans to the investors in the syndicates—who stood to make a handsome profit if the circle were completed. The Enterprise would keep the remaining profits on the deals (known as "residuals").

Botched deals put the financial arrangements in jeopardy. Khashoggi and a Canadian syndicate were owed $10 million or more on advances to the arms dealers because Iranians refused to pay The Enterprise for unacceptable deliveries. When the Canadians were not repaid by Ghorbanifar, they threatened to expose the arms deals. To get Khashoggi and Ghorbanifar out of the "second channel" deals, North was preparing to pay millions of dollars to square their finances—otherwise they could expect leaks to the newspapers.[30] By November 1986 the operation was about to come undone unless he could come up with the money.

Presidential Prerogative

The arms sales, and the subsequent diversion of $3.5 million of the profits to the Nicaraguan Contras, relied on presidential command and fiat, sometimes by skirting the statutory laws, sometimes by exploiting its loopholes and ambiguities, and sometimes by directly violating them. A president who plays fast and loose with domestic law, even in dealing with a foreign policy issue, will not always be shielded by courts or enjoy support in Congress.

Vetting the Operation for Legality

The important legal issues were never properly vetted by Justice Department or NSC lawyers. CIA Director William Casey and North turned to inexperienced junior counsel at the President's Foreign Intelligence Advisory Board—an unusual source for legal advice—for favorable opinions.[31] Thereafter officials assumed, based on judgments by Attorney General Meese, that the legal obstacles had been overcome. In fact, the magnitude of legal violations of law was unprecedented in intelligence operations. The following is just a small sample:

- The Arms Export Control Act of 1976 requires a dealer to obtain an end-user certificate and an export license for private arms sales, and it requires prior congressional notification, none of which occurred.[32] Section 4 limits sales to a "friendly" country, and such sale or lease must be for "legitimate self-defense." It states that the secretary of state "shall be responsible for the continuous supervision and general direction of sales . . . and exports" under the law. Secretary Shultz did not supervise the sales. It requires quarterly reports to the Speaker and Foreign Relations Committee of sales of $1 million or more. No such reports were submitted to Congress. It requires that decisions on issuing export licenses be made in coordination with the United States Arms Control and Disarmament Agency, taking into account the director's opinion about arms races in a region, escalation of conflict, or arms control arrangements.[33] There was no coordination.
- The Omnibus Diplomatic Security and Anti-Terrorism Act of 1986 was passed into law August 27, 1986, in the midst of the arms sales. It provided that items on the U.S. Munitions List may not be exported to any nation the secretary of state determines is providing support for acts of international terrorism.[34] Iran was on the list in 1984, 1985, and 1986. The prohibition can be waived under Section 40, provided Congress is given notice. Congress never received any notice of waiver from the

president, which in any event would have expired ninety days after being issued (unless Congress enacted the waiver into law). The president could have invoked section 3(f), which allows him to sell arms that otherwise would be prohibited to individuals or groups receiving sanctuary after committing acts of terrorism.[35] But that Finding has to be communicated to the Speaker of the House and the Committee on Foreign Relations in the Senate. Reagan never made such a Finding or communicated to Congress.

- The Export Administration Act of 1979 requires dealers to get a license from the Secretary of Commerce for certain technologies. If exports of any goods or technology to countries supporting international terrorism are contemplated, the secretaries of commerce and state must notify the Foreign Affairs Committee, Foreign Relations Committee, and Senate Committee on Banking, Housing, and Urban Affairs, for a thirty day "report and wait" period.[36] No licenses were received, and no committees were notified.
- The Foreign Assistance Act of 1961 prohibits assistance (including arms) to a nation granting sanctuary from prosecution or otherwise supporting international terrorism.[37] The president can waive the provision by notifying in writing the Speaker and Chair of the Foreign Relations Committee, if vital to national interest.[38] This was not done. No security assistance may be granted to a nation whose government engages in a consistent pattern of gross violations of internationally recognized human rights.[39] The State Department reports of 1985 and 1986 listed Iran as a violator of human rights and ineligible for arms or intelligence information.

To get around these and other laws, the Reagan administration relied on the Hostage Act of 1868, which provides that the president may "use such means, not amounting to acts of war, as he may think necessary and proper to obtain or effectuate the release" of a U.S. citizen.[40] The administration used this provision to claim a blanket authorization for actions that otherwise might have been illegal, such as the violations of export laws mentioned above. But all facts and proceedings relating to such presidential actions must be communicated by the president to Congress "as soon as practicable."[41] There were no communications to Congress under the act.

Poindexter told Reagan that if sales were part of an "intelligence operation," the laws would not have to be followed: "Some time ago Attorney General William French Smith determined that under an appropriate Finding you could authorize the CIA to sell arms to countries outside of the provisions of the laws and reporting requirements for foreign military sales. The objectives of the Israeli plan could be met if the CIA, using an authorized agent as necessary, purchased arms from the Department of Defense under the Economy Act and then transferred them to Iran directly after receiving appropriate payment from Iran."[42]

Yet even if that theory were true, other laws regulating intelligence operations were routinely ignored. For example: As of December 4, 1985 (before the U.S. direct sales began), transfers of arms exceeding $1 million *by an intelligence agency* to a recipient outside that agency was deemed a "significant anticipated intelligence activity" that must be reported to intelligence committees of Congress.[43] Congress intended that it receive notification of at least fifteen days before such a transfer occurred. No such notification was made when arms were transferred to the Israelis for shipment to Iran.

Bypassing Congressional Oversight

Reagan ignored his statutory duty to keep Congress informed of covert operations by violating the Intelligence Oversight Act of 1980.[44] The law requires the president to issue a "Finding" that an intelligence operation is in the national interest, based on the Hughes-Ryan Amendment of 1974, which prohibits the expenditure of funds to support covert action operations by the CIA abroad, "unless and until the President finds that each such operation is important to the national security of the United States and reports, in a timely fashion, a description and scope of such operation to the appropriate committees of the Congress. . . ."[45] Some sales were made in 1985, before the president signed any Finding. He then did so retroactively after the CIA was involved in the third transfer of Israeli arms and issued two more Findings to cover projected direct U.S. sales. But no Findings were issued on the diversion of funds from the arms sales to support the Contras.[46]

Once a Finding has been made by the president, the National Security Act of 1947 requires that congressional authorities be "informed of all intelligence activities which are the responsibility of, are engaged in by, or are carried out for or on behalf of, any department, agency or entity of the United States. . . ."[47] The director of the CIA must keep members of House and Senate Intelligence Committees "fully and currently informed" prior to the operation on all intelligence activities or "significant anticipated intelligence activity" undertaken by or on behalf of any "department, agency or entity of the United States."[48] "Fully and currently" in legislative language means at the time of the Finding and does not admit delay. Alternatively, under the law the Director might notify eight designated congressional leaders: the chair and ranking minority members of the House and Senate intelligence committees, the Speaker and minority leader of the House, and majority and minority leaders of the Senate. No notifications to Congress about the arms sales or the diversion of funds to the Contras were made. The law also requires the president to report any "illegal intelligence activity or intelligence failure" to Congress. None were reported.

If an intelligence operation commences without notification to the committees or leaders, the law requires that the president fully inform the intelligence committees in a timely fashion and/or provide a statement of the reasons for not giving prior notice. Notifications had been delayed only three times during the Carter administration, in connection with the failed rescue mission of American diplomats. Reagan's Finding for the arms sales ordered that the Director of Central Intelligence "refrain from reporting this Finding to the Congress as provided in Section 501 of the National Security Act, as amended, until I otherwise direct."[49] He did so to protect the lives of the hostages in delicate negotiations, yet it is likely that he did so also to prevent any interference from Congress.[50]

Reagan's decision to keep the information from Congress violated his own National Security Decision Directive (NSDD) 159, which he signed on January 18, 1985, and which specified that the president would approve *in writing* all covert action Findings made pursuant to Section 501 of the National Security Act. Reagan did not follow his own procedures when the Israeli arms transfers commenced without written Findings, and when a Finding was issued retroactively. Nor were there Findings for North's Contra activities. Moreover, neither the Executive Order nor NSDD 159 contemplated action in violation of statutory law, because nothing in the Executive Order "shall be construed to authorize any activity in violation of the Constitution or statutes of the United States."[51]

Violating the Gentleman's Agreement

Reagan's failure to notify Congress not only violated the law but also an informal "gentleman's agreement" between CIA Director Casey and the members of the Intelligence Committees of the House and Senate. After congressional outrage over CIA-sponsored attacks on ships at the Nicaraguan port of Corinto, "the Casey Accords" were agreed to by the CIA and the committees. The director would notify the Senate Select Committee on Intelligence of "new Presidential Findings concerning covert action" and of "any other planned covert action activities for which higher authority or Presidential approval has been provided . . . as soon as practicable and prior to implementation of the actual activity."[52] On June 17, 1986, the director signed the "Casey Addendum," which specified that he would notify the committees "of any instance in which substantial non-routine support for a covert action operation is to be provided by an agency or element of the U.S. Government other than an agency tasked with carrying out the operation, or by a foreign government or element thereof." Casey also promised to notify the intelligence committees prior to an operation when "significant military equipment actually is to be supplied for the first time in an ongoing operation, or there is a significant change in the quantity or quality of equipment provided." He never did so.

Reagan and Casey armed themselves with legal opinions from the Attorney General making their noncompliance of the legal-reporting provisions neither frivolous nor legally insupportable.[53] A president relying on an opinion of his Attorney General to interpret statutory language in a way that provides some deference to the president's constitutional powers is ordinarily not considered to be involved in an abuse of power or a conspiracy to defraud the United States.[54] In any event, there were no criminal penalties for violation of these laws, and the administration argued that since it ultimately did report to Congress (albeit after the arms deals became known in the media), it did not technically violate the reporting provisions.

Violating Funding Cutoffs

The diversion of funds to the Contras was more clear-cut. The secret mining of Corinto alienated Senate conservatives such as Barry Goldwater (R-AZ) and led to strict congressional restrictions on covert operations in Central America. Boland II, passed on October 10, 1984, specified that:

> During Fiscal Year 1985, no funds available to the Central Intelligence Agency, the Department of Defense, or any other agency or entity of the United States involved in intelligence activities may be obligated or expended for the purpose of which would have the effect of supporting, directly or indirectly, military or paramilitary operations in Nicaragua by any nation, group, organization, movement or individual.[55]

As Boland put it during the House debates, Boland II "clearly ends U.S. support for the war in Nicaragua. . . . There are no exceptions to the prohibitions."[56] By the fall of 1985, limited military aid was resumed. Reagan signed the Intelligence Authorization Act for FY 1986. It provided that funds available to CIA or the DOD, or any agency or entity involved in intelligence, could not be used for the Contras unless the funds were explicitly authorized under the act, approved for reprogramming by Congress, or approved by Congress in addition to $27 million designated for humanitarian aid.[57] None of the funds North diverted to the Contras was so authorized or reported back to Congress.

Officials in the Reagan administration exploited what they believed to be an ambiguity in the Boland amendments. The Counsel to the President's

Intelligence Oversight Board issued an advisory opinion holding that the NSC was *not* an intelligence entity under provisions of the statute. This gave North what he took to be a "green light," since it would mean that he and other NSC staffers were not covered by the prohibitions of the law.[58] But this was a misreading of the term "entity." Executive Order 12333, signed by Reagan when he entered office, organized the entire intelligence apparatus of the government and states that "the N.S.C. shall act as the highest executive branch entity that provides review of, guidance for, and direction to the conduct of all national foreign intelligence, counterintelligence and special activities, and attendant policies and programs."[59] The NSC was not only an intelligence entity—*it was the highest such entity, and therefore clearly covered by the funding prohibitions.*

In addition, the covert operations violated Reagan's regulations regarding national security matters, referred to as "special activity." Executive Order 12333 provides that the NSC must submit to the president "a policy recommendation, including all dissents, on each special activity."[60] These "special activities" were defined as:

> activities conducted in support of national foreign policy objectives abroad which are planned and executed so that the role of the United States Government is not apparent or acknowledged publicly, and functions in support of such activities, but which are not intended to influence United States political processes, public opinion, policies or media and do not include diplomatic activities or the collection and production of intelligence or related support functions.[61]

Only specified intelligence agencies may conduct "special activities" under the Executive Order, and the NSC is not listed as one of them. Government agencies other than the CIA are forbidden from carrying out covert actions unless there is a presidential determination that the use of another agency "is more likely to achieve a particular objective." Reagan never issued a directive assigning special activities or covert actions to the NSC with regard to the Contras, and his Finding on sales of arms to Iran did not contemplate either The Enterprise nor the NSC taking an operational role.

Unraveling Operations

Both covert operations unraveled within a month of each other. On October 5, 1986, a decrepit C-123K cargo plane used by The Enterprise was shot down by the Sandinistas in northern Nicaragua. Although the Americans on board had been told not to carry anything that might give away their identities, they had disobeyed orders, and their identity papers indicated some were U.S. citizens. The cargo "kicker," Eugene Hasenfus, was captured and under interrogation gave details about the operation, admitting that two CIA officers had been in charge. The CIA shut down the entire resupply operation almost immediately, bulldozing planes and other supplies into a deep pit. By October 11, Assistant Secretary of State Elliot Abrams was on CNN stating categorically, "This was not in any sense a U.S. government operation."[62]

Just as the Reagan administration was trying to contain information about its role in the Contra resupply operation, it was blindsided by news coming out of the Middle East designed to affect a power struggle among Iranian factions. After Rafsanjani orchestrated the arrest of radical leader Mehdi Hashemi, the Ayatollah Husseini Ali Montazeri decided to discredit the Speaker. His followers began leafleting in Tehran revealing McFarlane's mission. The story was picked up by a Beirut weekly magazine, *As-Shiraa* ("*The Sail*"), that published the account on November 3, 1986.[63] Rather than engage in a cover-up, Rafsanjani took the offensive two days later and confirmed the visit. In a major address commemorating the seizure of the U.S. embassy, he described McFarlane and other American officials in contemptuous tones. He claimed that McFarlane had come uninvited, that no responsible Iranian official had agreed to meet him, and that he and his delegation had spent five days in detention and then had been allowed to leave.[64]

Presidential Containment and Cover-up

Shultz's advice to Reagan was to go public and characterize the arms sales as a humanitarian action to free hostages. But Reagan decided to cover up American involvement. At a bill signing ceremony Reagan commented that the *As-Shiraa* news article involved "a story that came out of the Middle East and that, to us, has no foundation," and referred to the magazine as "that rag in Beirut."[65] On November 7 he welcomed former hostage Jacobsen to the White House and cautioned the press on harmful speculation as to how he had been released. On November 8, McFarlane and White House press secretary Larry Speakes warned that speculating on arms sales in the Middle East might harm the hostages. On November 9, Bush discussed matters with Shultz, emphasizing that the sales had been undertaken to reestablish the strategic relationship with Iran; Shultz reminded Vice President Bush that it had been an arms-for-hostages deal and that Bush had known that.[66]

On November 10, at a White House meeting, the Reagan administration decided to claim that the long-term strategic relationship with Iran was the rationale for the sales. The president called for a solid front—a denial that the sales involved an arms-for-hostages deal. They would not acknowledge the

HAWK missile shipment nor mention the retroactive Finding of December 5, 1985. Following the meeting, the White House issued a press statement, neither confirming nor denying arms sales to Iran. Instead, the White House merely stated that "no U.S. laws have been or will be violated and . . . our policy of not making concessions to terrorists remains intact."

On November 13, Reagan made a speech to the American people about the arms sales. Instead of portraying the sales as a humanitarian gesture to release hostages, which would have gained him public understanding and perhaps support, he chose to cast it as a geostrategic decision. He claimed that the United States had delivered some arms to influence moderates and wean Iran from Soviet influence: "We did not—repeat—did not trade weapons or anything else for hostages, nor will we." The arms were defensive in nature, and "taken together (the arms) could easily fit into a single cargo plane." Reagan made no mention of the Israeli arms sales or the United States's role in them. Seventy-nine percent of the public believed that the speech was misleading, and Reagan began to sink in the polls.

On November 19, Reagan held a televised news conference. Again he denied that the United States had traded arms for hostages. Again he reiterated that all the arms could have been placed in a single cargo aircraft. Again he denied any U.S. role in the 1985 HAWK transaction, claiming only that arms shipments occurred after the January 17 Finding. This last statement was corrected twenty minutes after the conference ended when the White House issued a statement in Reagan's name admitting that a third country had been involved, although it claimed that its shipment had not been authorized by the U.S. government.[67]

The next day Secretary of State Shultz met with Reagan. He said that the president had made a number of erroneous statements in the prior day's news conference. Shultz reminded Reagan that they had been engaged in an arms-for-hostages trade, even though Reagan now was trying to deny it. He pressed Reagan to initiate an inquiry. In the next few days, Chief of Staff Don Regan, as well as Meese and Bush, all tried to figure out how to get Shultz on board, and above all, how to come up with accounts that would pass muster with Congress, the media, and the State Department.

The Meese Inquiry

Reagan directed Attorney General Meese to conduct an inquiry. As the Independent Counsel later put it, Meese conducted "more of a damage-control inquiry than an effort to find the facts."[68] He used a small group of personal aides and political appointees within the department, rather than investigators from the criminal division, and he did not initiate a criminal investigation. He did not seal or secure NSC files. He told FBI director William Webster that the bureau's assistance would not be needed, and for several days key files were not secured. He did what he could to move the investigation's focus away from Reagan, and what he might or might not have authorized, and onto lower-level officials.

While the White House was attempting to protect itself, officials involved in the covert operations attempted to cover their tracks. On November 17, NSC staffers (North, Poindexter, and McFarlane) and CIA officials prepared a chronology of events to be used by Poindexter and Casey in their scheduled November 21 appearances before the House and Senate Intelligence Committees in order to conceal Reagan's involvement in the 1985 arms shipments. The chronology claimed the United States had no prior knowledge of the first two Israeli shipments, that Israel had misled the United States by airlifting a cargo described as "oil-drilling equipment," and that no one in the U.S. government knew that missiles were aboard. But Secretary Shultz and his legal adviser Abraham Sofaer (a former Columbia law professor and federal judge) refused to go along and insisted that these false passages be deleted. But there were still omissions: The final chronology made no mention of the December 1985 Finding signed by the president nor of the third Israeli shipment. It stated that the entire cabinet had been consulted about U.S. arms shipments and that the mission was within the law.

On November 20, Meese, Casey, and other officials met at the White House to discuss Casey's forthcoming congressional testimony. Casey wanted to deny knowledge of the HAWK shipment of November 1985 and drafted a passage that "no one in the CIA" knew of that transaction in advance. North, to protect The Enterprise, revised and broadened Casey's language to read, "No one in the USG [U.S. government] knew." The following day Poindexter destroyed Reagan's December 7, 1985, retroactive Finding: "I thought it was a significant political embarrassment to the President, and I wanted to protect him from possible disclosure of this."[69] Poindexter told North that, contrary to North's assumption, the president had not known of the diversion of funds to the Contras. Though North had written six memoranda to the president about the diversion, Poindexter claimed he had sent none on to the Oval Office.

Casey lied to the Intelligence Committees in his November 21, 1986, testimony. He did not acknowledge that the CIA knew about or helped out on the HAWK transfer, claiming that he did not learn about them until the Iranians told the CIA sometime in January 1986. He claimed that all funds from the arms sales made by the United States were accounted for by the CIA, conveniently ignoring the role of The Enterprise in appropriating profits from the resupply and arms sales operations. The following afternoon, at a White House meeting designed to coordinate everyone's version of events and to protect the president, Meese reviewed the 1985 shipments, described the U.S. involvement, and indicated that they might have been illegal because there was no prior Finding by the president. He also "reported" that Reagan did not know of the November shipment and that Reagan didn't issue a Finding because he had not been informed. Meese was trying to lay down the White House line, and understanding this to be the case, no one corrected him about Reagan's role at this meeting.

Disclosure of the Diversion

Fortunately for Reagan, Meese had come up with something the day before that might divert attention from the White House. On November 23, Meese had interviewed North, who told him that funds had been diverted from the arms sales and sent to the Contras. He claimed that only he, McFarlane, and Poindexter had known of the transfers. On the morning of November 24, Meese reported to Reagan, Bush, and Regan in the Oval Office about the diversion of funds. The following day, President Reagan held a televised noon press conference and disclosed the diversion, claiming that he had been unaware of it until Meese had uncovered it. Reagan announced that Poindexter was retiring and that North had been "reassigned" from the NSC staff. He turned the news conference over to Meese, who tried to distance the president from both the arms sales and the diversion. The arms sales involved an Israeli plan, according to the Attorney General. The president had not had "complete knowledge" of the 1985 shipment of HAWKs to Iran. North knew of the diversion, Meese reported, but had not told Reagan. "So far as we know at this stage," Meese added, "no American person actually handled any of the funds that went to the forces in Central America" because funds had gone from Israel to the Contras. This statement was not true, since Hakim and Secord had handled the funds for The Enterprise and they reported to North.[70]

The news conference could not contain the political damage because the Israelis—the administration's designated "fall guys"—were unwilling to take the blame for the diversion of funds. The U.S. government itself was divided about a cover-up. Shultz was quick to distance himself, and he had notes indicating that President Reagan had been aware of the first Israeli arms shipments. "Reagan administration officials deliberately deceived the Congress and the public about the level and extent of official knowledge of and support for these operations," the Independent Counsel was later to conclude.[71] There was ample evidence that Reagan himself, in the first three weeks of November, "knowingly participated or at least acquiesced in efforts of Casey, Poindexter, and North to minimize or hide his advance approval of and participation in the 1985 arms shipments to Iran without notice to Congress."[72]

Reagan's Role

The Iran-Contra affair was a fiasco for the administration. Reagan's approval ratings plummeted. From fall of 1986 until the end of his term, his administration was convulsed with internal investigations, resignations of top officials, congressional investigations, and thereafter with court cases against North and Poindexter. Reagan was unable to focus on governance at times, his legislative program stalled, and he became in many respects a caretaker president. The investigations never focused on Reagan but rather on the arms dealers and on low-level operatives. And so the question remains: What did the president know and when did he know it? What orders had he given and when had he given them?

These were not questions that anyone pursued with any zeal, either inside or outside of the administration. After the most exhaustive investigation, Independent Counsel Lawrence Walsh concluded, in a somewhat vague formulation, "The policies behind both the Iran and Contra operations were fully reviewed and developed at the highest levels of the Reagan Administration."[73] According to Walsh, "The investigation found no credible evidence that President Reagan violated any criminal statute. The OIC [Office of Independent Counsel] could not prove that Reagan authorized or was aware of the diversion or that he had knowledge of the extent of North's control of the Contra-re-supply network."[74]

Reagan directly testified to the Tower Commission (a presidentially appointed panel that investigated the affair) that he had approved the first shipment in August 1985, but then he retracted and said "he did not recall authorizing the August shipment," and finally on February 20 he wrote a letter to the Tower Commission: "My answer and the simple truth is 'I don't remember—period.'" He also claimed that he did not know that the NSC staff was helping the Contras. Independent Counsel Walsh could not prove that Reagan wasn't telling the truth, though he had his suspicions: "It was doubtful that President Reagan would tolerate the successive Iranian affronts during 1986 unless he knew that the arms sales continued to supply funds to the Contras to bridge the gap before the anticipated congressional appropriations became effective."[75]

Given the Independent Counsel's strong suspicion that some such activity—even if not provable in a court of law—might have involved the president, one can consider three mutually exclusive hypotheses about the president's role in the Iran-Contra affair: First, that national security officials, operating on their own initiative and advancing their own agendas, engaged in a rogue operation; second, that Reagan's subordinates did what he wanted in the resupply and arms sales operations without waiting for his orders and without involving him in order to give him maximum protection while carrying out his wishes; third, that Reagan was directly involved in ordering and supervising these operations, but national security managers covered for him with "plausible denial."

Rogue Elephants

The first hypothesis starts with the assumption that national security managers were, in the words of the congressional committees, "a cabal of zealots," neither carrying out President Reagan's direct orders nor providing him with political cover. Instead, they were pursuing their own agendas with reckless disregard for the risks for the White House. Constantine Menges, a national security staffer, recounted a conversation in which he remarked to North that the role of the NSC was to give President Reagan facts and policy options. "No, we have to make the right things happen and make sure that the President goes the way we want," North replied. "We have to box him in so there's only one way he can go—the right way."[76]

Reagan's closest advisers found him "inattentive, unfocused and uncurious," according to his biographer Lou Cannon.[77] "Reagan's operating style, delegating many of his oversight duties to his subordinates," observed press secretary Larry Speakes, "gave his aides more power, for better or worse, than they would have had under any other president in memory."[78] The Tower Commission concluded that Reagan "did not force his policy to undergo the most critical review of which the NSC participants and process were capable. At no time did he insist upon accountability and performance review. Had the president chosen to drive the NSC system, the outcome could have been different."[79]

In this scenario the CIA and its bureaucratic allies within the NSC and State Department functioned as "rogue elephants," abusing the discretion Reagan had lodged in them. Blocked by Congress from using the CIA for operations in Central America, Casey decided to bypass congressional restrictions by "handing off" the Contra program to the NSC staff.[80] As McFarlane suggested, "It was Bill Casey and North, operating out of Casey's office in the White House complex in the Executive Office Building, who put together the Hakim-Secord "off-the-shelf" Contra-support operation."[81] Reagan had been deceived by his subordinates, who failed to give him timely and accurate briefings and manipulated him to obtain his consent for the record.

North and McFarlane were both Vietnam veterans, both "true believers" in the American mission to redeem the world for democracy. They were determined never to let politicians betray the U.S. fight against communism again by imposing needless restrictions on national security operations. They shared the "stab in the back" resentments that afflicted German veterans of the

Freikorps after World War I and the French forces in Algeria in the 1950s.[82] As McFarlane described North in his congressional testimony, "I believe that he [North] committed himself to assuming that he would never be party to such a thing [an American defeat] . . . again if he could prevent it."[83]

North and others on the NSC therefore played an operational role in covert operations rather than restrict themselves to an analytic and oversight role. This led to an inversion of policy that completely eliminated accountability to higher authority.[84]

Meanwhile the CIA was using the NSC staff as its own "cutout" within the government to get around the Boland Amendments. Casey orchestrated the administration's massive public relations campaign on behalf of the Contras, led by former CIA agents he had brought into the State Department's Office of Public Diplomacy for Latin America and the Caribbean.[85] Casey interceded with Attorney General Meese so that North would not be sent back to the marines and could have his tour at the NSC extended. After Saudi Arabia pledged $1 million a month for the Contras (with Casey playing a hand by making a pitch for the funds to King Fahd bin Abdul Aziz at the royal palace), McFarlane directed North to find out from Casey which Contra leaders the CIA wanted to support. Casey arranged with CIA legal counsel Stanley Sporkin and Attorney General William French Smith for the key opinion in June 1984 that U.S. efforts to obtain third-party funding of Contras would be lawful. Casey introduced North to all CIA senior field officers in July 1984 so that North would be able to coordinate their activities on behalf of the Contras. Casey insisted that CIA operatives share agency intelligence and policy papers with North about Central America. Casey got CIA operative Alan Fiers to "dovetail" CIA intelligence operations with North's resupply efforts. CIA operatives were involved in all phases of Contra aid.

Casey was helpful to North on the arms sales to Iran. He had North sound out wealthy contributors about the possibility of private funds to ransom William Buckley. Casey supported the decision to use the arms dealer Ghorbanifar, over objections of Clair George, deputy director of the CIA's Directorate of Operations. Casey helped put together the syndicates to advance funds to arms dealers and recommended that Secord be used as the "commercial cutout." He authorized CIA assistance in the logistics of the Israeli transport of HAWKs to Iran in November 1985, and in December he prevented the sales from being terminated by suggesting that the United States convert them into a direct operation, with the CIA purchasing the arms from the Pentagon. To clinch his argument, Casey had given Reagan misleading information about the Iran-Iraq war (claiming Iraq was winning) so that Reagan would believe the arms sales were crucial to Iran. Casey tutored the neophyte North about covert operations: He suggested that North keep a diary and log, take funds from the "residuals" for expenses, and set up secret bank accounts. He gave North a fake identify, "Goode," complete with CIA-furnished passport, driver's license, and other identification. When the operations unraveled, Casey told North to destroy his expenditure ledger.

Casey was interested in more than just the Contra operation. As of the time of the disclosures, $7 million remained in Enterprise bank accounts. North was trying to sell the assets of the resupply operation to the CIA for $4 million at the time when the mission was being closed down. Casey may have wanted to use the funds available to The Enterprise for other missions, possibly in Africa. But is there conclusive evidence that Casey knew of the diversion of funds from the arms sales to the Contras? North claimed he did, but only after Casey's death. When questioned by Meese on November 23, 1986, he did not mention Casey as someone who knew of the diversion. The Independent Counsel concluded that there was no credible proof, but that Casey's behavior, in not trying to get to the bottom of it when there were rumors of a diversion but instead meeting with Poindexter and North, suggests he was "aware of the diversion and concerned with keeping it concealed."[86]

Casey himself denied advance knowledge of the diversion.[87] There is no direct evidence that Casey knew the amount of funds in The Enterprise or that he intended to set up an illegal set of covert operations with these funds. We have North's testimony on this point, but North is an interested source.[88] North was warned by Poindexter on May 15, 1986, to keep information from Casey, particularly about the diversion of funds. "From now on, I don't want you to talk with anybody else," Poindexter ordered North, "including Casey, about any of your operational roles."[89] Poindexter testified that Casey had not known of the diversion. Casey died on May 6, 1987, as the congressional hearings were getting under way: Legislators, according to Senators Cohen and Mitchell, "openly speculated on how much blame would now be shoveled into Casey's grave."[90]

The Becket Scenario

The second hypothesis is the Becket scenario. In the movie adapted from playwright Thomas Bolt's version, King Henry II of England is embroiled in a feud with his former chancellor Thomas á Becket, the Archbishop of Canterbury. "Will no one rid me of this meddlesome priest?" a drunk Henry asks his Norman nobles. "A priest who mocks me? Are all around me cowards, like myself? Are there no men left in England?" They need no direct orders to enter Canterbury Cathedral and murder Becket as he celebrates Mass—the goading hint from their sovereign will do. In the same manner Reagan seemed to be asking his aides: "Who will rid my hemisphere of these troublesome Sandinistas?" No command is issued, but Reagan's men know what must be done.[91] As the Independent Counsel put it, "The President's disregard for civil laws enacted to limit presidential actions abroad—specifically the Boland Amendment, the Arms Export Control Act, and congressional-notification requirements in covert-action laws—created a climate in which some of the Government officers assigned to implement his policies felt emboldened to circumvent such laws."[92]

In this scenario, McFarlane and Poindexter, Reagan's national security advisers, were the key players. "I don't want to pull our support for the Contras for any reason," Reagan tells his national security aides. "This would be an unacceptable option."[93] It is up to them to figure out what to do. Poindexter later testified about the proposal for the diversion of funds: "I also felt I had the authority to approve it, because I had a commission from the President which was in very broad terms, my role was to make sure that his policies were implemented. In this case, the policy was very clear, and that was to support the Contras."[94] In this scenario, Reagan did not have to give Poindexter direct orders to go beyond the Boland restrictions, and Poindexter did not have to give North direct orders to divert funds.

Plausible Deniability

A third hypothesis is that the president ordered the entire operation, including the diversion of funds to the Contras. "I was very definitely involved in the decisions about support to the freedom fighters," Reagan boasted on May 15, 1987, adding, "It was my idea to begin with."[95] But what kind of support did he mean? Reagan spoke to wealthy donors and "third-party" heads of state and government to obtain funding for the Contras. Reagan later denied that he knew such funds were spent for lethal aid. He claimed that he had believed that domestic funding was going for pro-Contra advertisements in newspapers to influence congressional and public opinion.[96] But North, in a memo to Poindexter, recalled that Reagan was aware of the resupply operation, observing "the President obviously knows why he has been meeting with several select people to thank them for their support for Democracy in CentAM."[97]

Presidential aides could have set up a system of plausible deniability. Poindexter led North to believe that Reagan had approved the Contra operation, including the diversion, so that North wouldn't have qualms in the operation. But Poindexter claimed later that he didn't fully brief the president. Reagan corroborated this version with the claim that he was never informed of the transfer of funds by Poindexter and never received any of North's memos (though if he had been briefed, there was no reason why he would have been sent memos from a lower-level operative).

North testified at the Iran-Contra hearings that the president had authorized all his activities and that North had been only a "good Marine" following
orders through the chain of command:

> Throughout the conduct of my entire tenure at the National Security Council, I
> assumed that the President was aware of what I was doing and had, through my
> superiors, approved it. I sought approval of my superiors for every one of my ac-
> tions and it is well-documented. I assumed that when I had approval to proceed
> from either Judge Clark, Bud McFarlane or Admiral Poindexter, that they had in-
> deed solicited and obtained the approval of the President.[98]

North later claimed that Reagan knew of the diversion of funds to the Contras: "I have no doubt that he was told about the use of residuals for the Contras and that he approved it. Enthusiastically."[99] When Reagan fired North, he
did not ask him for an explanation about his illegal activities. Nor did he ask
Poindexter. Reagan's lack of investigatory zeal and his appointment of Meese
to conduct an initial investigation are both actions consistent with the idea
that he already knew what Meese was supposed to find out.

North testified to Congress that he initially believed that Reagan had
known what he was doing, but he later learned from Poindexter that the president had not been told. North would have been willing, he claimed, to take a
"spear in the chest" for the president, but as it turned out that would not be
necessary, given Poindexter's role. North's self-serving testimony, as Senators
Cohen and Mitchell pointed out, "carefully steered the spear into Admiral
Poindexter's chest."[100]

A Smoking Gun?

"There ain't no smoking gun," Reagan pointed out.[101] But there is a document that comes tantalizingly close. North's "shredding party" to destroy evidence missed a document that was discovered in a folder marked "W. H." by
two Justice Department officials, William Bradford Reynolds and John
Richardson, when they began their investigation under Meese. The unsigned
document, entitled "Release of the American Hostages in Beirut," was dated
April 4, 1986. On the last page, it said, "The residual funds from this [arms
sales] transaction are allocated as follows . . . $12 million will be used to pur-
chase critically needed supplies for the Nicaraguan Democratic Resistance
Forces." There were "approve" and "disapprove" signature spaces on the
memo—but no initials or signature on the document.

North was asked by Justice Department investigators to name the recipients of this memo, and he responded by asking them if they had found a
"cover memo" or routing sheet. When they told him they had not, he replied

that "the memorandum had been shown to Poindexter," but that "it was not to be circulated beyond Poindexter." After an interview with Attorney General Meese, which ended at 5 p.m. on November 23, North spent the next eleven hours in his office shredding documents. There is no evidence that he shredded the original of the diversion document with Reagan's signature or initials on it, but had he wished to protect the president, he had the opportunity as well as the motive to do so.[102] North denied that he had shredded "any document which gave me an indication that the President had seen the document or that the President had specifically approved."[103] Poindexter also denied that this memo ever went to Reagan, although all similar memos with "approve or disapprove" had been sent to the president. He testified that in this instance he made "a very deliberate decision not to ask the President" about the diversion in order to "insulate [the President] from the decision and provide some future deniability for the President if it ever leaked out."[104]

Yet there is more to the story. There was an attachment to the diversion document: "Tab A—U.S.–Iranian Terms of Reference" dated April 4, 1986, which referred to McFarlane's mission to Tehran. McFarlane later testified that Reagan had approved the "terms of reference."[105] Did Reagan see the entire document, including the diversion memo? Or was he given just the Teheran mission attachment? Reagan himself denied seeing the memorandum spelling out the diversion, and no one can prove that he did see both parts of the document. Other separate copies of the "Terms of Reference" were found in NSC files, indicating that Reagan could have been given the "Terms of Reference," or been briefed from it, without having been given the diversion memo.

Yet even had Reagan's signature or initials appeared on the diversion document, it might not be taken by some as conclusive evidence that Reagan had known of the diversion. Reagan sometimes was unaware of the details of his briefings, and his attention span was limited. He might have signed such a memo without understanding the significance of the paragraph about "residuals." It also is possible that his initials could have been forged, a practice not unknown in the Reagan White House.[106]

Plausible deniability cannot wash away some inconvenient facts. Reagan was briefed regularly by McFarlane and Poindexter. He approved third-party funding efforts for the Contras and personally solicited Saudi contributions to the Contras. He made decisions about expediting weapons and intelligence to them. He gave the go-ahead for U.S. arms transfers to Iran in January 1986, and in the White House meetings the president was fully engaged in the discussions and clear in his wishes to go ahead with the sales. He signed Findings preventing Congress from being notified. He pushed for the loosest interpretation of the Boland Amendment.[107] Most important of all, Reagan had been an active participant in the meetings. He chose from options presented to him, narrowed down the circle of advisers and operatives, and kept information from those opposed. At all times the final decisions on arms sales and aid to the Contras can be traced back to the president, even though the Independent Counsel correctly concluded that there was not enough evidence for a court of law to conclude that the president had conspired to violate the laws.

Prerogative Power: Overshoot and Collapse

In the Iran-Contra affair the decision to bypass the framework laws regarding arms sales and intelligence operations resulted in a policy fiasco. There was no trade-off here between efficacy and restraint; it is precisely because the policymakers had no sense of restraint that they were able to develop mechanisms such as The Enterprise that left key aspects of the negotiations outside of any presidential control and accountability. Risky business, particularly intelligence operations, may require dealing with unsavory characters, but the controllers must not be the bad characters themselves. That requires distancing, which leads to policy inversion and privatization.

Framework legislation was passed by Congress for a reason, usually in the aftermath of prior fiascoes, and if it creates a hurdle for policymakers, they might consider that the hurdle has been placed there by Congress for good reason. Consultation and collaboration provisions require the president and his aides to demonstrate their authority—their knowledge of the issue and their capacity to formulate policy—before congressional committees that are less likely to be impressed with presidential wisdom than are officials within the executive branch. Policy inversion or privatization are less likely to occur if framework laws are adhered to because top officials know they will be held accountable. The delays that are usually built into the framework laws also serve a useful purpose, preventing precipitate action before full consultation occurs within the executive branch and between the executive and congressional committees.

Most importantly, framework legislation tends to encourage processes that are functional and discourage practices that are dysfunctional in small group decision making because they require continued justification of policy before a skeptical audience. To the extent that they discourage illegal action, they may also be discouraging action that is not operationally viable or politically supportable.

Notes

1. P.L. 98–473 (1984).

2. Robert McFarlane, *Special Trust* (New York: Cadell and Davis, 1994), 350.

3. P.L. 99–83 (1985).

4. International Security and Development Cooperation Act of 1985, Sec. 722(d).

5. P.L. 99–160 (1985).

6. Lawrence Walsh, *Iran-Contra: The Final Report* vol. 1 (Washington, DC: U.S. Court of Appeals for the District of Columbia Circuit, 1993), 6.

7. Oliver North entry of August 9, 1985, summarizing meeting with Robert Owen (North's handwritten notebooks). See National Security Archive Electronic Briefing Book, No. 2.

8. David Corn, "Following a Trail of Powder," *Washington Post National Weekly Edition* (August 24, 1998): 32.

9. Peter Kornbluh and Malcolm Byrne, eds., *The Iran-Contra Scandal: The Declassified History* (New York: New Press, 1993), 130.

10. Walsh, *Iran-Contra* vol. 1, 161. Had arms sales been legal and handled by the U.S. government, commissions to arms dealers would have been limited to $50,000.

11. Walsh, *Iran-Contra* vol. 1, 141.

12. Michael Ledeen, *Perilous Statecraft: An Insider's Account of the Iran-Contra Affair* (New York: Charles Scribner's Sons, 1988), 102.

13. "Draft National Security Decision Directive: U.S. Policy toward Iran," June 11, 1985.

14. Report of the congressional committees investigating the Iran-Contra Affair: With supplemental, minority, and additional views. 100th Congress, 1st session (Washington, DC: U.S. Government Printing Office, 1987), 167; hereinafter cited as Committee Report.

15. President's Special Review Board, Report of the Special Review Board (Washington, DC: U.S. Government Printing Office, 1987), B-83.

16. Kornbluh and Byrne, eds., *The Iran-Contra Scandal*, 215.

17. FBI summary of December 7, 1985 meeting, in Walter Pincus and George Lardner Jr., "Iran-Contra's Moral for Presidents," *Washington Post National Weekly Edition* (February 7–13, 1994): 23.

18. "Memoranda for the Attorney General," in Walsh, *Iran-Contra: The Final Report* vol. 1 (Washington, DC: U.S. Court of Appeals for the District of Columbia Circuit, 1993): 469–70.

19. Ronald Reagan, "Finding Pursuant to Section 662 of the Foreign Assistance Act of 1961, as Amended, Concerning Operations Undertaken by the Central Intelligence Agency in Foreign Countries, Other Than Those Intended Solely for the Purpose of Intelligence Collection," January 17, 1986.

20. President's Special Review Board, Report of the Special Review Board (Washington, DC: U.S. Government Printing Office, 1987), 217. Reagan acted based on a recommendation from North: "Because of the extreme sensitivity of this project, it is

recommended that you exercise your statutory prerogative to withhold notification of the Finding to the congressional oversight committees until such time as you deem it to be appropriate."

21. Committee Report, 208.

22. Weinberger Diary, January 24, 1986.

23. John Poindexter to Oliver North, "Private Blank Check," April 16, 1986, PROFS Notes.

24. U.S. Congress, Joint Hearings before the Select Committee on the Iran-Contra Investigation vol. 100–107, part 1 (Washington, DC: U.S. Government Printing Office, 1988), 8.

25. Walsh, *Iran-Contra*, 199; Jane Mayer and Doyle McManus, *Landslide: The Unmaking of the President, 1984–1988* (Boston: Houghton Mifflin, 1988), 181.

26. Kornbluh and Byrne, eds., *The Iran-Contra Scandal*, 248, quoting North's tapes of a talk with Ghorbanifar in London.

27. Joseph Persico, *Casey: The Lives and Secrets of William J. Casey: From the OSS to the CIA* (New York: Viking, 1990), 483.

28. Kornbluh and Byrne, eds. *The Iran-Contra Scandal*, 244.

29. Kate Stith, "Congress' Power of the Purse," *Yale Law Journal* vol. 97, no. 7 (June 1988): 1343–96.

30. Walsh, *Iran-Contra*, 21, 22, 170.

31. Richard K. Willard, "Law and the National Security Decision-Making Process in the Reagan Administration," *Houston Journal of International Law* vol. 11, no. 1 (Fall 1988): 129–48, 138.

32. 22 USC secs. 2751–2796(c) (1976).

33. 22 USC sec. 2778(a)(2) (1982).

34. P.L. 99–399 sec. 509(a) (1986).

35. 22 USC sec. 2753(f)(1).

36. 50 USC sec. 2405(j)(1) (Supp. III, 1985).

37. 22 USC sec. 2371(a) (Supp. III, 1985).

38. 22 USC sec. 2364(a)(2) (1982).

39. 22 USC sec. 2304(a)(2) (Supp. III, 1985).

40. 15 U.S. Stat. 223 (1868) at 224.

41. 22 USC sec. 1732 (1982).

42. John M. Poindexter, "Memorandum for the President, Covert Action Finding Regarding Iran," January 17, 1986.

43. 50 USC sec. 415(a)(3) (Supp. 1987).

44. 94 U.S. Stat. 181 (1980), 15 USC sec. 413 (1982). See "Note: Intelligence Oversight, National Security, and Democracy," *Harvard Journal of Law and Public Policy* vol. 12 (Spring 1989): 285–609.

45. 88 U.S. Stat. 1804 (1974); P.L. 93–559 (1974).

46. Walsh, *Iran-Contra*, 379, 400–41; Philip L. Gordon, "Undermining Congressional Oversight of Covert Intelligence Operations: The Reagan Administration Secretly Arms Iran," *New York University Review of Law and Social Change* vol. 16, no. 1 (Winter 1987–1988): 229–76.

47. 50 USC sec. 413(a), sec. 501(a) (1982).

48. 50 USC sec. 413(a) (1982).

49. President's Special Review Board, Report 217, 228, Findings of January 6 and January 17.

50. Independent Counsel Lawrence Walsh did not find the administration's actions illegal, finding that "the President's professed motive for secrecy—a desire to protect the lives of the hostages and to effect their rescue—had at least a surface plausibility." Walsh, *Iran-Contra* vol. 1, 456.

51. Executive Order 12333, sec. 2.8. (1981).

52. "Procedures Governing Reporting to the Senate Select Committee on Intelligence (SSCI) on Covert Action," June 6, 1984.

53. "Memoranda for the Attorney General," in Walsh, *Final Report Vol. III: Comments and Materials Submitted by Individuals and Their Attorneys Responding to Volume I of the Final Report* (Washington, DC: U.S. Government Printing Office, 1993), 445–70.

54. Walsh, *Iran-Contra* vol. 1, 455.

55. P.L. 98–473 (1984).

56. Congressional Record vol. 130, H11980 (1984).

57. P.L. 99–169, sec. 105; 99 U.S. Stat. 1002, 1003 (1985).

58. Yet North was a salaried employee of the Marine Corps (Department of Defense) and was on nonreimbursed status while assigned to the NSC. The Boland Amendment ban therefore covered his activities on Department of Defense expenditures.

59. President Ronald Reagan, Executive Order 12333, sec. 1.2(a).

60. 46 Federal Register 59941 (December 4, 1981); 50 USCA 59–67 (Supp. 1998).

61. Executive Order 12333, sec. 1.4(d) (1981).

62. Theodore Draper, *A Very Thin Line: Iran-Contra Affairs* (New York: Hill and Wang, 1991), 356.

63. Hasan Sabra, "Between Reason of State and Reason of Revolution," *As-Shiraa* (November 3, 1986): 24–26.

64. Foreign Broadcast Information Service, *Daily Report* vol. 8 (November 5, 1986): 11–16.

65. Walsh, *Iran-Contra Affair,* 297; Daniel Pipes, "Breaking the Iran/Contra Story," *Orbis* vol. 31 (Spring 1987): 135–39.

66. George Shultz, *Turmoil and Triumph: Diplomacy, Power, and the Victory of the American Ideal* (New York: Charles Scribner's Sons, 1993); William Safire, "Truth from Shultz," *New York Times* (February 4, 1993): A-23.

67. Presidential News Conference, "Statement by the President, November 19, 1986."

68. Walsh, *Iran-Contra,* xviii.

69. U.S. Congress, Joint Hearings on the Iran-Contra Investigation, "Testimony of John M. Poindexter," vol. 1 (Washington, DC: U.S. Government Printing Office, 1988): 18.

70. Meese, in his congressional testimony, claimed that North, Poindexter, and Casey had misled him.

71. Walsh, *Iran-Contra* vol. 1, xiv.

72. Walsh, *Iran-Contra* vol. 1, 467.

73. Walsh, *Iran-Contra* vol. 1, xiv.

74. Walsh, *Iran-Contra* vol. 1, xvii.

75. Walsh, *Iran-Contra* vol. 1, 446.

76. Constantine Menges quoted in Anthony Lewis, "North by Northwest," *New York Times* (December 4, 1988): E-31.

77. Lou Cannon, *President Reagan: The Role of a Lifetime* (New York: Simon & Schuster, 1991), 718.

78. Lawrence Speakes, *Speaking Out: The Reagan Presidency from Inside the White House* (New York: Charles Scribner's Sons, 1988), 54.

79. President's Special Review Board, Report vol. 4, 4. It concluded that the president did not seem to be aware of how the operation was implemented or of the consequences of U.S. participation and that there was no evidence he knew of the diversion of funds, at 55, 79.

80. These conclusions were reached by journalist Haynes Johnson, *Sleepwalking through History: America in the Reagan Years* (New York: W. W. Norton, 1991), 284; see also Casey's sympathetic biographer, Persico, *Casey*, 399.

81. McFarlane, *Special Trust*, 352.

82. Godfrey Hodgson, "Not for the First Time: Antecedents to the 'Irangate' Scandal," *Political Quarterly* vol. 58 (April/June 1987): 134.

83. U.S. Congress, "Testimony of Robert C. McFarlane," vol. 1, *Joint Hearings on the Iran-Contra Investigation* (Washington, DC: U.S. Government Printing Office, 1987), 146.

84. Harold Hongju Koh, *The National Security Constitution: Sharing Power after the Iran-Contra Affair* (New Haven, CT: Yale University Press, 1991), 101–16.

85. "National Security Decision Directive no. 77: Management of Public Diplomacy Relative to National Security"; Robert Parry and Peter Kornbluh, "Iran-Contra's Untold Story," *Foreign Policy* no. 72 (Fall 1988): 3–30.

86. Walsh, *Iran-Contra* vol. 1, 221.

87. Walsh, *Iran-Contra* vol. 1, 212.

88. Persico, *Casey*, 564.

89. Persico, *Casey*, 501.

90. William S. Cohen and George J. Mitchell, *Men of Zeal* (New York: Viking Press, 1988), 69.

91. Hodgson, "Not for the First Time," 133.

92. Walsh, *Iran-Contra* vol. 1, xvii.

93. Persico, *Casey*, 411.

94. U.S. Congress, "Testimony of John M. Poindexter," vol. 1, *Joint Hearings on the Iran-Contra Investigation* (Washington, DC: U.S. Government Printing Office, 1988), 37. On most of the details, however, Poindexter in his testimony was vague, with 184 formulations such as "I don't recall" and "I don't recollect."

95. *Newsweek* (May 25, 1987): 6.

96. Walsh, *Iran-Contra* vol. 1, 96.

97. President's Special Review Board, Report 476.

98. U.S. Congress, "Testimony of Oliver L. North," vol. 1, *Joint Hearings on the Iran-Contra Investigation* (Washington, DC: U.S. Government Printing Office, 1988), 10.

99. Oliver North, *Under Fire: An American Story* (New York: HarperCollins, 1991), 14–15.

100. Cohen and Mitchell, *Men of Zeal,* 159.

101. Quoted in David E. Rosenbaum, "Reagan Insists He Never Saw Contra Fund Memo," *New York Times* (June 17, 1987): A-11.

102. Cohen and Mitchell, *Men of Zeal,* 193.

103. "Testimony of Oliver North," Congressional Hearings, July 8, 1987. This is an artful way of saying that he had not destroyed a document with Reagan's initials or signature. It is not a flat denial that Reagan had been given, and had seen, such a document. Nor is it a flat denial that North had shredded such an (unsigned) document.

104. Cohen and Mitchell, *Men of Zeal,* 196.

105. Walter Pincus and Dan Morgan, "What Did North Write and When Did He Write It?" *Washington Post National Weekly Edition* (June 29, 1987): 13–14.

106. Steven V. Roberts, "Former Aide Questions Signing of Reagan's Initials," *New York Times* (September 16, 1988): A-16.

107. According to McFarlane, the president "had a far more liberal interpretation of that [amendment] than I did." *New York Times* (May 14, 1987).

7

Gamesmanship

Bush 41 and the Budget Summit

IN 1990 PRESIDENT GEORGE H. W. BUSH went back on the "no new taxes" promise he had made two years earlier at the Republican National Convention. After a brief government shutdown a deal was hammered out between Bush and the Democrats at a budget "summit." Bush's compromise with the Democrats established a new budget process with serious spending limitations, stabilized the spiraling deficits, and cleared the decks for his successful confrontation with Iraq over its invasion of Kuwait. Yet politically it was a disaster: The president divided his party, his budget compromise laid the groundwork for the rise of the right-wing Republican leaders in the House, and it contributed to his own re-election defeat two years later.

By contrast, after losing control of Congress in the midterm elections of 1994, President Bill Clinton spurned a Republican offer to compromise on budget and taxes and presided over a lengthy government shutdown during the Christmas season. He and his Democratic allies left the budget process in shambles for the entire fiscal year—yet Clinton united his party behind him and began a remarkable political comeback, culminating in his re-election victory. Clinton then stalled the Republican-controlled Congress in its fiscal policy in 1997, maneuvered Republicans into accepting his spending increases in 1998 (in the midst of his impeachment crisis), and by 1999 spooked the opposition leaders so badly that they accepted a deal on Clinton's terms rather than risk another shutdown.

These two disparate outcomes call into question the conventional wisdom of budget politics: that process is important; that it is better to get something done in a bipartisan manner than to act confrontationally or unilaterally; that it is better for the president, because he is "Chief Executive," to act more responsibly in budget negotiations than Congress does. Bush's failure, taken by itself, is also a case study in both the limitations inherent in gamesmanship and in the use of power stakes analysis in framing presidential choice.

The Deficit Crisis of 1990

By 1990 the legacy of Reagan's supply-side economics—soaring deficits and mounting debt—had put Bush into a box. There was no way the government could grow out of these deficits, given the Federal Reserve's tight money policy that restrained an economic boom in order to control inflation. Bush was constrained in his budget preparation to meet progressively diminishing deficit targets that Congress had set in 1985 in the Gramm-Rudman-Hollings Act (hereafter GRH) for deficit reduction and which had been amended in 1988 to require a balanced budget by fiscal year 1993. If projected deficits exceeded the authorized fiscal year's deficit number, the president was required to issue a "sequester" order to cut spending across the board—half in defense and half in discretionary domestic programs.

In his Fiscal Year 1991 budget (running from October 1990 through September 1991), Bush forecast a $100.5 billion deficit but proposed to get under the deficit target of $75 billion with a combination of minor taxes ($13.9 billion), user fees ($5.6 billion), and spending cuts. Bush had previously proposed $6 billion in tax hikes in 1990 (with political cover from both President Gerald Ford and Jimmy Carter), which Congress had passed, without being hurt politically, and he thought he could do it again. His optimistic budget scenario forecast corporate profits up 16.9 percent (yielding higher revenues), though private economists saw a drop of 1.9 percent for the fiscal year. He projected that interest rates would decline to 6.7 percent for Treasury Bills and that this would lower outlays for debt service. The Savings and Loan bailout costs (involving a government funding of a reorganization of an insolvent segment of the banking system) and other government operations were estimated at their low range. Bush called for reduction in the capital gains tax, claiming it would stimulate sale of long-term assets and produce an additional $12.5 billion through 1995, with $4.9 billion collected in FY 1991.

During the winter the deteriorating economic situation put an end to this rosy scenario. Interest rates went up from 7.5 to 8 percent and increased Treasury borrowing costs. The Treasury projected lower revenues, and the Office of Management and Budget (OMG) projected higher expenditures for the coming fiscal year. On March 5, the Congressional Budget Office (CBO) estimated a $131 billion deficit even if Bush's proposals passed and a $161 deficit if existing spending provisions and tax laws remained constant—way over the deficit reduction targets mandated by GRH. Chief of Staff John Sununu said the Bush "no new taxes" pledge would hold, "as long as the climate of this country is appropriate for that commitment to stay in place."[1] But White House political advisers were firm that Bush should not abandon his tax pledge: A Bailey, Deardourff and Associates poll taken in March found a 52 majority opposed to tax increases if the goal were to reduce the deficit and a 32 percent minority in favor.[2]

Democrats sat on their hands. "The first action has to be taken by the president," House Speaker Tom Foley (D-WA) insisted. "First with the president, then with us."[3] Resolutions setting overall fiscal policy were due from the Democratic-controlled House and Senate Budget Committees by April 15, but the Democrats did not issue the required reports. In the policy vacuum OMB Director Richard Darman sensed an opportunity for policy and political gain, arguing that a White House decision to face up squarely to the deficit would have several advantages: Bush could gain political points for presenting honest numbers about the budget; he could put pressure on Democrats to cut social welfare programs, thus gaining support from Republican conservatives; and he could get the bad economic medicine over with in the midterm period, rather than propose tax hikes and spending cuts in his re-election year.

Democrats played a waiting game: The House and Senate Budget Committee passed resolutions that contained no tax or spending proposals but permitted the appropriations committees to get to work and have their spending bills considered—a suspension of the rules of the budget process, under which the Budget Resolution was supposed to set overall policy and appropriations could not be considered beforehand. This was a game of chicken: It involved Democrats removing a preexisting constraint (the GRH deficit targets) and a preexisting duty to set fiscal policy in order to convince Republicans that unless agreement could be reached, an irrational outcome would occur. The maneuver was the opposite of the Ulysses approach to decision making: Ulysses had himself bound to the mast of his ship to resist the lure of the Sirens. In game theory this is called "pre-commitment": A weak-willed player intentionally seeks an external constraint in order to be able to make decisions of his free will based on an inferior position.[4] Democrats were unshackling themselves from constraints to warn Republicans that the lure of the Sirens could sweep everyone overboard unless a compromise on new taxes were reached.

The Democratic strategy of putting pressure on Bush to make the first move worked. Council of Economic Advisers (CEA) Chair Michael Boskin gave the president the bad news: The economy was slowing, tax receipts were less than the Treasury expected, and unemployment was increasing. Bush agreed to pursue Darman's "BUBBA" (Big Bipartisan Agreement) strategy, calling for bipartisan commitment to tax increases (also known as a fiscal Immaculate Conception), and phoned Senate Majority Leader George Mitchell (D-ME) to ask for a budget "summit" with congressional leaders. At Mitchell's insistence, Bush told a news conference that he would "talk process" with the Democrats with "no preconditions"—which was code for consideration of tax increases.[5] "Everything is on the table," Bush told Democratic leaders at a White House meeting. Democrats insisted that Bush make that pledge even more explicit. The following day, Bush's press secretary Marlin Fitzwater said that discussions would start with "no preconditions" and would occur "unfettered with conclusions about positions taken in the past."[6] "The assumption is that everything is on the table," reiterated Speaker Foley.[7] Press secretary Marlin Fitzwater told reporters that in the negotiations either party could propose anything "without being politically castigated for it."[8]

White House aides put the best spin they could on the upcoming talks. They argued that without a deal, the economy would topple into a recession. They wanted to reduce the deficit *now*, they claimed, to bring down interest rates and sustain economic growth. In fact, the administration was desperately trying to stem a rushing tide of red ink (the projected deficit was now estimated at over $200 billion) that threatened to take the economy over the cliff. Taxes would have to be raised and spending from the projected baseline cut, and neither seemed politically palatable to the administration without bipartisan political cover. But conservatives were not reassured. "If everything is on the table, then everything is on the table," warned House whip Newt Gingrich (R-GA), including "every appropriation, every piece of pork, all the micromanagement, all of the various built-in, mandated waste. . . ." Tom DeLay (R-TX) reassured conservatives: "He ain't gonna raise taxes—believe me," in a veiled warning to the White House. Connie Mack (R-FL) and seventeen other Republican senators sent Bush a letter warning against tax increases.

Summit Negotiations

The White House wanted a deal more than Democrats, and its weak hand going into the negotiations can be gauged by what happened after Chief of Staff John Sununu told the *Washington Post* that if Democrats could propose new or higher taxes, "It is their prerogative to put them on the table, and it's our prerogative to say no. And I emphasize the no." Sununu was immediately undercut by Marlin Fitzwater, who responded to reporters' questions about the remarks by saying "I disavow every remark that doesn't represent the President. The President speaks for himself."[9] Democrats charged that Sununu was "poisoning" the talks and threatened to walk out even before negotiations had begun. House Speaker Foley told reporters, "We view this incident as an extremely serious one because it could, if repeated, threaten the success of these talks."[10] To keep negotiations on track, Bush went public again, telling reporters on *Air Force One* that "there's no conditions, and that's the way it is."[11] Bush telephoned Foley to reassure him that no preconditions meant just that. Sununu backed down on *Meet the Press*, using the phrase "no preconditions" himself.

The administration pursued what Darman called "multiple contingency planning." Dropping his calls for deep cuts in domestic spending and ending the onerous deficit caps would be Bush's bait once the negotiations got under way. "It was the right thing to do," Darman later cracked, "and also the politically sound thing to do if the right thing didn't work out."[12] A deal would provide Bush with necessary political cover, but if negotiations fell apart, the Democrats could be blamed for the resulting mess.

Summit negotiations began at the White House on May 15. Democratic congressional leaders asked Bush to make a nationwide television speech outlining the economic issues and setting forth his own proposals. But Bush refused, saying that he did not intend to be the first to call for a tax increase. Darman tried to pressure the Democrats by painting a gloomy picture: If Social Security surpluses were removed and bailout costs for the savings and loan industry were included, the deficit for the coming fiscal year would be about $337 billion.[13] Darman thought these numbers would put pressure on Democrats to accept major reductions in spending. But it worked the other way; the worsening fiscal situation put the onus on the president to find a way out.

The numbers also created new divisions among Republicans. Darman wanted a deal, as did CEA Chair Boskin. Ed Rollins, cochair of the National Republican Congressional Committee, urged caution because House candidates were running on Bush's "no new taxes" pledge. Sununu remained suspicious about any deal that might include higher taxes because he was skeptical of Democratic motives and wary of a trap. He was more willing to walk away from negotiations than Darman. Nevertheless, in mid-May there was a consensus among White House aides that Bush held the high cards: Sooner or later the Democrats would have to come to the table and call for higher taxes to protect their spending for social programs from a sequester.

Republicans insisted that the Democrats go first. On a May 24 news conference Bush observed, "Congress appropriates all the money and raises all the revenues. That's their obligation," and "People understand that the Congress bears a greater responsibility for this." But the Democrats continued with their tactic of abandoning the budget process rather than propose new taxes: Congress failed to pass a budget reconciliation bill by the June 15 deadline (setting tax and overall spending policy) and failed to complete work on appropriations by the June 30 deadline. By that time the projected deficits for the next fiscal year were soaring: OMB raised its estimate by $21 billion just in that month. Defense Secretary Dick Cheney presented the Pentagon budget requests, and his proffered cuts were too small to solve the problem. The White House would have to make a deal or, under existing budget laws, Bush would be required to sequester funds, resulting in a 20 percent cut in discretionary domestic programs and a 27 percent cut in the defense budget. Spending cutbacks of this magnitude might trigger a recession.

Darman continued the game of budget chicken, hoping he could paint the Democrats as the high-tax party that had pressured Bush into concessions. Changing tactics, he now proposed deep cuts in domestic programs favored by Democratic constituencies. Democrats did not blink. Senator Lloyd Bentsen (D-TX), chair of the Senate Finance Committee, told Darman and Treasury Secretary Nicholas Brady that "the talks were going to come apart, that the Democrats were not going to come up with taxes, and that the President had to make a high-profile move."[14] Conservative Republicans wanted Bush to call the Democratic bluff. "If congressional Democrats could not live with the cuts," White House domestic staffer Charles Kolb was later to write, "that was their problem. Forcing them to face up to the continued need for spending restraint (as distinguished from a tax increase) would have been a net plus for the Republicans."[15]

Bush invited the congressional budget negotiating group to the White House with the hope that an agreement could be reached before the August recess. Foley told the president he would have to make "some kind of public commitment" on new taxes. "Like what," responded Bush. "What would make you satisfied?"[16] Foley dictated the gist of a statement on "tax increases," but Sununu insisted on the phrase "tax revenue increases" (which could be taken to mean increased revenues without higher taxes) to make it an easier sell among Republicans in Congress.[17] It didn't necessarily mean tax hikes, but it could mean an increase in revenues based on a thriving economy. The decision about whether or not to go for tax hikes could still be left to the negotiators. After the Democrats caucused briefly, Foley and Mitchell insisted that Bush begin with the phrase "It is clear to me" at the beginning, thus putting the onus squarely on the president.

Bush refused to make a televised speech, but he agreed to release his statement to the White House press corps. (It was pinned to the White House press office bulletin board at the end of the meeting, so there would be no possibility that it could be edited and changed by the president's aides.) In its entirety it read as follows:

> It is clear to me that both the size of the deficit problem and the need for a package that can be enacted require all of the following: entitlement and mandatory program reform; tax revenue increases; growth incentives; discretionary spending reductions; orderly reductions in defense expenditures; and budget process reform—to ensure that any Bipartisan agreement is enforceable and that the deficit problem is brought under responsible control. The Bipartisan leadership agrees with me on these points.

The White House had bungled the first set of negotiations. It had abandoned its main goal, which had been Darman's "immaculate conception," when Bush had agreed to make a statement about taxes. It had made the most important concession at the beginning of summitry, before it had wrapped up a deal, and had paid a high price without getting anything in return. Bush had gone back on his pledge and didn't yet have a deal he could justify and sell. And it had all happened by happenstance, since neither Darman nor Sununu had planned for Bush to issue a statement at the end of the meeting and neither had thought in advance about what to do if the Democrats asked for a statement.

"Don't tax you, don't tax me, tax that fellow behind the tree," went an old ditty in the House Ways and Means Committee. If "revenue enhancements" were in the offing, then who would be behind the tree? Democrats wanted the tax system to become more progressive, and as they were gearing up for battle, a book by Kevin Phillips, *The Politics of Rich and Poor,* came out, just in time for Beltway summer reading.[18] Phillips argued that wealth had been redistributed upwards in the Reagan years because of tax cuts and rate changes favoring the wealthy. Democrats pounced on "income inequality" to reframe the deficit issue as an issue of fairness—as a question of redistributive politics in which they could attack "the overclass" on behalf of a resentful middle class. Democrats intended to channel voter rage about taxes upward, against the rich, rather than focus on spending downward, against the urban and minority poor, as Republicans had been able to do in the 1980s with rants about "welfare queens" driving Cadillacs. Senate Majority Leader Mitchell put down the Democratic marker: There would be no lowering of capital gains unless there was a rise in the income tax rates for the wealthy. Republicans countered by calling for higher taxes on consumption along with capital gains cuts.

Darman continued to use "honest numbers" as a bludgeon: OMB over the summer predicted a huge forthcoming deficit of $231.4 billion. The required sequesters in the $80 to $100 billion range would be impossible for the White

House since $40 to $50 billion would hit the Defense Department budget.[19] "If these negotiations fail, it will have major implications for virtually everything the Federal Government touches," Darman warned.[20]

Darman was putting pressure on Republicans to agree to a tax hike, but the party's right-wing wasn't buying. The House Republican Conference passed by a 3 to 1 margin a nonbinding resolution circulated by Texas representative Dick Armey opposing increases in "all rates on all existing taxes under Federal jurisdiction" and opposing "new taxes and all tax-rate increases as a means of reducing the federal budget deficit."[21] Supporters of the measure wore buttons saying "Read Armey's Lips." DeLay told his colleagues that by passing their resolution, "House Republicans had stood up for the American people and sent a clear message to the Democrats in the budget summit negotiations—stop trying to raise taxes. . . ."[22] Gingrich was the only House conservative still straddling the fence. He told his colleagues that if there were a capital gains cut, no increase in income tax, adequate spending for defense, real cuts in discretionary spending, cuts in entitlement spending, and presidential spending controls, "House Republicans I believe will consider appropriate revenue increases."[23]

Gamesmanship

The summit negotiators met eighteen times before the August recess but never got into questions of tax increases or cuts in entitlements. They discussed proposed cuts in discretionary spending and how they would be "scored" against budget targets. Darman had called for $16 billion in such savings, and Democrats countered with $5.6 billion. Each side still waited for the other to fold. Unfortunately for Bush, the budget game was soon to be eclipsed by a much bigger game: an Iraqi invasion of Kuwait and Bush's response, Operation Desert Shield. After Bush decided in early August to send troops to Saudi Arabia to defend its oil fields and borders, his bargaining position eroded. He would need funds and could not abide by cuts in the Defense budget as a result of automatic sequesters if the talks failed.

According to the timetables in the budget process, on August 25, the president was supposed to receive an OMB report, issue an initial sequester order, and then by September 6 send an explanatory message to Congress. Bush didn't comply with the law because neither he nor Secretary of Defense Cheney could engage in a military buildup in Saudi Arabia while simultaneously sequestering Defense Department funds. Likewise, Congress did not meet its September 10 deadline to pass new tax legislation, nor its September 15 deadline for appropriations, nor its September 27 deadline to pass a reconciliation bill on all taxing and spending in order to start the fiscal year that would begin October 1.

The budget process had evaporated and in its place was more ad hoc summitry, with a meeting on September 7 at Andrews Air Force Base of congressional party leaders, committee chairs, and ranking minority members from the budget, taxing, and appropriations committees. With Bush preoccupied with the Gulf crisis, Sununu, Darman, and Brady represented the administration. Republicans entered negotiations in disarray. House conservatives pushed a plan cooked up by Gingrich and DeLay, an Economic Growth Package dubbed the "4 percent solution," calling for increases of no more than 4 percent in federal spending for the next six years and a balanced budget by the end of that time. The White House thought that Senator Phil Gramm (R-TX) on the Senate Finance Committee would agree to a deal with the Democrats, because otherwise the draconian cuts in spending would be known as the "Gramm Sequesters" (since Gramm's name was on the budget law requiring adherence to deficit reduction targets) and that would hurt him in his own Texas reelection campaign. The White House was convinced that Democrats would make a deal, probably involving $30 billion in spending cuts, perhaps less than half of that in domestic spending, in return for an agreement to get rid of the GRH deficit targets, now unsupportable as the country was moving toward a war footing.

Speaking to a joint session of Congress about his decision to send 100,000 troops to Saudi Arabia, Bush told the legislators that "most Americans are sick and tired of endless battles in the Congress and between the branches over budget matters. It is high time we pull together and get the job done right." He called for a budget agreement so the United States can "function effectively as a great power abroad." Then, violating a cardinal rule of politics, he got into specifics and detailed his bottom line before entering negotiations: "To the extent that the deficit-reduction program includes new revenue measures, it must avoid any measure that would threaten economic growth or turn us back towards the days of punishing income tax rates." He also violated another rule of negotiation by announcing a self-imposed deadline: He warned that everything had to be wrapped up by September 28 or he would be forced to sequester.

At Andrews, Bush was poorly served by his negotiating team. Sununu blustered and ranted at Democrats. He antagonized the courtly Senator Robert Byrd (D-WV) by putting his feet up on the table near the senator's face. Byrd told the conferees after Sununu left the meeting that he had never been treated with such disrespect in all his years in the Senate—at the next meeting the senators put Sununu and Darman at the foot of the table. By September 14, with no visible progress, Senator Robert Dole threatened to end the summit, accusing the Democrats of bad faith and of leaking and distorting Republican proposals. Gramm went to the Senate floor and called Democratic behavior "a raw attempt to grasp some partisan advantage."[24] With negotiations stalled, party leaders devised a new format: A core group, consisting of Senators Mitchell and Robert Dole (R-KS), Speaker Foley, Reps. Richard Gephardt (D-MO) and Robert Michel (R-IL), and the three White House negotiators, Darman, Sununu, and Brady (with Bush again taking no direct part), met through the week of September 24 in the Capitol.

The Democrats, led by Mitchell, campaigned to "burst the bubble" on tax rates that hit the middle class hardest. A 33 percent marginal tax rate applied to single filers on taxable income in a "bubble" between $44,900 and $93,130, and to joint filers on taxable income between $78,400 and $185,760. On both prior and additional income the rate dropped to 28 percent. Democrats said they would accept the capital gains cuts that Bush wanted, provided he agreed to tax income above those levels at the same rates as income in the "bubble." But the White House saw a trap: Capital gains cuts were unpopular with most voters and would raise the fairness issue once again, and Bush would face a revolt from conservatives in his party if he raised the highest income tax rates on the wealthy from 28 to 33 percent. As news of the Democratic offer circulated, "Junk the Summit" buttons appeared in the House on Republican lapels.

How to disengage from the trap? Dole suggested to Democrats that capital gains cuts be taken off the table. Negotiations then proceeded quickly, and on September 30 (just as the Fiscal Year 1990 deficit came in at $220.4 billion, the second highest in the nation's history) a budget deal was announced by President Bush in the Rose Garden. The negotiators agreed to cut $40 billion in projected spending from the FY 1991 baseline budget and to cut $500 billion over five years (with most of it coming in the last two years). There would be no increases in the income tax, no capital gains cut, no tax increase on social security benefits, and no delay in cost of living increases. Instead, ten new regressive excise taxes and tax increases on luxury consumer goods and user fees would bring in $147.7 billion. People in the top income quintile would have their tax burdens increase 0.9 percent, while the lowest quintile's tax burden would go up 2 percent. Democrats accepted the deal because the proposed cuts in domestic spending were illusory; the deal actually allowed between 4 and 6 percent annual *increases* in outlays (since the "cuts" were merely reductions from the previously projected budget increases). Darman was willing to allow for some continued growth in domestic spending, but he insisted that "they would have to let him manipulate the baseline so it would look like there were no growth, which he did."[25]

Revolt in the Ranks

After being briefed by Bush, a bipartisan group headed for a Rose Garden ceremony. Minority Whip Gingrich intercepted Bush at the door and told him "I can't go outside," adding, "I feel it's my duty to tell you it won't pass the House."[26] Bush responded that he would make sure it did pass.[27] Vin Weber (R-MN), an ally of Gingrich and the head of the National Republican Campaign Committee, told Republican House challengers, "They should take on this agreement, label it a Democrat tax increase agreement that was basically stuffed down our president's throat."[28] Dan Burton (R-IN) called for "guerrilla warfare" against the package.[29] DeLay argued that "the numbers released by the Office of Management and Budget are so confusing that few Senators and Congressmen can figure out exactly what it is they are being asked to vote on. The agreement is the most successful use of blue smoke and mirrors to date by those budget summiteers."[30]

Conservatives claimed domestic spending in the next three years would go up by 12 percent, that defense would bear the brunt of any cuts, that projected savings in the "out years" were not to be trusted, and that indeed the numbers *were* suspect. GNP growth was projected at 3.8 percent between 1992 and 1995, enabling the negotiators to overstate projected federal revenues. They claimed interest rates on Treasury Bills would decline to 4 percent, not very likely if the growth rate were as high as they were projecting, but an estimate that enabled them to claim a reduction in interest rate costs of $64 billion. The out-year cuts in spending were left unspecified. While the negotiators claimed the budget would be balanced by FY 1995, independent economists were predicting deficits of up to $250 billion for that fiscal year.

"This agreement will also raise revenue," Bush told the American people in a nationwide address. "I'm not, and I know you're not, a fan of tax increases. But if there have to be tax measures, they should allow the economy to grow. They should not turn us back to higher income tax rates, and they should be fair." He pointed out that the agreement "will not raise income tax rates, personal or corporate." He urged his audience to "tell your congressman and senators you support this deficit-reduction agreement. If they are Republicans, urge them to stand with the president. Urge them to do what the bipartisan leadership has done: come together in the spirit of compromise to solve this national problem."[31] Bush had made no stirring call for sacrifice, and commentators pointed out that the measure also contained several tax breaks for the wealthy. The Democrats played on the fairness issue: "We'd prefer a budget that asks more from the wealthy and less from the elderly," Mitchell told the nation in his televised response to the president's address, even as he reiterated his support for a budget agreement the Democrats were clearly labeling a

White House plan. A *Time*/CNN poll taken just after Bush's speech had 59 percent of the public saying it should be passed and only 31 percent saying "voted down."[32] But only 32 percent said it was fair to the middle class, and 63 percent said it was unfair.

Republican conservatives were infuriated by Bush's call on voters to put pressure on them. "I'll take sequestration," Armey said, adding, "Sequestration hurts the government, and this package hurts the American people and their economy."[33] Sununu, addressing the Republican conference, alienated and antagonized the legislators. "By the way, none of you guys want to have the President come to your district, to be on a platform with him with a big audience of constituents and have him turn and say, 'Why aren't you with me on this deal?'" he blustered.[34] "I know George Bush and he would never do anything like that," an infuriated Bill Goodling (R-PA) responded. "George Bush is a much nicer guy than I am," Sununu shot back.[35] House Republicans rose and applauded Carl Pursell (R-MI) when he told Sununu, "We don't appreciate your coming up here to threaten us."[36]

Because the White House legislative liaison, communications, and public liaison staffers had not been given any advance notice of the budget agreement, they were unprepared to lobby for it in Congress. Some aides complained that they found it hard to coordinate their efforts with Darman. But it is doubtful they could have made much headway against the groundswell of feeling against it. Bush himself brought a dozen undecided Republicans to the White House, but Sununu ruined his attempts to patch things up: When Fred Upton (R-MI) told Bush he couldn't vote yes because agreement was "a rotten deal," a furious Sununu berated him. "What are you smoking?" he demanded.[37]

The next few days were filled with bad news for the president. The General Accounting Office concluded that cuts in spending would be much less than predicted, a conclusion also reached by the Congressional Budget Office. The administration won the support of the Federal Reserve, however. Chair Alan Greenspan called it a "credible" plan, claiming it would drive down interest rates. He warned, "Failure to enact the agreement would produce an adverse reaction in financial markets that could undercut our economy."[38] House Republicans thought otherwise, and Gingrich and Senator Trent Lott (R-MS) began rounding up the opposition. Conservative Republicans pointed out to the White House the political risks in the agreement: Democrats were saying that they opposed the agreement but would vote for it, leaving the onus for raising taxes on the Republicans.

The Democratic House took up the budget bill under a rule that barred floor amendments. Democrats were insistent that Republicans would have to vote for higher taxes in the agreement as the president had signed onto it, and there would be no opportunity for the minority to offer amendments to cut

spending and jettison tax increases. Either the White House would deliver on
the tax increases or the deal would fall apart. The Democratic caucus told its
members to hold back and let Republicans vote first: Only if Republicans
backed the agreement would the Democratic leaders make an effort to put it
through. Speaker Foley was forty votes short of a Democratic majority according to his own head count. But if Republicans voted for it, he was prepared to make an appeal in the well of the House to turn his party around.

The House voted on the plan on October 5, and Bush managed to get thirty-
six Republicans who had been undecided to vote for the bill through personal
lobbying.[39] Sununu convinced none of a dozen or so GOP conservatives he lob-
bied. The House voted overwhelming to turn the agreement down, 179–254.
Republicans rejected it, 71 in favor and 105 opposed. Democrats had stayed on
the sidelines while Republicans voted, but as they saw the Republicans defect,
many protected themselves and voted against the agreement as well, with only
108 in favor and 149 opposed. Only fourteen of twenty-seven Democratic committee chairs voted for it, the other thirteen protesting the exclusion of key committee leaders from the budget summit. For the same reason only six of the thirteen Democratic Appropriations Subcommittee chairs voted for it. Democrats
facing tough challenges from the Republicans in the upcoming elections all
voted against it. There was a "BUBBA" in the House, but it was a bipartisan
agreement to throw Bush, Darman, and Sununu under the bus.

The Senate also voted the agreement down, and afterwards, in a gibe at Gingrich, a disappointed Dole said, "You pay a penalty for leadership. If you don't
want to pay the penalty, maybe you ought to find some other line of work."[40]
But it was the party leaders, not the conservative rank and file, who had paid
the penalty. Voting against the measure was in tune with public opinion: By
the time the vote was taken a Gallup poll indicated that 33 percent of public
supported the deal, 20 percent were undecided, and 41 percent were opposed.

Congress passed a continuing resolution to keep the government running.
Bush leaned toward signing it, then decided to veto it after Dole told him a
veto could be sustained. Democrats, Bush believed, would not be able to take
the pressure of a government shutdown in an election year and with war
looming. "The hour of reckoning is at hand," Bush proclaimed in his veto
message, claiming that Congress had to pass an acceptable budget resolution.
Democrats and some moderate Republicans in the House failed by six votes
to override the Bush veto, 260–138. But Republican willingness to "shut it
down" was not well received, with a Gallup poll indicating that however much
the public had opposed the original agreement, 52 percent said Congress
should have passed it rather than close down the government. The White
House was blamed for the mess: Only 36 percent approved Bush's handling of
budget crisis, while 48 percent disapproved. [41]

Faced with these numbers, Bush worked to patch things up with Congress. Secretary of Defense Dick Cheney was brought in to smooth things over with his former House colleagues. Congressional leaders and the president made new efforts to cobble together an interim agreement to keep the government running, and on October 8, stopgap spending resolutions passed the House (305–105) and the Senate (by unanimous consent) to keep the government open through October 19.

Along with these stopgap resolutions was a "budget framework" establishing a new budget process. It set binding limits (expenditure caps) on annual spending authority and outlays for the next three fiscal years and called for specific amounts in new revenues to be settled later by the House Ways and Means and Senate Finance committees—both Democratic controlled. It passed with forty-two Democrats and twenty-four Republicans in favor, and thirteen Democrats and twenty Republicans opposed. Every one of the senators facing a close election in the fall, whether liberal or conservative, voted against the package. In the House it passed on a party vote, with all but twenty-eight Democrats voting yea and all but thirty-two Republicans voting nay. At the urging of Darman and Sununu, Bush signed the resolution. A confrontation would be useless, since if Bush vetoed the resolution it would not be sustained. The Democratic majorities in Congress were now free to craft a reconciliation bill (incorporating all tax and spending measures reported by committees) on a partisan basis and then cut a final deal with the White House. The White House had ceded the details of the budget to liberal Democrats, provided their plan stayed within the new spending caps. Best of all from their point of view (and perhaps the White House as well), the Democrats could cut out the conservative House Republicans without fear of Bush's veto.

The budget process had been restructured, but the political game Darman and Sununu had played collapsed. The president started in a weak position but hadn't understood that, and because of Bush's awkward positioning his party was in disarray. By excluding many Republican leaders from negotiations, he had further eroded his position. Democrats were holding the high cards and were willing to back off a deal unless it suited them. Republicans had gotten into a hole because they thought they could negotiate with Democrats along a single "more or less" dimension of deficit reduction and had forgotten the "fairness" valence dimension (a valence is a value not susceptible to compromise but expressed in absolute "yes or no" terms). They had miscalculated by creating a crisis atmosphere: If it really were a crisis, how could the president have justified shutting the government down?

Flip-Flops

Democrats set to work to exploit their advantages, with Speaker Foley observing that any new tax measure would have to place a greater burden on the rich. They dangled a deal: burst the "bubble" on income tax rates in return for a lower capital gains tax (19 percent). The White House had no idea how to handle this gambit, because although the strategists understood that it was a trap, Bush was eager for the bait. He was concentrating on the Persian Gulf, not well briefed, and somewhat "out of the loop" as developments moved rapidly on the Hill. He failed to attend to the details, which proved disastrous. At his October 9 morning news conference, Bush was asked if he would trade higher income tax for a capital gains cut. "That's on the table," he replied. "That's been talked about. And if it can be worked in proper balance between the capital gains rate and income tax changes, fine."

Republicans were feeling heat from their constituents and conservative groups, more concerned about the possibility of income tax increases than of capital gains reductions. Seventeen Republican senators met at the White House to tell Bush to get the tax trade off the table. Bob Packwood (R-OR) came out of the meeting to announce, "The President agreed, our unified position was we will not go up on the rate, not 1 percent, not 2 percent, not one penny . . . we will leave the rates where they are, drop capital gains and do nothing about the rates."[42] When asked by reporters about the president's response, Marlin Fitzwater responded, "It's fair to say he acquiesced in their views." Bush had actually been noncommittal at the meeting; Sununu tried to steer things by ordering Fitzwater to give that answer. But Sununu and Fitzwater had gone further than Bush intended.[43] Fitzwater, concerned about his own credibility, went to Bush and got Sununu off his back. "Publicly, we're not taking a position on any specific items," he was able to tell reporters later at the noon briefing. "This morning he says he'll consider the trade and this afternoon we have this statement that there's no way they'll do it," Democratic senator Lloyd Bentsen of Texas gibed to the press: "I wonder what his position will be tomorrow morning."[44]

Bush continued to give the impression of being out of the loop. On October 10, jogging in St. Petersburg, Florida, he was asked by reporters about the tax trade. He turned away from the television camera and sashayed off, saying, "Read my hips." Though not exactly the same thing as "let them eat cake," the media image of Bush airily dismissing the question had a strong impact. Bush's gesture seemed a parody of effeminate body language, as if to say that a *real* man doesn't have to worry about campaign promises and a *real* man doesn't have to answer media questions. *Time* ran an article that had a picture of Bush pointing to his rear, with the caption, "How could the man who confronted Saddam be so indecisive?" Its subhead was "Bush's flip-flops add new confusion to the budget battle and raise doubts about his domestic leadership."[45]

More flip-flops were to come. Bush met with a delegation of House Republicans to clear up the confusion, and Bill Archer (R-CA) reported that Bush was willing to make the trade. Several hours later, after Bush met with Senate Republicans, a White House spokesperson said the president "did not believe that such a compromise was now possible." Next the White House issued a "clarification" written by Darman, saying that Bush was in favor of the compromise but did not think it was feasible, and so he had recommended to Congress that the idea be dropped. One hour later, when the president was asked about efforts by congressional Republicans to cut a deal, he commented, "If they can get that done, fine."[46] Reporters raced to Darman, who commented facetiously, "I have no idea what White House statement was issued, but I stand behind it 100%."[47]

By the end of the week Bush was being portrayed by the media as an inconsistent, incomprehensible, effete goofball, and not only a wimp, but a waffling wimp. On the foreign exchange markets the dollar sank, and the stock and bond markets slumped. By October 22, *U.S. News and World Report* referred to the president as "the man who deftly rounded up a posse to stop Saddam Hussein now can't seem to organize a two-car funeral back home."[48] *Time* said: "Bush's flip-flops add new confusion to the budget battle and raise doubts about his domestic leadership."[49] *Newsweek*'s story, headed "Bush League," claimed that "between their flips and flops over the budget, the president and Congress looked like a bunch of stumblebums."[50] "It took only two breathtaking weeks for George Bush to sink into a quagmire of indecision and ineptitude. It could take him the rest of his presidency to dig out," *U.S. News and World Report* concluded.[51]

How was Bush to get back on track? Vice President Dan Quayle and Cheney argued for brokering a tax deal with Ways and Means Chair Dan Rostenkowski (D-IL), who came up with a plan for a 33 percent tax rate on the wealthy to "burst the bubble" and a 10 percent surtax on millionaires. Bush refused the deal. The Democrats now passed their own partisan budget, in the form of a reconciliation bill, on October 16. It was close to a party-line vote, 227–203. It included Rostenkowski's boost in the marginal tax rate and his surcharge on millionaires, a higher alternative minimum tax rate, up from 21 to 25 percent, and an increase in wages subject to Medicare from $51,300 to $100,000. The only capital gains provision was an annual exclusion of the first $1,000. The plan dropped the hikes in gasoline and petroleum taxes to gain support of Northeastern liberals. The tax increases were progressive: The richest 1 percent of the population would have its average federal income tax burden raised from 25.2 percent of income to 27 percent. Republican conservatives were unfazed, expecting Bush to continue the confrontation: "We on the Republican side of the aisle take heart in our President who declared his intention of vetoing the Democrats' tax and spend budget package," DeLay said to his House colleagues after the vote.[52] The Senate approved its own version of a reconciliation bill on October 19, on a more bipartisan 54–46 vote. It had various consumption taxes, and even established new tax breaks, but it did not raise the income tax rates.

Darman tipped the administration's hand just prior to the final talks on *This Week with David Brinkley* when he said that Bush would accept a 31 percent top tax rate if the rest of the package were satisfactory. The remaining sticking point was how to tax the rich. Democrats held the high ground, because the "fairness" issue seemed to be sticking with the public. Dole offered to reduce itemized deductions benefiting upper-income filers. Democrats had insisted on a 33 percent tax rate, but now they put their last best offer on the table: a 31 percent tax rate on the highest income, *plus* a 7.5 surtax on millionaires, in return for Bush's capital gains cut. When Dole reported this to Sununu he balked, sensing another Democratic "fairness" trap as well as open Republican revolt over the tax hike.

Dole was convinced that the Republicans could not afford to be seen as the party of the rich and that a capital gains cut would be poison. He was willing to accept Mitchell's insistence on a rise in income tax rates, as was Bill Archer, the leading House conservative dealing with tax policy. But they wanted to get rid of Rostenkowski's surtax. And so they traded: Democrats would drop the surtax, and Republicans would drop Bush's capital gains cut. On the spending side Republicans made some gains: Discretionary spending could rise by only $20 billion in the next three years, under a set of spending caps designed to keep almost all spending "flat." This was to be a serious limitation, not a cover for increased spending, as had been the case in the previous plan.

The deal was embodied in the Omnibus Budget Reconciliation Act of 1990. It provided for only $28 billion in deficit reduction in FY 1991 and $236 billion in five years—only *half* of what had been called for in the earlier agreement. Less than half of the goal would be accomplished by raising taxes: $137 over five years. Personal exemption and itemized deductions for upper-income taxpayers would be phased out. The proposed 10 percent surtax on income over $1 million was dropped. The top marginal income tax rate was raised to 31 percent, starting at $82,000, with a 28 percent ceiling on capital gains.[53] This meant that the tax rate would rise from 28 to 31 percent on income for 600,000 of the wealthiest taxpayers. There would be an increase from $51,300 to $125,000 in the wage base subject to a 1.45 percent Medicare payroll tax, an increase for upper-income wage earners and professionals. There would be new luxury taxes. The telephone excise taxes, set to expire at the end of 1990, would be made permanent. The increase in the gasoline tax was halved from the prior agreement, only rising five cents a gallon, which would be popular with western senators, while the tax on home heating oil was dropped, which would be popular with Northeast and Midwest senators. As with all tax measures, lobbyists managed to slip in tax breaks for businesses, to the tune of $27.5 billion in lost Treasury revenues.

The final accord accomplished three things for the Democrats. First, it was progressive and accorded with party principles. The wealthy would pay the most: Half of the total increases, the middle 60 percent of the population, would pay 40 percent, and the bottom quintile of the working poor, while paying 10 percent of the increases, would actually gain some income because of increases in the Earned Income Tax Credit refunded to them (a program to provide funds to wage earners whose income was below the poverty line). Second, it expanded some welfare state measures: It made more poor children eligible for Medicaid up to the age of 18, expanded Medicare, and even created a five-year, $22-billion child care program.[54] Third, the Democrats had forced the Republicans not only to accept hikes in income and excise taxes but also to accept political responsibility for higher taxes. Bush had been left vulnerable to charges within his own party that he had broken his promise.

With Bush's backing the agreement passed the House on October 27 by 228 to 200 and the Senate shortly thereafter by 54 to 45. In both chambers, a large majority of Republicans voted against it.[55] Most Democrats voted in favor, though the leadership counseled that those in close election races vote no.[56] Bush now was slumping in the polls with a 48 percent approval rating—the lowest scores of his presidency. The compromise was opposed by the public: 24 percent thought it was fair and 49 percent unfair. Bush's handling of the economy was approved by 33 percent and disapproved by 56 percent.[57]

Why would Bush agree to back a Democratic budget that would leave him so vulnerable? Doing so would secure Bush's domestic flank during an international crisis, and it might help him gain bipartisan support for his foreign policy. The tax increases would demonstrate to our allies that the United States was doing its part to finance the effort against Iraqi president Saddam Hussein. The agreement would avoid a sequester of military funds during this crisis. But Bush underestimated the fissures within his party. Republican challengers running for the House felt betrayed, since the White House had assured them that the president would resist Democratic efforts to raise income taxes. Republican candidates stopped using commercials featuring Bush in their media campaigns. Bush continued to sink in the polls, from 76 percent approving in September (and 16 percent disapproving) to 53 percent approving in October (and 37 percent disapproving).[58] Fund-raising appeals by the

Republican Senate and House campaign committees proved disastrous, as conservatives refused to contribute. Ed Rollins, director of the National Republican Campaign Committee (the campaign arm of House Republicans), sent out a memo to Republican candidates telling them to disassociate themselves from the deal. "I have a great deal of respect for this President, and I obviously want to help him," Rollins explained. "But my job today is to help House Republicans survive and help other Republican candidates. I have to give the best political advice I can and in this case, it's to run away from the budget package." Marlin Fitzwater responded that "it would be the understatement of the decade to say that the White House was unenthusiastic about Rollins' memo."[59]

With an agreement in place, Bush devoted his efforts to reuniting the party: Rollins would not be fired (for a while) and Gingrich and other dissidents in the House would not face reprisals. To punish dissidents would destroy his party's chances just before the following week's elections, so Bush held his fire. But within the White House staff morale sank, and acrimony increased. Everyone other than Sununu and Darman had been cut out of the action and felt angry, particularly those in the Domestic Policy, Communications, and Congressional Relations offices. Darman was soon to be engaged in trench warfare against "New Paradigm" believers (those who favored a supply-side program and devolution of programs to the states) in the Domestic Policy shop. The biggest cuts came in defense, not domestic programs, they claimed: Not a single domestic program was to be eliminated. There were *real* tax increases, they claimed, but only *illusory* spending cuts (except for Defense, where the spending cuts seemed to be real).[60] Armey and many other conservatives attacked the new budget process.[61]

Defining Moments

From Bush's perspective, the months leading up to the agreement had produced a squall that would soon blow over. Bush portrayed the tax increases as something the Democrats had foisted on him. On November 7, after Republicans had been pasted in the midterm elections—particularly those who had voted for the first agreement, such as Senator Rudy Boschwitz (R-MN)—he told reporters he'd had "serious regrets" about "being forced" to abandon his pledge and promised he would "absolutely" refuse to accept further tax rate hikes.[62] He told reporters that he would say to the American people, "Look, I've reluctantly signed this." Others in the administration echoed the line: "The president has made it clear he was forced to pay the tax ransom once in order to save the economy. He will not be forced to pay again," Sununu told the National Press Club. But this approach backfired. It made the president look weak and irresolute, a man who could be rolled by the opposition party. Trotting out "Bush the Wimp" as a White House strategy was the height of foolish media spin, since it played into a vulnerable aspect of Bush's public persona.

Bush argued that the tax increases amounted to only 0.6 percent of the GNP. But the White House itself had puffed up a minor adjustment of spending and taxes into a national emergency requiring a "summit" to resolve. Darman had insisted throughout that he and he alone was "serious" about the budget and that the problems had to be resolved, and resolved *now*. The White House believed that fiscal policy could not get into better balance without a crisis. This strategy was contradictory: Bush and Congress dropped already existing institutional checks and balances in the budget process designed to balance the budget in favor of a new precommitment rule on spending ceilings. The new rules would reduce the discretion of both the White House and Congress—hardly what one does in crisis management, which by definition requires executive leadership and discretionary policies.

If budget politics were transmuted into crisis politics, then the American people would evaluate the president according to his skills at crisis management. Bush would have to get a deal, and he would need to do so more than the Democrats, though this seems never to have been understood by his conservative critics who kept counseling him to walk away from negotiations, to sequester, and to use his veto. When Bush did veto, closing down the government, it backfired.

The Democrats knew from the start that they were playing politics with the budget. White House aides and the president never quite "got it" because they kept thinking that by defining the situation as a crisis and by hectoring everyone to be "serious," they would get the Democrats to play their game—eventual compromise in the context of a national security emergency in the Persian Gulf. But the Democrats were able to define the issue in a way that would show up the president, *even if he negotiated successfully*. The winning issue for Democrats was not the specifics of fiscal policy—it was the valence issues involving fairness, trust, and keeping promises. Bush not only lost the trust issue: He would be unable to use the credibility issue against President Bill Clinton in the 1992 elections. The worst of it was that Bush divided his own party on the character question. Charles Kolb, one of Bush's own domestic policy aides, later asked: "If he could so easily relinquish the central plank of his 1988 election campaign and cave in to the Democrats, then what did he really stand for?"[63]

The White House had handled the negotiations with the Democrats as a question of spatial positioning along two dimensions (more or less spending, higher or lower tax rates) along which compromises could be fashioned. But Bush never understood the key point: The question of a tax increase had become a defining ideological issue of a principal, rather than a pragmatic, question about raising revenues. The ideological issue that had divided Democrats from Republicans during the Reagan years involved taxation for the welfare state, and with one agreement in 1990 Bush had thrown away the Republican edge. Fairness once again became an issue as Democrats claimed to have fought for a progressive tax system while Republicans called for lower capital gains and protection of high income from Democratic proposals. The Democrats were able to leave Bush holding the ideological bag, even though it was the *Democrats* who had insisted on income tax hikes as early as the first Rostenkowski plan in April, and it was *Democrats* who had proposed income tax increases throughout the negotiations. The split in his own party and condensed media reporting seemed to leave an impression with the American people that Bush had developed the plan to raise taxes. In February 1990, before the budget process collapsed into summitry, Bush had 54 percent of the public believing he could avoid raising taxes, up from 24 percent when he had taken office.[64]

Republicans lost ground in the 1990 midterm elections, though candidates who put distance between Bush and themselves did better than those who defended the president's decision to raise taxes. Republicans lost eight House seats, not a lot for a midterm contest, and one senator and one governor. But antitax Democrats beat Republican governors in Nebraska and Kansas. Antitax Republican gubernatorial candidates won in Ohio and Michigan. The Republican National Committee let go one-third of the 250 member staff after the elections because campaign contributions dried up. By 1992, Democrat Bill Clinton could campaign against Bush on the promise of a middle class tax cut. And Bush would have no credible reply.

Bush's motivation in accepting a budget deal was that it would stimulate the economy, but Bush's pragmatic economic policies did not produce the desired results in time. The promised deficit reduction was supposed to result in a decline in real interest rates, a decline that would keep the economy in high gear. And that assumed serious deficit reduction (which would not be achieved). But spending cuts in the first year would be $30 billion at most (even though the announced number was $42.5 billion)—0.5 percent of gross domestic product. How much impact could *that* have on interest rates? None, the Federal Reserve thought, and it didn't plan to make large rate reductions. The White House thought that lower interest rates would stimulate the economy, but new investments are not made by companies simply because rates have gone down. They are made when companies think there are growth opportunities. After the deal was announced, the economy went into the tank: A drop of about \$30 billion in federal government spending, coupled with a multiplier effect, actually reduced stimulus and caused a downturn in investment. Unemployment and inflation went up, automobile and home sales declined, and the nation remained in recession. Receipts were also lower than projected. The deficit for FY 1991 shot up to \$300 billion—actually \$400 billion if the Savings and Loan bailout costs were included—setting a new record.

In the longer run the new budget rules did spark a recovery in the presidential election year, but by that time public and media impressions of a year's worth of a weak economy after the budget deal had been enacted had been set in stone. Republicans were on the defensive, once again defined as the "eat your peas" party of balanced budgets, high taxes, and low growth—completely reversing the electoral allure of Reaganomics. By 1992 Bush himself would be a casualty of the budget agreement. Pat Buchanan entered the Republican race and won one-third of the vote in New Hampshire before fading. Ross Perot entered as an independent candidate and drained votes from Bush in the general election.

"Listen, if I had to do that over, I wouldn't do it. Look at all the flak it's taking," Bush admitted during the campaign, but he didn't mean that he felt he had done the wrong thing. This comment only reinforced the public's sense that he had done things politically in the first place and that he lacked conviction. If in Bush's mind politics should have trumped economic principles in March 1992, in the view of the public his politics had trumped his principles in October 1990. "I went along with one Democratic tax increase and I'm not going to do it again—ever, ever," Bush told an audience in September 1992 on the campaign trail. White House aides quickly backtracked because it sounded ridiculous. "It wasn't a pledge, no," Fitzwater warned off reporters.[65] In mid-October, 1992, Bush announced that in his second term he would replace his economic team of Brady, Darman, and Boskin with Jim Baker.[66] By then it was two years too late.

Was the budget crisis the "defining event" for the Bush presidency, demonstrating a failure of leadership?[67] George Will posed the question about the physics of Bush's presidency: "How can something lighter than air fall so fast?"[68] Yet it is hard to believe that the tax hikes, in and of themselves, meant the end of George Bush. For one thing, the tax hikes raised income taxes on only 2.3 percent of filers. The final agreement raised the kind of taxes people seemed most willing to accept, blunted the "fairness" issue that Democrats otherwise would have used, and demonstrated a willingness to compromise that is usually applauded by the public. In recent years presidents have often raised taxes (while cutting expenditures). Tax hikes didn't kill Reagan in 1982 or Clinton in 1993. Neither did positional politics, pragmatic deal making trumping ideology, or complaints from the congressional party over the final

deals worked out by the White House. Why then were tax hikes, a budget im-
broglio, and a presidential veto so damaging to Bush? Why couldn't he have
just ridden it out?

The answer is that he did. The tax hikes did not do him in, and he was right
about public opinion: The tax hike ruckus did blow over. Going into the summit negotiations, on July 11, a Gallup survey showed 63 percent approval rating for Bush, down from 69 percent in June, with 54 percent disapproving of
his statement on the need for additional revenues and 41 percent approving.
But Bush's poll standing remained higher than Reagan's and Carter's after a
comparable 18 months in office.[69] The negotiations hurt Bush, but not fatally:
A September *Time*/CNN poll had 29 percent of respondents blaming Bush for
the failure to get a budget agreement, but 42 percent said the Democrats in
Congress were to blame.[70] The deal was unpopular, but it was not fatal.

It wasn't the tax increase per se that hurt Bush, it was how it defined him with
a specific group of conservative voters. The issue for the "base" in the Republican Party was Bush's leadership and character; not his tax policy. "Read my
hips," became the defining image of a politician who could not care less about
the people. Bush's image management, more than his fiscal management, put
his presidency at risk. But did Bush's negative image in the budget negotiations
fatally weaken his presidency? That would seem overstated. There is no question
that Bush had declined in the polls during the budget negotiations, but the decline was not precipitous, and some of it may be laid on declining support for
Desert Shield, with much of the public concerned he might take the nation to
war before all avenues of negotiation had been exhausted.

By the end of the Desert Storm war in 1991, Bush enjoyed a 91 percent approval rating. He was ahead of any conceivable Democratic opponent and
thought he would benefit from what he believed was a weak opposition field.
No one through 1991 thought of him as a lame duck who had irretrievably
blown his presidency. The conservative journal *Policy Review* in November
1990 asked leading conservatives to assess the Bush presidency, in a feature entitled "Sophomore Slump."[71] Some commentators graded him F or D, based
on the budget deal, but others graded him higher, particularly in foreign affairs, and Vice President Quayle and cabinet secretaries got good grades.

But the polls and the pundits missed a point that had not been lost on Gingrich, DeLay, and other Republicans in the House. The budget deal was nom-
inally about taxes and spending, but those were always negotiable. What was
not negotiable were questions of character, of promises, of attitude. Bush had
broken his word on a pledge that he had made to the conservative wing. He
had shut them out, taken them for granted, negotiated fairly with the enemy
but unfairly with his friends. He had left conservative challengers out on a
limb, and had cost the party in the midterm elections. He had not given

conservatives a vision of the future or a flag to rally round. Even when Bush regained his credibility with the nation after the Persian Gulf War, he seemed to have lost it, perhaps irretrievably, with the conservative wing of his party, who never forgave him for mortgaging the future of the party for what they saw as short-term political gain. By the 1992 elections, only 12 percent of the strong Republican identifiers gave money or worked for the campaign compared with 23 percent in 1988—and the lowest figure by far since 1952 when these figures began to be compiled.[72]

The 1990 Budget Summit illustrates the problems a president faces when he doesn't rely on a power stakes analysis at the appropriate time, when he turns over the definition of public policy to the institutionalized presidency instead of guarding his stakes himself, and when he compounds these problems by getting way out of step with an antipolitics mood, thus having the worst of all possible worlds. "There is a terrific cost to this kind of out-of-control performance," Meg Greenfield observed, "it is paid in the coin of government credibility."[73] Bush offered conservatives the worst of all possible worlds when he accepted a budget deal: the prospects of a high tax, low service state. Who could rally around that?

"Remember, there have been lots of great one-term presidents," John Sununu kidded Bush at the start of the negotiations.[74] Ultimately the give and take of legislative horse-trading, conducted by seasoned Republican politicians in the leadership like Dole and Michels, led their party to an agreement. The system "worked," but a success in revamping the process produced perverse economic and political results. The economic result was to drain demand from the system, reduce business confidence, and provide mixed signals leading to a recession. Between 1989 and 1992, constant per capita income (in 1987 dollars) fell $100.[75] The political effect was to reduce the authority of the president, increase public cynicism about his motives, and raise questions about his character among his party's ideological base.

"We had to have some compromise," Bush later observed, "and I paid one hell of a price for it."[76] Bush still didn't get it. It wasn't a question of compromise. In an antipolitical era, a president who defines policy according to his power stakes, who makes and then breaks a symbolic promise as he maneuvers to cut a deal, who engages in pointless gamesmanship, will fall victim. Bush failed not because he was a bad politician, and not because he brokered a bad deal, but because he went back on a promise he should not have made in the first place and therefore breached a promise he had made with the American people that had been one of the most important factors in his election. To breach trust is fatal, particularly when the president does not pay sufficient attention to repairing the breech. That too must be one of the president's stakes in decision making.

Clinton's Summitry

"Bill Clinton vetoed our budget bill and shut down the government. He shut it down. But he got away with convincing the American people that Congress did it. That won't happen again."[77] So promised Republican Senate Majority Leader Trent Lott (MS) after President Bill Clinton had parlayed a budget summit victory into a second term in office. Nevertheless, Clinton not only outfoxed Republicans in 1995, winning a budget game that in many respects was a replay of the situation President George H. W. Bush had found himself in 1990, he was also able to defeat them on spending issues in 1998 in the midst of an impeachment crisis and then pin them to the wall in 1999, when they were so spooked by his skills that they refused to negotiate, fearing yet another defeat.

Why Clinton succeeded where Bush failed can tell us a great deal about how the game of budget politics is best played. Clinton in 1995 managed to position himself correctly along three separate dimensions: the "liberal versus conservative more or less" dimension on taxes, spending, and deficits; the "open versus shut" dimension on government shutdowns and continuing resolutions; and the "caring versus uncaring" dimension involving government programs benefiting the Democratic electoral coalition. He too was involved in gamesmanship, but in Clinton's case each move had a point.

By November, months past the deadline for passage of spending bills for the FY 1996 budget, Clinton had vetoed several appropriations bills and had accepted a continuing resolution from the Republican Congress to keep the government open. On November 13, Clinton refused to sign a new Republican continuing resolution: "If you want to pass your budget, you're going to have to put somebody else in this chair. I don't care if I go to five percent in the polls. I am not going to sign your budget," he told Republican leaders. "It is wrong. It is wrong for the country."[78]

On November 15 a continuing resolution expired, and the government shut down. The following day Republican congressional leaders and Clinton aides agreed on a framework for negotiations, and a few days later Congress reopened the government with a continuing resolution that Clinton signed. Events seemed a replay of the aftermath of the budget shutdown of 1990, but it soon took a different turn: Republican leaders claimed victory because the framework would require a balanced budget with CBO scoring. The White House replied that the deal did not necessarily require CBO scoring; merely that CBO scoring would be taken into account. Furious Republicans thought the White House was reneging.[79]

As negotiations began on November 28 in the Mansfield Room of the Capitol, Republicans borrowed their strategy from the Democratic 1990 playbook:

They insisted (as Speaker Tom Foley had insisted in 1990) that the other side go first, that the president put his budget and tax plans on the table. But White House chief of staff Leon Panetta refused to do so. Democrats knew they would eventually have to agree to CBO scoring, but they wanted to hold off until the final outline of a deal was in place. Unlike the Bush negotiators in 1990, they had no intention of giving away the prize just to get into the game. Republicans tried to get Panetta and Treasury Secretary Robert Rubin to state their intention to produce a balanced budget with CBO numbers. After a week of haggling, Democrats agreed to submit a budget, but not one necessarily based on CBO numbers.

Unlike Bush, Clinton did all he could to control the climate of public opinion. In the midst of negotiations Clinton vetoed a reconciliation bill passed by the Republican Congress, using the pen that President Lyndon Johnson had used to sign Medicare in 1965. At a news conference he observed that Republicans had sought "to make extreme cuts and other unacceptable changes in Medicare and Medicaid, and to raise taxes on millions of working Americans." He contrasted it with his own balanced budget plan, which "reflects the values that most Americans share—work and family, opportunity and responsibility." Clinton had painted Republicans as ideological extremists unwilling to come to a sensible compromise; he also had seized the high ground of "values." Americans are operational liberals, loathe to cut programs that provide them with benefits; they are ideological conservatives when it comes to balanced budgets; and they are strongly supportive of family values. Clinton had framed a three-dimensional centrist position in which he felt he held the high cards on the two dimensions—health care and family values. He had labeled his plan "a balanced budget plan" to blunt the Republican advantage on the third dimension. His message also contained an "exit strategy" in case negotiations failed.

When Panetta brought the administration's budget proposals to Republicans gathered in Bob Dole's Senate conference room, his numbers were based only partly on CBO estimates. Panetta offered no movement on Medicaid or Medicare—the White House had agreed only to small cuts. Instead, the White House came up with a balanced budget within seven years by making its economic assumptions more optimistic. Republicans thought the Democrats had reneged on the November 19 agreement, which they had interpreted as requiring CBO scoring in exchange for the continuing resolution on reopening the government.

Why was there no movement from the White House side? Clinton felt politically secure (he had recently had some foreign policy accomplishments in Northern Ireland), he was moving up in the polls, and he was in the mood to settle scores. Vice President Al Gore insisted on holding firm, perhaps because of the problems he would inherit as Clinton's successor in the Oval Office if most of the cuts being discussed were to come *after* Clinton's second term. Clinton's advisers believed they should slow down the pace of the negotiations. Once again, as in 1990, Democrats understood that time was on their side.

Republicans were unsure of their ability to pressure Clinton, in part because their congressional leaders were on the defensive. Gingrich no longer seemed to be a leader in full command of House Republicans, some of whom were urging him to lower his profile. Dole had been dubious from the start about the House strategy; he had wanted a continuing resolution to keep the government open while he and Clinton negotiated. But the House Republican leaders opposed passing a continuing resolution: They would force the issue with a government shutdown if necessary, just as they had done in 1990. If there were any evidence necessary that elephants may forget nothing but they also learn nothing, Republican tactics at this point would suffice. Newt Gingrich (R-GA) asked Dole to come to one of the House Republican Conference meetings, where Dole posed the key questions: "What's the end game? Shut down the government and that's the whole story? We don't win."[80] The House Republicans were not convinced when Dole argued for a continuing resolution. Right in the middle of the meeting, members turned on the television to listen to a Clinton news conference. The president warned that he wouldn't give into Republican threats: "It is wrong for the Republicans to insist that I make deep cuts in Medicare and Medicaid or they'll shut the government down." In response the entire Republican conference supported the leadership call for a shutdown, and they let the existing resolution expire. Within days Clinton vetoed his sixth and seventh spending bills (in all he would veto ten) on December 18 and 19, citing environmental protection, worker safety, and crime programs that would be cut by Republicans, all hot button issues.

Gingrich understood that continuing the crisis was a high stakes gamble. He sent a fax to his own Republican House leaders that indicated he would talk tough to the opposition: "We want them to understand that if they want a long-term standoff, we are prepared to stay the course for as long as it takes." But Gingrich argued, "The White House wants a situation in which they can continue to portray us as extremists. They want to blame the government shutdown on us as irresponsible partisans." He proposed that a continuing resolution reopen the government through January 3, through the Christmas season. But the Speaker's advisory group, led by Dick Armey (R-TX) and Tom DeLay (R-TX), disagreed. Instead the leaders began working on a strategy to continue the shutdown and negotiate from there.

As in 1990, the Republicans were on the wrong side of the shutdown. House Republicans believed the public would blame Clinton for not negotiating seriously and for not using CBO numbers, just as the public had blamed Bush in 1990. But Bush had allowed the government to close down in the midst of a perceived deficit crisis combined with a real national security crisis. In 1995 Republicans had neither crisis to exploit. Their charges about "CBO scoring" were too technical and too complicated for the public to follow. Worse, House Republicans were flying blind: They had taken no polls and had no focus groups to tell them how their tactics would play. Over on the Senate side, Dole had polls and political assessments telling him that the shutdown wouldn't work, but the House leadership ignored him. So for 21 days the shutdown continued, with 620,000 federal workers off the job. When Congress passed appropriations bills to fund the government, Clinton vetoed them on grounds of "fairness" and "family values." The focus shifted from cutting programs and reorienting fiscal policy (spatial issues involving political compromise) to "who is responsible for the shutdown of government?" This was a "yes or no" valence issue that would weaken the Republicans, just as it had done in 1990. The Democratic National Committee press release for December 15 was headlined "Will Republicans Shut Down the Government Again Because They Insist on Cutting Medicare?" Democrats warned, "The Republican budget is packed with extremist, dangerous cuts that aren't necessary to balance the budget." The media ran stories about government workers who were not being paid just before Christmas and whose families would do without presents. As Republican legislator John Kasich (OH) put it, media were demonizing the "Gingrich who stole Christmas."[81] Republicans countered with claims that the First Lady had supported deep Medicare cuts similar to those in the GOP budget plan. This prompted senators Ted Kennedy (D-MA) and Jay Rockefeller (D-WV) to point out that these ads had distorted Hillary Clinton's position, which had involved new efficiencies in Medicare with the funds going into increased health benefits and universal coverage.[82]

"The most extreme members of the House" were keeping the government closed, Clinton charged at a news conference, in an unstated parallel with extremists who had bombed the Oklahoma City federal building. Senator Patrick Leahy (D-VT) made it explicit when he observed how sorry Americans were when "so many of those federal workers died" in Oklahoma, in the context of calling for a budget agreement to put their coworkers back on the job.[83] The salient issue for the public was not reigning in "Big Government" or "promoting fiscal responsibility," as the Republicans had assumed, but the identification of a government shutdown with "extremism." White House pollster Stanley Greenberg reported that the public was supporting Clinton and the Democrats. At a news briefing Clinton talked of "a plan that is passed, that is credible, and that is ultimately certified by the Congressional Budget Office." This was a new formulation, with the qualifier "ultimately" masking his refusal to use CBO numbers in the negotiations.

Republicans charged that the shutdown was being orchestrated by the White House to frighten the American people, and that it was arbitrary (some agencies were kept open) based on political costs and benefits. After Treasury Secretary Robert Rubin had taken interest-bearing Treasury securities from the Civil Service Retirement Fund, replacing them with a Treasury "IOU" for $60 billion so he could keep the essential activities of government functioning, Republicans charged that he was tampering with Social Security and that the transfer was illegal. Democrats pointed out that similar borrowing had been done by the Reagan administration and that legislation guaranteed that the retirement fund would be fully reimbursed. Rubin also had other contingency plans to borrow from the Federal Financing Bank and the Exchange Stabilization Fund, which would enable the Treasury to fund the government for months into 1996. Republicans could not wait Clinton out.

Summit negotiations resumed after a Christmas break. Clinton welcomed the negotiators back at a news conference by saying, "I think that people ought to go back to work, and I think they ought to be paid," adding that his goal was "to protect Medicare and Medicaid, education and the Environment."[84] Feeling the heat, Gingrich and Dole no longer insisted that Democrats put up a balanced budget with CBO scoring. But with polls showing the Democrats gaining, House Republicans agreed that if there were no progress, they would blow up the negotiations, though they had no clear idea what such a move would accomplish.

They were too late: Clinton had lost interest in compromise. As a White House aide put it, "The more this became up or down on specific issues, the more the President took traditional Democratic positions." Clinton's priority was to stay within the liberal Democratic framework as best he could. With the public blaming Republicans for the shutdown and the deadlock, it was a no-lose position for the president. The talks remained at an impasse as the Democrats refused to yield. Gingrich later admitted that "we expected that there would be a slump in our poll numbers, but we didn't calculate that a surge in Clinton's numbers would cause him to dig in even more."[85] With the public blaming Republicans by a margin of 2 to 1 for the shutdown, the Democrats prepared to stand on the Daschle Budget (named for the Democratic Senate minority leader, Tom Daschle of South Dakota), which Clinton would support in his State of the Union Address. It would be popular with his congressional party: Democrats in the House were doing their own polling and sampling public opinion in their districts and they didn't want Clinton to deal, and they wanted to sharpen the differences between themselves and the Republicans, especially on Medicare, believing it would help them in the 1996 congressional elections.

Moderate House Republicans wanted a way out, and on January 3, fifty-four of them voted in the Republican Conference to end the government shutdown. Meanwhile, without consulting Gingrich, Dole won a continuing resolution from the Senate to send government workers back to their jobs. Clinton praised the Senate and again attacked the House Republicans for the shutdown. On January 4 Gingrich presented a plan that would have all federal workers go back to their jobs through March 15; the House Republicans rejected it, but Gingrich had had enough, and the following day all pretense at democracy among House Republicans ended: Gingrich told legislators what they were going to do, did not permit them to vote on his plan in the Conference, and warned that he would remember anyone who did not support the leadership. The members then trooped down to the floor of the House, and under the watchful eyes of the leadership, voted to reopen the government.

On January 6, the leaders went back to the White House to negotiate. Republicans remained under the delusion that after having caved on the shutdown they could still negotiate a deal. Clinton did not give them the compromises they were expecting. He offered a seven-year balanced budget "eventually" scored by CBO, but with a catch: The plan used his own numbers and not CBO estimates. On January 9, each side made its last best offer. Republicans went as low as $152 billion in tax cuts. The administration was willing to increase cuts in Medicare, Medicaid, and welfare. Clinton had moved quite far toward the Republicans, and vice versa. The final differences in spending per beneficiary on Medicare were only $150 apart, and Medicaid funding differences were only $6 billion a year in programs spending $178 billion annually by 2002. Yet Clinton turned down the opportunity to close the deal.

Even though the two sides were close, ultimately neither would go the distance. There were too many hardcore conservatives in the GOP, too many liberals among the Democrats. Clinton would not do a deal without half the Democrats voting for it, but no deal that could get half the Democrats could also get half the Republicans. Neither Clinton nor Gingrich thought a deal was worth a party split or worth giving up the differences that defined them. Republican negotiators in the Roosevelt Room decided to end the talks. Clinton continued to bait the Republicans, saying that he was in favor of a balanced budget, and that this could be achieved "in fifteen minutes" if only the Republicans would return to negotiate.

Why couldn't the two sides come to closure? As they got closer to a deal, each experienced anxiety about moving away from the more extreme position of core supporters. Their own movement toward the middle raised their anxieties and their uncertainties about the risks they would assume. Each believed that they were making more concessions than the other side; that the opposition would pocket gains and offer nothing in return. They wondered if they could trust the other side to come to closure. They were uncertain that they could maintain their own coalition after the deal was announced. The strategy for concluding negotiations is to broaden the range of issues and interests and enlarge the scope of a potential agreement. Clinton never did that, preferring a "blame game."

Given Clinton's choice, the budget process evaporated. Congress could not get a reconciliation bill past the White House, so merely a hodgepodge of prior appropriations, continuing resolutions, and OMB directives determined spending levels through the remainder of the fiscal year. The public blamed Congress, particularly Republicans, for the pointless Christmas shutdown. "When the leadership in Congress insists on going it alone, one party alone, we get gridlock, stalemate, vetoes, government shutdowns," Clinton opined at a press conference—misleading to the last. Republicans had gone more than halfway toward compromise, and Clinton had led them on. It was a classic example of "pursuit and avoidance," in which Republican leaders did what they could near the end of the game to come to an agreement, just at a point at which Clinton decided he held the high cards and refused to make the deal.[86]

Consider the different outcomes for Bush and Clinton. Bush lost, even though eventually he struck a deal and reformed the budget process; Clinton won even though he backed away from a deal and let the process disintegrate. Political choice trumps rational choice in the budget process every time, and Clinton knew it. The outcome of the budget game was irrational for fiscal policy, but the political strategy laid the groundwork for Clinton's resurgent presidential reelection campaign of 1996.

The big difference between the two presidents seemed to be the way they played the budget game. Clinton was always immersed in the details; Bush allowed staffers to run the negotiations. Clinton never allowed himself to move far enough to split his party; Bush moved far enough to provoke a backbencher and conservative revolt. Clinton understood the nature of the game he was playing; Bush never even understood he was engaged in a game. Clinton struck early and hard in the media wars; Bush had no control over his image and lost it entirely with the "read my hips" fiasco. Clinton played fast and loose with the budget process; Bush played according to the rules. Clinton was prepared to scuttle the budget process itself; Bush tried hard to improve it. Clinton always played a political game; Bush thought politics had to be deferred during a national crisis. The irony is that careful attention to the *real* game led Clinton to a victory and Bush to failure.

Notes

1. Quoted in *New York Times* (May 10, 1996): B-12.

2. *The National Journal* (May 19, 1990): 1240.

3. *Congressional Quarterly Almanac, 1990* (Washington, DC: CQ Press, Inc., 1991), 127.

4. Jon Elster, *Ulysses and the Sirens: Studies in Rationality and Irrationality* (Cambridge, UK: Cambridge University Press, 1979).

5. Robert D. Hershey Jr., "Bush Seems Concerned That Economy May Slip," *New York Times* (May 9, 1990): B-8.

6. Maureen Dowd, "Bush Eases Stand, Saying New Taxes Can Be Discussed," *New York Times* (May 7, 1990): A-1.

7. Susan Rasky, "Tax Rise 'On the Table' in Talks on Federal Budget," *New York Times* (May 7, 1990): 4.

8. Andrew Rosenthal, "Budget Chief Warns of Cutbacks if Congress Does Not Drastically Reduce the Deficit," *New York Times* (May 9, 1990): B-8.

9. Eleanor Clift and Ann McDaniel, "After You! We Insist!" *Newsweek* (May 21, 1990): 19.

10. Maureen Dowd, "Bush, Trying to Quell Tax Debate, Insists Budget Talks Will Be Open," *New York Times* (May 12, 1990): A-1.

11. Dowd, "Bush, Trying to Quell Tax Debate," A-1.

12. Michael Duffy, "Man in the Muddle," *Time* (October 15, 1990): 41.

13. Susan Rasky, "Bush Aides Increase Estimate of Projected Deficit," *New York Times* (May 23, 1990): A-27.

14. *New York Times* (June 29, 1990): A-12.

15. Charles Kolb, *White House Daze: The Unmaking of Domestic Policy in the Bush Years* (New York: Free Press, 1994), 92.

16. George Church, "Eating His Words," *Time* (July 9, 1990): 16.

17. Richard Darman, *Who's in Control?: Polar Politics and the Sensible Center* (New York: Simon & Schuster, 1996), 263.

18. Kevin P. Phillips, *The Politics of Rich and Poor: Wealth and the American Electorate in the Reagan Aftermath* (New York: Random House, 1990).

19. Darman, *Who's in Control?*, 225.

20. David Rosenbaum, "Estimate on Deficit Is Raised Sharply," *New York Times* (July 17, 1990): A-14.

21. William McGurn, "Mr. Outsider," *National Review* (October 15, 1990): 28–29.

22. *Congressional Record* vol. 136, H5126, July 20, 1990.

23. *Congressional Record* vol. 136, H5129, July 20, 1990.

24. *Congressional Record* vol. 136, S13161, September 14, 1990.

25. Aaron Wildavsky and Naomi Caiden, *The New Politics of the Budgetary Process* (New York: HarperCollins, 1992), 492.

26. Fred Barnes, "Copped Lips," *New Republic* vol. 203, no. 17 (October 22, 1990): 10.

27. Richard Berke, "Rebellion Flares among Republicans over Accord," *New York Times* (October 2, 1990): A-22.

28. Berke, "Rebellion Flares," A-22.

29. Berke, "Rebellion Flares," A-22.

30. *Congressional Record* vol. 136, H8588, October 1, 1990.

31. *New York Times* (October 3, 1990): A-1.

32. *Time* (October 15, 1990): 35.

33. *Congressional Quarterly Almanac* (Washington, DC: CQ Press, Inc., 1990): 136.

34. Bill Whalen, "For Republicans, a House Divided," *Insight* (November 12, 1990): 5.

35. Laurence Barrett, "1,000 Points of Spite," *Time*, October 15, 1996, 39.

36. Eloise Salholz, "A Payback for the President's Enforcer," *Newsweek* (October 15, 1990): 30.

37. Maureen Dowd, "Bush Aides' Big-Stick Tactics Drove Away Many in House," *New York Times* (October 6, 1990): A-8.

38. Barrett, "Spite," 35.

39. Fred Barnes, "Knives Out," *New Republic* vol. 203, no. 18 (October 29, 1990), 10.

40. Barrett, "Spite," 36.

41. *CBS News* poll, October 7, 1990.

42. R. W. Apple Jr., "Bush Hints at Rise in Top Tax Rates, Then Backs Away," *New York Times* (October 10, 1990): A-1.

43. Maureen Dowd, "Bush's Woes Stir G.O.P. Grumbling over Sununu," *New York Times* (October 29, 1990): B-8.

44. Apple Jr., "Bush Hints," A-19.

45. Dan Goodgame, "Read My Hips," *Time* (October 23, 1990): 26.

46. John Cassidy, "Laurel and Hardy Take Charge at the White House," *Sunday Times* (October 14, 1990): 14.

47. Cassidy, "Laurel and Hardy Take Charge," 14.

48. *U.S. News and World Report* (October 22, 1990): 34.

49. *Time* (October 22, 1990): 26.

50. *Newsweek* (October 22, 1990): 20.

51. *U.S. News and World Report* (October 29, 1990): 24.

52. *Congressional Record* vol. 136, H10502 (October 18, 1990).

53. In effect this was a slight cut in capital gains taxes for people "in the bubble," down from 31 percent to 28 percent, if one viewed their capital gains as their marginal income subject to bubble rates.

54. Sally Cohen, *The Politics of Childcare Legislation, 1970 to 1990* (New York: Columbia University Dissertation, 1993).

55. In the House 47 Republicans supported it while 126 voted against. In the Senate 20 Republicans voted for and 25 against.

56. In the House 181 Democrats for, 74 against. In the Senate 35 Democrats for and 20 against.

57. *Newsweek* poll, October 28, 1990.

58. Gallup polls, September 10–11, 1990, and October 18–21, 1990. Since the Gulf crisis was going on at the same time, one cannot disentangle the effects of the two crises on his popularity.

59. Andrew Rosenthal, "Bush Tries to Quell G.O.P. Rebellion," *New York Times* (October 25, 1990): A-22.

60. Tom Bethell, "Smoke, Mirrors and the Adversary Press," *American Spectator* (December 1990): 14.

61. Dick Armey, "Our Kingdom for a Deal," *American Spectator* (December 1990): 35.

62. *CQ Almanac, 1990* (Washington, DC: Congressional Quarterly, 1990), 166.

63. Kolb, *White House Daze*, 99.

64. Terry Eastland, *Energy in the Executive* (New York: Free Press, 1992), 60.

65. Stephen Robinson, "Tax Pledge Shadow on Bush Plan for Growth," *Daily Telegraph* (September 11, 1992): 14.

66. Dan Goodgame, "Anatomy of a Fumble," *Time* (October 26, 1992): 32.

67. David Mervin, *George Bush and the Guardianship Presidency* (New York: St. Martin's Press, 1996), 154.

68. George Will, "Flippant Style, Trivial Pursuits," *Newsweek* (November 5, 1990): 88.

69. Gallup poll, July 6–8, 1990. Reagan had 42 percent and Carter 40 percent in comparable periods.

70. *Time*/CNN poll (September 23, 1990).

71. "Sophomore Slump," *Policy Review* no. 55 (Winter 1991): 32–44.

72. Data compiled by the Center for Political Studies, American National Election Studies, 1992 (University of Michigan, Survey Research Center, 1993).

73. Meg Greenfield, "Ringside at a Pillow Fight," *Newsweek* (October 29, 1990): 88.

74. Darman, *Who's in Control?*, 249.

75. U.S. Department of Commerce, *Statistical Abstract of the U.S., 1996*, table 709, 456 (Washington, DC: U.S. Government Printing Office, 1996).

76. David E. Rosenbaum, "In Balanced-Budget Deal, Bush Is off the Seesaw," *New York Times* (August 8, 1997): A-23.

77. Richard L. Berke, "Trent Lott and His Fierce Freshmen," *New York Times Magazine* (February 1, 1997): 48.

78. David Maraniss and Michael Weisskopf, *"Tell Newt to Shut Up!"* (New York: Simon & Schuster, 1996), 148.

79. Clinton projected growth of 2.5 percent and price rises of 3.1 percent and Medicare health costs increasing by 9.8 percent; Republicans projected growth of 2.3 percent, price increases of 3.2 percent, and health care costs rising by 10.3 percent. Clinton's projections had a balanced budget in a decade; Republicans projected Clinton's budget would lead to $200 billion deficits.

80. Maraniss and Weisskopf, *"Tell Newt to Shut Up!"* 165.

81. Maraniss and Weisskopf, *"Tell Newt to Shut Up!"* 163.

82. *Congressional Record* vol. 141, S19183 (December 22, 1995).

83. *Congressional Record* vol. 141, S19314 (December 29, 1995).

84. *Federal News Service*, December 29, 1995.

85. Elizabeth Drew, *Showdown: The Struggle Between the Gingrich Congress and the Clinton White House* (New York: Simon & Schuster, 1996), 360.

86. John B. Gilmour, *Strategic Disagreement* (Pittsburgh, PA: University of Pittsburgh Press, 1995), 51–95.

8

Program Innovation

Clinton and Health Care

"THIS HEALTH CARE SYSTEM OF OURS is badly broken," President Bill Clinton proclaimed in a 1993 address to Congress, "and it is time to fix it." He appealed for bipartisan support: "For the first time in this century, leaders of both political parties have joined together around the principle of providing universal, comprehensive health care. It is a magic moment and we must seize it."[1] It was a typical Clinton performance: because the Teleprompter operators had put the wrong speech up, Clinton could not use the screens, and because he didn't have his reading glasses on, he couldn't see the hard copy of the speech on his podium—he improvised until the right speech came up on the screens. The foul-up on the podium was a portent of things to come: Clinton would improvise, but in the end he would not reform health care—a failure defining his first term. "The most stunning fact about this entire effort," journalists Haynes Johnson and David Broder later observed, "is that when the Democrats controlled both houses of Congress and had in the White House in Bill and Hillary Clinton the two most knowledgeable and committed advocates of universal health care coverage in history, they failed over two years even to bring the measure to a vote."[2]

The conventional wisdom is that Clinton delegated too much authority to Hillary Clinton and her health reform task force; the task force produced a bill far too complicated and cumbersome to win passage. The lesson learned was that presidents should reform incrementally rather than comprehensively. But this is too simplistic: Presidents delegate the responsibility to innovate to task forces all the time, and blockbuster initiatives always involve national commissions or task forces and often succeed. Why then did the Clintons fail?

Health Care as an Issue

In the early 1990s health care costs were increasing 6 to 9 percent, and individual premiums and employer contributions were up as much as 20 percent annually. The federal government paid one-third of health care costs, constituting more than 16 percent of its budget, and states allocated 12 percent of their budgets. Per capita national expenditures in the United States were $2,900 in 1992, compared with Canada's $1,600, France's $1,500, Germany's $1,500, Japan's $1,200, and the United Kingdom's $1,000. Americans were not getting the best health care for their high expenditures: In infant mortality the United States ranked nineteenth, below Ireland and Spain; in life expectancy the United States was ranked twenty-fourth for men and twentieth for women, in spite of the American emphasis on high-technology medicine carried out by trained specialists. Other industrial countries provided better access to care for their low-income populations.[3] The number of uninsured Americans at any given time had increased from 24 million in 1980 to 40 million by 1992; about one-quarter of workers lost insurance temporarily each year because of job loss or cuts in benefits. The proportion of Americans with any kind of private health care insurance had declined from 83 percent in 1980 to 70 percent in 1991.[4] Americans with private insurance found that their benefits were being reduced and their freedom of choice curtailed when their employers moved their coverage into HMO's or preferred provider plans. Many faced cutoffs if they had to change carriers and had preexisting conditions. Given these statistics, it is not surprising that an August 1991 Gallup poll reported that 91 percent of Americans thought there was a health care crisis, and 60 percent thought they might not be adequately covered in the future.[5]

The origins of Clinton's health care plan go back to the 1992 New Hampshire primary contest. One of his advisers, James Carville, had worked for Harris Wofford (D-PA) in a Senate race in 1990. "I think working Americans should have the right to a doctor. That's why I'm fighting for national health insurance in the Senate," Wofford had intoned in commercials, and he had come from behind and won with 55 percent of the vote.[6] Two years later in the New Hampshire presidential primary Carville coined the slogan for his campaign staffers: "It's the Economy, Stupid. Don't forget about health care." Clinton proposed a modified "pay or play" plan (a corporation would have to offer private health insurance to its workers or pay a quit tax) to counter Senator Bob Kerrey's (D-NE) competing proposal for a single-payer system (the national government would finance all health services through a 5 percent payroll tax and higher cigarette and top-bracket income taxes).[7] "Bill Clinton's American Health Care Plan: National Insurance to Cut Costs and Cover

Everyone," a six-page issue paper vague on details, did not specify how he would pay for universal coverage nor how quickly it would be phased in.

Kerrey and other proponents had argued that single-payer would be less expensive because it would replace premiums to private insurers with a less costly tax and that its savings (no profits to insurance companies and lower administrative costs) would provide universal coverage.[8] The General Accounting Office (GAO) estimated that administrative savings from all sources in the health care system could total $67 billion, enough to finance the estimated $64 billion needed for comprehensive coverage.[9] But Clinton had two reasons not to endorse single-payer: First, as a centrist "New Democrat" and founder of the Democratic Leadership Council, he wanted to distinguish himself from liberals who proposed or defended government solutions rather than public-private partnerships and regulated market approaches; second, he was not going to propose in New Hampshire *anything* that would require the tax increases required for the single-payer plan.

After winning the Democratic nomination, Clinton gave a speech at Merck Pharmaceuticals promising to expand coverage to the 38 million people without insurance and to do so without raising taxes. Employers would pay for workers' insurance, the government would provide coverage for the unemployed, and it would also subsidize premiums for small businesses. A system of "managed competition" among private insurance providers would hold health care costs down; there would be national caps on overall federal spending for health care, dubbed "competition within a budget."[10] He spoke of saving "hundreds of billions per year" and using the plan to lower the deficit.

Clinton's campaign proposals touched on many values and embraced many goals. Based on Stanley Greenberg's polls, the campaign de-emphasized "managed competition" and pushed "comprehensive coverage," a term that implied more benefits for those already covered, which would appeal to middle class swing voters. Greenberg found that the public wanted health care security: a guarantee that private insurance would not be canceled or denied because of preexisting conditions.[11] At no point in the presidential campaign did Clinton provide hard numbers. Experts such as Henry Aaron of The Brookings Institution warned that costs would be higher and new taxes might be necessary. When he released his economic plan in June after the primary season had ended, Clinton decided not to cost out his health plan but to present only general principles.[12]

Postelection surveys after Clinton's victory indicated that Americans ranked health care third on the list of national concerns, just after the economy and the deficit—and ranked second among Clinton's supporters.[13] As Clinton took office a Gallup poll found that 68 percent of Americans said they were very or somewhat confident that he could make health care available and affordable for all Americans.[14] Although Americans were generally satisfied with their own coverage, they no longer believed that health care should be left completely to the private sector, favored some form of universal coverage, and were willing to pay more in taxes to get a better health system. Most Americans believed the government should help those who could not pay for health care; three-quarters agreed that the president should veto any bill that didn't provide for universal coverage. The percentage who felt major changes were needed were increasing, while those who disagreed was declining.[15] The nation was ready for major new initiatives in health care, seemingly along the lines of Clinton's ideas.[16] Even so, polls showed respondents were worried that reform might negatively affect cost of care, quality of treatment, access to advanced technology, and freedom of choice.[17] Any plan would have to deal with these fears.

Clinton might win support from the business community: Employers were concerned about health benefit costs increasing so fast that they were eating up profits, and large corporations, whose costs per worker's family averaged $4,000, wanted cost containment. Companies with unionized workforces formed the National Leadership Coalition for Health Care Reform, which recommended price controls, mandatory coverage, or payment of a payroll tax to finance health care for workers. The Health Insurance Association of America (HIAA), representing 270 small- and medium-sized health insurance companies, presented a plan called the "Campaign to Insure All Americans," calling for an employer mandate to provide health insurance for workers, seeing it as a way to increase its pool of premium payers (especially reasonably healthy workers) and spread the risk of increasing coverage, a position that was also supported by the American Medical Association (AMA) and the U.S. Chamber of Commerce.[18] The National Federation of Independent Businesses (NFIB) endorsed insurance market reforms. Republican governors and legislators, responsive to their local industries, might help create a bipartisan coalition if Clinton could win them over.[19]

Program Planning

In his first week in office Clinton made several decisions about health care reform.[20] First, his plan would be comprehensive rather than incremental because so many things that required change were interrelated. Second, he would meet a campaign pledge to introduce health care legislation within one hundred days, and he would get Congress to pass it by the second year. Third, he would establish a White House task force rather than delegate drafting of the plan to the Department of Health and Human Services, whose new secretary, Donna Shalala, Clinton did not consider knowledgeable on health policy. Fourth, the task force would be supervised by his wife Hillary Clinton and run by Ira Magaziner, an innovative "out of the box" business consultant and social policy planner. Fifth, the plan would be based on a variant of managed competition and not on a single-payer approach used by every other industrialized nation. Sixth, the plan would limit expenditures: Federal funds would be allocated to regions by a national health board.

Right from the start there were skeptics about the task force. "Everyone thought Ira's process paper was a joke," one adviser recalled, "because nobody's ever seen anything like it in their whole career, and everybody suddenly realized that Clinton had never seen a first-rate policy process."[21] Secretary Shalala, for example, couldn't raise the single-payer issue because innovations from the departments were strictly excluded from consideration according to the process. Her department would do the number crunching and errand work, but it would be divorced from the policy formation.

Nevertheless, five days after taking office Clinton established the President's Task Force on National Health Care Reform.[22] He directed Hillary Clinton to submit proposals to Congress within one hundred days. "She's better at organizing and leading people from a complex beginning to a certain end than anybody I've ever worked with in my life," the president said about his appointee.[23] There were other reasons for giving her the assignment: Health care would be a project that could take up most of her time—this had its advantages for the president, as well as for the White House staff, which had already won an internal battle to keep her from being named chief domestic adviser. Hillary Clinton would be able to articulate the goals in a caring, sympathetic way, humanizing the numbers, and she did have some experience in policy formulation and in the field of public health, since she had led a rural health care task force in Arkansas and had served on the board of the Arkansas Children's Hospital. The Task Force not only included executive officials but also outside experts (primarily academic), several governors, and representatives of women's health organizations and minority groups (at Mrs. Clinton's suggestion). Some five hundred government officials formed its eight "cluster groups" and within them thirty-four "working groups," which were also attended by private-sector representatives of insurers and health care providers. After congressional leaders complained, more than one hundred congressional staffers were invited to participate in these groups.

The process created by Magaziner was highly complex. The Working Groups would broaden their analysis to consider all options. "Toll gates" at weekly and biweekly intervals were set up, at which time each Working Group's recommendations would be reviewed and options narrowed down. The leaders of the Task Force would make over 1,100 individual decisions, with the final decisions on trade-offs that divided liberals from conservatives (i.e., free market versus regulation; health care as universal right versus health care as market commodity; fiscally neutral versus redistributive outcomes) remaining in the hands of the president and his top policy and political advisers. Seasoned Washington hands Shalala and Alice Rivlin (deputy director of OMB) went to the Clintons to voice their reservations about the process, but they were ignored.

As the Task Force began work it enjoyed a surge of support: 82 percent of the public favored requiring employers to offer a health care plan; 78 percent favored limiting increases in premiums; 76 percent were for emergency short-term price controls on doctors, hospitals, and drug companies; and 86 percent said they supported the concept of managed competition.[24] But these poll results were meaningless: Respondents were registering support for a "free lunch" of benefits, without mention of costs and trade-offs.

The Task Force squandered the opportunity to win support from the business community and from Republicans. From the outset Magaziner excluded Republican staffers and made no attempt to keep Republicans legislators informed. The AMA and other health care provider interest groups kept trying to get the Clintons to give them more participation in the Working Groups, since the AMA had already come out with its own version of universal health care insurance.[25] Magaziner did not bring provider groups into the process. He was secretive even with task force members and used a "back channel" to the Clintons to discuss issues with them privately. He often indicated that the president had already made the basic decision, so the Task Force discussions did not cover all options.

The Task Force operated in strict secrecy, and Magaziner imposed a news blackout. Republicans on the House Government Operations Committee claimed that the Federal Advisory Committee Act (FACA) had been violated: The law provided that any task force not entirely composed of government employees must hold all meetings in public after a fourteen-day advance announcement. They argued that since Hillary Clinton was not a public employee, the law applied to the Task Force and its working groups. The White House responded that the First Lady was exempt from the provisions of FACA. A lawsuit was brought by the American Council for Health Care Reform, the American Association of Physicians and Surgeons, and the National Legal and Policy Center: Federal judge Royce Lamberth decided that the Task Force would have to comply with FACA and hold public sessions, though the working groups could continue closed-door meetings because they consisted solely of government employees and were not making recommendations to the president.[26] When the Clinton administration appealed the decision, the original plaintiffs were joined by news organizations, including the American

Society of Newspaper Editors and the Associated Press. The Court of Appeals reversed the lower court and found that the Task Force could conduct its meetings in secret because "Hillary Clinton was a 'de facto' [federal] officer or employee." But it also found that some of the working groups had permitted representatives of health care organizations to attend meetings (later the number of such people was put at more than three hundred) and therefore they might have to open their proceedings and release their papers.[27]

Magaziner was dogged by Clinton officials dealing with the economy, all of whom had been cut out of the deliberations and none of whom bought his arguments about saving money. They shot down his scheme to impose price controls on medical care, although Magaziner claimed it would save $101 billion in four years. They blocked Hillary Clinton's idea of attaching health care reform to their economic proposals. If it had been part of a budget reconciliation measure, health care would have gone into the Senate under privileged budget rules requiring only a majority vote at any stage; considered as stand-alone legislation, it would have to withstand a Senate filibuster and would need sixty votes. But the president did not want to hold his economic plan hostage to the fortunes of health care, and so sixty votes it would be.

Magaziner began talking about $50 to $100 billion in extra costs in the short term to provide universal coverage, figures that would require a sales tax, payroll tax, a cap on employer and employee tax deductibility for health care benefits, or some other large tax increase—any or all of which would likely be politically suicidal. Because the numbers didn't add up without a tax increase that the president had ruled out, the Task Force could not complete work in the one hundred days as Clinton had promised. Magaziner himself was becoming the issue. He had been a management consultant (his clients included the Greenhouse Commission in Rhode Island and the General Electric Corporation) whose firm specialized in innovative—some would say offbeat—solutions to problems. In each case, his proposals involved highly complex and comprehensive plans, and in several previous unsuccessful efforts to make public policy he had presided over what critics had called "a chain of disasters."[28] Now he had gotten bogged down in a fight with the economists and budget analysts and slipped his deadline.

The Task Force went back to the drawing boards: It came up with a financing scheme that health care expert Paul Starr called a payroll tax dressed up to look like an insurance premium. The Task Force fared no better with cost containment: Starr wanted it to recommend that the president be granted authority by Congress to freeze health care costs if inflationary increases could not be controlled by other means, while Magaziner suggested instead strict limits on reimbursement to providers. Clinton's economic and budget advisers fought hard to keep both ideas out of the plan. But Clinton did not side

with his economic advisers when they proposed their own incremental proposal for a slow phase-in of universal coverage. He pointed out to them that
all he was moving through Congress were a Republican-style deficit reduction
budget, along with trade legislation that would probably win more support
from Republicans than Democrats. He disputed the economists' arguments
that his reelection would turn on economic performance alone. In thinking
about his power stakes, he realized that he and his congressional party needed
a *Democratic* program: "We must have something for the common man. It
won't hurt me in '94, and I can put enough into '95 and '96 to crawl through
to reelection," he told them, adding, "At least we'll have health care to give
them, if we can't give them anything else."[29]

The Task Force produced a complex set of recommendations in thirty
loose-leaf binders, and on May 20 there was a showdown on the plan between
Magaziner and Clinton's National Economic Council. Hillary Clinton was
present and had already pronounced herself in favor of the Magaziner plan.
Clinton followed the advice of his wife as well as the political operatives in the
White House staff.[30] They wanted it big and they wanted it now, and they rejected "Plan A," backed by the economic advisers, that would have limited coverage to serious and catastrophic illnesses. But Shalala warned the Clintons
that if they went ahead with Magaziner's plan, "All the interest groups will be
mad—the doctors, the hospitals, the labs. You're building on all the nega-
tives."[31] The warning went unheeded: A few days later Hillary Clinton met
with a group of union leaders. "We have to be willing to take on every special-
interest group," she told them.[32] In a reprise of the Truman 1948 campaign
chant "Give 'em hell Harry," they roared back "Give 'em Health, Hillary."

Clinton formed three White House groups (one for budgets, one for legislation, and one for political strategy) to take over from the disbanded Task
Force. His next decisions, designed to reduce his own political risks, made the
work of these groups vulnerable. He rejected new broad-based taxes (having
already had to raise taxes in his economic plan), and a cigarette tax increase
was the only option he would consider. But the increase would cover only
some of the new costs, while leaving conservative southern Democrats from
tobacco states ready to bolt. He insisted, against the advice of the economists,
on capping individual insurance premiums for health insurance policies, en-
suring that insurance companies and their congressional allies would oppose
his plan. To finance universal coverage for lower and moderate-income workers who had been part of his electoral coalition, Clinton would call for cuts in
Medicare and Medicaid that would alienate liberal Democrats. Even if he won
passage of his plan, health care costs would increase from 14 to 17 percent of
GDP by the year 2000. Worst of all, costs in 1996 would be higher *with* reform
than without it. His plan would achieve universal coverage, but everything else

seemed to involve political costs for his congressional party and measures designed to alienate potential Republican backers.

Some observers later claimed that Clinton had created a "technically compelling" plan but had not paid enough attention to his political advisers, who might have induced him toward a more popular approach, perhaps by making health alliances voluntary or by better explaining the health alliances.[33] This is doubtful: While political aides did not work on the mechanics of the plan, their strategic advice informed every aspect of it. The First Lady was not in the business of promoting legislation designed to make her husband a one-term president, and the president would not have signed off on such a version. If anything, the Clintons' plan was *not* technically compelling, but rather politically expedient, without any compelling economic or policy rationale. Clinton had been too clever by half: He had boxed himself in by rejecting "single-payer" and "tax increases." Clinton had framed his choices in terms of his own power stakes, ignoring both the advice of his economic team and the needs of his congressional party to lower what he perceived to be his own vulnerabilities if he raised taxes.[34]

Over the summer Clinton concentrated on his economic program, including the North American Free Trade Agreement. Health care seemed stalled, and Magaziner, in a memo to top White House staffers, warned that the delay was leading to negative media stories, which he summarized: "Too complex or secretive a process devised by Magaziner, a plan being watered down, a feud between the First Lady and the economic team, a program where $100 billion of new taxes can't be sold to the President and he can't make decisions, etc."[35] Ironically, that memo was close to the truth of the matter.

Clinton's Choice

In his televised address to Congress on September 22, Clinton proposed compromises along three dimensions: government regulation versus market forces; national versus state administration; and public versus private financing. Government regulation would provide a mix of incentives to send "signals" in the marketplace; change would be nationally directed but health alliances would be organized and to some extent regulated at the state level; the government would provide some public funding but would require employer mandates and private financing or premiums for most workers.

Clinton's plan would guarantee comprehensive health care insurance for everyone. A National Health Care Board would establish standards for quality and service. Health Alliances in each state would contract with insurance companies, which in turn would contract with providers to deliver services.

Large corporations operating in more than one state could opt out and set up their own corporatewide Health Alliances. Private insurers would offer a choice of plans, including basic services provided by a health maintenance organization (HMO), as well as more expensive plans, including a traditional fee for service and plans involving networks of doctors or Hospital/Preferred Provider organizations. All participants would be covered in the basic plan at the same rate (referred to as a community rating) rather than at a rate based on their individual health histories. No one could be denied coverage for a preexisting condition. Medicare and Medicaid would be incorporated into this new state-oriented structure.

Congress would not pass a plan with new taxes: A proposed payroll tax had been blocked by Clinton economic advisers; a value-added tax (taxing every stage of production of goods) was shelved as politically risky, as was a national sales tax proposed by Shalala. By the time Clinton addressed Congress, the cost burden in the plan had been shifted back to employers (80 percent) and employees, along with a new cigarette tax of seventy-five cents per pack. There would be subsidies for small business, a measure intended to win support from the NFIB. Families with income up to 150 percent of the poverty line could apply for subsidies to help pay for the premiums. The National Health Care Board would set an overall annual budget for federal funding, and within the caps, spending would be controlled by competition and by limits on increases in premiums each year—an indirect form of price controls.

The plan relied on market incentives: Regional health alliances would pool premiums and negotiate with insurance companies for lower premiums, and insurance companies would negotiate with service providers to hold down costs. There would be considerable pain to share: The overall budget would constrain the regional alliances; they in turn would put insurance companies under the gun by negotiating to limit premium increases; insurance companies in turn would pass the financial pressure on to the medical groups and the doctors employed by them.

Driven by his pollster's findings, Clinton's speech bypassed the complexities of cost-containment (although it was mentioned), and focused on health care security, quality, responsibility, choice, and—of all things—simplicity. Clinton called for "health care that's always there, health care that can never be taken away."[36] He held up a Health Security Card modeled on the Social Security Card. Although the president received the usual standing ovations, he had not won Congress over, particularly not the Republicans. House Republican Leader Robert Michel (IL) warned that the plan would "impose on American families a very complex system that cannot work efficiently, a maze in which individuals will be lost."[37]

Greenberg's tracking poll reported 66 percent in favor after the speech, and Clinton's approval went up in the polls from 46 to 56 percent. Even so, a survey by the Kaiser Family Foundation and the Harvard School of Public Health, conducted September 30 to October 5, found that most Americans did not know what the term "managed care" meant (68 percent) and could not define managed competition (80 percent). They were less convinced the more they learned about it. On October 14, a "Citizens Jury" organized by a Minnesota think tank issued its verdict: Health care needed reform, but not according to the Clinton blueprint. The twenty-four citizens of the "jury" had spent five days in Washington learning about health care, then voted 19–5 against the Clinton plan.[38] They recoiled from terms used by Clinton such as health care alliances, managed competition, and employer mandates, which they found incomprehensible.

Only ninety-nine Democrats in the House and twenty-nine in the Senate sponsored Clinton's 1,342-page Health Security Act. The bill was divvied up among several House committees: Ways and Means, Energy and Commerce, and Education and Labor, and smaller parts went to seven other panels, with none of their leaders favoring the essential principles in Clinton's plan. In the Senate, Daniel Patrick Moynihan's (D-NY) Finance Committee had jurisdiction over the bulk of the proposal; Moynihan thought that the health care problem was part of the welfare problem, and if anything were to be done, it should probably involve extension and improvement of health care for the poor, and whatever should be done should come after comprehensive welfare reform.

Ten committees in the House and seven in the Senate would hold approximately 150 hearings on health care issues yearly. The power of decision was dispersed and fragmented (with no committee holding more than one-quarter of the hearings), which meant that any Clinton plan would involve many different players, making negotiations complex.[39] It is hard to fathom how the Clinton people expected anything good to come out of such fragmented committee referrals. They could have asked the Democratic congressional leaders to create an ad hoc joint committee, or they could have insisted that the party leaders refer the bill to party caucuses, as had been done with President Jimmy Carter's energy proposals, but by relying on standing committees, they guaranteed that the strains within the Democratic Party would intensify and that little would be done until the spring of 1994. By that time enemies of Clinton's proposals would have had time to organize.

The Backlash

At the 1992 Democratic nominating convention Clinton had called for a government with "the courage, finally, to take on the health care profiteers and make health care affordable for every family."[40] Clinton and vice presidential candidate Al Gore had claimed in a campaign book that "instead of putting people first, Washington favors the insurance companies and drug manufacturers and health care bureaucracies."[41] Hillary Clinton had bashed drug companies for excessive profits and insurance companies for not containing costs, raising premiums, and keeping people with preexisting conditions from obtaining coverage. This heated rhetoric had made them many enemies: Insurance companies (organized in the Alliance for Managed Competition), hospitals, and pharmaceutical and "medibusiness" companies had no interest in reforms that would limit health care expenditures.

The Clintons thought that the business community would support a plan that lowered medical costs by allowing consumers and companies to pressure the health care providers in a "regulated market" system of "managed competition." They also thought they would gain significant support from doctors; the AMA by 1990 had endorsed a plan that would have required an employer mandate. But once health care providers understood the plan would cap expenditures they struck back: The Pharmaceuticals Manufacturers Association hired the Sawyer Miller Group, the Medical Rehabilitation Education Foundation hired Hill and Knowlton, and the HIAA hired Bill Gradison, a former Republican member of the House. HIAA aired "Harry and Louise" commercials in September 1993, attacking the new "health care bureaucracy" with the tagline "They choose, we lose." The insurance industry created the Coalition for Health Insurance Sources to mobilize grassroots opposition and organize a letter- and fax-writing campaign to Congress.[42] The American Hospital Association enlisted hospital administrators and their boards of directors in thousands of local hospitals against the plan. The NFIB began a grassroots fax campaign to its 600,000 member firms, a majority of which did not offer health insurance to their workers. The Federation of American Health Systems, representing more than 1,400 private (for profit) hospitals, and the Health Care Leadership Council, representing the fifty largest health care companies (hospitals, insurers, and health maintenance organizations), spearheaded the health industry's opposition to Clinton's plan. Between January 1, 1993 and July 31, 1994, candidates for Congress, most of them incumbents, received $38 million from the health and insurance industries.

Some groups withdrew their initially favorable response: Late in 1993 the AMA House of Delegates withdrew its prior support for employer mandates, in large measure because state chapters responded to pressure from the NFIB, which was opposed to the mandate provision. Similarly the Washington leadership of the Chamber of Commerce was unable to continue with its initial negotiations with the White House on a compromise because of pressure from its state chapters, pressure orchestrated by the NFIB and Republican congressional leaders. The conservative Christian Coalition weighed in with a grassroots mobilization in evangelical and fundamentalist churches against the plan. This "reverse lobbying"—starting from the grassroots and working up to national organizations—defeated the White House strategy of winning interest group endorsements from the top down.[43] Lulled by an increase in his own approval ratings between September and late November of 1993, Clinton failed to mobilize support either in Congress or among interest groups, ending up with only his core liberal supporters. To keep them on board Clinton had to up the ante, backing away from a cap on premium deductibility, adding prescription drug benefits to Medicare, and adding provisions for home-based care for the elderly. None of these concessions to the liberals would help him forge a winning coalition in the center.

The Clintons hoped for strong endorsements from corporations, but at best they won tepid support for general principles. The National Leadership Coalition for Health-Care Reform, with former presidents Carter and Ford serving as honorary chairs, supported cost containment, universal coverage, and employer mandates—but not the Clinton plan. The Small Business Legislative Council, consisting of one hundred trade and professional associations, favored price freezes. The five largest health insurers, organized as the Alliance for Managed Competition, supported competition among service providers. The Corporate Health Care Coalition (big business) would accept an employer mandate. Businesses with older, manufacturing, and unionized workers tended to favor some reform, but those with younger service and nonunionized workers did not. HMOs held off on supporting the president because of doubts about provisions that would prevent actuarial enrollment and that would require "community rating" and access for everyone.[44] Clinton never won business endorsement for his plan.

Congress Fragments

As Clinton's support among the public ebbed and the possibility of interest group support evaporated, Congressional Republicans went for political advantage rather than compromise. In December 1993 a memo from neoconservative strategist William Kristol to Republican legislators argued that Clinton was engaged in "a brazen political strategy of fear-mongering, conducted on a scale not seen since the Chicken Little energy crisis speeches of President Carter." He warned that "the urge to negotiate a 'least bad' compromise with the Democrats, and thereby gain momentary credit for helping the president 'do something' about health care should . . . be resisted." Kristol went on to observe that Clinton's plan is "a serious threat to the Republican party. Republicans must therefore clearly understand the political strategy implicit in the Clinton plan—and then adopt an aggressive and uncompromising counter strategy designed to delegitimize the proposal and defeat its partisan purposes."[45] House Republicans organized fifty town meetings in late December in twenty-four states to demonstrate public opposition to the Clinton plan.[46]

Republicans followed their standard tactic in blunting Democratic social welfare initiatives: introduce an alternative approach to establish their bona fides as problem-solvers with the public, then simultaneously characterize the presidential plan as a radical departure from accepted principles as well as a bureaucratic nightmare that would lead to red tape and corruption. Republican House Minority Leader Michel introduced a measure that would require insurance companies to end bars on preexisting condition coverage and prohibit the cancellation of coverage for people with illnesses. But this ban would mean little without universal coverage and community rating; by admitting sicker people into the pools, insurance companies would have to raise premiums, which in turn would induce young and healthy workers and their families to drop coverage, which then would drive premiums for remaining policyholders higher, thus driving even more healthy young people out of the pool. Insurance companies referred to this as the "death spiral." Michel's proposal would also provide for tax-advantaged "Medisave Accounts," irreconcilable with Republican calls for a balanced budget. There was no way these proposals would ever pass Congress, but that was never the point.

Close to half of the Senate Republicans, including minority leader Bob Dole (R-KS), signed onto Senator Lincoln Chafee's (R-RI) proposal, which would require those without insurance to purchase coverage and would subsidize those who could not. The plan would be funded by reductions in Medicare and Medicaid—another proposal likely to go nowhere, since Democrats would never agree. Some Republicans later backed a bill proposed by Dole, also crafted for political effect, which would guarantee access to insurance and provide subsidies for poor Americans but with no universal coverage and no cost-containment.

Clinton did not have to worry about these nonstarter Republican proposals, provided he could keep Democrats in line. After his bill was introduced, the White House held a two-day "health care university" for members of Congress to explain its provisions, but the session failed to bring the party together. One hundred liberal Democrats broke away and sponsored the American Health

Security Act, a single-payer plan sponsored by Jim McDermott (D-WA) in the House and by Paul Wellstone (D-MN) in the Senate. It would create a Medicare-style program for the entire nation, with uniform benefits and universal coverage. It would bypass the insurance companies, since everything would be funded by the national government, financed through payroll and income taxes. They claimed taxpayers would save $1,500 annually because they would no longer pay private insurance premiums, and federal and state governments would save $100 billion or more annually on administrative costs. At the other end of the spectrum, conservative House Democrats backed the Cooper-Grandy bill, which would not provide universal coverage, would not have premium caps, and would use managed competition to hold costs down.

Clinton hoped to bring the single-payer faction in with his party's moderates and then negotiate a final compromise with the Republican leadership. "We'll work something out," Dole kept reassuring Clinton.[47] The White House established its "war room" (dubbed the Delivery Room) in room 108 on the main floor of the Old Executive Office Building, with seventy-five aides to handle the media campaign, congressional and party liaison, instant response to news stories, speech scheduling for Hillary Clinton and cabinet members, publicity events, liaison with friendly interest groups (such as unions and hospital workers), and daily coordination with the Department of Health and Human Services. The Democratic National Committee assigned twenty staffers to coordinate mailings to party members, in an effort headed by former Ohio governor Richard Celeste. These efforts, known as the National Health Care Campaign, were top-down and media-oriented, but most groups they approached gave at best a "yes but" response, filled with further demands to move health care reform in their direction. Grassroots organizing for the plan did not go beyond some labor union and surrogate organizations representing the poor. The health care effort was soon relegated to a "special project" of the party.[48] Eventually the White House media consultants pulled the plug on the funding for grassroots work, preferring to concentrate on television advertisements.[49]

The White House lost the initiative over the winter months. Clinton was preoccupied with erupting foreign crises and domestic scandals, and Harold Ickes was then taken off health care issues and assigned to contain the scandals and to coordinate the political operations at the Democratic National Committee for the midterm elections. On the defensive, Clinton neglected to explain to the public the particulars of the plan, and to the extent it was being explained, it was by its critics. With evidence that price pressure on insurance premiums were moderating, with an increase in managed competition, with greater use of generic drugs, and with the consolidation of health care organizations, the public had less reason to believe that health care was in crisis.

Between September 22, 1993 and January 31, 1994, public support for the Clinton plan dropped from 67 percent to 48 percent, according to *Washington Post/ABC News* polls.

Clinton's opportunity to rebound came in January 1994, when he delivered his State of the Union address. He talked of 58 million Americans who lacked health care at times during the year and of the 81 million with preexisting conditions. Then, based on the advice of his political advisers, Clinton brandished a pen, and warned: "I want to make this very clear. . . . If you send me legislation that does not guarantee every American private health insurance that can never be taken away, you will force me to take this pen and veto that legislation, and we'll come right back here and start all over again." For a president who lacked the votes, it was not a good idea to deliver that challenge.

Senator Dole delivered the Republican response, claiming that "America has the best health care system in the world" and that there was "no health care crisis." He argued that the complex Clinton plan would mean "more cost. Less choice. More taxes. Less quality. More government control. Less control for you and your family." He warned that "the president's idea is to put a mountain of bureaucrats between you and your doctor," and called for health reform "without triple bypass surgery." In the House, Richard Armey (R-TX) produced a chart with spaghettilike strands, showing the bureaucracy that would oversee the doctors—even the White House had counted more than ninety new bureaucracies in its plan.

Media coverage turned sour, as George Will unfairly claimed that under the Clinton plan patients would face 15-year jail terms for trying to obtain medical care they needed that the government did not deem necessary. His analysis disregarded the provisions to allow individuals to purchase any health care services they wished, as well as any supplemental insurance they might choose.[50] Elizabeth McCaughey, a policy analyst at the Manhattan Institute, weighed in with "No Exit" in the *New Republic,* claiming that coverage would decrease, costs would rise, doctors could only be paid by the government (ending fee-for-service care), and patients could not choose their own doctor.[51] Clinton seemed to be losing ground. Instead of mounting a sustained counterattack, he and media advisers relied on vague rhetorical gimmicks and slogans such as "health care that can never be taken away."

Even worse, the Congressional Budget Office (CBO) reported that the Clinton numbers didn't add up: His plan would not reduce the deficit but would add $74 billion to it in the first six years (though it did find savings after seven years in overall health costs). The CBO wanted the employer mandate to be considered a tax, as the Republicans had suggested, because the payments were mandatory and would fund a new entitlement to health care.[52] The amount would involve more than half a trillion dollars—a nice round sum that Republicans began referring as the Clinton tax increase. The Republican attacks and the difficulties with the CBO either caused or coincided with a drop in public support for Clinton's plan into the low 40s.[53] The focus by early February had shifted from the Clinton plan as the solution to the Clinton plan as the problem. The Republican National Committee spent $500,000 on advertisements promoting its own approach, though it protested a policy by the three networks that banned "advocacy" advertising, a policy that prevented it from reaching a national audience in a $2 million campaign that was to be paid for by entrepreneur and former presidential candidate Ross Perot.

Clinton also lost all chance of gaining interest group support. On February 3, the Business Council endorsed the Cooper bill (later followed by the Business Roundtable), under pressure from the health insurers in its membership. The following day the Chamber of Commerce withdrew its support for the principles in the Clinton plan. The day after that the National Association of Manufacturers governing board declared its opposition, and soon thereafter the Chamber of Commerce came out against the Clinton plan. The AMA began its advertisements: "Would you rather trust your life to an M.D. or an MBA?"

Throughout the spring and summer interest groups went on the offensive in a $100 million lobbying, campaign contribution, and public relations campaign against Clinton's bill.[54] In addition to the HIAA's "Harry and Louise ads," Americans for Tax Reform came up with a radio spot in which a desperate mother is required to call "1-800-Government" and get a "health-care representative" on the line before she can get a doctor to see her seriously ill baby. "Why did they let the government take over?" she cries. "I need my family doctor back." Citizens for a Sound Economy ran radio ads in which a mother, trying to reach "Dr. Murray," her family doctor, hears a "government gatekeeper" tell her: "Under health reform all Americans, and that includes you and your son, will have to go through government health alliances with gatekeepers like me. We will decide who, when, or even if you need to see a doctor." Hillary Clinton, responding to this media barrage, remained on the defensive, with lame comebacks such as: "The only choice we're trying to take away is from those insurance companies that are funding the ad so they can no longer choose to disqualify you from health care because they want to do so or charge you more than they would have otherwise."[55] President Clinton urged audiences not to listen to actors who were paid to deliver their lines: "We want to talk about real people and real medical problems. . . ."[56]

The terms of the debate had been changed: "Freedom to choose" seemed to many people to be in jeopardy under the Clinton plan. There is little evidence that the ads by themselves changed many minds, but coverage of the campaign by the media left the impression that the health insurers were winning over the public, and their lobbyists gained influence in Congress.[57] White House poll data in March indicated that the public still did not understand the plan, so spokespersons discussed specifics: the guarantee of private insurance that could never be taken away; a choice of doctor and health care plan; new regulations on insurance companies; protecting Medicare for the elderly; and guaranteed health benefits for workers. Clinton explained how the plan would work and denied that the slump of public support for the plan was anything more than a temporary fluctuation. In town hall meetings Clinton would "take testimony" from doctors, patients, and hospital administrators describing the problems they faced making the existing system work. He would then affirm that things would be different after his plan was enacted.[58] These town meetings went badly: Clinton was often distracted by questions about his character and the Whitewater scandal (charges involving Clinton's tenure as governor in Arkansas in the 1980s). "What's really going on in the heartland of America gets lost in a cloud of hot air" in Washington, Clinton complained, imploring voters to tell Congress "to deal with this issue and not fool with it anymore."[59]

But interest groups were drowning out the White House message. A National Right to Life advertisement warned that "The Clinton Plan equals involuntary euthanasia" requiring "your child or grandmother to die against her will." The Christian Coalition mobilized its chapters in opposition. The American Council for Health Care Reform mailed brochures to millions of people warning that if they bought additional care, above and beyond the choices from the Health Care Alliance, they would face five years in jail. In fact, criminal penalties in Clinton's bill referred only to bribing a doctor, and under the plan people would still have had the right to purchase any health care services they wished.[60] A study by the Annenberg School for Communications at the University of Pennsylvania found that more than one-quarter of the print advertisements and more than half of the broadcast spots were "unfair, misleading, or false" and failed to disclose the origins and interests of their sponsors.[61]

Most Americans remained confused and skeptical, believed Clinton's plan had too many bureaucratic layers, and were unconvinced that their health care options would be improved and their costs contained.[62] A majority of people thought the plan would cost far more than the president had estimated.[63] Clinton was never able to allay fears that the mechanisms would raise costs, reduce coverage, and increase taxes, and his attempts to explain the specifics seemed to backfire; for reasons the White House could not explain, the problem seemed to be more with Clinton than with the principles his plan embodied. In March 1994, *Wall Street Journal*/NBC polls found a majority opposed to the Clinton plan, 45–37. But when his proposals were presented without identifying them as Clinton's, opinion shifted, with 76 percent saying it had some or great appeal.[64] By June, voter opposition to any plan with Clinton's name on it had risen to 49 percent, although 76 percent of Americans supported guaranteed coverage for all.[65] Newt Gingrich (R-GA) taunted Democrats: "We're told by pollsters you lose 20 to 30 points automatically if you put Clinton's name in front of the term 'plan.'"[66]

Polls indicated that more Americans trusted Congress than the president to handle health care reform.[67] Several congressional committees took that as a green light to develop their own plans. Pat Williams (D-MT), chair of the Subcommittee on Labor-Management Relations, submitted a liberal revision of the Clinton plan, containing more benefits for employers and more subsidies for employees. His committee also reported (without recommending it) a single-payer plan, as a sop to the fifteen liberals on the committee who were dissatisfied with the Clinton approach. Chair Sam Gibbons (D-FL) had a revised bill ready for the Education and Labor Committee; the CBO said that it was revenue neutral (at least until 1998), and Democrats beat back Republican attempts to drop employer mandates and universal coverage. When the committee voted on the revised Clinton plan, not a single Republican voted in favor. A House Ways and Means subcommittee dropped the regional alliances and instead wrote up a plan to extend coverage to the uninsured based on revisions in the Medicare program. Then the full Ways and Means committee approved a version involving private insurance and with universal coverage, on a party line vote, 20–18, with all Republicans and (ominously) three conservative Democrats opposed, along with one liberal Democrat who favored single-payer. The abortion issue split House Democrats: Thirty-five would not vote for a bill *with* coverage for abortions, while sixty-eight indicated they would not vote for a bill *without* it.

In the Senate, Ted Kennedy (D-MA) came up with a version based on Clinton's plan that made participation in the health alliances voluntary, exempted small businesses from the mandate (but required a payroll tax), and allowed anyone to join the federal workers plan, the Federal Employees Health Benefits Plan. But even as centrist amendments passed, Kennedy failed to attract Republicans, with only Jim Jeffords (R-VT) joining. In the Finance Committee the situation was just as bad: After Dole moved toward confrontation rather than negotiation, Moynihan took Republicans up to the White House to convince Clinton that the committee could not report out any bill with universal coverage. Sure enough, the weakened bill it reported set a goal (but not a requirement) of 95 percent coverage by 2002 and called for a new national commission to study universal coverage.

The public wanted more benefits and less regulation and believed that with the Clinton plan they would get the reverse: By July only 17 percent of those surveyed thought Clinton's plan would be an improvement, while 43 percent believed they would receive less care. The interest groups and Republicans had shifted the 10 to 20 percent of public necessary to block Clinton's proposals. To change these poll numbers the Democratic National Committee ran a $250,000 ad campaign featuring its own "Harry and Louise" characters. They lay in bed, Louise with a broken arm, and Harry with a cast from head to toe. Because Harry had lost his job, they didn't have any health insurance. "You said universal coverage was too complicated," Louise complained to Harry. "You said you'd never lose your job so we'd always be covered." The narrator then advised viewers to ask members of Congress "for what *they* already have: the security of affordable, universal health care." Ads were targeted to run in states with wavering Democratic lawmakers, such as Nebraska's Bob Kerrey—who responded negatively to the pressure.[68]

The First Lady and the vice president were enlisted in August for radio and television appearances and newspaper and newsmagazine interviews. Cabinet secretaries talked about universal coverage ("Health Care That's Always There") at "health care forums" timed to coincide with the congressional summer recess. Once Congress returned, the White House organized a "Health Security Express" consisting of bus caravans of Clinton supporters (many of them organized by the American Federation of State, County, and Municipal Employees) joined at various stops by cabinet secretaries. Clinton told crowds that the only way to be assured of health care if his plan didn't pass was to "go on welfare, go to jail, get elected to Congress, or get rich."[69] Dubbed the "phony express" by its critics, Republican hecklers and protesters drowned out speeches at each stop, and media coverage emphasized poor planning, disorganization, and controversies in the caravan.[70] Wags noted that the caravan itself was symptomatic of the health care system, because it kept breaking down.[71] By the end of July, by a two to one margin, Americans agreed with the statement that Congress should "start over next year."[72]

Clinton folded his hand at the summer meeting of the National Governors Association in Boston. In response to a question from Governor Ben Nelson of Nebraska, Clinton talked about a phase-in to universal coverage of "somewhere in the ballpark of ninety-five percent upwards" and that he was open to suggestions about how to pay for it, thus seeming to abandon the idea of an employer mandate. Although he was immediately criticized for having abandoned his own position even before bargaining had begun, in reality little damage had been done, because he was abandoning a plan that was already dead. Everyone jumped ship after Clinton's statement. Mitchell D-ME introduced a bill that would go for 95 percent rather than universal coverage by the year 2000, an employer mandate starting in 2002 that would not exceed 50 percent of any employees premiums (only in states with less than 95 percent coverage), and an exemption for companies with less than twenty-five workers. Clinton said he would sign the Mitchell bill, but neither liberals nor conservatives could work up any enthusiasm for it.

The fate of health care in the Senate was now in the hands of a bipartisan Mainstream Coalition consisting of twenty or so senators looking for something that could pass. Its proposals involved guaranteed access to insurance, encouragement of purchasing cooperatives, subsidies for the poor, and a national commission that would make new recommendations if coverage did not come close to being universal by 2002. To attract fiscal conservatives, it also contained cuts of $50 billion in the deficit in five years, deep cuts in Medicare and Medicaid, a sixty-nine cent cigarette tax, and a tax on high-benefit insurance plans. But liberals and conservatives refused to endorse the plan because of the tax increases, though Clinton seemed amenable if the votes could be rounded up. They could not. On September 20, House and Senate Republican leaders administered the coup de grace: They told Clinton that if health care were considered further in the session, they would block consideration of new legislation to create a World Trade Organization, one of the president's top priorities. Comprehensive health care reform was dead for the remainder of Clinton's presidency.

"What Ifs"

Allen Schick, one of the most acute analysts of Washington politics, has laid out all the "what ifs?":

> What if Clinton had accepted incremental reform at the start rather than at the very end; if he had sent Congress an outline rather than an overdetailed plan; if he had introduced the legislation earlier and not squandered scarce congressional time; if he had reached out more to Republicans and depended less on Democrats; if he had proposed smaller subsidies and less redistribution; if the subsidies had been targeted more strategically to supporters of reform rather than being spent on some who opposed it anyway; if he had attacked drug and insurance companies less and had worked for support from doctors and other affected groups more; if he had steered clear of health alliances and other novel arrangements and relied on familiar institutions instead; if his plan had less regulation and more competition; if, rather than entrusting reform to a special task force, he had worked at the outset with congressional committees and leaders. . . .[73]

Yet had Clinton done most or all of these things, it would have made little difference to the ultimate fate of health care reform in the 1990s.

Viewed in historical perspective, the odds of any major health care innovation were poor, and Clinton's actually got farther than most: The House dealt with several different versions of fundamental reform, and committees reported several different bills; the Senate held an extended debate for two weeks. Most presidents have neither the political capital nor the nerve even to try it.[74] President Franklin Roosevelt removed medical benefits in his Social Security proposals due to opposition from state medical societies and business leaders, lukewarm support from unions, and divisions among his advisers; he did not support a compulsory health insurance plan promoted during the war years by several liberal members of Congress due to stiff opposition from southern conservative Democrats, state medical societies, and a lack of consensus among his economic advisers.[75] President Harry Truman's health insurance plan went nowhere in the "do-nothing" 80th Congress, and although he made political hay out of it in the 1948 election, the Democratic majority in the next Congress stalled health care reform because of opposition from the AMA and its southern Democratic allies. President Lyndon Johnson, armed with a landslide electoral victory and liberal majorities in Congress, nevertheless proposed health insurance only for the elderly and the poor. Because he got Medicare and Medicaid, the separation out of the elderly and the indigent would make it even harder to cover the remaining uninsured population. He had picked all the low-hanging fruit, and viewed from the vantage point of subsequent presidents the policy choices were tougher and the political risks and costs greater to get the rest.

The one major change in health care approved by Congress after 1965 confirms the point. In 1988 Congress by large bipartisan majorities provided Medicare recipients with coverage for catastrophic illness: Within eighteen months the health insurance industry and AMA won repeal of the measure. Senior citizens opposed the measure because many had already bought "medigap" insurance policies covering catastrophic illness—they preferred a market solution to a governmental program that would have required them to pay additional premiums for "universal coverage" (i.e., for other elderly) that would not benefit them. In microcosm, the interest group campaign against the measure and the drop in public support for this redistributive approach presaged Clinton's failure.

Could Clinton have operated incrementally? Paul Starr suggested that Clinton's team tried to do too much and that the lessons of reform are to try for less and do it faster.[76] Clinton himself, looking retrospectively at his efforts, said that he should have taken three years rather than attempt to get the entire package through in a single year.[77] But there is no reason to believe Clinton would have fared any better with that approach. Presidents have not found this to be a winning strategy: President Richard Nixon was unable to get a bill through Congress in 1971 requiring employers to offer all employees a minimum level of medical benefits. Carter had a cost-containment proposal targeted at hospital revenues and capital spending, to be followed by a second stage of comprehensive coverage. The attempt to contain hospital costs was blocked by the AMA and the American Hospital Association, and the bottom line for Congress was that Medicare could not be tampered with—and neither could the hospital reimbursements. A coalition of narrowly based groups, each looking out for itself, defeated President Jimmy Carter's proposal that narrowly distributed sacrifice in order to obtain a broadly based good. This pattern seems to hold whether the changes proposed are comprehensive or incremental.

Health care contained valence issues, not necessarily resolved along a "more or less" compromisable continuum of government funding and involvement but involving fundamental and noncompromisable "yes or no" decisions about values such as the right to choose a family doctor or the right to have abortions covered. Health care was also bound up with the question of Bill and Hillary's character. Clinton had called himself a "New" Democrat, in effect rejecting traditional Democratic programs and approaches, particularly those championed by leaders of Congress. In proposing what in effect was a middle way between Democratic liberalism and Republican conservatism, Clinton left himself open to charges that he lacked any principles at all. Health care, as Clinton himself understood, was not only an attempt to win over congressional Democrats and public opinion but was also an attempt to define himself and his administration. Conservative and liberal Democrats would fight not only over the details of the plan Clinton proposed but also over its overall orientation, understanding themselves that it was more than a fight over legislation but involved the soul of the Democratic Party. Republicans were prepared to have it both ways: If Clinton moved toward the liberals, they would attack him on his ideological positioning. If he presented a conservative plan (market-oriented with cost-containment), they would attack him for being unprincipled and lacking character.[78]

Health care reform was not about how health care was to be provided, it was primarily about how it would be financed. Eighty-five percent of the American people already had some form of health care insurance. Only 15 percent needed the universal coverage to replace either the publicly subsidized care they received from clinics or emergency rooms. The majority was being asked to make fundamental changes and accept more regulation and higher costs but would receive no tangible benefits for themselves. At best there would be lower medical costs for the country and a public good (better health for those now uninsured). Gallup polls indicated that nine out of ten Americans were "very or somewhat" satisfied with their medical care.[79] Until a plan was proposed, people worried about the health care crisis and claimed they wanted reform; once specifics were offered people could weigh the costs (lower benefits or higher premiums) if it were adopted. The White House would find it difficult to distribute the losses fairly or even to acknowledge publicly that there would be losses.

Policy Carts before Party Horses

President Thomas Jefferson once warned that "great innovations should not be forced on slender majorities."[80] Yet Clinton was doing exactly that. He had won office with 43 percent of the vote in a three-way race, was a newcomer to the Washington community, and had no committed following in Congress. Democrats had lost ten seats in the House and two in the Senate, then would lose a succession of special House elections, as well as gubernatorial and mayoralty elections, in his first year in office.

Managing the trade-offs in health care policy are insurmountable unless a president presides over a political realignment or has won a large party margin in Congress. Clinton proposed a complex health care plan involving the rearrangement of one-seventh of the American economy. He was attempting to pass a "breakthrough" policy without having had a breakthrough election.[81] In spite of his political weakness, Clinton put a comprehensive health care bill on the national agenda in 1993, even though other measures had failed six times in the twentieth century. Congress would not have dealt with health care without a White House initiative: Clinton was making strong demands on his colleagues for action and strong demands on a vulnerable party. One memo by Magaziner suggested that to win the president would have to hold all liberal and moderate Democrats, win most conservative Democrats, and then attract fifteen to twenty Republicans in the House and eight to ten moderate Republicans in the Senate.[82] Treasury secretary Lloyd Bentsen, budget director Leon Panetta, and communications strategist George Stephanopoulos all hoped to delay action until 1994, believing that the legislative agenda was too full, with economic issues paramount. But Clinton made the key decision to move forward based on his political stakes. He had to get out in front of Senators Kennedy and Wofford and other liberal Democrats; he had to fashion a health care program to secure his liberal base and to demonstrate party leadership.[83] Health care became his touchstone issue to create a dominant political coalition; he would use it to fashion a resounding victory for his party in 1994 that would open up the rest of his legislative agenda.

Making health care the defining issue for a reinforcing midterm election put the legislative cart before the electoral horse. To attempt to get a comprehensive health care plan through Congress would require that party government already be in place in order to overcome the constraints that had defeated all major health care initiatives (with the exception of Medicare and Medicaid). Clinton acted as if he already had some of the advantages of party government—as if the votes would be there if he needed them. He did have a nominal Democratic majority in both chambers, and since the mid-1980s party voting and party cohesion in Congress had greatly increased. Yet to the extent that Clinton had party government, he had the disadvantages without the advantages. He had a party platform that expressed concern for the poor and pledged action to improve the lot of the middle class. Health care was an issue that Democrats were expected to deal with, expected to deliver on. Yet it was a deeply partisan and ideologically polarizing issue in the party. With fewer southern Democratic conservatives the Democrats had become more ideologically consistent and cohesive on many issues—but not on health care.

Democrats were split three ways: Liberals wanted a single-payer nationalized system; centrists wanted increased coverage within the existing system; and conservatives were not prepared for anything more than minor modifications and were responsive to the interest groups. None of these factions trusted Clinton to protect their interests: All believed, correctly, that Clinton's own strategy might leave them hanging out to dry if they supported his plan, since sooner or later he would modify the provisions they cared about to come up with votes from other groups for the final deal. The problem of forging party unity in Congress was exacerbated by the divisions in the White House. While the First Lady and Magaziner were trying to forge a coalition of Democrats around their plan, Chief of Staff Mac McClarty, counselor David Gergen, and some of the economic advisers were quietly urging centrists to "hang in there," presumably as a counterweight to the more liberal plans and as an eventual anchor for a bipartisan compromise.[84] Bipartisan consensus building would also be difficult: What would be in it for the Republicans that would be better than leaving Clinton out to dry?

"A lot of people . . . say it would be an outright miracle if we passed health care reform," Clinton observed in his September 22 address to Congress. "But . . . in a time of change you have to have miracles. And miracles do happen." Then again, most times they don't. In retrospect (it is always easier to see things in retrospect) the only chance Clinton might have had involved Moynihan's original advice on timing: First deal with welfare reform and construct a bill that would cement the Democratic coalition. Having established his authority in domestic policymaking, Clinton then might have been able to build the party coalition for health care reform. Of course, the more likely outcome was that welfare reform itself would split the party asunder, making the larger issue of health care reform a nonstarter.

Spatial Positioning versus Valence Politics

Was Clinton an amateur in health care? Did he develop a policy that he
thought was the most technically compelling and effective, and *then* try to
round up the votes? Some who have studied these events believe that Clinton
had proposed a technocratic, professional solution that was designed to be
above partisan dividing lines and that he and his advisers erroneously believed
that their proposal was an "efficiency" solution, dominating inferior options,
and could eventually be sold to Congress as the most effective policy solution
to a national crisis.[85] But there is considerable evidence that Clinton acted as
a professional, defining his policy proposals in terms of what it would take to
create and hold a congressional coalition.

Given the splits in the party and Republican opposition, Clinton would
have to zig and zag to create a coalition. Clinton moved to the right during his
presidential campaign by embracing managed competition, then moved to
the left when the plan was being framed by the task force by approving comprehensive benefits, inclusive purchasing alliances, coverage for abortions,
drugs, home and mental health services, and universal coverage. Clinton's
strategy *was* political, because it was built around "compromisable issues."
Even Ira Magaziner understood early on that the plan would require bipartisan support and the endorsement of business and health provider groups. The
80 percent mandate on employers was to be negotiable, and Clinton could
pick up support as he moved the mandate down to 50 percent. The plan required all employers except those with five thousand workers or more to join
the health alliances, a number that many expected to be lowered during congressional negotiations. In trying to build a winning coalition, large corporations were promised that the administration would pick up the medical costs
of their early retirees; small businesses were promised subsidies to defray costs
of insuring employees. The administration expected to continue bargaining
over the details until groups signed on, much as Carter had done with his energy package.

As it turned out, Clinton was positioned too far to the left as the congressional game began to quickly pick up the moderate to conservative Democrats
from border and southern states—Clinton's own political base. In the Senate,
his position meant that he could never get sixty votes past a filibuster.[86] Perhaps he would have been better off starting closer to the bipartisan centrist
position, but to do so he would have had to jettison the White House task
force apparatus and would have had to contend with Hillary Clinton and her
allies.

The real problem was that Clinton did not understand the game the Republicans were playing. It was not *spatial* politics, in which adroit positioning

on "more or less" issues would count; rather it was *valence* politics, in which highly charged themes would be used to encourage a "thumbs down" judgment on a health care initiative taken as a whole—and on the president who had proposed it. In a valence game, maneuver and changes in position do not bring additional support but rather are signs of weakness. Movement begins a process of erosion. This was the way Bill Kristol advised Republicans to play the game: "We want to use the health care debate as a model for routing contemporary liberalism and advancing an aggressive conservative agenda."[87] This was the way Representatives Michel, Gingrich, and Armey and Senator Dole played it. Their game was about building a conservative majority in the next national election and not about coalition building to pass a compromise bill.

Strategic and Tactical Failures

On any given issue, as the Clinton's health care fiasco demonstrates, a president who lives by the media may die by the media: An effort to gain public support may lead to a backlash and end with public opposition. A White House attempt to reach the people directly calls forth a reaction by opponents who often have greater media resources. In an antipolitics culture, when public confidence in government was at one of its lows, a plan as comprehensive as the Clintons' would be vulnerable. Unlike foreign policy crises, there is no "rally round the flag" effect in domestic affairs when crisis rhetoric is deployed.

The Clinton "testimonial" approach was wrong-headed: It emphasized emotional moments and empathetic bonding—"I feel your pain"—rather than information, analysis, and choice. It was organized as a campaign, with mass advertising, town meetings, talk show appearances, and bus caravans. The administration's discussion was scripted to sound-bite dimensions. The testimonials were organized in advance, as were the responses. By not giving audiences anything of substance, the administration also gave the media little of substance to report. Clinton substituted assertion and testimony for argument. He failed to provide historical context, to define terms, to describe mechanisms. He did not lay out alternatives or discuss their costs and benefits. He offered two choices for the people: the right way and the wrong way. The reaction was inevitable: No one wants to be subject to a high-pressure sales pitch masquerading as a religious revival.

The White House erred by taking public opinion polls at face value, because what people *said* in the polls is not what they *felt*. The middle class was looking for more security and benefits, and at lower cost, and an end to waste in the system—and that is what respondents meant by health care reform. They had no urge to pay more, to make sacrifices, and consider trade-offs or to extend benefits—even when people answered yes when asked if they supported reform. The wording of the polls didn't indicate the "stop signs"—the choices that people would *oppose* once they became aware of them. Nor did polls indicate the sentiment that would soon emerge against "big government" running health care programs. People were worried that their choice of doctor or hospital would be curtailed, that they would not be able to receive certain services, that their taxes would go up, that there would be fraud and abuse, that quality would decline, that the bureaucracy would increase. The polls didn't indicate the worries people had that the Clinton plan would hurt people like themselves. They didn't indicate that the public had not understood the trade-offs that might be involved. Clinton would have to allay these fears to win over public opinion, but he was unable to do so. The more the issues were discussed, the more people tuned out: Between September and December 1993, the proportion of people reporting that they knew a lot about Clinton's plan dropped from 21 to 13 percent.[88]

The Clintons themselves became the issue. The plan should have been the Shalala plan, or the Moynihan plan, but certainly not the Clinton plan, which personalized the policy. And because Clinton assigned innovation to his wife and Magaziner—the latter portrayed in the media as a combination oddball wonk and Svengali—the cast of characters didn't help. President Truman was able to get European reconstruction through a Republican Congress by identifying it as the "Marshall Plan," thus borrowing the prestige of General of the Army George C. Marshall; Clinton was unable to get health care through a Democratic Congress in part because it was identified so closely with himself. If it were to be the Clinton plan, and if were to be a plan to help the Clintons politically, to energize his presidency and strengthen the Democratic majority—why would Republicans want to do anything to help?

It was precisely *because* this plan was so well crafted to fit into the president's power stakes, and precisely *because* it fit into the model of a "professional" president defining the national interest in terms of his own, that it could not get through Congress. It offered a great deal to the Clintons but not enough to legislators, interest groups, or the American voter. "We will make history by reforming the health-care system," Clinton told Congress in his 1994 State of the Union Address. But unable to understand or negotiate effectively within a labyrinthine legislative process he was just beginning to master, Clinton was his own worst enemy. "I set the Congress up for failure," he admitted after the legislative struggle had ended.[89] By seeking always a middle ground when there was no middle ground, by attempting to overcome poor initial spatial positioning when it is doubtful there was any space for any version of comprehensive reform, by proposing a bill that could not be sustained by his party without modifications that would cut out its heart, each of Clinton's interventions only made matters worse, particularly each ill-timed effort to negotiate, all of which involved giving up principles (such as universal coverage in late June) that had supposedly been inviolate.

Had Clinton understood the game he was in, he would have recognized that absent a party realignment in the 1992 elections, health care reform would be a losing game. He then could have made health care a pure "valence" play as a prelude to the realignment he would be seeking in the 1996 elections. He would not have gotten health care reform passed, but he would have gotten political credit for the attempt. His proposal would have simply been a piece on the political board. Clinton never asked, "What can I get by sacrificing this piece?" So perhaps Clinton's problem was not that he didn't act as a "professional" in proposing health care reform; rather, it was that he did not take the "professional presidency" calculations far enough. It might have been possible for him at least to have used health care to make major political gains. Then conceivably in his second term, flush with large Democratic majorities more prepared to implement his program, he might have gotten a large part of the health care program passed. Instead, Clinton wound up with less than zero for his pains, having lost the valence issues to the opposition, especially the traditional Democratic "fairness" issue. When asked if the plan would be "fair to people like you, or not?" in the *CBS News/New York Times* polls, the proportion indicating it would be fair went from 51 percent when the plan was introduced by the president to 38 percent by April 1994, while those saying unfair went from 21 percent to 48 percent.

In part due to the health care fiasco, Democrats lost the 1994 midterm congressional elections. An election night exit poll sponsored by the Henry J. Kaiser Family Foundation indicated that a large majority of those who voted Republican believed that the Democratic plan had too much bureaucracy and would have reduced the quality of their health care.[90] A majority said they wanted incremental change rather than comprehensive reform, and wanted Congress, rather than the president, to take the lead. Democrats, but not Republican voters, felt cross-pressured by their party's position on the issue. No Republican who opposed health care lost a seat. But Senator Wofford lost and Rep. James Cooper (D-TN) lost, and so did many other Democrats identified with health care reform.

Clinton had not only lost his congressional majorities but also his chance to reshape health care. Subsequent changes were "de-incremental," as cuts in Medicaid at the state and national level became the most significant "reforms." Health care seemed to be evolving into a three-tier system, with the best professional care that money could buy for the affluent; managed care, HMOs, preferred provider and other health insurance plans for the middle class and working class; and overstaffed public hospital emergency rooms and clinics for the working poor ineligible for Medicaid. After the Clinton debacle, 31 percent of Americans lacked health insurance—and 70 percent of them were employed.

Clinton thereafter signed incremental health measures he once had vowed to veto. Even more ironic, the president who had stumbled politically when trying to enact health care reform in 1994 gained political strength by defending the existing health care system. "I won't let government mess with your Medicare," became Clinton's rallying cry, one that propelled him to political successes in 1996. By his second term, millions of American workers were enrolled in managed health care plans that raised costs, cut benefits, and imposed stringent requirements. Clinton had come full circle, proposing a major overhaul of Medicare, with the same dubious fiscal assumptions and unwieldy administrative approach that doomed his first plan, and no restructuring of the rest of the health care system, which remained in danger of fiscal collapse. By the end of his presidency there were 44.3 million Americans without coverage, 4.5 million more than when Clinton first proposed his health care plan. Corporations were cutting benefits to retirees and workers, and small employers were canceling health benefits. The World Health Organization ranked the United States 24 in life expectancy and 15 in overall effectiveness in delivering services, although it continued to rank first in per capita expenditures.

Notes

1. William Jefferson Clinton, "Address to Joint Session of Congress on Health Care Reform," *Weekly Compilation of Presidential Documents* vol. 29 (September 22, 1993): 1837–38.

2. Haynes Johnson and David Broder, *The System: The American Way of Politics at the Breaking Point* (Boston: Little, Brown, 1996), 622.

3. Lawrence R. Jacobs, "Politics of America's Supply State: Health Reform and Technology," *Health Affairs* (Summer 1995): 143–57.

4. Henry Aaron, *The Problem That Won't Go Away: Reforming U.S. Health Care Financing* (Washington, DC: Brookings Institution, 1996).

5. R. J. Blendon and K. Donelan, "Public Opinion and Efforts to Reform the U.S. Health Care System: Confronting Issues of Cost-containment and Access to Care," *Stanford Law and Policy Review* (Fall 1991): 147.

6. Harris Wofford, "In 1991, Pennsylvania Sen. Harris Wofford Rode His Support for Health Care Reform to Election. This Year, Wofford Sees Parallels to His Race in the Presidential Contest. Health Care, After a Hiatus During the Primaries, Is Back as a 'Sharp, Defining Issue.'" *Roll Call*, September 28, 1992.

7. T. Hamburger, T. Marmor, and J. Meacham, "What the Death of Health Reform Teaches Us about the Press," *Washington Monthly* vol. 26, no. 11 (November 1994): 35–41.

8. Robert J. Blendon, J. N. Edwards, and A. L. Hyams, "Making the Critical Choices," *Journal of the American Medical Association* vol. 267, no. 18 (May 13, 1992): 2509–20.

9. "Canadian Insurance: Lessons for the United States," General Accounting Office (Washington, DC: U.S. Government Printing Office, 1990).

10. William Clinton, "The Clinton Health Care Plan," *New England Journal of Medicine* (September 10, 1992): 804–6. On "managed competition" see Alain C. Enthoven, "A Consumer-Choice Health Plan for the 1990s: Universal Health Insurance in a System Designed to Promote Quality and Economy," *New England Journal of Medicine* vol. 320, no. 2 (January 12, 1989): 94–101.

11. Elizabeth Drew, *On the Edge: The Clinton Presidency* (New York: Simon & Schuster, 1994), 191.

12. Bob Woodward, *The Agenda: Inside the Clinton White House* (New York: Simon & Schuster, 1994), 44–50.

13. Robert Blendon et al., "Public Opinion and Health Care," *Journal of the American Medical Association* vol. 268 (1992): 371–75.

14. George Gallup, *The Gallup Poll 1993* (Wilmington, DE: Scholarly Resources, 1994): 19.

15. Allen Schick, "How a Bill Did Not Become a Law," in Thomas E. Mann and Norman J. Ornstein, eds., *Intensive Care: How Congress Shapes Health Policy* (Washington, DC: AEI and Brookings Institution, 1995), 233.

16. Lawrence Jacobs and Robert Shapiro, "Questioning the Conventional Wisdom on Public Opinion toward Health Reform," *PS* vol. 27, no. 2 (June 1994): 208–14.

17. Roper Center poll, November 3, 1992.

18. James Todd et al., "Health Access America—Strengthening the U.S. Health Care System," *Journal of the American Medical Association* vol. 265, no. 19 (May 15, 1991): 2503–6.

19. Julie Rovner, "Governors Ask Relief . . .," *Congressional Quarterly Weekly Report* (February 16, 1991): 3303.

20. Ira Magaziner, "Preliminary Work Plan for Interagency Health Care Task Force," unpublished manuscript, 1993.

21. Drew, *On the Edge*, 192. For a contrary view claiming Magaziner's memo called for consultation with all affected interest groups and a serious communications strategy, see Theda Skocpol, *Boomerang: Health Care Reform and the Turn against Government* (New York: W. W. Norton, 1996), 51.

22. For a full narrative see Jacob Hacker, *The Road to Nowhere: The Genesis of President Clinton's Plan for Health Security* (Princeton, NJ: Princeton University Press, 1997).

23. *New York Times* (January 26, 1993): A-1.

24. Polls cited in Julie Rovner, "Congress and Health Care Reform 1993–1994," in Mann and Ornstein, eds., *Intensive Care*, 185.

25. American Medical Association, *Health Access America: The AMA Proposal to Improve Access to Affordable, Quality Health Care* (Chicago: AMA, 1990).

26. *Association of American Physicians and Surgeons, Inc., v. Clinton*, 813 F. Supp. 82 (D.D.C. 1993).

27. *Association of American Physicians and Surgeons, Inc., v. Clinton*, 997 F. 2d. 898 (D.C. Cir., 1993).

28. Jacob Weisberg, "Dies Ira," *New Republic* (January 24, 1994): 10.

29. Woodward, *The Agenda*, 165.

30. These included pollster Stanley Greenberg and strategists Mandy Grunwald and Paul Begala. Elizabeth Drew, *On the Edge*, 193.

31. Drew, *On the Edge*, 306.

32. Woodward, *The Agenda*, 200.

33. Skocpol, *Boomerang*, 115.

34. Richard Neustadt, *Presidential Power and the Modern Presidents: The Politics of Leadership from Roosevelt to Reagan* (New York: John Wiley, 1960).

35. Johnson and Broder, *The System*, 150.

36. William Jefferson Clinton, "Address to Joint Session of Congress on Health Care Reform," *Weekly Compilation of Presidential Documents* vol. 29, no. 38 (September 22, 1993): 1836–46.

37. Clifford Krauss, "Congress Praises President's Plan but Is Wary of Taxes and Costs," *New York Times* (September 23, 1993): A-20.

38. Rovner, "Congress and Health Care Reform 1993–94," in Mann and Ornstein, eds., *Intensive Care*, 194.

39. Frank R. Baumgartner and Jeffery C. Talbott, "From Setting a National Agenda on Health Care to Making Decisions in Congress," *Journal of Health Politics, Policy and Law* vol. 20, no. 2 (Summer 1995): 441.

40. William Jefferson Clinton, "Nomination Acceptance Speech," Democratic National Nominating Convention, July 16, 1992.

41. Bill Clinton and Al Gore, *Putting People First: How We Can All Change America* (New York: Times Books, 1992), 19.

42. Sven Steinmo and Jon Watts, "It's the Institutions, Stupid! Why Comprehensive National Health Insurance Always Fails in America," *Journal of Health Politics, Policy and Law* vol. 20, no. 2 (Summer 1995): 364.

43. Schick, "How a Bill Did Not Become a Law," in Mann and Ornstein, eds., *Intensive Care*, 242–43.

44. Robert Pear, "HMO Leaders Express Doubts on Health Plan," *New York Times* (October 18, 1993): A1.

45. William Kristol, "Defeating President Clinton's Health Care Proposal" (Washington, DC: Project for the Republican Future, 1993).

46. Robin Toner, "Foes Take to the Grass Roots on Clinton Health Proposal," *New York Times* (December 5, 1993): A38.

47. Johnson and Broder, *The System*, 35.

48. Ceci Connolly, "The DNC Aims to Approach Hill from Ground Up," *Congressional Quarterly Weekly Reports* (1994): 2809.

49. Johnson and Broder, *The System*, 294.

50. George Will, "The Clintons' Lethal Paternalism," *Newsweek* (February 7, 1994): 64; for provisions of the law contradicting Will's assertions see Health Security Act, Title I, sec. 1003.

51. Elizabeth McCaughey, "No Exit," *The New Republic* (February 7, 1994).

52. "An Analysis of the Administration's Health Proposal: A CBO Study" (Washington, DC: U.S. Government Printing Office, 1993).

53. Lawrence R. Jacobs and Robert Y. Shapiro, "Don't Blame the Public for Failed Health Care Reform," *Journal of Health Politics, Policy, and Law* 20 (Summer 1995): 411–23. See "Table 3: Evaluation of Clinton's Plan," 419.

54. Rovner, "Congress and Health Care Reform 1993–1994," in Mann and Ornstein, eds., *Intensive Care*, 217; also Kathleen Lewton, "The Death of Health Care Reform," *Public Relations Tactics* (December 1993); Thomas Scarlett, "Killing Health Care Reform: How Clinton's Opponents Used a Political Media Campaign to Lobby Congress and Sway Public Opinion," *Campaigns and Elections* (October/November 1994): 34–37.

55. Robin Toner, "Hillary Clinton Opens Campaign to Answer Critics of Health Plan," *New York Times* (January 16, 1994): A-11.

56. Douglas Jehl, "Clinton Asking Elderly to Support Health Plan," *New York Times* (February 17, 1994): A-20.

57. Kathleen Hall Jamieson, "When Harry Met Louise," *Washington Post National Weekly Edition* (August 22–28, 1994): 20.

58. Lisa Disch, "Publicity-Stunt Participation and Sound Bite Polemics: The Health Care Debate 1993–1994," *Journal of Health Politics, Policy and Law* vol. 21, no. 1 (Spring 1996): 1–32.

59. *New York Times* (April 6, 1994): A-18

60. Rick Wartzman, "Truth Lands in Intensive Care Unit as New Ads Seek to Demonize Clinton's Health-Reform Plan," *Wall Street Journal* (April 29, 1994): A-14.

61. Adam Clymer, "The Overview," *New York Times* (July 26, 1994): A-16.

62. Richard Morin, "Don't Know Much about Health Care Reform," *Washington Post National Weekly Edition* (March 14–20, 1994): 37.

63. Robert J. Blendon et al., "What Happened to Americans' Support of the Clinton Plan?" *Health Affairs* vol. 14, no. 2 (Summer 1995): 16.

64. Hilary Stout, "Many Don't Realize It's the Clinton Plan They Like," *Wall Street Journal* (March 10, 1994): B-1.

65. Richard Berke, "On the Stump, Not Much Talk of Health Care," *New York Times* (July 10, 1994): A12.

66. Katharine Q. Seelye, "Some House Democrats Like Plan but Not Political Risks," *New York Times* (July 30, 1994): A-8.

67. Schick, "How a Bill Did Not Become a Law," in Mann and Ornstein, eds., *Intensive Care*, 236.

68. Joe Klein, "The Religious Left," *Newsweek* (July 25, 1994): 23.

69. Adam Clymer, "Clinton Opens Drive to Push Health Care Plan," *New York Times* (July 19, 1994): A-8.

70. Skocpol, *Boomerang*, 128–29.

71. Catherine Manegold, "Health Care Bus: Lots of Miles, Not So Much Talk," *New York Times* (July 25, 1994): A7.

72. *Newsweek* poll, August 1, 1994.

73. Schick, "How a Bill Did Not Become A Law," in Mann and Ornstein, eds., *Intensive Care*, 228.

74. Steinmo and Watts, "It's the Institutions, Stupid!" 329–69.

75. Jaap Kooijman, "Sooner or Later On: Franklin D. Roosevelt and National Health Insurance, 1933–1945," *Presidential Studies Quarterly* vol. 29, no. 2 (June 1999), 336–50.

76. Paul Starr, "What Happened to Health Care Reform?" *American Prospect* no. 20 (Winter 1995): 20–31.

77. Johnson and Broder, *The System*, 127.

78. Stephen Skowronek, "President Clinton and the Risks of 'Third-Way' Politics," in *Extensions* (Spring 1996): 10–15.

79. American Medical Association, *Public Opinion on Health Care Issues* (Chicago: AMA, 1994); also see Daniel Yankelovich, "The Debate That Wasn't: The Public and the Clinton Health Care Plan," in Henry Aaron, *The Problem*, 76.

80. Letter to General John Armstrong, May 2, 1808.

81. Hugh Heclo, "The Clinton Health Plan: Historical Perspective," in *Health Affairs* (Spring 1995): 86–98.

82. Johnson and Broder, *The System*, 301.

83. Drew, *On the Edge*, 189.

84. Johnson and Broder, *The System*, 315.

85. Johnson and Broder, *The System*, 177.

86. David W. Brady and Kara M. Buckley, "Health Care Reform in the 103d Congress: A Predictable Failure," *Journal of Health Politics, Policy and Law* vol. 20, no. 2 (Summer 1995): 447–54.

87. "Kristol Ball: William Kristol Looks at the Future of the GOP," *Policy Review* no. 47 (Winter 1993): 15.

88. Yankelovich, "The Debate That Wasn't," in Aaron, *The Problem*, 79.

89. Johnson and Broder, *The System*, 609.

90. Henry J. Kaiser Family Foundation, "National Election Night Survey," November 5, 1994.

9

Parallel Governance

Bush and Iraqi Weapons of Mass Destruction

PRESIDENTS RELY ON THEORIES OF GOVERNANCE and doctrines of constitutional law to legitimize their actions. Bush administration lawyers (political partisans for the most part) in the White House Counsel's Office and in the Office of Legal Counsel of the Department of Justice relied on the doctrine of the "unitary executive," developed in the 1980s and 1990s in reaction to the so-called imperiled presidencies of Gerald Ford and Jimmy Carter in the decade before. In brief, this doctrine claimed that both as a matter of constitutional law and practical governance, the executive must be granted what amounts to plenary authority in foreign affairs, national and domestic security matters, intelligence and covert operations, and war powers. To the extent that Congress would play a role, it should confine itself to a "perfecting power" (in a parliamentary sense): It should support the initiatives and policies of the duly elected and appointed administration. It should not (and these lawyers argued that constitutionally it *could* not) fashion framework laws to establish inter-branch policy codetermination.

The Bush administration claimed the prerogatives of the unitary executive, but in fact there was little that was "unitary" about its conduct in national security affairs. As with all other presidents, there were conflicts between career officials and political appointees, among cabinet secretaries (State and Defense especially), and between the staffers of the institutional presidency (such as the National Security Council [NSC]) and everyone else. But what marked a departure from business as usual was an extension of what the Reagan administration had developed in the Iran-Contra affair: The Bush administration established "parallel governance" in gathering, evaluating, and disseminating intelligence in the War on Terrorism. Parallel governance, as described and analyzed in this chapter, led to grave miscalculations about Iraqi capabilities and intentions after the 9/11 attacks, as the administration made the claim that Iraq must be disarmed of weapons of mass destruction—if necessary by military force.

The Run-up to an Invasion

Several months before the United States and its allies invaded Iraq, President George W. Bush addressed the United Nations General Assembly and set forth the rationale for possible military action: "Our greatest fear is that terrorists will find a shortcut to their mad ambitions when an outlaw regime supplies them with technologies to kill on a massive scale. Saddam Hussein's regime is a grave and gathering danger."[1] The administration sent to Congress a nonclassified 92-page National Intelligence Estimate (NIE), predicting with "moderate confidence" that Iraq "probably will have a nuclear weapon during this decade." The report, which had input from fifteen intelligence agencies, stated that Iraq was pursuing chemical, biological, nuclear, and missile programs contrary to United Nations Resolutions that had required their termination. In a speech to the American public a week after delivering the NIE to Congress, the president drew the connection between Iraqi weapons of mass destruction (WMD) and the war on terrorism: "We've learned that Iraq has trained al Qaeda members in bomb-making and poisons and deadly gases. . . . Iraq could decide on any given day to provide a biological or chemical weapon to a terrorist group or individual terrorists."[2] Three days later, on October 10, 2002, Congress passed a resolution authorizing hostilities against Iraq at a date to be determined by the president.

The Iraqi nuclear program had been dismantled under United Nations auspices after the Gulf War in 1991. It took seven years to level the facilities and eliminate all associated equipment, along with radioactive materials. Gamma detection emitters were installed in former facilities to ensure that the program was not reconstituted at these sites. But Bush alluded to intelligence that indicated that the Iraqis were not abiding by their obligations. In Bush's January 2003 State of the Union Address, the president noted that British intelligence had reports that Iraq was attempting to purchase "uranium from Africa." He stated that Iraq had a huge arsenal of WMD, including 26,000 liters of anthrax; 38,000 liters of botulinum toxin; one million pounds of sarin, mustard, and VX nerve agent; 30,000 munitions to deliver these toxic agents; and mobile biological warfare weapons laboratories. The president warned that these weapons could be delivered to terrorists for use against the American people.[3] When the president issued the orders to go to war against Iraq, he sent a report to Congress consistent with provisions of the War Powers Resolution, stating, "I have also determined that the use of armed force against Iraq is consistent with" the need to act against "persons who planned, authorized, committed or aided the terrorist attacks that occurred on September 11, 2001."[4]

The military phase of the war took only a few weeks, as American and British military units moved up from their bases in Kuwait, advancing on the highways along the Tigris and Euphrates rivers, seizing towns along the way, and eventually capturing the "Green Zone" in Baghdad, which was the main compound of the Iraqi government. The Iraqi military sometimes fought and sometimes surrendered; Fedeyeen guerrillas fought rearguard actions but were subdued or melted away to fight again during the years of occupation.

As combat wound down, military and civilian units of the Iraq Survey Group (ISG) fanned out across Iraq looking for the WMD. They found next to nothing. They did find occasional arms caches with shells that were or could be equipped for chemical warfare, but these were old stashes of weapons and were not in good condition. There were no nuclear facilities. There were no chemical processing facilities or bioweapons laboratories. Members of the group prepared a report concluding that Iraq had not had WMD at the time of the invasion, nor had it restarted WMD programs since its 1991 defeat in the Persian Gulf War. Top American and British intelligence officials removed these conclusions out of the ISG reports.[5]

Failure to find WMD became a partisan issue. Democrats charged that Bush had deceived Congress and fraudulently gained its authorization to use force. In a Veteran's Day speech on November 11, 2005, Bush responded angrily to charges that he had misled the American people about these weapons: "While it's perfectly legitimate to criticize my decision or the conduct of the war, it is deeply irresponsible to rewrite the history of how that war began. Some Democrats and anti-war critics are now claiming we manipulated the intelligence and misled the American people about why we went to war. These critics are fully aware that a bipartisan Senate investigation found no evidence of political pressure to change the intelligence community's judgments related to Iraq's weapons programs."[6] Vice President Dick Cheney, speaking before the American Enterprise Institute ten days later, said, "Any suggestion that prewar information was distorted, hyped or fabricated by the leader of the nation is utterly false."[7] But the questions would not go away, and they struck at the legitimacy of the president's decision making. Helen Thomas of Hearst, the dean of Washington news correspondents, challenged the president at a 2006 press conference: "Every reason given, publicly at least, has turned out not to be true. My question is, why did you really want to go to war?"[8]

Why did the Bush administration fail to find WMD in Iraq? The Senate investigation did not find that the judgments of the intelligence community were distorted by political pressure. But that does not answer the question as to whether the administration distorted, hyped, or fabricated evidence. As it turned out, Bush, Cheney, and Secretary of Defense Donald Rumsfeld found ways to bypass the intelligence community, by setting up parallel intelligence gathering and analysis groups that would assist the administration to make its case.

Prewar Intelligence

The United States and Iraq did not have diplomatic relations prior to the war, and so there was no American embassy that could gather information. American intelligence agencies had few Arabic speakers. Much of the intelligence gathering relied on three approaches: electronic surveillance of telecommunications and high-resolution satellite imagery; monitoring of Iraqi and other Gulf newspapers, radio, and television reportage; and the use of informants in the country or exiles, many of whom were brought to intelligence agencies by an exile organization, the Iraqi National Congress (INC). From these sources, intelligence agencies gathered a picture of Iraqi weapons development since the Persian Gulf War. They focused on several worrisome developments. But professional intelligence analysts in the CIA, the military, and the State Department all found reasons to doubt that the information about Iraqi WMD development was credible.

Yellowcake from Niger

In President Bush's State of the Union Address in 2003 he told the American people that "the British Government has learned that Saddam Hussein recently sought significant quantities of uranium from Africa." The evidence involved letters on Niger government letterhead and contracts of sale to Iraq. The American embassy in Rome had been given these letters by the Italian magazine *Panorama*.[9] The magazine in turn had received them from Rocco Martino, an executive and a former freelance spy for Italian military intelligence. He claimed to have gotten them from a friend who worked in Niger's Italian embassy.[10] The International Atomic Energy Agency (IAEA) took a look at the documents and concluded they were forgeries: A Niger official who had signed them was no longer in office on the date he supposedly signed, and the seals were incorrect. A French mining company tightly controlled the yellowcake uranium, and it would have been impossible for the Iraqis to negotiate a contract with that company. In December 2002 IAEA director Mohammed el-Baradei communicated his doubts to the White House. German intelligence and the U.S. State Department's Bureau of Intelligence and Research all thought the sales were "unlikely and the documents were a forgery."[11] A four-star general, Carlton W. Fulford Jr., went to Niger to investigate and concluded that the sales had never taken place.[12] The CIA on three occasions warned Stephen Hadley, the deputy director of the NSC, not to use the documents to make the claim that Iraq was developing nuclear weapons.[13] Alan Foley, the director of the CIA counterproliferation effort, tried to get the White House to remove the yellowcake claim from the President's State of the Union Address. But the NSC staff inserted it into the draft of the presidential address, even after Foley's warning. (The intelligence on the purchase was so suspect that Secretary of State Colin Powell refused to use it when he addressed the United Nations.)

Aluminum Tubes for Centrifuges

If the Iraqis were trying to build nuclear weapons, they would need to turn the yellowcake uranium into a gas, which then could be converted into enriched uranium used for bombs. This would require arrays of tens of thousands of centrifuges. American intelligence determined that the Iraqis were purchasing thousands of aluminum tubes, and "Joe T," an engineer at the CIA with no experience in nuclear engineering, suspected that the tubes would be used for the gaseous diffusion. Centrifuge experts at the Oak Ridge National Laboratories who were familiar with the diffusion technology said the tubes were unsuitable as centrifuges but were well suited for casings in the manufacture of artillery rockets. By mid-September 2002 CIA Director George Tenet informed Bush that both the State Department and the Energy Department had their doubts about the use of the tubes, and so did other analysts in the CIA.[14]

Chemical and Biological Weapons Labs

After the Persian Gulf War Iraq admitted that it had secretly produced 30,000 liters of anthrax, botulinum toxin, aflatoxin, and other lethal biological warfare agents, as well as the nerve gases sarin and tabun. American bombing during the Persian Gulf War in 1991 had obliterated the Muthanna State Establishment that had produced these weapons. Thereafter UN weapons inspectors supervised the complete demolition of these facilities. There was no evidence that the Iraqis reconstituted any fermenting facilities. Whatever stocks they possessed would have turned into the equivalent of a bad but harmless pudding within five to ten years.[15]

But some evidence surfaced that Iraq might have been reconstituting its program. Late in 2001 an Iraqi defector in Germany, Rafid Ahmed Alwan, was debriefed by German Federal Intelligence Services (BND). He claimed to have been a chemical engineer at Djerf al Nadaf outside of Baghdad. The facility was supposedly involved in "seed purification," but "Curveball," as he was known by the intelligence agents, claimed it was developing biological weapons. The BND was skeptical of his story because others who had worked at the plant did not corroborate it. Satellite imagery showed a solid wall where Curveball claimed trucks picked up shipments. Curveball seemed psychologically unstable and was rattled when he learned that another defector had worked at the facility. It turned out he had fabricated other information, including the dates of his supposed service at the facility; he had been fired from the Iraqi government years before any alleged germ warfare research could have started.

The CIA Berlin station chief interviewed Curveball and warned about using his information. But his supervisor told him: "Let's keep in mind that this war's going to happen regardless of what Curveball did or didn't say, and the powers that be probably aren't terribly interested in whether Curveball knows what he is talking about."[16] That seemed to be the case, as the Bush administration used Curveball's information about mobile laboratories. "We have firsthand descriptions of biological weapons factories on wheels and on rails," Secretary of State Powell said in his February 5, 2003, speech to the United Nations. "We know what the fermenters look like. We know what the tanks, pumps, compressors and other parts look like." The trailers Curveball talked about were said by other Iraqis to be producing hydrogen for weather balloons. After the war this was corroborated, and testing revealed no traces of chemical or biological agents in the trailers.[17]

If Iraq did have chemical or biological agents, it would need a way to deliver them. Iraq purchased a number of unmanned surveillance drones that came equipped by the manufacturer with aerial mapping coordinates that included the United States. Some CIA intelligence analysts seized on this fact to claim that Iraqis intended to disperse their biological agents through these unmanned planes in the United States. The Director of Air Force Intelligence dissented from a CIA briefing, and the Defense Intelligence Agency, after examining the evidence, agreed that there was no threat to the United States from these tiny drones.

The al-Qaeda Connection

Until the 9/11 attacks American policy toward Iraq involved containment. Under UN resolutions Iraq was disarmed of WMD and subject to inspections. Its air force could not fly in "no fly zones" in two-thirds of the country's airspace, enforced by American and British fighter jets. Its oil exports were controlled by the United Nations, which used funds from sales in an "oil for food" program to fulfill basic needs of the Iraqi people. In the aftermath of the 9/11 attacks, the Bush administration claimed there was a connection between Saddam Hussein's secular Ba'athist regime in Iraq and Osama bin Laden's fundamentalist Islamic al-Qaeda terrorist network. This seemed implausible on its face, but Cheney and others claimed that the pilot of the first 9/11 plane, Mohammed Atta, had met in Prague with senior Iraqi intelligence agent Ahmed Khalil Ibrahim Samir al-Ani in Prague, five months before the attacks.[18]

The information had come from an al-Qaeda informant, a senior military trainer in the organization, Ibn al-Shaykh al-Libi, who claimed that there was an alliance between Saddam Hussein and bin Laden.[19] The FBI and CIA discounted his story because credit card and phone records placed Atta in Virginia Beach, Virginia, at the time of the alleged meeting in Prague. The Defense Intelligence Agency (DIA) demolished the credibility of the informant as well.[20] The DIA claimed in January 2003 that al-Libi provided "intentionally misleading data." He didn't know the details of the supposed training in WMD that Iraq was giving to al-Qaeda.[21]

Al-Libi had initially been interrogated by the FBI, using standard interviewing protocol, and had not talked. The CIA took over the case and took him to a secret facility. Although the Bush administration has never confirmed it, there are news accounts claiming that he was subject to "waterboarding" (a simulation of drowning) and that he began talking thereafter. But he may have talked to get the waterboarding and other mistreatment to stop and may have told his interrogators what they wanted to hear.[22] There was another source: As of September 2002 the CIA received contradictory information from an informant in Saddam Hussein's inner circle. This informant claimed that Saddam had no past or present contact with bin Laden and considered al-Qaeda an enemy. Although al-Libi's information was given to Bush and Cheney, the second informant's information was not passed on to the president.[23]

Top-level counterterrorism officials in the Bush administration told their superiors that there was little or no evidence for an Iraqi link to al-Qaeda. Former White House counterterrorism director Paul Kurtz wrote a memo to National Security Adviser Condoleezza Rice indicating that "no compelling case" could be made. Richard Clarke, a counterterrorism adviser, told the White House the same thing using the same phrase.

The Bush Administration's Use of Intelligence

Tenet briefed the president and his "war cabinet" on December 21, 2002. Bush later recalled, "Tenet said, 'Don't worry, it's a slam dunk.' And that was very important."[24] Yet in the fall of 2002, many intelligence professionals were upset and angry about the way the Bush administration was collecting and using intelligence about Iraqi WMD. One news story, based on interviews with many of these professionals, is worth quoting at length:

> These officials charge that administration hawks have exaggerated evidence of the threat that Iraqi leader Saddam Hussein poses—including distorting his links to the al-Qaida terrorist network—have overstated the amount of international support for attacking Iraq and have downplayed the potential repercussions of a new war in the Middle East. They charge that the administration squelches dissenting views and that intelligence analysts are under intense pressure to produce reports supporting the White House's argument that Saddam poses such an immediate threat to the United States that pre-emptive military action is necessary. "Analysts at the working level in the intelligence community are feeling very strong pressure from the Pentagon to cook the intelligence books," said one official, speaking on condition of anonymity. A dozen other officials echoed his views in interviews. No one who was interviewed disagreed. None of the dissenting officials, who work in a number of different agencies, would agree to speak publicly, out of fear of retribution. But many of them have long experience in the Middle East and South Asia, and all spoke in similar terms about their unease with the way U.S. political leaders are dealing with Iraq.[25]

Although the Bush administration did not pressure or distort intelligence findings from the intelligence agencies, it "cherry picked" for intelligence that would back up its views. It also established parallel sources of intelligence separate and apart from sources cultivated by intelligence agencies and then disseminated its raw intelligence and analysis. In that way it was able to ignore and bypass the intelligence community when it did not back up assumptions held by the president, the vice president, and other top officials. These efforts were carried on by three groups.

The Policy Counterterrorism Evaluation Group

In the spring of 2002, Vice President Cheney began to visit the CIA to question analysts working on WMD intelligence. Dissatisfied with their efforts, Cheney and Rumsfeld directed Douglas Feith, a senior Pentagon official heading the Office of Special Plans (OSP), to establish a unit in the Pentagon to analyze and question the intelligence community's work. This "Policy Counterterrorism Evaluation Group" was initially headed by two civilians, then revamped in January 2002 with two naval reserve officers. The unit focused particularly on the "Prague Connection" and other Iraqi links to al-Qaeda. It circulated the yellowcake intelligence.[26] It received information about WMD development from the Iraqi National Congress (an exile group based in London) and other exile sources. Its work product was submitted to Feith, who in turn would brief Cheney, Rumsfeld, Hadley, and Cheney's aide Lewis "Scooter" Libby. After receiving a written report from Feith detailing purported links between al-Qaeda and Hussein, Cheney in barely legible handwriting wrote in the margin: "This is very good indeed. . . . Encouraging. . . . Not like the crap we are all so used to getting out of the CIA."[27] The CIA, in response to Rumsfeld's request in May 2002 to see if there was an al-Qaeda/Iraq link, reported back that it could not find one. Undeterred, Rumsfeld relied on his own group, and on September 26, 2002, claimed, "We have what we consider to be credible evidence that Al Qaeda leaders have sought contacts with Iraq who could help them acquire . . . weapons-of-mass-destruction capabilities."[28]

Feith's briefings called into question the expertise of the intelligence community, and the administration suggested that further analysis of the al-Qaeda link was called for.[29] But Feith would go further: In "Facilitation: Atta Meeting in Prague," his unit created a PowerPoint slide show alleging that Mohammed Atta and Iraqi intelligence officer Ahmad al-Ani met in April 2001 in Prague. Even though the CIA had called the evidence "inconclusive," Feith's briefings put it out as fact.[30] A subsequent report prepared by the Inspector General of the Department of Defense concluded that Feith's briefers should have noted all deviations from the consensus of the intelligence community. Senator Jay Rockefeller (D-WV), chair of the Senate Intelligence Committee, noted that the Inspector General considered the work of Feith's unit to be "intelligence activities," and that the unit may have violated the National Security Act of 1947 by not reporting its activities to Congress. The report did not charge the unit with violating any laws or knowingly misleading Congress.[31]

The Information Warriors

The CIA and the Pentagon funded a nongovernmental effort to develop intelligence sources that would back the administration's policies. The Rendon Group received a $16 million contract to "create the conditions for the removal of Saddam Hussein from power." Led by John Rendon (a former campaign worker for Democratic presidential candidates who refers to himself as "an information warrior and perception manager"[32]), the group helped to establish the INC, which was then subsidized to the tune of $326,000 per month by the CIA through intermediaries. The INC in turn found defectors, and the Rendon Group would debrief them, help them organize and prepare their testimony, arrange for government polygraph tests, and send them and their transcripts on to both intelligence agencies and the media. The INC brought in Curveball with information on the mobile labs, the nuclear engineer with information about the reconstituted nuclear program, and a defector who described training for non-Iraqi terrorists at the Salman Pak base. Its "Source Five" claimed that Saddam had met with bin Laden in Baghdad. "Source Eighteen" described nuclear reactors for the nuclear weapons program. Most of the information didn't pan out, and eventually the Senate Intelligence Committee concluded that the INC had fed false information to American intelligence analysts.[33]

The White House Intelligence Group

The Bush administration created a public relations group consisting of chief of staff Andrew Card, deputy chief of staff Karl Rove (chairing the group), presidential counselors Karen Hughes and Mary Matalin, Libby, and Condoleezza Rice and Stephen Hadley of the NSC. In fall 2002 all the way through to the beginning of the war, the The White House Iraq Group was at the center of efforts to make the administration's case to the media about WMD.[34] The administration would leak information to the media, such as the September 8, 2002, story on the aluminum tubes, which then would be followed by top administration officials going on Sunday talk shows to discuss the news stories.

While Rumsfeld bypassed his own DIA analysts through Feith's parallel group, Secretary of State Powell relied on the regular State Department analysts. This meant that as he prepared his speech for delivery to the United Nations, he would have to make a choice: rely on the intelligence and analysis from the intelligence community; rely on the White House and Defense Department groups; or take a critical stance toward the intelligence and do some "cherry picking" of his own. He chose the third option. Cheney aides Libby and John Hannah turned up with three books of "allegations" along with what they described as raw intelligence.[35] Powell and his deputies Richard Armitage and Lawrence Wilkerson went through and challenged the material, discarding about 80 percent. When the White House Iraq Group, the vice president, and the NSC deputy director tried to get him to keep the Prague connection in his speech, Powell took it out. "I personally vouch for this, it's good," Tenet told Powell about the material that remained. "It better be, because you are going to be sitting behind me tomorrow. Right behind me, in camera," Powell replied (according to Wilkerson).[36] What Tenet vouched for was the Niger uranium sale and the mobile labs for biological warfare. "What we're giving you are facts and conclusions based on solid intelligence," Powell told his audience at the United Nations. "We have first-hand descriptions of biological weapons factories on wheels and rails," he told the delegates. "We also have satellite photos that indicate that banned materials have recently been moved from a number of Iraqi weapons of mass destruction facilities."[37] Later Wilkerson was to acknowledge that he and others had been misled: "My participation in that presentation at the UN constitutes the lowest point in my professional life. I participated in a hoax on the American people, the international community and the United Nations Security Council."[38]

Bush was not nearly as skeptical as Powell, and he used the conclusions from the parallel intelligence groups uncritically. (Moreover, he never asked the intelligence community for a NIE before making his decisions about war. The only NIE that was produced about WMDs came about because Congress requested it.) So Bush talked about the Niger uranium sales, even though CIA and State Department analysts had told him at least fourteen times that there were serious doubts about the documents.[39] Bush used the suspect al-Libi's intelligence when he claimed that "we've learned that Iraq has trained al Qaeda members in bomb making and poisons and deadly gases."[40] He brought up the al-Qaeda connection repeatedly, even though he had been told in classified briefings as early as September 21 that there was no evidence linking Iraq to the 9/11 attacks and no evidence that there were ties between Iraq and al-Qaeda.[41] Bush referred to the NIE, which concluded that a link was possible but assigned a "low confidence" to it. Bush warned in three major televised addresses that Iraq might attack us, although the NIE held it unlikely except if "ongoing military operations risked the imminent demise of his regime" or if he intended to "exact revenge" for a prior American assault on him. The State Department dissented from the presidential assessment, holding that Iraq would be "unlikely to conduct clandestine attacks against the U.S. homeland" in any scenario. Bush made these charges even though he had been given four briefings on the low probability of such attacks, beginning in spring 2002.[42]

The White House was never interested in intelligence that cast doubt about its own analysis. Tyler Drumheller, who headed CIA covert operations in Europe, later revealed that Iraq's foreign minister, Naji Sabri, had been a CIA informant. Sabri told the CIA that there were no WMD programs, but as Drumheller recalls it in an interview on CBS, "The (White House) group that was dealing with preparation for the Iraq war came back and said they were no longer interested," Drumheller recounted. "We said: 'Well, what about the intel?' And they said: 'Well, this isn't about intel anymore. This is about regime change.'" Drumheller's CIA operation had been assigned the task of debriefing the Iraqi official. "It just sticks in my craw every time I hear them say it's an intelligence failure," he later told CBS. "This was a policy failure."[43]

Intelligence Failure or Policy Failure?

Some of the blame for the failure to assess Iraqi capabilities and intentions does go to the intelligence community. As summarized by the Senate Committee on Intelligence, the efforts of the community resulted in incorrect NIE assessments:

> Postwar findings do not support the [NIE] judgment that Iraq was reconstituting its nuclear weapons program; . . . do not support the [NIE] assessment that Iraq's acquisition of high-strength aluminum tubes was intended for an Iraqi nuclear program; . . . do not support the [NIE] assessment that Iraq was "vigorously trying to procure uranium ore and yellowcake" from Africa; . . . do not support the [NIE] assessment that "Iraq has biological weapons" and that "all key aspects of Iraq's offensive biological weapons program are larger and more advanced than before the Gulf war"; . . . do not support the [NIE] assessment that Iraq possessed, or ever developed, mobile facilities for producing biological warfare agents; . . . do not support the [NIE] assessments that Iraq "has chemical weapons" or "is expanding its chemical industry to support chemical weapons production"; . . . do not support the [NIE] assessments that Iraq had a developmental program for an Unmanned Aerial Vehicle "probably intended to deliver biological agents" or that an effort to procure U.S. mapping software "strongly suggests that Iraq is investigating the use of these UAVs for missions targeting the United States."[44]

Sometimes the agencies got things wrong, because intentions might be misinterpreted even when the information was accurate. In 1996 for example, American intelligence intercepted a memo from the Iraqi Intelligence Service to "insure that there is no equipment, materials, research, studies or books related to manufacturing of the prohibited weapons (chemical, biological, nuclear and missiles) in your site." U.S. intelligence agencies viewed the memo at the time as proof that the Iraqis intended to deceive arms inspectors. But it turned out that the Iraqis wanted to make sure that UN inspectors would not come across materials from the terminated programs. The regime wanted to ensure that UN inspectors would realize that it was in compliance with the disarmament regime, so the United States would not have a pretext for "regime change."[45]

Sometimes it wasn't a question of competence but of agency discretion. Consider the CIA's decision about briefing top officials just before the start of the war. The CIA had recruited Dr. Sawsan Alhaddad, an Arab American woman in Cleveland, to travel to Baghdad and visit her brother, Saad Tawfiq, an electrical engineer whom the agency believed was involved with reconstituting the nuclear program. He confided to his sister that there was no program. She was debriefed by the CIA upon her return, along with thirty other

Iraqis and Iraqi Americans who had been similarly recruited. All said the same thing: There was no Iraqi nuclear program. The CIA did not attempt to include this information in the NIE. Instead, the NIE stated that Iraq was "reconstituting its nuclear program."[46]

Was there political pressure from Bush or Cheney or Rumsfeld to alter the conclusions of the intelligence community? The Senate Intelligence Committee concluded the following in a report adopted unanimously by Republicans and Democrats:

> The Committee did not find any evidence that intelligence analysts changed their judgments as a result of political pressure, altered or produced intelligence products to conform with Administration policy, or that anyone even attempted to coerce, influence or pressure analysts to do so. When asked whether analysts were pressured in any way to alter their assessments or make their judgments conform with Administration policies on Iraq's WMD programs, not a single analyst answered "yes."[47]

A bipartisan commission, cochaired by Republican Appeals Court Judge Laurence Silberman and former Senator Charles Robb (D-VA), concluded the following about the question of political pressure:

> These (intelligence) errors stem from poor tradecraft and poor management. The Commission found no evidence of political pressure to influence the Intelligence Community's pre-war assessments of Iraq's weapons programs. As we discuss in detail in the body of our report, analysts universally asserted that in no instance did political pressure cause them to skew or alter any of their analytical judgments. We conclude that it was the paucity of intelligence and poor analytical tradecraft, rather than political pressure, that produced the inaccurate pre-war intelligence assessments.

The conclusions of the Senate Committee and of the Silberman-Robb Commission are somewhat beside the point. There was no need to put pressure on the intelligence community or distort its work because its consensus product could be used when it backed the administration line and bypassed in favor of a parallel intelligence network when it did not.

Intelligence as Input or Output

The Bush administration inverted the way intelligence is supposed to be used by decision makers: Instead of using intelligence as an input to make rational decisions supported by evidence, the administration used intelligence as an output to justify decisions it had already made.

Early Military Planning

There is considerable evidence that President Bush and other top officials intended to further "regime change" in Iraq even prior to the 9/11 attacks. Bush's first Secretary of the Treasury, Paul O'Neill, recalls that planning began ten days after the inauguration. In his memoirs he wrote that at the first NSC meeting on January 30, 2001, Bush assigned tasks relating to Iraq to everyone. Rumsfeld and Joint Chief of Staff Chair Hugh Shelton "should examine our military options," including use of ground forces in the north and south of Iraq. "From the very beginning, there was a conviction, that Saddam Hussein was a bad person and that he needed to go."[48] Over the summer the NSC began planning for the liberation of Iraq, with a deputies committee meeting to discuss the subject five times *before* the 9/11 attacks. Barely five hours after American Airlines Flight 77 plowed into the Pentagon, Rumsfeld was calling on his aides to plan for striking Iraq.[49] Rumsfeld told General Richard Myers to find the "best info fast . . . judge whether good enough [to] hit S. H. at the same time—not only UBL." (The initials referred to Saddam Hussein and to bin Laden.) Notes taken by Rumsfeld's deputy Stephen Cambone indicate that the defense secretary was thinking: "Go massive. . . . Sweep it all up. Things related and not."[50] The following day, according to White House antiterrorism director Richard Clarke, President Bush "grabbed a few of us and closed the door to the conference room. 'Look,' he told us, 'I know you have a lot to do and all . . . but I want you, as soon as you can, to go back over everything, everything. See if Saddam did this. See if he's linked in any way. . . .'" When Clarke replied that it was an al-Qaeda operation, Bush told him: "Just look. I want to know any shred. . . . Look into Iraq, Saddam."[51] The president issued a NSC directive on September 17, 2001, to begin military planning for an invasion of Iraq.

Nine days after the attacks Bush met with British Prime Minister Tony Blair at the White House. According to British ambassador Sir Christopher Meyer, Bush asked Blair to support regime change in Iraq. Blair replied that retaliating against al-Qaeda in Afghanistan must come first. "I agree with you Tony," Bush responded. "We must deal with this first. But when we have dealt with Afghanistan, we must come back to Iraq."[52] Bush received a classified briefing from the CIA the following day in which the agency reported it could not find al-Qaeda links to Iraq, and in conversations they monitored Saddam, who referred to al-Qaeda as a threat.[53] Dissatisfied with the CIA response, Bush sent former CIA director James Woolsey to the United Kingdom to obtain any evidence British intelligence might possess.

Military planning accelerated. CENTCOM, the Pentagon's command for the Middle East, designated the Third Army as its headquarters for a coalition land force. On November 27, after Bush asked Rumsfeld for military options,

Rumsfeld ordered General Tommy Franks to develop these options. The first Op Plan was presented to Bush by the Christmas holidays. The timing preceded most of the intelligence about WMD subsequently developed by the administration.[54] Franks reportedly told Senator Bob Graham (D-FL) as of late February that CENTCOM was no longer engaged in Afghanistan. "Military and intelligence personnel are being redeployed to prepare for an action in Iraq."[55] In the early summer troops from the Fifth Special Forces Group were pulled away from the hunt for Osama bin Laden in Afghanistan and redeployed to train for a new mission—hunting down Saddam Hussein after an invasion. On June 19, 2002, Franks briefed the president on the war plan, and the president signed a directive on June 30, 2002, that the Joint Chiefs of Staff should implement the war plans. By the summer the Pentagon reprogrammed $750 million from Afghanistan to make preparations for a large force to be billeted in Kuwait. Condoleezza Rice told State Department official Richard Haass in July (as he recalled it). "Essentially, that that decision's been made, don't waste your breath."[56] Throughout the second half of 2002, there was a sharp escalation in bombing raids by the United States and United Kingdom to degrade Iraqi air defenses as a prelude to invasion. In early September a U.S. and UK 100-plane combined raid (known as the "Blue Plan") attacked western air defenses in Iraq and signaled a huge new air offensive.[57] The raids were illegal under international law. The only authorization for American and British combat aircraft involved UN resolutions for "no fly zones," and these were authorized under Resolution 688 only to protect civilian Kurds in the North and Shiites in the South—not to pressure the Iraqi regime for disarmament or prepare for an invasion and regime change.

The Downing Street Memos

The American and British strategy to force "regime change" in Iraq were detailed in the "Downing Street Memos," prepared by national security aides to the British government. They are secondhand reports, summarizing interactions between officials of the two nations, and they report solely on what the British believe to be American intentions. One memo reports on a March 14, 2002, dinner between Condoleezza Rice and Sir David Manning, who served as Prime Minister Blair's national security adviser. According to the memo, Manning reported to Blair that Rice only wanted to talk about regime change in Iraq, and as Manning put it, "Condi's enthusiasm for regime change is undimmed."[58] He added, "I said that you would not budge in your support for regime change, but you had to manage a press, a parliament, and a public opinion that was very different than anything in the States. And you would not budge either in your insistence that, if we pursued regime change, it must be very carefully done and produce the right result. Failure was not an option." Manning then added that the Bush administration "has yet to find answers to the big questions," one of which he posed as: how to persuade international opinion that military action against Iraq is necessary and justified.

On March 18, Ambassador Christopher Meyer met with Deputy Defense Secretary Paul Wolfowitz. He reported back to Manning: "On Iraq I opened by sticking very closely to the script that you used with Condi Rice last week. We backed regime change, but the plan had to be clever and failure was not an option. . . . The U.S. could go it alone if it wanted to. But if it wanted to act with partners, there had to be a strategy for building support for military action against Saddam."[59] The British did not think that the WMD issue would garner much support. A memo from British intelligence analysts prepared for Foreign Secretary Jack Straw concluded, "But even the best survey of Iraq's WMD programs will not show much advance in recent years on the nuclear, missile or CW/BW (chemical or biological weapons) fronts: the programs are extremely worrying but have not, as far as we know, been stepped up."[60] And Straw in turn cautioned Prime Minister Blair that other parts of the case against Saddam were weak: "If 11 September had not happened, it is doubtful that the U.S. would now be considering military action against Iraq. In addition, there has been no credible evidence to link Iraq with OBL (Osama bin Laden) and al-Qaida."[61]

On April 6–7, Bush and Blair met at Bush's ranch in Crawford, Texas. They talked about how to present the best case for regime change. Two months later a Downing Street briefing paper referred to these talks: "When the prime minister discussed Iraq with President Bush at Crawford [Texas] in April, he said that the UK would support military action to bring about regime change." It noted, "The U.S. Government's military planning for action against Iraq is proceeding apace." The paper then discussed ways in which the British might influence American policy "to create the conditions in which we could legally support military action." Referring to the Bush administration, it reported: "Although no political decisions have been taken . . . U.S. military planners have drafted options for the U.S. Government. . . ." The paper noted that both governments would have to "shape public opinion" to make war politically feasible.[62] From the British perspective, the Americans had not made a final decision to go to war as of July, though American military planning anticipated that it was likely war would ensue.[63]

On July 23, 2002, senior British officials met with Prime Minister Blair to discuss Iraq. Matthew Rycroft, a national security aide, wrote up a memo of the meeting. The memo summarizes the visit of "C" (Sir Richard Dearlove, the head of MI6, the British equivalent of the CIA) to Washington and his talks with high-level American national security officials:

C reported on his recent talks in Washington. There was a perceptible shift in attitude. Military action was now seen as inevitable. Bush wanted to remove Saddam, through military action, justified by the conjunction of terrorism and WMD. But the intelligence and facts were being fixed around the policy. The NSC had no patience with the UN route, and no enthusiasm for publishing material on the Iraqi regime's record. There was little discussion in Washington of the aftermath after military action.[64]

After "C" gave his assessment, Foreign Secretary Jack Straw agreed that the Americans had decided on war, but observed, "The case was thin." Saddam posed little threat to the security of the West. His WMD capability was less than Libya's, North Korea's, or Iran's. Then Blair spoke: "The Prime Minister said that it would make a big difference politically and legally if Saddam refused to allow in the UN inspectors. Regime change and WMD were linked in the sense that it was the regime that was producing the WMD. . . . If the political context were right, people would support regime change. The two key issues were whether the military plan worked and whether we had the political strategy to give the military plan the space to work."

The Downing Street Memos indicated that the Americans had no patience with going to the United Nations or with the British insistence that Saddam be given an ultimatum about complying with UN inspections. Blair was insistent on how to "fix the political context," likely because he was worried about criminal liability in cases before the International Criminal Court—something the American government did not have to consider because the United States did not accept jurisdiction of the court.[65] Blair proposed that the United States and the United Kingdom call for inspections. He expected Saddam to turn down the call, which then would provide the casus belli for the invasion. Bush later claimed that Iraq refused to allow the UN weapons inspections required by Security Council Resolutions. But that was not true: The inspectors were in Iraq. They were obtaining good cooperation from the Iraqis as the threat of war loomed. They only left Iraq because the United States warned them to get out before the start of a bombing campaign.

Bush agreed to go to the United Nations to obtain its authorization. This was to help Blair with his own Labor Party and with British public opinion. A first resolution, 1441 was passed on November 8, 2002, with the United States arguing that if Saddam did not abide by its terms there was no need for further UN authorization. The British differed with the United States on this point, with British UN ambassador Sir Jeremy Greenstock stating that in his government's view: "There is no 'automaticity' in this Resolution. If there is a further Iraqi breach of its disarmament obligations, the matter will return to the Council for discussion as required. . . . We would expect the Security Council then to meet its responsibilities." But months later when the UN

Security Council was unable to pass a second resolution authorizing hostilities (due to opposition from France, Russia, and China), the British changed position to conform to the American view. On January 31, 2003, in a two-hour meeting between Blair and Bush, the prime minister told Bush that he was behind the use of force. They discussed the failure to find hard evidence of WMDs or a breach of UN resolutions. Bush nevertheless made it clear to Blair that he intended to invade, with or without a new UN resolution. He even raised the idea of orchestrating an incident to get Saddam to fire on American reconnaissance planes to justify American retaliation.[66] David Manning wrote in a memo summarizing the discussion and paraphrasing the words of Bush: "The start date for the military campaign was now penciled in for 10 March. This was when the bombing would begin."[67]

From the Downing Street Memos and other documents, it appears that Bush had made up his mind early on to bring regime change to Iraq. Going to the United Nations was not, as Blair claimed, a way to prevent war, but rather was a way to legitimize it. Insisting that Saddam had not allowed inspectors and therefore had something to hide also legitimized the war, even though just prior to hostilities the Iraqi regime had made it clear that it would let inspectors see everything. On March 7, 2003, UN chief weapons inspector Hans Blix informed the UN Security Council that Iraq was cooperating and that inspectors would need only a few months to certify that Iraq did not possess WMD.

Administration Denials

Throughout the summer and fall of 2002 the Bush administration denied that it had made decisions about hostilities and regime change. Bush met with Saudi ambassador Bandar bin Sultan on August 26, 2002, after which White House spokesperson Ari Fleischer told CNN, "The president stressed that he has made no decisions, that he will continue to engage in consultations with Saudi Arabia and other nations about steps in the Middle East, steps in Iraq." On September 8, 2002, Vice President Cheney was interviewed by Tim Russert on *Meet the Press*. Russert asked, "Will militarily this be a cakewalk? Two, how long would we be there and how much would it cost?" Cheney replied, "First of all, no decision's been made yet to launch a military operation."

Both Bush and Blair have stated flatly that they made no decision for war until shortly before hostilities began. Years later, at a joint news conference with Bush and Blair on June 7, 2005, Steve Holland of *Reuters* asked, "On Iraq, the so-called Downing Street memo from July 23, 2002 says intelligence and facts were being fixed around the policy of removing Saddam through military action. Is this an accurate reflection of what happened? Could both of you respond?" Bush replied, ". . . somebody said, well, you know, we had made up our mind to go to use military force to deal with Saddam. There's nothing farther from the truth. My conversation with the prime minister was, how could we do this peacefully? what could we do?" Then Blair responded: "Well I can respond to that very easily, No, the facts were not being fixed in any shape or form at all." He added, "And let me remind you that that memorandum was written before we then went to the United Nations. Now, no one knows more intimately the discussions that we were conducting as two countries at the time than me. And the fact is, we decided to go to the United Nations and went through that process, which resulted in the November 2002 United Nations resolution to give a final chance to Saddam Hussein to comply with international law. He didn't do so. And that was the reason why we had to take military action."

The Bush administration argues that members of Congress had the same intelligence and that they too were convinced about WMD. The president pointed to the assessments of other intelligence agencies around the world, to UN resolutions citing Iraq's development and possession of WMDs. "That's why more than a hundred Democrats in the House and Senate—who had access to the same intelligence—voted to support removing Saddam Hussein from power."[68] But if the case had been made by the parallel groups rather than the intelligence community, and if they had hyped and distorted the data and reached conclusions beyond the evidence, then Congress would have been misled and the delegation of authority would not have been obtained by force of reasoned argument.

The only group in the Senate that saw the work produced by the regular intelligence community, the fully classified NIE, was the Senate Select Intelligence Committee. Members of that committee voted in fall 2002 *against* the authorization of the use of force against Iraq. CIA director George Tenet then sent an unclassified "summary" of the NIE to Congress—a summary that exaggerated the Iraqi threat. The unclassified version claimed that Iraq would have nuclear weapons in the decade and that it had resumed its nuclear program. It claimed Iraq had chemical and biological weapons, along with sprayers and unmanned vehicles for biological weapons. Senator Graham, who was chair of the committee that had received the classified version, and his committee colleagues were barred by classification rules from discussing the contents of the classified report with the full Senate: They could not explain to their colleagues that what the full Senate had received contained none of the caveats and qualifications about the intelligence or the doubts of the intelligence analysts who had prepared the NIE.

Paul Pillar, a senior CIA analyst, wrote years later:

In the wake of the Iraq war, it has become clear that official intelligence analysis was not relied on in making even the most significant national security decisions, that intelligence was misused publicly to justify decisions already made, that damaging ill will developed between policymakers and intelligence officers, and that the intelligence community's own work was politicized.[69]

WMD: Rationale or Reason

Nothing about President Bush's decision to invade Iraq turned on the accuracy of intelligence about WMD. This raises the question: If not WMD, what did the invasion turn on? If Iraq was a war of choice rather than a preemptive war (to prevent a terrorist attack using WMD transferred by Iraq to al-Qaeda), what was the choice about?

There are several competing hypotheses, and as yet not enough is known about decision making in the Bush presidency (and not enough documentary sources have been made available to scholars) to come up with definitive answers. But we can make educated guesses as to the elements of decision.

Democratization and the Neocons

One hypothesis is that regime change in Iraq was part of the "democratization" project of the "neoconservatives" in the Bush administration. The political theorist Leo Strauss, based at the University of Chicago, had a Manichean worldview (i.e., there is Good and there is Evil), and several of his former students had achieved high places in the administration, including Deputy Defense Secretary Paul Wolfowitz; head of the intelligence advisory board, Richard Perle; Cheney assistant Scooter Libby; Zalmay Khalilzad (ambassador to Afghanistan after the war); and Abe Shulsky in the State Department, among others. In 1992 at the tail end of the first Bush presidency, Wolfowitz, Libby, and Khalilzad had produced a "Defense Planning Guidance" document that posited America as the only superpower. In a volume published in 2000, as a critique of the first Bush presidency, neocons called for use of this superpower status in the service of promoting democracy throughout the world. In the first Gulf War, President George H. W. Bush had "failed to see the mission through to its proper conclusion: the removal of Saddam from power in Baghdad." They argued that American forces should have been kept in the area "long enough to ensure that a friendlier regime took root." They called for "a broad strategy of promoting liberal democratic governance throughout the world."[70] Ensconced in Washington think tanks during the Clinton presidency, neocons developed the "Project for a New American Century." Their plans for Iraq called for regime change, followed by a permanent American military presence in the region. This would give the United States leverage on the oil-producing gulf states.[71] Once appointed to positions in the second Bush administration, neoconservatives developed a strategy embodied in a document produced by the NSC in September 2002, "The National Security Strategy of the United States of America."[72] They recognized "the single sustainable model for national success: freedom, democracy, and free enterprise." They claimed this model applied to the entire world. The strategy document proclaimed that the "values of freedom are right and true for every person, in every society—and the duty of protecting these values against their enemies is the common calling of freedom-loving people across the globe and across the ages." It warned that the United States would hold to account "nations that are compromised by terror, including those who harbor terrorists." And it concluded, "The United States welcomes our responsibility to lead in this great mission." If ideology drove the decision to invade Iraq and topple Hussein, the existence or nonexistence of WMD made no difference; the goal was democratization in the Middle East and expansion of American influence in the region.

Petropolitics

An alternate (but not mutually exclusive) theory has been expressed by former Federal Reserve Board chair Alan Greenspan, who in his memoirs wrote, "I am saddened that it is politically inconvenient to acknowledge what everyone knows: the Iraq war is largely about oil." Iraq has 112 billion barrels of proven reserves and the possibility of 220 billion barrels to be discovered. Costs of extraction are low: $1.50 per barrel versus $8 in many other parts of the world. Only 125 of the 526 potential oil field sites have been explored. The western desert region remains to be developed. The two major American companies who work in the Middle East, Exxon Mobil and Chevron-Texaco, along with the British companies BP Amoco and Royal Dutch Shell, would directly benefit from the invasion. The energy task force that Vice President Cheney chaired before the invasion paid attention to the exclusion by the Saddam Hussein regime of American companies. The State Department's "Future of Iraq Project" had an "Oil and Energy Working Group" that planned for the privatization of the Iraqi oil industry.

After the war, the American government pressed Iraq to conclude "Production Service Agreements" with American oil companies, which would lock in the right to exploit the fields on favorable terms for up to forty years.[73] The American government pressed the Iraqi parliament to pass an oil law (which as of late 2007 it had not yet done) that would allow private companies to exploit 85 percent of the Iraqi fields, leaving only 15 percent to be developed by the Iraqi National Oil Company. The total value of the oil could be as much as $30 trillion.[74] Control of this much oil would allow the United States to put downward pressure on the OPEC price cartel. The United States was building five superbases in Iraq, and after the "Surge" of 2007 was planning to leave perhaps as many as 35,000 troops in the region, including rapid reaction forces that could be used to protect the oil fields.

The Limits of Hypothetical Reasoning

It is clear that neocons wishing to democratize the Middle East had influence within the Bush administration, and it is just as clear from the draft oil legislation (and the signing of contracts by Kurdistan with American oil companies in 2007) that America gained access to Iraqi oil production as a result of the war. But neither democratization efforts nor petropolitics are mutually exclusive with the proposition that the Bush administration did believe that Iraq had WMD. Indeed, the additional motives are in this instance reinforcing rather than contradictory. *So they do not, in and of themselves, provide evidence that the Bush administration falsified its reasons for entering the war.* Scholars must await the release of documents and the (admittedly self-interested) testimony of participants to the decision making. At that point we will know better whether ignorance and self-delusion, enthusiasm and exaggeration, or deliberate falsehood of intelligence led to the failure to find WMDs. What we know now is that parallel governance contributed greatly to the flawed decision making process.

Parallel Governance

The Iraqi intelligence fiasco is symptomatic of a pattern of governance in which presidents claim concurrent powers that circumvent the powers of Congress and the courts, based on their commander in chief powers, their inherent and implied executive powers, or their responsibilities stemming from the oath of office. When taken to its extreme, the result is not merely claims of a "unitary executive" in which all *executive* powers are to be exercised by the president and his subordinates, but rather *parallel governance*, in which the president exercises what he considers to be the necessary executive, legislative, and judicial power himself to control policymaking, and in doing so bypasses the legislatively constituted departments of government, as well as Congress and the courts.

The irony is that the justification for parallel governance comes, not just from the Hamiltonian conception of "energy in the executive," but also from the Madisonian doctrine of *partial* separation of powers developed in *Feder-*

alist No. 47. James Madison observed (following Montesquieu) that the "accumulation of all powers legislative, executive and judiciary in the same hands, whether of one, a few or many, and whether hereditary, self appointed, or elective, may justly be pronounced the very definition of tyranny." He pointed out, however, that if a *complete* separation of power had been planned for the new Constitution (so that Congress exercised all legislative power and only legislative power, the president exercised all executive power and only executive power, and the Supreme Court and lower courts exercised all judicial powers and only judicial powers), the institution assigned all legislative power would be so powerful it would suck the other institutions into the legislative "vortex." This is what the Framers believed had already happened in many of the states after constitutions were written incorporating complete separation clauses: Legislatures were dominant, and the postcolonial governors and courts were too weak to keep legislative power in check.

How to prevent the erosion of separation of powers? Madison's solution involved *partial* separation of powers. Some powers would overlap and some would blend, and in some instances one branch of government could exercise powers considered to be a part of another branch. And so, in spite of the fact that the Constitution assigned "the judicial power" to a Supreme Court, Congress has a power of subpoena, it may hold witnesses at hearings in contempt, and it conducts impeachments as a trial; similarly, the president has the power to issue reprieves and pardons for offences against the United States. Congress does not exercise all legislative powers: Presidential executive orders, executive agreements, military orders, and proclamations all have the force of law.

Presidents have used partial separation doctrines to legitimize their claims of concurrent foreign affairs and war powers. In practice this means that presidents can cobble together a set of concurrent powers and institutional practices, first to set policy, then to implement it, and finally to pass judgment on it. Facilitating a unitary executive was the antithesis of Madison's thinking, but yet a line of argument from Madison's own conception of *partial* separation of powers does lead to just that outcome—and to the possibility that all significant war powers and national security powers will fall into an "executive vortex."

Presidents (including Bush) have superimposed their own version of law through signing statements and at times asserted a dispensing power when they decided they would not enforce provisions of laws in bills they had signed.[75] Presidents have supplemented diplomats consented to by the Senate with an "invisible presidency" of unofficial envoys who convey presidential messages "under the radar."[76] They have bypassed the congressional power of the purse, as Reagan did in the Iran-Contra affair through Colonel Oliver North's "Enterprise," self-funded through receipts from arms sales. They have bypassed the declaration of war clause with congressional resolutions of support, UN resolutions, NATO resolutions, congressional authorizations and what they considered to be self-executing treaty provisions, relying on whatever was at hand.[77]

In the "war on terrorism," Bush extended parallel governance. He ignored the requirements of the Foreign Intelligence Surveillance Act of 1978 that required the Foreign Intelligence Surveillance Court to issue a special court order (the equivalent of a warrant) for surveillance of foreigners who communicate from abroad into the United States, and instead directed the National Security Agency to conduct surveillance on the president's authority.[78] He bypassed military court martials established by Congress by issuing a military order establishing military tribunals with far fewer due process guarantees.[79] He delegated power through the military's chain of command to establish interrogation procedures in ad hoc detention facilities that violate international law commitments and authorize intelligence agents to exercise the power of extraordinary rendition so that detainees in the war on terror can be interrogated in other nations, without direct participation by Americans, and in ways that directly violate Geneva Convention Common Article III and the Anti-Torture Act.[80] In all these matters he exercised his prerogatives to establish parallel processes (bypassing the warrant requirements for foreign surveillance), powers (executive agreements for treaties), and institutions (military tribunals for court martials).

What distinguishes parallel governance is its substitution of enthusiasm for expertise and experience, of expedience for legality, of ad hoc and often surreptitious procedures for the standard operating procedures of complex organizations. In the WMD case President Bush and Vice President Cheney established a parallel processing unit within the department of defense to obtain information from the Iraqi National Congress.[81] Parallel governance may have led to groupthink within the top levels of the administration (if they believed in what they were being briefed on), or else it was simply a device used by an administration that knew—and did not care—that Iraq did not have WMD programs in place. Either way, the parallel governance of the WMD case resembles the Iran-Contra policy inversion case: Privatization combined with the establishment of ad hoc units using alternate processes led to incorrect information moving through the system, which led to decisions about WMD that lacked moral authority, policy viability, or legitimacy in international law.

Notes

1. "President's Remarks at the United Nations, September 12, 2002," http://www.whitehouse.gov/news/releases/2002/09/20020912-1.html.

2. "President Bush Outlines Iraq Threat, October 7, 2002," www.whitehouse .gov/news/releases/2002/10/20021007-8.html.

3. "President Delivers 'State of the Union,' January 28, 2003," http://www .whitehouse.gov.edgesuite.net/news/releases/2003/01/20030128-19.html.

4. Letter to Congress, March 21, 2003.

5. Antony Barnett, "Secret Emails, Missing Weapons," *Observer* (May 15, 2005).

6. "President Bush Veteran's Day Speech, November 11, 2005," www.whitehouse .gov/news/releases/2005/11/20051111-1.html.

7. "Vice President Cheney Address to American Enterprise Institute, November 21, 2005." http://www.whitehouse.gov/news/releases/2005/11/20051121-2.html.

8. Quoted in Joe Conason, "Saddam Chose to Deny Inspectors," www.salon.com (March 31, 2006).

9. Peter Eisner, "How Bogus Letter Became a Case for War," *Washington Post* (April 3, 2007): A-01.

10. Elaine Sciolino and Elizabetta Povoledo, "Source of Forged Niger-Iraq Uranium Documents Identified," *New York Times* (November 4, 2005): A-1; Peter Wallsten, Tom Hamburger, and Josh Meyer, "FBI Is Taking Another Look at Forged Prewar Intelligence," *Los Angeles Times* (December 3, 2005): 4.

11. Memo, Bureau of Intelligence and Research, January 12, 2003. For an analysis see Murray Waas, "What Bush Was Told about Iraq," *National Journal* (March 2, 2006).

12. Eric Lichtblau, "2002 Memo Doubted Uranium Sale Claim," *New York Times* (January 18, 2006). After the war CIA director George Tenet retracted the CIA charge that Saddam had been buying yellowcake from Niger. Some American officials charged that the documents had been produced in Italy by former agents of the Italian Intelligence Service (SISMI). Jonathan S. Landay, "Italy Provided U.S. with Faulty Uranium Intelligence, Officials Insist," *Knight-Ridder Newspapers* (November 6, 2005).

13. Judd Legum et al., "The Stephen Hadley Connection," *Progress Report* (October 28, 2005).

14. Murray Waas, "Insulating Bush," *National Journal* (March 30, 2006); Waas, "What Bush Was Told."

15. William Rivers Pitt, "Yes, They Lied," Truthout/Perspective, www.truthout.org (November 8, 2005).

16. Ray McGovern, "Proof Bush Fixed the Facts," May 4, 2005, posted on www .TomPaine.com.

17. Joby Warrick, "Lacking Biolabs, Trailers Carried Case for War," *Washington Post* (April 12, 2006): 5.

18. "It's pretty well confirmed that [Atta] did go to Prague and he did meet with a senior official of the Iraqi intelligence service last April, several months before the attack." Vice President Cheney, *Meet the Press*, December 9, 2002.

19. Robert Scheer, "Lying with Intelligence," *Los Angeles Times* (November 8, 2005).

20. Defense Intelligence Agency DITSUM No. 044-02.

21. Michael Isikoff and Mark Hosenball, "Al-Libi's Tall Tales," *Newsweek* (November 10, 2005): 15.

22. Rosa Brooks, "In the End, Torture Hurts Us," *Los Angeles Times* (November 25, 2005).

23. Walter Pincus, "CIA Learned in '02 That Bin Laden Had No Iraq Ties, Report Says," *Washington Post* (September 15, 2006).

24. Bob Woodward, "What We Have Here Is a Failure to Communicate," *Washington Post* (May 6, 2007): BW01. Tenet later claimed he was referring to the public relations impact of the claims, not to the quality of the intelligence.

25. Warren Strobel and Jonathan Landay, "Some Administration Officials Expressing Misgivings on Iraq," *Knight-Ridder Newspapers* (October 8, 2002).

26. Office of Special Plans, "Iraq and al-Qaida: Making the Case," July 25, 2002.

27. Waas, "What Bush Was Told."

28. Waas, "What Bush Was Told."

29. Douglas Feith, "Inside the Inside Story," *Wall Street Journal* (May 6, 2007).

30. Matt Renner, "Pentagon Office Created Phony Intel on Iraq/al-Qaeda Link," Truthout/Report, www.truthout.org (April 6, 2007).

31. Inspector General United States Department of Defense, Deputy Inspector General for Intelligence, "Review of the Pre-Iraqi War Activities of the Office of the Under Secretary of Defense for Policy," Secret/Noform/MR20320209, Report No. 07-INTEL-04, February 9, 2007.

32. Speaking to cadets at the Air Force Academy in 1996, as quoted in James Bamford, "The Man Who Sold the War," www.rollingstone.com/politics/story/8798997/the_man_who_sold_the_war/ (November 17, 2005).

33. U.S. Senate, *Report of the Select Committee on Intelligence on the Use by the Intelligence Community of Information Provided by the Iraqi National Congress*, September 8, 2006. 109th Congress, 2nd sess.

34. John Prados, "Blindsided or Blind?" *Bulletin of the Atomic Scientists* (July/August 2004); John Prados, ed., *Hoodwinked: The Documents That Reveal How Bush Sold Us a War* (New York: New Press, 2004).

35. Joseph L. Galloway, "'Dishonest and Reprehensible' Words from Dick Cheney," *Knight-Ridder Newspapers* (November 24, 2005).

36. William E. Jackson Jr., "Foggy Bottom Memos: The Hemorrhaging of Iraq War Minutes," Huffington Post.com (August 23, 2005).

37. "U.S. Secretary of State Colin Powell Addresses the U.N. Security Council, February 5, 2003," www.whitehouse.gov/news/releases/2003/02/20030205-1.html.

38. Interview with Lawrence Wilkerson, Public Broadcasting System, "Now" (hosted by David Brancaccio), February 5, 2006.

39. Craig Unger, "The War They Wanted, the Lies They Needed," *Vanity Fair* (July 2006).

40. "President Bush Outlines Iraq Threat, October 7, 2002," www.whitehouse.gov/news/releases/2002/10/20021007-8.html.

41. Murray Waas, "Key Bush Intelligence Briefing Kept from Hill Panel," *National Journal* (November 22, 2005).

42. Waas, "What Bush Was Told."

43. "CIA Warned Bush of No Weapons in Iraq," *Reuters* (April 22, 2006).

44. *Report of the Select Committee on Intelligence, on Postwar Findings about Iraq's WMD Programs and Links to Terrorism and How They Compare with Prewar Assessments*, 109th Congress, 2nd Session, September 8, 2006.

45. Kevin Woods, James Lacey, and Williamson Murray, "Saddam's Delusions," *Foreign Affairs* (May/June 2006).

46. Sidney Blumenthal quoting James Risen in "Bush's War on Professionals," http://www.salon.com/opinion/blumenthal/2006/01/05/spying/ (January 5, 2006).

47. *Select Committee on Postwar Findings*, 273

48. CBS *60 Minutes*, January 11, 2004.

49. *CBS News*, September 4, 2002.

50. Cambone Notes, 9.11.2001. Available on outragedmoderates.org.

51. Richard Clarke, *Against All Enemies: Inside America's War on Terror* (New York: Free Press, 2004), 15.

52. "The Path to War," *Vanity Fair* (May 2004).

53. Waas, "Key Bush Intelligence Briefing."

54. John Prados, "The Man Behind the Curtain," TomPaine.com (July 19, 2004).

55. Bob Graham and Jeff Nussbaum, *Intelligence Matters: The CIA, the FBI, Saudi Arabia, and the Failure of America's War on Terror* (New York: Random House, 2004), 127.

56. Quoted in Warren P. Strobel, "British Documents Portray Determined U.S. March to War," *Knight Ridder Newspapers* (June 17, 2005).

57. Michael Smith, "British Bombing Raids Were Illegal, Says Foreign Office," *Sunday Times* (June 19, 2005).

58. Downing Street Memos, March 14, 2002.

59. Meyers to Manning, "Iraq and Afghanistan: Conversation with Wolfowitz," March 18, 2002, Downing Street Memos.

60. Thomas Wagner, "Memos Show British Fretting over Iraq War," *Associated Press* (June 18, 2005).

61. March 25 Straw memo to Blair on legality, "PM/02/019 Crawford/Iraq."

62. "Iraq: Conditions for Military Action," July 19, 2002, Downing Street Memos.

63. David E. Sanger, "Prewar British Memo Says War Decision Wasn't Made," *New York Times* (June 13, 2005).

64. Matthew Rycroft, "S 195/02 Iraq: Prime Ministers Meeting, 23 July 2002," Downing Street Memos.

65. "Confidential Iraq: Legal Background," Memo for the Cabinet, Downing Street Memos.

66. David Corn, "The Mother of all Downing Street Memos," posted at www .davidcorn.com/archives/2006/02/the_mother_of_a.php.

67. Don Van Natta Jr. "Bush Was Set on Path to War, Memo by British Adviser Says," *New York Times* (March 27, 2006).

68. President Bush Veteran's Day Speech, November 11, 2005, www.whitehouse .gov/news/releases/2005/11/20051111-1.html.

69. Paul Pillar, "Intelligence, Policy and the War in Iraq," *Foreign Affairs* (March/April 2006).

70. Defense Planning Guidance, February 18, 1992, reprinted in *New York Times* (March 7, 1992); a revised version dated April 16, 1992, reprinted in Patrick Tyler, "Defense Policy Guidance, 1991–1994," *New York Times* (May 23, 1992).

71. Project for a New American Century, "Rebuilding America's Defenses," September 2000, as posted at www.newamericancentury.org.

72. "The National Security Strategy of the United States of America," www.white house.gov/nsc/nss.html.

73. Joshua Holland, "Bush's Petro-Cartel Almost Has Iraq's Oil," Alternet.org (October 16, 2006).

74. Jim Holt, "It's the Oil," *London Review of Books* (October 18, 2007).

75. Marc V. Garber and Kurt A. Wimmer, "Presidential Signing Statements as Interpretations of Legislative Intent: An Executive Aggrandizement of Power," 24 *Harvard Journal of Legislation* 363 (1989); also Christopher Kelley, "Contextualizing the Signing Statement," *Presidential Studies Quarterly* vol. 37, no. 4 (December 2007).

76. Louis Koenig, *The Invisible Presidency* (New York: Rinehart, 1960).

77. Richard Pious, "Inherent War and Executive Powers and Prerogative Politics," *Presidential Studies Quarterly* (Spring 2007).

78. Richard Pious, "Warrantless Surveillance and the Warrantless Presidency," in Christopher Kelley and Ryan Barillaux, eds., *The Unitary Executive and the Modern Presidency* (College Station: Texas A&M Press, 2008).

79. Richard Pious, "The President and Military Tribunals," in Joseph Bessette and Jeffrey Tulis, eds., *The Constitutional Presidency* (Baltimore, MD: Johns Hopkins Press, 2008).

80. Anti-Torture Act, 18 USC sec. 2340A. Richard Pious, "Torture of Detainees and Presidential Prerogative Power," in George Edwards, ed., *The Polarized Presidency of George W. Bush* (New York: Oxford University Press, 2007).

81. Seymour Hersh, "The Stovepipe," *New Yorker* (October 27, 2003).

10

Presidents Unbound

Crises of Authority and Legitimacy

W HY DO PRESIDENTS FAIL? Not because of the *kinds* of problems they tackle. A listing of presidential failures would include covert operations, limited wars, and domestic innovation, but so would a listing of presidential successes: Kennedy failed in the Bay of Pigs, but Bush 43 succeeded in Afghanistan with a proxy force; Johnson failed with compellence in Vietnam, but Clinton succeeded in the Balkans; Clinton failed with his health program, but Carter won passage of much of his energy program; Bush 41 failed in budget summitry, but Clinton won with his budget brinksmanship.

Nor do presidents fail because of a particular *style* of decision making. They fail when they centralize command and control (Ford with the *Mayaguez*), but also fail when they distance themselves (Reagan with Iran-Contra); they fail when they propose global solutions (Clinton with health care), but several presidents failed with incremental approaches to health care (Carter). They fail when they have overheated rhetoric (Carter) and when they are too understated (Ford and Bush 41); they fail when they assert controversial prerogatives (the imperial presidencies of Johnson and Nixon); and they fail when they do not assert prerogatives in emergencies (Buchanan and Hoover).

Risk Assessments

"Luck is the residue of design," Brooklyn Dodgers general manager Branch Rickey once observed. Conversely, poor design may lead to bad presidential luck.[1] Presidents fail either because they micromanage *or* they delegate excessively, go global *or* go incremental, talk too grandiloquently *or* to modestly, assert prerogative *or* hold back. What these opposite approaches have in common is that *in each case presidents adopt a strategy they believe will lower their risks.* Ford in the *Mayaguez* incident gave direct orders to military commanders. But, when presidents constrain military commanders, what appears to be a rational effort to minimize risk actually maximizes the likelihood that a constrained operation will fail. Micromanagement raises costs of complying with demands for information for field operatives; they are less able to move information horizontally, so coordination suffers. As performance declines, vertical information flow becomes degraded with noise or deliberate falsifications, leading to self-destructing rather than self-correcting feedback loops.[2]

As we saw in the *Mayaguez* case, horizontal communication and dissemination of "local knowledge" by troops on the ground—even when improvised out of desperation—offers a high yield of valid information at low cost. Cases of "perfect failure" such as Vietnam usually involve the hierarchy discouraging lateral flows. Shortcut communication (in which people at different levels in the hierarchy meet each other randomly or systematically to pass on information) is also likely to be discouraged by those at the top when they wish to manage risk themselves.[3] (In both the *Challenger* and *Columbia* space shuttle disasters, knowledge of significant risk did not reach those in command.) What makes Hollywood thrillers so dramatic—and so unrealistic—is that impending disaster is averted just in time because out in the field an operative always finds a way around the chain of command to reach the president with information that saves the day.

To avoid accountability the president may delegate, but excessive delegation may be counterproductive: Military commanders at one point in the Vietnam escalation were considering widening the conflict to include China. In covert operations excessive delegation of responsibility within the White House to provide plausible deniability for the president does not reduce his risks. What results is an inversion and privatization of functions, as in the Iran-Contra affair: Policy is made by default as low-level officials or nongovernmental "cutouts" take actions fraught with policy consequences while nominal superiors look away or are taken out of the loop.

The further out an operation moves from the bounds of legality, the higher the White House stakes but the lower presidential control of these stakes, even (or because) of plausible deniability. Had Eisenhower's U-2 flights been vetted by the National Security Council (NSC), it is doubtful that the presummit flight over Russia would have been approved. The resupply operation for the Contras mounted by "The Enterprise" involved poorly trained crews and rust bucket cargo planes—such an operation would never have been approved if it had gone through the normal State, Defense, and CIA reviews.

When policies are inverted and operations privatized, they attract lowlifes as middlemen and brokers, as in Iran-Contra arms sales. Presidential attempts to minimize risk with plausible deniability increase the risk, because inexperienced, overly eager, or unstable operatives are recruited to do the work. They may go off the deep end or decide they have been poorly treated and betray their handlers. Blackmail is always a possibility, because if these operatives are ever caught in any illegality, their ace in the hole is to give up their White House sponsors. Such are the staples of Hollywood plots: The irony is a president who had been an actor himself but never mastered the genre.

Hard Problems

Presidents get to decide on risky business. *What is easy does not reach the White House for decision* (even though presidents take credit for problems being solved by executive departments). Issues become "presidential" because no one knows what to do about them, because they have a pedigree of failure, because proposed solutions are risky (a situation in which odds are known) or are uncertain (a situation in which even the odds cannot be stated).

Satisficing versus Satisfiability

American politicians by vocation usually downplay fixed principles and ideology in favor of pragmatic, often incremental, searches for solutions. They are usually willing to "satisfice," accepting a solution that "solves" a problem, even though is it not likely to be a maximal solution. They have an intuitive sense that the best is the enemy of the good. But presidents, because of their unique vantage point as national leaders and because of the multiplicity of conflicting pressures they face, get the problems that do not admit of "satisficing" solutions. The problems that reach their desk involve webs of conflicting demands by stakeholders and a multiplicity of trade-offs along different spatial dimensions, and they also involve "valences" that lead to judgments that their proposals are "moral or immoral" or "honest or dishonest." Many problems that reach the White House lack "satisfiability" in the mathematical sense: They lie on or beyond a mathematically defined frontier between the solvable and the impossible, because solving problems with multiple constraints is often impossible.

Two things might help a president deal with these frontier problems. First, the White House could bring advisers with the quantitative skills to help the president recognize where on the solvability dimensions the public policy issue as he has defined it is located. These advisers might in some instances suggest comprehensive or partial solutions to the trickiest (known as 3-SAT) problems.[4] Second, the political advisers can help the president navigate the valence issues that create emotional responses in the electorate so that they navigate with the political winds at their back. This raises the larger issue of how presidents utilize their advisers.

Experts and Expertise

"What presidents do every day," presidential scholar Richard Neustadt once observed, "is to make decisions that are mostly thrust upon them, the deadline all too often outside their control, on options mostly framed by others, about issues crammed with technical complexities and uncertain outcomes."[5] For each problem the White House tackles, presidents need a theory about how the world works so that they can understand the odds, the trade-offs, the costs versus the benefits, and so that they can effectively manage their risks. One might assume that the advisory units located in the Executive Office of the President, such as the Council of Economic Advisers or the Domestic Policy Council, give presidents a unique vantage point and greater expertise than any other institution involved in public policy. Yet there is no evidence that these units—known collectively as the institutionalized presidency—have improved any president's ability to make domestic policy. If anything, in the past thirty years, there has been a growing gap between what experts claim to be able to discover, describe, and predict, and what they actually deliver.

Presidents routinely have problems obtaining valid information, in part because their advisers tend to discount any "local knowledge," however expert, that does not fit their preconceived data formats. Their data, particularly involving complex economic and social statistics and trends, are highly imperfect approximations of real-world quantities. Even when good data are available, experts in and out of government use theories about the real world that often have little validity: One thinks of the discredited Phillips Curve and NAIRU (specifying the supposed relationships between the unemployment rate and inflation and the supposed point at which inflation will accelerate), and the two supply-side programs of Reagan and Bush 43, respectively. Economists in and out of government have had dreadful track records predicting the basics: rates of inflation, rates of productivity, rates of growth, revenue streams, deficits—with the "consensus" forecasts having become a national embarrassment.[6] Scorecarding units such as the Office of Management and Budget and the Council of Economic Advisers are unable to forecast turning points and crises (Savings and Loan, Internet bubble, subprime mortgages, to name three), and budget forecasting has been getting progressively worse in the past three decades. As late as 1995 the Congressional Budget Office and the Office of Management and Budget were forecasting $200 billion deficits into the indefinite future, while just three years later they were forecasting a decades' surplus of $1.5 trillion, and three years after that the projected surpluses had turned into $400 plus billion deficits for the foreseeable future, while two years after *that* (near the end of the Bush 43 presidency) deficits were shrinking dramatically but then seemed to be rising again.

After leaving his presidency, Gerald Ford was scathing in his assessment of the predictions the CIA had made in the late 1960s that in ten years the United States would be behind the Soviet Union in military capability and economic growth. "The facts are," Ford observed after leaving the presidency, "they were 180 degrees wrong. These were the best people we had, CIA's so-called experts."[7] The CIA later studied its own forecasting problems, coming to the conclusion that its "single outcome forecasting" had been to blame for serious miscues because trend extrapolation had failed and the agency had been unable to predict the discontinuities that had actually occurred.[8] Defense Department officials who saw a missile gap in favor of the Soviets in the 1950s got it wrong; they were succeeded by officials who saw a gap in favor of the United States, and they eventually got it wrong as well. Hardly any Reagan-era national security managers or Sovietologists predicted the collapse of the Soviet Union. In the 1999 Balkans conflict, experts in the State Department and the NSC claimed that a few days of bombing would bring Milosevic to the bargaining table to sign an agreement on Kosovo; no one advising the president predicted that the Yugoslav leader would order mass expulsions of the 1.6 million Kosovars.

In domestic affairs the experts are no better. Consider their predictions about energy use and petroleum prices. In 1978, Carter's Energy Secretary James Schlesinger provided a chart at a congressional hearing entitled "Free World Oil Demand and Supply, 1966–1985" that projected that without government intervention oil demand would outstrip supply by 8 million barrels by 1985 and result in higher energy prices. In 1985 prices declined to their lowest levels in more than a decade, and there was an oil glut, not the shortage Schlesinger and most other energy experts had predicted.[9]

Kenneth Arrow, one of the founders of rational choice theory and the science of risk management, warned, "When developing policy with wide effects for an individual or society, caution is needed because we cannot predict the consequences."[10] It is well to keep Arrow's caution in mind. Nowhere is the failure of expertise more apparent than in domestic program formulations that rely on contributions from the social sciences. Incomplete and faulty data, overreliance on trend extrapolations, and use of unproven theories based on causal fallacies are typical. Lyndon Johnson's attempt to make war on poverty with an untested "community action" concept (which no one including his planners understood) was matched later by Carter's presentation of an energy program whose assumptions he didn't understand, which was matched even later by Clinton's health care program, with an organizational chart that became a national joke. When confronted with evidence that their predictions are incorrect, most experts deny the obvious, claiming that they were "almost" right or their timing was just a little bit off and that their analysis nevertheless was sound.[11]

Complexity in the Advisory System

One expects any organism or social system in which information is entering to increase its complexity, even if a general rule of survival is that nature in the long run prefers the simplest and most elegant solutions.[12] The development of the "modern" presidency is in large measure a history of the increased complexity of the White House Office and the Executive Office of the President. The presidential workload has increased in consequence, and routine presidential performance has improved with all the hired help. But the risks of failure have also increased, especially when limited expertise of presidential aides intersects with poor planning and ill-conceived operations. One response is to add to the complexity: hire more experts and consultants; gather more data; develop more sophisticated models. But there is no evidence that substituting a multifaceted and complex planning process, as was done in health care, to replace the looser BOGSAT (bunch of guys sitting around a table) method in the War on Poverty, will improve domestic planning. Increasing the complexity of the advisory system did not reduce risk for Clinton—it compounded it. The health care task force panels got tangled up in White House court politics over disagreements with cabinet officials and economic advisers. The White House experts were challenged by countervailing expertise; presidential claims of policy viability were diminished in the cacophony of other voices. Presidential authority diminished because of the gap between presidential promises to solve problems and the task force's inability to propose viable policy.

Failure occurs when the president games the advisory system from the top; it also occurs when operatives game it from the bottom. In Vietnam both kinds of gaming occurred. Johnson permitted a semblance of debate on real options. But he ignored the good advisers and their good advice. His advisory system might have worked had the president not manipulated and sabotaged it. Delegating out is no solution. A complex autonomous advisory system takes on an organizational life of its own, and the more resources it commands, the greater its dysfunctions. An advisory system will fail when those with local knowledge are marginalized and when those supplying information up the chain of command are themselves "gaming" the system for their own promotions.

Presidential decisions will be flawed when there are too many grand theorists and not enough practitioners with local knowledge and operational expertise. The more complex the system the more there will be policy distortion based on the "learned incapacity" and "tunnel vision" of a narrow group of experts. Issues will be compartmentalized and controlled by claims of professional expertise, and then there will be less room for freelancing by generalists. The process itself may become controversial, as happened with the court case to open up the health care task force, or the advisers as much as the advice may become the issue: In Vietnam the "best and the brightest" became a synecdoche for the failed policies; Ira Magaziner became a poster boy for opponents of the health care plan. The White House finds itself spending political capital to defend the planners, which diverts public attention from the merits of the proposal. The complexity of the process itself may be caricatured by opponents as a Rube Goldberg contraption that doesn't work and that will produce failed policies.

The displacement of policy formulation from the departments into the institutionalized presidency does not serve the president's interests. The White House aides should be the *consumers* of policy and not its *producers*: albeit well-educated consumers who evaluate proposals produced by departments or task forces based on their own evaluation of the quality of analysis and its political viability. Their stance should be that of the skeptic, not the advocate.

Gamesmanship

Presidents are game players: They make moves and defend against the moves of their adversaries, they try to win by getting opponents to lose materiel, abandon options, give ground, and concede. But sometimes gamesmanship is a losing proposition. In his Vietnam escalation Johnson tried to compel his enemy to negotiate on American terms. The North Vietnamese played a better game of compellence: They saw and raised the bet, and their actions compelled us to match them each step of the way to avoid total disaster.

Gamesmanship presupposes cool, calm, and collected decision making, but presidents often fail because they rigidify in crises; they ignore, discount, deny, forget, or misinterpret information; they deceive themselves; they do not correctly calculate the responses of other parties; they attempt to achieve contradictory goals. They rely on poor information about adversaries, fail to understand their intentions, misinterpret and misunderstand their messages, see imaginary dangers where none exist, and miscalculate real dangers. Presidents assimilate information that bolsters their prior beliefs while rejecting information that might contradict their assumptions. They devalue competing interests, bolster their own preferred options, miscalculate costs and benefits, and spread out alternatives so that it seems that only one decision is viable. They procrastinate, or alternatively, engage in a burst of hyperactive search followed by premature decision. They make bad calculations about probabilities and odds and about costs and benefits: There is often an inverse relationship between the importance of the goal and the calculation of the cost of obtaining it. If they recognize how costly a decision may be, they may believe that any means are justified because of such costly ends, and that too may lead to faulty risk calculations based on wishful thinking. Such were some of the problems involved in Bush 43's foray into Iraq.

Presidents rely on poor historical analogies and learn the wrong lessons or overgeneralize lessons from the past into inflexible axioms for future behavior; they are wedded to methods that worked in the past and are resistant to innovation more suited to a new situation, or they are too swayed by their own personal experiences or those that marked their generation's coming of age. They are influenced by a consensus of advisers who have negotiated their own arrangements to protect their own interests. They plan unrealistically, and their plans are overtaken by events. They "normalize" risk (i.e., devalue the problems associated with poor odds) because of the culture of risk within the organizations that make up the institutionalized presidency, because of negotiation of risk that takes place among officials, or because of a consensus or coalition of officials that may form in support of a proposed decision. The anarchic and chaotic interactions among nations may leave the president with hostile images of other parties to disputes, and cognitive rigidity in the White House may reinforce these images, while decision makers discount information that might reduce tensions. The result may be tragic, when in the fog of decision making all sides to a potential conflict are drawn into the maelstrom of events none preferred, none foresaw, and none controlled.[13]

These decision dysfunctions are well known, but the worst of it is that presidents and their advisers tend to overvalue their own rationality and devalue the rationality of their adversaries: Their view of the world and the information they use is reliable; their opponents are ignorant, irrational, immoral, and irresponsible.

Rational Decision Making and System Complexity

These *sufficiency* explanations for flawed operations are logically and intuitively satisfying: Nevertheless, flaws in information gathering and dysfunctional decision making by the president or the small group surrounding him are not *necessary* conditions for presidential failure. Presidents do not always fail because they and their advisers act irrationally, and conversely sometimes they may succeed in spite of irrational calculations. Obversely, sometimes their efforts to make rational choices, based on concepts from game theory, compound their problems and contribute to their failures.

In the Vietnam escalation, presidential gamesmanship involved a high degree of systemic complexity, with many advisory units interacting with each other and many operational units interacting with advisory groups. It also involved tightly coupled operations. Every local initiative of Vietcong and North Vietnamese forces was considered by U.S. policymakers to be part of Hanoi's overall strategic game. Small incidents resulted in major U.S. escalations, completely out of proportion to the provocations or even the intentions of the other side. Presidential gamesmanship intersected with complexity or chaotic effects in ways that made it unlikely that rational choices could long be maintained. Because policymakers in Vietnam succeeded in keeping the level of threat below the nuclear threshold, their incentives to drop their games of escalation and compellence were lessened.

The Limits of Rational Choice

Presidents do not engage in formal game theoretical modeling, but they do use elements of rational decision making, and some of their advisers do make explicit use of game theoretic concepts and models. There is something beguiling about the prospect of "rational choice" in the White House, about formalizing the gamesmanship style into a "science" of decision making, about using a scientific discipline to overcome the messy dysfunctions that now exist. But presidents must beware of a "revenge effect": The application of formal game theory is likely to *increase* the odds of failure.

Fortunately presidents do not play "games" that correspond to the properties of formal models. For one thing, they have intentional rather than transitive preferences and rank choices only in the context of situations as they are presented to them, feeling free to change their rankings and valuations in new and evolving situations. But at least some of the elements of rational choice— particularly "war gaming" simulations and two-player "rational actor" simulations of diplomatic negotiations—are associated with presidential decision making in foreign policy crises.[14]

Presidential gamesmanship differs from formal game theory in several crucial respects. In game theory the ideal case follows the assumption that all players have equivalent (even if incomplete) knowledge about each other's preferences and intentions. In the rough and tumble world of politics, as in war, no game begins when these circumstances prevail: Adversaries maneuver until they are satisfied that they have an advantage, and then they initiate the game. Presidents assume, as most of us with real-world experience would assume, that a game is a competition that people come to with different aptitudes and abilities and resources—an assumption not found in most formal game theoretic models. Presidents make moves based not on a universal mathematical rationality but on their own situation as they experience and feel it. They assume that the side equipped to make the better moves, diplomatic or military, and with the better crisis management, will come away with a win—or at least avoid a loss. They are interested in asymmetric games that they can play with a mismatch in resources or rules in their favor.

Presidential gamesmanship takes place in a messy and complex world, not in a controlled laboratory situation. Games are not completely bounded: Participation is not limited, the rules of the game are not fully developed or known, participants and rules may change as the game progresses, and odds cannot be set until the game is in progress. There are surprises in the real world that are excluded from formal game models: quantitative surprises that occur when we know that something will happen, but not how much of it; qualitative surprises that occur when something happens that we did not anticipate. Rational choice models do not take these factors into account, but presidents and their advisers must do so.

In the real world (unlike the assumptions of game theorists), a game usually is nested in one or more larger games: Even if the initial and small game is amenable to rational choice theory, it is impossible to use the approach with nested games. Larger games constrain smaller games: Vietnam was partly constrained by superpower nuclear capabilities and by presidential election politics; Bush 41's budget summitry was constrained by an emerging Gulf crisis; Clinton's budget game was informed by the upcoming presidential election. The staple of the Hollywood movie's crime or political formula is the game that gets out of hand, as players transgress and as rules go by the wayside. Novelists and screenwriters know intuitively that no game can be contained and that there are always games within games, and so they fashion their plots accordingly. So do some politicians. "He's not six moves ahead of you," Bill Paxon (R-NY) once remarked about his mentor Newt Gingrich (R-GA), "he's six chess boards ahead of you."[15]

From the White House perspective, one game blends into another, both in terms of space and time. This creates a tendency to suboptimize play in any individual game by invoking norms of "fairness" and reciprocity in future engagements that lower present payoffs or by conceding a position now as part of a transaction to gain support for another game later or by understanding that moves may be linked. In 1998 budget summit negotiations, Republicans had to consider a concurrent impeachment game, and so they abandoned efforts to win in the budget game, eschewing threats to shut down the government, because they did not want to give Clinton an opening. Clinton won much more in that year's budget summit than he would have had he not faced impeachment—a counterintuitive outcome, albeit one that is obvious if one thinks through the logic of nested games.

Just as in competitive sports, "running up the score" against an opponent, or "hot dogging" to the crowd, may result in reprisals at a later date. What might seem suboptimal, or irrational, when viewed as a move in a single game, can actually be considered a form of optimal integrated rationality when considered in a multiple-game, long-term perspective. Even if a president could achieve a maximum payoff, he might be better off with a "satisficing" and suboptimal result when the game is considered as merely a step in a larger game. Kennedy and Nikita Khrushchev understood this point in the Cuban Missile Crisis, and it is also why Clinton did not order massive bombings on Belgrade: The Kosovo game was embedded in larger games of NATO unity and NATO-Russian relations. General Wesley Clark exhibited great flexibility at the tactical level, improvising new targeting approaches (using forward air rather than ground controllers to develop targets and then subjecting proposed targets to a variety of military assessments), but his strategic latitude was curtailed by NATO Secretary General Javier Solana and by Clinton, so that by lowering operational risks, the political risks could be reduced as well.

Often the president is playing one game with his information, his resources, his political position and his motives, while opponents are playing a different game, as was the case in Vietnam or in the Bush budget summits. Because the games are not the same, neither are the rules, and neither are the payoffs. Even the definition of winning and losing may differ, or the motives for winning or losing in situations in which a player may wish to bluff and get caught, or play a hidden hand, or use other stratagems to deceive one's opponent.

Presidents are better off not relying on formal game theory because odds and probabilities cannot be calculated from idiosyncratic situations. There are not enough cases at the presidential level to make game theoretic generalizations, leaving the chief executive with what John Maynard Keynes called "uncertain knowledge." Much presidential decision making involves "wicked problems," in which the best the White House can do is "fuzzy gambling"; since the problems cannot be formulated with exactitude, solutions cannot be tested ceteris paribus because there are too few cases and laboratory conditions do not prevail, risks cannot be calculated, and outcomes cannot be specified in advance.[16] They may well be better off using what some behavioral scientists refer to as "bounded rationality": using decision strategies based not on sophisticated models, but rather on calibrated adjustments, on preexisting "rules of thumb" (heuristics), on local knowledge.[17]

Presidents may fail when they use gamesmanship in inappropriate situations and when they fail to understand that gamesmanship might be used just as effectively against them. But if they attempt to use game theory as a more sophisticated variant of gamesmanship, they will be reducing their local knowledge, their flexibility, and their ability to calibrate responses along multiple dimensions and for multiple nested games. They will receive nothing of value in return except for the illusory comfort given by models of rational choice, and that comfort will not last long.

The Antipolitical Culture

In both domestic and foreign affairs, presidents constantly negotiate with their allies and adversaries. Presidents succeed or fail depending on their skill at moving toward or away from the center and on their negotiating techniques: their ability to understand their interests, to define their positions, to select a bargaining strategy, to frame and justify a proposal, to bluff and deceive, to threaten or cajole, to exploit time pressures, to set the agenda, to influence the rules, and to decide whether and when to negotiate.[18]

Positioning

Skill at positioning and bargaining are not the only determinants of success or failure for presidents. Americans may have invented the art of the deal, but politics is the game that Americans love to hate. The public has two contradictory moods: Its grudging admiration for wheeler-dealers and "Slick Willies" alternates with its moral fervor and a reformist bent. Since the mid-1960s, an *antipolitical* culture has prevailed: A majority of Americans assume that politicians are not trustworthy, ethical, or honest, that they are only out for themselves, not for the public interest, and that they play the angles for their own gain and not because of honest differences in policy. Consider the proportion of Americans in the mid-1990s giving high ratings for honesty and ethical standards to college teachers (50 percent) and the clergy (54 percent) compared with politicians (10–20 percent).[19] Worse, half the public in the 1990s believed that corruption and dishonesty had increased in the past twenty years. More than half the voters in a 1999 survey thought of "the" government rather than "our" government. Only one in four thought the government pursued the public interest rather than the agenda of special interests or its own agenda.[20] This culture has created a legitimacy crisis for the political practitioner: Voters dislike conflict, compromise, and bargaining, thinking all of it is simply pointless partisan bickering.[21] They see lobbying by interest groups and legislative accommodation as immoral and evil.[22] The public's loss of trust in politicians affects the way the public perceives presidents and in turn limits their ability to win over the public.[23]

The antipolitical culture affects those with whom the president must deal in two ways. First, it changes the cast of characters, particularly in Congress, as new cohorts of true believers are elected pledging to "clean up the mess." There are fewer legislators who position themselves in the center, and fewer who have the aptitude or inclination to craft compromises. In the 1990s ideological activists among the newly elected House Republicans made it more difficult for a Democratic president to engage the opposition in routine bargaining, compromise, and negotiation; similar polarization in Democratic ranks affected Bush 43, even after the 9/11 tragedies and the proclamation of a war on terror. Second, leaders have to take extreme positions or spend their energy defending the principle that compromise is a good thing. In the midst of the 1995 budget negotiations a mystified Gingrich commented on the position taken by the newer members of the House Republican Conference against negotiating with the Clinton White House: "The psychology of where we're at makes no sense to me."[24] In New Hampshire he lashed out at party leaders who opposed his compromises: "I think some people would rather sit out there on the right flank and say, Don't do anything, don't agree to anything."[25] But Gingrich and his fellow Republican leaders themselves had not gained power through compromise. They had been ideologues and revolutionaries, self-styled bomb throwers during the Bush presidency, interested in knocking down the structure of governance, not working within it. Both conservative and liberal ideologues are adept at moralizing the claims of their own constituents and demonizing their opponents, which makes it even more difficult for a president to influence Congress.

When an antipolitical culture dominates the country, compromisable issues on a "more or less" dimension (*spatial issues*) are transformed into noncompromisable moral issues (*valence issues*) susceptible only to a "yes" or "no" determination. Abortion, prayer in schools, flag-burning, and gays in the military fit into that category. Although it is possible to specify a "middle position," the compromise cannot satisfy true believers on either side. Even traditional spatial issues such as budgets and taxes become framed as valence issues and are moralized, so that positions become "nonnegotiable" and compromise is viewed as a sin, as a dishonorable betrayal of principles and of followers, as godlessness.[26] Candidates for president feed into the antipolitical culture by promising that if only they are elected, policies based on principle will prevail.[27] Once in office they are vulnerable, because their attempts at compromise are immediately suspect, and they are called wafflers and sellouts for attempting to negotiate with the enemy—as Bush learned after the budget summit. Civility toward opponents, give and take between honorable adversaries, reciprocal concessions granted by equals to equals—all that Ralph Waldo Emerson meant when he said that, "men descend to meet"—is misunderstood or mischaracterized by true believers. Presidents then become defined by the compromises they make, not by the goals they seek. Even worse, they become negatively defined by their willingness to compromise.

Compromise as a Liability

Presidents have no choice: They must position and negotiate. They must look for common and complementary interests to form a coalition, they must try to bring in those who are indifferent with side payments, and they must try to defeat or neutralize those with divergent, contrary, and conflicting interests. But in doing all this, they must protect themselves from the antipolitical culture. And sometimes they fail, because their search strategy itself has costs and benefits that must be taken into account. Presidents have to *get* from here to there. They have to shift from positions they have taken, as Bush did from his "Read my lips" pledge and Clinton did in redefining his health care proposals. Often the president's willingness to move becomes a valence issue: Is the president demonstrating needed flexibility and pragmatism? Or is his movement simply the unprincipled opportunism of a Slick Willy? One might argue that from the Eisenhower to Kennedy presidencies, spatial movement to the center was considered a positive valence; in the period encompassing Nixon through Clinton, such positioning has increasingly been characterized with a negative valence.

When both parties are constrained by leadership considerations, spatial positioning is only one factor involved in the prospects for a deal: Either a positive or negative valence created by the movement toward the center is another. The public mood sets the context in which negotiations can take place: When politics is legitimized, movement to the center and an eventual compromise leads to "thumbs up" approval; when it is delegitimized, movement to the center is viewed as an unprincipled tactic.

Values and McIssues

Like battlers of forest fires who learn to set backfires to contain the blaze, a president may be successful by converting spatial issues into valence issues. Through 1995 into the election year Clinton moved from programmatic politics to values politics, from the partisan presidency to head of state, from the substantive role of legislator-in-chief to the symbolic role of mourner-in-chief after the Oklahoma City bombing and the firebombing of black churches. He went after Hollywood, attacking producers for making movies that "romanticizes violence and killing." In a speech at Georgetown University, he stressed the need for communal effort, not individualism. He called for a national consensus rather than partisan divisiveness, for "more conversation and less combat." He called on the American people to find common ground as "Democrats and Republicans debate the proper role of government." In a school in the District of Columbia he announced an initiative to help religious children to pray on school grounds without amending or violating the Constitution.

Clinton attempted to straddle the deep divide in race relations with what the White House billed as "common ground" speeches. He came out with a "mend it, don't end it" stance on affirmative action in a speech at the National Archives. On the same day as the Million Man March was held in Washington, Clinton observed in Austin, Texas, that "One million men are right to be standing up for personal responsibility, but one million men do not make right one man's message of malice and division"—a way of distancing himself from the march's organizer, Elijah Muhammad. In June 1996, when several black churches were torched, Clinton spoke out against racial violence, set up a federal task force to deal with racially motivated arson, and got Congress to pass the Church Arson Prevention Act.

A president can succeed by controlling the scale of his agenda. Because Clinton could not rally the nation for major new initiatives after the health care fiasco, he substituted a set of small initiatives and a shift to incremental policymaking, dubbed by Washington reporters "the Incredible Shrinking Agenda": a set of "McIssues" on crime, handguns, school discipline, television violence, tobacco advertising, teenage curfews, school uniforms, truancy enforcement, drug tests for driver's licenses, wiring of classrooms for the Internet, regulation of obscenity on the Internet, deadbeat dads, drive-through deliveries of children, cellular phones for crime-watch groups, the 911 emergency call system, V-chips for parents to control television programming—all of which polls showed were more important to voters, particularly uncommitted voters, than economic issues.[28] Many of these were designed to preempt Republican legislative agenda: If Republicans insisted on tax cuts, he would advance his educational goals with targeted tax cuts. If Republicans were intent on cutting entitlements, the White House would figure out how to get new programs and services in these bills. Instead of talking about a "health-care crisis," in his 1997 state of the Union address, Clinton talked of "step-by-step" gains in access to health care, especially for uninsured children. His liberal critics derided these efforts as Governing Lite, but they missed the point, which was that these initiatives were emotionally heavy (as seriously ill children rightfully are).

Clinton's success with "McIssues" and failure with comprehensive initiatives demonstrates that scaling issues to the right proportions and identifying with positive valences helped him overcome the consequences of poor initial spatial positioning and disastrous program planning. Clinton's success argues for the proposition that presidential decision making must consciously transcend "rational choice" positioning models because presidents make decisions that go against stated probabilities of success or involve trade-offs dominated by better positions or are measured with a poor ratio of costs to benefits. All this is complicated by the fact that much of what divides the participants does not lie along one or two issue dimensions and cannot be resolved by movement along these dimensions, however rational such movement might be. Much of what constrains agreement is not even on the table, and off-the-table issues are more likely to be vulnerable to antipolitical characterizations. The nominal issues to be compromised may not be the fundamental issues at all. The paradox of negotiation is that the closer the parties come to spatial compromise, the farther apart they may draw on valence issues, making it less likely that agreement can be reached.

And so presidents must make decisions on multiple dimensions and position themselves in a complex policy space that combines spatial and valence positioning. Presidents and their adversaries are likely to increase the number of dimensions involved in any important issue in an attempt to gain leverage. This is what Republicans did to Clinton in the health care conflict, when bureaucratic complexity and "big government" became the salient dimension rather than universal coverage.

Bounded Rationality

Presidents may not rely on formal rational choice, but they do engage in a *quasi-rational* approach, in "bounded rationality," in what decision theorists call an "orderly choice" of alternatives. Presidents limit their searches by relying on one or more heuristics: their own ideology, or experience, or political stakes. Or they act as a "clerk" and advance the interests and agendas of others. They make decisions that affect fundamental values of the community, including its political or religious culture or its sense of history. They substitute valences for weakness along the "more or less" dimension. Valence positioning, which is increasingly more amenable to media portrayal than spatial positioning, substitutes for and trumps rational choice and spatial positioning. When all else fails, a politician should operate according to "Gestalt hunches"—a fancy way of saying that the politician must use experience and judgment rather than analytical techniques.[29]

Power Stakes

But is explicitly making decisions based on political calculations a sufficient condition to guarantee against failure? One approach suggests that the president should come up with his conception of the public interest, then innovate policies or make decisions to further that interest, choosing the appropriate strategy and tactics. The opposite approach would be for the president to define his power stakes first and define his own political interest as the public interest. He would innovate policies and make decisions about programs, but do so in order to maximize his power. Even the way the president defines his program would be framed initially by a power stakes analysis. Presidential scholar Richard Neustadt argued that the first approach is used by the "amateur" and that the second approach defines the "professional" president. By seeking to maximize power while managing his personal risks, Neustadt claims, the president not only gains political influence for himself but also furthers the public interest. The president's attempt to maximize his power produces policies that are in the public interest. As Neustadt put it in *Presidential Power:*

> And because the president's own frame of reference is at once so all-encompassing and so political, what he sees as a balance for himself is likely to be close to what is viable in terms of public policy. . . . The president who sees his power stakes sees something very much like the ingredients that make for viability in policy. . . . In a relative but real sense, one can say of a president what Eisenhower's first secretary of defense once said of General Motors: what is good for the country is good for the president, and vice versa.[30]

Neustadt argued that the president must understand his *power stakes*: that means he or she must think ahead, about future moves, and about keeping options open. His choices today must be made with the recognition that they can boost his chances for mastery tomorrow. He must make moves that open up the field, that give him the chance to make big plays, that prevent him from being constricted, hemmed in, merely reacting to the moves of opponents. The power stakes approach to public policy is by far the most influential paradigm for presidency scholars, and rightly so. It prescribes a strategic way of thinking that is of immediate use to presidents and those who advise them.[31] As Neustadt later put it, his main purpose was to answer the question of what might the president do "in his own defense against the mediocre choices, muddled options, unexamined premises, unintended consequences pressed upon him by associates? Theirs the substantive expertise, his only the accountability! What questions might he ask? Deriving from what clues? And what, reliably, could he treat as a source of clues?"[32] What he could treat as clues turned out to be his own stakes in decisions, his own measurement of how his choices would increase or decrease his power to make choices in the future, given his decisions made today.

There have been many critiques of this approach.[33] Some pointed out that taken to its extreme (which Neustadt never did), it smacks of the doctrine that kings can do no wrong. "If the president does it, that means it's legal," Nixon informed British television host David Frost in his only televised interviews about the Watergate break-ins and burglary that had taken place during the 1972 campaign. Neustadt never meant his analysis to be taken to that extreme, but his approach does lend itself to devaluing the expertise and authority of other institutions: If the president has already considered his power stakes, guarded his reputation, and developed his policy based on his professional expertise, and the policy he proposes is the most viable for the country, what role does that leave for the rest of the government? By implication, public policies defined by others (read Congress) must be less viable and less in the public interest.

There is a bit of slight of hand in the Neustadt model. The president is to define public policy in terms of his own power stakes, because that is the professional way to develop the most viable public policy. But if his definition of public policy fits his own political situation like a hand in a glove, it must by definition be ill-suited for those with whom the president must deal. The president is supposed to persuade others *to do of their own volition and on their own authority* what he wants of them. But if what he wants is good for him but not necessarily for them, why would they comply? How would a president persuade? As Neustadt's own examples often illustrate, the president would not be able to do so. If presidential power consists primarily in the power to persuade, then the job may be harder, not easier, if policies are designed with only the president's power stakes in mind.

Some presidents have been successful not when they guarded their reputation but when they allowed others to underestimate them, as Eisenhower did with a "hidden hand" style of leadership he developed in the army and applied to his presidency.[34] One can win just as often through deception, guile, and pretended weakness as through a reputation for success and skill. Eisenhower wished to act when two conditions existed: He knew what there was to know of his opponent; his opponent was deceived about him. Dodger general manager Branch Rickey had the same idea about major league pitching: "We want to produce delusions, practice deceptionism, make a man misjudge. We fool him—that's the whole purpose of the game."

The presidential power model of the 1960s may have given way to a postmodern presidency of the post-Vietnam and post-Watergate era, as the political resources of the White House diminished. Presidents may influence the national agenda, but often they will be checked by outside advocacy or interest groups, as Clinton was in the health care battles, and there is no guarantee that they will even command a national audience, particularly in a distrustful and antipolitical mood.[35] Neustadt assumed that others in the Washington community anticipate the reactions of the president and modify their behavior accordingly. But what happens when it is the president who modifies his behavior because of the anticipated reactions of others? What happens when we have a Rodney Dangerfield ("I can't get no respect") presidency? At that point, epitomized by Clinton midway through his first term, the president drops an ambitious legislative agenda in favor of minor but highly symbolic initiatives, makes unilateral modifications to avoid congressional gridlock, or converts gridlock into campaign themes. Neustadt was on the mark when he talked of the danger that a president might become nothing more than a clerk: always busy with the agenda of others. But it may be the very professionalism of a president attempting to define public policy through his power stakes that does him in.

The professional president sometimes compounds his own problems. A Johnson who guarded his power stakes in Vietnam came up with a policy that provided neither victory nor a successful stalemate procured at a "reasonable" cost but did lead to a credibility gap and a stalemate that was not politically viable. A Ford who guarded his power stakes rushed into a rescue mission costing many American lives, when waiting would have produced the same result at no cost. A Clinton who guarded his power stakes defined his health care reforms in ways that helped him win the nomination and election but left him vulnerable once in office.

Perhaps the most telling critique of the Neustadt approach is that the power stakes model concentrates the attention of the president on acquisition or retention of power itself, rather than on substantive goals and governing principles. Fortunately, most if not all presidents do bring with them goals that are not derived merely from their power stakes; a president who relied solely on the Neustadt model would be operating without any compass or any constraints. Because the model is so self-contained and self-referential, the power stakes approach no longer seems fully legitimate. The power stakes approach toward many issues seems flawed because it is incomplete: It fails to take into account the values of the American people and their noncompromisable valences.

In Neustadt's "political power" paradigm the president fails because he is an amateur, doesn't understand his power stakes, doesn't guard his reputation, lacks institutional resources, is behind the curve of technological innovation, does not organize his White House staff effectively, lacks effective command and control, and is caught in an expectations gap (the public expects what he cannot deliver). But in an *antipolitical* culture presidents fail *because* they maneuver politically, *because* they rely on their White House aides, *because* they guard their power stakes, and *because* they define their positions in terms of these stakes.

The Loss of Authority

A president may try to control the national agenda by going public. When he does, he may gain the trust of the American people or lose all credibility and authority. Washington columnist Meg Greenfield observed that the fundamental issue for Bush and congressional leaders was not budget numbers, but "the loss—or diminution anyway—of their general overall credibility as leaders who deserve respect, whose advice carries a presumption of seriousness, logic and good faith." Even as a deal was being cut, she pointed out, there was "a tremendous hidden cost to government—a cost in authority, trust and believability."[36] A president may know what he is doing, but can he communicate his reasoning in a way that will bring him support and trust of the people?

Authority in America has always involved explaining and justifying reasoning behind action: The Declaration of Independence does more than declare the intentions of those who met in Philadelphia; it pays "a decent respect to the opinions of mankind" by providing a lengthy list of their complaints against the king. Presidential authority requires justification as well. The president initially guarded the Framers' intentions and justified his actions in terms of their constitutional principles. By the 1830s presidential authority had been transformed by Andrew Jackson: "Majority rules" and "to the winners go the spoils" justified policy. By the early twentieth century, through the efforts of Roosevelt, Taft, and Wilson, the basis of authority shifted again to expertise in the service of the public interest—presidents proposed policies developed by task forces and national commissions. During the Cold War, "reasons of national security" justified many presidential actions, just as "homeland security" did at the start of the twenty-first century.

"Your trust is what gives a President powers of leadership," Reagan told the American people, and he was right, because he understood that authority is a *relationship* that flows from the people to the White House—it is not an attribute presidents possess. *Who* is asserting authority is as important as *what* is being asserted: It is the speaker as much as the speech that determines audience acceptance. To do his job the president must convince as much of the public as he can, not only that he knows what he is doing, and not only that what he is doing is in the national interest, but also that he is worthy of being entrusted with the power of decision.

Presidents may fail with misguided attempts to maintain their authority. They may lie or dissemble, as Lyndon Johnson did with his Vietnam escalation and Bush 41 did in his charges of weapons of mass destruction in Iraq, creating "credibility gaps" that haunt their administrations. They may duck issues. Their rhetoric may raise expectations they cannot meet or transgress popular values. When they lose authority, they lose the aura that creates, motivates, and inspires followers, and their supporters hedge or desert while opponents multiply and take the offensive. Within the White House a phony courtier spirit is replaced with a sense of betrayal, a bunker mentality prevails, the staff attempts to circle the wagons, and their inner circle fragments. Presidents whose decisions are under attack will defend their authority by attacking their critics' lack of expertise, qualifications, and knowledge, and attack their faulty reasoning and suspect motives. They claim that critics do not, and cannot, have a presidential vantage point. When this argument fails, as it often does, their authority crumbles.

The president may be defeated by his opponents because they trample on his message. The president has polls and focus groups, so do they; he has speechwriters, a communications office, and spinmeisters, and they have public relations firms; he has access to networks for prime-time speeches to propose his programs, and they have access to the editorial and op-ed pages to respond; he can stage "pseudoevents" to dramatize his themes, and they can spend million of dollars on commercials attacking them. The selling of the Clinton health care plan demonstrates that a president well versed in communications skills, with a staff perhaps unequaled in American history in its sophisticated approach to policy debate, employing all of his resources in an attempt to win the battle for the national agenda, may still be defeated. The president played his rhetorical hand just the way the experts prescribe: He called for a program in the public interest, for a policy good for all, and not just for a deprived part of the population. He cast his rhetoric in the framework of struggle between the public and the private interest. Yet the White House was outspent, outmaneuvered, and outgunned, an indication that at least one reason for presidential failure is due to the diminished resources a president can bring to bear when compared with the resources of his opponents.

"As one looks to the future," political scientist Samuel Kernell wrote in 1993 as Clinton assumed office, "the prospect for the continued use of going public as a presidential strategy shines bright."[37] Kernell assumed that the strategy of going public would continue to be important "in the strategic repertoire" of presidents. Yet he also noted that the president would face countervailing use of the media by opponents in Congress. As it turned out, in the 1990s these opponents maximized their strength when they combined their resources with interest groups that used a grassroots media strategy against the White House. On any given issue a president that lives by the media may well die by the media, and an effort to gain public support for an initiative may lead to an interest group backlash. Clinton found this to be true not only with health care reform but also with gun control, tobacco regulation, and other health issues. By 1999 the "Harry and Louise" commercials were replaced by "Maude," a character in a $30 million media campaign produced by the pharmaceutical industry. Her tagline was "I don't want big government in my medicine cabinet," and Maude helped block Clinton's proposal to provide prescription-drug benefits under Medicare. Bush 43 followed Clinton's failures with many of his own: He went public on Social Security reform and immigration reform and was handily defeated on both.

One should not equate authority with truthfulness. Ford converted the *Mayaguez* rescue from an operational fiasco into a political success by selectively omitting the most important facts. Kennedy and his circle never admitted they had bargained with the Soviets for removal of missiles from Cuba, insisting instead that "it was eyeball to eyeball, and the other fellow blinked," in the words Secretary of State Dean Rusk. One might wish for hard and fast rules about such deceptions, particularly rules embodying moral precepts, but one of the dirty little secrets about presidential power is that such rules are hard to come by, but one does seem to hold true: The underlying dimension involved in authority relationships is the consonance or dissonance of presidential action with American values. Eisenhower was able to rebound from his own deceptions in the U-2 incident because commentators contrasted his fundamental honesty (however belated) with Soviet trickery. Kennedy was able to restore his authority after the Bay of Pigs with claims that he had learned a valuable lesson about crisis management. Reagan maintained his moral authority with many people even after he had lost credibility; those who elected him twice understood him to be "right" about the big picture involving the Soviets, even though he had trouble explaining the arms sales to Iran.

Authority is increasingly difficult for presidents to sustain. As we have seen, their attempts to solve complicated problems are not matched by the expertise at their disposal. Their gamesmanship, positioning, compromising, and power stakes decision making compound their problems in an antipolitical culture. Their maneuvers become the focus of media reporting, so that even when they do make a serious attempt to argue their case, the media will not report it, preferring to focus on some dramatic moment, or some personality issue, followed by an ironic and detached analysis of the "How's he doing?" or "Watch the spin" variety.

Clinton, victimized by this style of reporting, complained of a Washington insider culture "too much into the day-to-day gamesmanship of politics."[38] But the White House itself feeds the media frenzy: Presidential rhetoric is designed to further presidential gamesmanship, and it greatly contributes to the weakening of presidential authority.[39] Kennedy's speechwriter Theodore Sorensen bemoaned a "long-term decline over several administrations in the quality of English spoken at the White House," and it got worse under Reagan, Clinton, and the two Bushs, but there is more to it than that.[40] Presidents often choose media strategies designed to increase support for their leadership rather than support for particular policies, lest they suffer the kind of defeat meted out to Clinton in the health care fight. Their deliberative role takes a backseat to their ceremonial role. They transform substantive arguments into symbolic appeals and stances, they *assert* rather than *argue* their cases, with shorter, simple sound bites and slogans. Presidents have shifted their rhetoric, from constitutional to partisan to public policy and finally to confessional. Presidential candidates have followed the Clinton style, combining the detached expertise of the policy wonk with the emotive "I feel your pain" patter of talk-show hosts. This entertains the nation, but does not move it.

"Governing with public approval requires a continuing political campaign," Pat Caddell advised Carter. The president becomes a storyteller, a stump speaker in permanent "campaign mode," an Oprah wannabe. But there are two dangers in going public in this vernacular. The first is overexposure: At a time when people don't want to be bothered with Washington, a president calling for their attention may wind up merely nagging rather than leading, and like Carter with his energy speeches, he may simply lose his audience. The second is that the problem of authority parallels the problem of command: To order someone to do something is an indication that persuasion has failed; to go public time and time again in an effort to rally public support is to acknowledge that rhetoric has failed; to speak in a completely common vernacular is an indication that an authority relationship has been diminished.

Socrates observed that had people not been able to speak, and had they wanted to communicate, they would have copied the dumb: They would have talked with their hands, head, and body. In effect, television and televisual images enable presidents to do all that and more, by staging pseudoevents, those designed just for a television audience. But once a president becomes an entertainer, he runs the risk of devaluing his mystique as a leader. As actor John Travolta put it in the early 1980s: "I can do all that President Reagan does. I do it all the time and have a bigger audience."[41] Presidents have lost *their* audience through overblown rhetoric and pseudoevents that has not been matched by substantive achievements. In the 1960–1980 period, according to Neilsen ratings, presidents could count on audiences ranging from 40 to 65 percent, averaging around 53 percent. Since that time, their audiences for prime-time speeches have declined to a range of 25 to 40 percent, with each president from Nixon through Clinton enjoying less audience share than his predecessor (Nixon averaged 50 percent share while Clinton's was barely above 30 percent).[42] The audience for White House sound bites on nightly network news has shrunk to less than 20 percent of households. Coverage of nominating conventions went down from 142 network hours in 1976 to 24 in 1996, with only fifteen million households tuning in. In the aftermath of his impeachment Clinton seemed to be banished from the front pages of the newspapers, the first president ever "exiled" since the presidency became headline news during World War II and its Cold War aftermath.

To the extent that there is an audience for presidential rhetoric, it is mediated by television and radio commentators and by newspaper reporters and magazine journalists. Increasingly the coverage of the president (and other political leaders) is negative, from the initial campaign through their term in office. Reporters dissect and question the president's strategies and motivations. Any maneuver, any rhetorical shifting of ground that can be detected over the course of an entire term, any attempt to exercise the art of political compromise, becomes a bad-news story, with a negative valence: The president is waffling, pandering, or posturing.[43] And there are plenty of bad-news stories in the antipolitics era: In the 1960s, less than one-third of the media's evaluations of top national political leaders were negative; that figure rose to more than two-thirds by the 1990s.[44]

The main problem comes when media coverage shifts a personality trait from a positive to a negative. The president's authority is usually at greatest risk when a decision he makes can be personalized so that an aspect of his personality and character is illuminated. He loses far less (or nothing at all) when his decisions merely confirm what everyone already knows about him. Eisenhower, Reagan, and Bush 41 were not very vulnerable when they fumbled on facts or seemed less than energetic: They all were hurt when their credibility was threatened. Carter was terribly vulnerable when his moralistic stance toward governance was undercut by his transparently political cabinet reshuffle maneuvers. Clinton did not lose popularity on issues involving character: The public always understood that his marriage was problematic and that he had been unfaithful. He did lose points when his adroit political maneuvering became transformed into an indictment; to wit, that he lacked sincerity or the ability to tell the truth in his public and private life.

The Loss of Legitimacy

"Public sentiment is everything," Lincoln said as he took emergency actions during the Civil War, "with public sentiment nothing can fail; without it, nothing can succeed." A successful assertion of authority and a demonstration of popularity reinforces presidential legitimacy and allows the president to expand the powers of his office. When authority is weakened, however, legitimacy may be questioned as well.

The president's conduct in office is considered legitimate by the American people when he has the right to be in the Oval Office (by popular election, constitutional selection, or constitutional and legally sanctioned succession), when he exercises his powers constitutionally and lawfully, and when his decisions seem fair and in conformity to fundamental values. Most presidents have had no problem claiming right of place, but because the Constitution and statutory law is often silent, underdefined, or ambiguous at key points, presidents must often define their powers for themselves, and the president is free to interpret his powers as he chooses until checked and balanced by Congress or the courts—which rarely happens. The real determinant of the legitimacy of presidential prerogative rests with its consonance or dissonance with fundamental American values, where constitutional law and public opinion intersect.

Presidents have gone beyond the black-letter text of the Constitution to lay claim to powers that the government may exercise by virtue of the sovereignty of the American people. Thomas Jefferson decided to acquire the Louisiana Territory by treaty from France, although the Constitution makes no mention of a power for the Union to acquire territory and only lays out the method by which states may join the Union. "The less said about any constitutional difficulties, the better," Jefferson cautioned his attorney general.[45] They exercise *emergency powers*, also known as Lockean Prerogative, after John Locke, who referred to the power of the executive "to act according to discretion, for the publick good, without the prescription of the Law, and sometimes even against it."[46] To defend his suspension of habeas corpus, Lincoln put the question to Congress in his message of July 4, 1861: "Are all the laws, *but one*, to go unexecuted, and the government itself go to pieces, lest that one be violated? Even in such a case, would not the official oath be broken, if the government should be overthrown, when it was believed that disregarding the single law, would tend to preserve it?"[47] Presidents claim the right to preserve the "peace of the United States" by intervening with the military in civil disorders or strikes, by using warrantless wiretaps and surveillance against suspected foreign and domestic enemies, and by holding unlawful combatants indefinitely, treating them without Geneva Convention protections and trying them before presidential tribunals.[48]

Presidents through their signing statements may claim a *dispensing power:* the right to refuse to execute the provisions of a law, if obeying those provisions might be harmful to the nation, even in the absence of an emergency. While they have an obligation to "take care that the laws be faithfully executed," that obligation does not appear in the oath of office. They claim that when laws conflict, their oath grants them the prerogative to decide which laws are to be enforced. These claims are American variations of long-standing claims of arcana imperii—the secrets of rule possessed by the prince, which led to claims of raison d'état in matters of national security.[49]

"The president is at liberty, both in law and in conscience, to be as big a man as he can," Woodrow Wilson concluded. "Only his capacity will set the limit."[50] Presidents claim vast executive and legislative powers, including the *inherent powers* of a "chief executive" based on an expansive reading of specific constitutional clauses. They claim *implied powers*, arguing that, like Congress, they may take actions "necessary and proper" to put their executive powers into effect, having all the means at their disposal that are not forbidden by the Constitution. They combine their constitutional powers with statutes passed by Congress to expand their administrative, diplomatic, and military powers. They issue executive orders, in effect creating a *legislative power*, and their orders may go way beyond the scope of the laws Congress passed to deal with a subject, sometimes covering matters on which Congress has not legislated at all.

Some uses of prerogative power involve ambiguities or silences in the Constitution. In these cases presidents may not act covertly; they may boldly claim what no past presidents have claimed before. If a president succeeds his claim of prerogative is likely to be incorporated into the Constitution. The president may benefit from a *frontlash* effect: The successful assertion of power will not only yield dividends in the form of enhanced authority but it will also strengthen the office itself. The Mount Rushmore presidents and the great twentieth-century presidents used prerogative power successfully in their most important decisions: Washington in instituting a pro-British neutrality policy in 1792; Jefferson with the Louisiana Purchase of 1803; Lincoln with the preparations for Civil War; Franklin Roosevelt with preparedness, the Destroyer Deal with Great Britain, and the use of the military before Pearl Harbor in an undeclared naval war against Germany in the Atlantic. The presidents' followers united while the opposition split; they won their next elections and their parties maintained majorities in Congress; and in no case was there partisan turnover in the White House in the election held after their second term. Congress did not check them but passed laws supporting their actions, and the courts did not interfere. The powers asserted by these presidents become part of the "living Constitution" because they were legitimated by Congress, the party system, and the people. The Cuban Missile Crisis resulted in a frontlash outcome: The precedent was set that the president, unilaterally, could commit the United States to regional peacekeeping, could control the nuclear arsenal for compellence as well as deterrence, and could do so without prior authorization from the United Nations. The expansion of constitutional prerogatives was matched by an expansive interpretation of U.S. sovereign rights and regional security rights under international law.

The Madisonian concept of a constitution of partial separation of powers, collaborative government, interior contrivances, and checks and balances assumes that before the president makes a decision he will review it with his top aides, take it before the cabinet or another policy council, and then present his decision to Congress for prior legitimation in the form of a law, an appropriation of funds, or a resolution of authorization or support. The Hamiltonian concept of prerogative power, of "energy in the executive," is the antithesis of Madisonian principles: It involves governance by faits accomplis. When a president institutes prerogative government he often imposes tight secrecy, confining his deliberations to a very small group. When he is ready to act, he issues proclamations, executive orders, and national security directives; institutes a chain of command flowing from the White House directly to the officials who will carry out his orders; and gives commands to subordinates to execute his orders and follow his policy. He usually does not consult with members of Congress in advance, nor does he ask for legislative authorization.

A president's decision to use prerogatives precedes the actual operation itself and has a bearing on how the operation itself is planned and implemented. The more the president anticipates that his use of prerogative will be controversial, the greater his incentive to act first and explain later. The president decides, his subordinates implement his policy, and he then informs Congress and the American people. At that point the politics of prerogative government begins: The president must defend the legitimacy and authority of his actions.

No president has ever admitted that he violated the Constitution or usurped the power of Congress or the courts. All obtain opinions from their Attorneys General, White House Counsel, and counsel for the relevant departments (especially State, Defense, and the CIA) arguing for the constitutionality and legality of their actions. The Solicitor General of the Justice Department defends the constitutional prerogatives of the president before the Supreme Court if necessary. Yet for every argument a president makes, a counterargument exists. "A century and a half of partisan debate and scholarly speculation," Justice Robert Jackson concluded in a case involving presidential prerogatives, "yields no net result but only supplies more or less apt quotations from respected sources on each side of any question. They largely cancel each other."[51] Another half-century of jurisprudence confirms Jackson's comment.

Presidents know that if they can defend the wisdom of the policy and its consonance with American values, most of the constitutional criticism will not harm them. Winning in the court of public opinion is often more important than winning in a court of law. Even so, the odds in court are usually with the president: The federal courts usually abstain from deciding cases involving presidential prerogatives using procedural rules or the doctrine of political questions, or else declare them to be constitutional exercises of power. The courts check and balance presidents only when their own prerogatives are at stake, such as the right to obtain evidence in spite of a claim of executive privilege or to maintain jurisdiction and reject broad claims of presidential immunity or when presidents make claims of national emergency.[52] Although courts rule against presidential claims of testimonial privilege, they uphold State Secrets Doctrine claims that allow the president to withhold sensitive information in lawsuits against the government.

Presidents in most controversies usually have little to fear from judicial review of their prerogative power. Yet many who won in court later found themselves politically damaged or destroyed after their exercise of such powers. Both Truman and Johnson successfully defended presidential war-making powers in the courts, yet these victories did not save them from the loss of public support that ended their chances to win second elective terms. Although Clinton lost in the courts on his broad claims of testimonial privilege, these cases had no impact on public opinion or on the outcome of his impeachment.

Prerogative governance has a direct bearing on operational viability; the president's negotiation of risk may involve constitutional considerations. This is a variation of the law of anticipated reactions: The president, knowing in advance that his use of prerogatives will be controversial, protects his stakes even as it lowers the odds of success. Kennedy shifted the location of the Bay of Pigs landing and put conditions on tactical air support in order to preserve his "deniability." The Reagan administration protected the president in planning the transfer of arms to Iran and ended up with "an operational nightmare." The president has an even greater incentive to minimize his own risk when one risky operation is linked to others. The Watergate burglary, for example, was part of a series of illegal operations conducted against political opponents; the Iran transfer of arms was linked to the Contra transfers of funds and to the third-party transfers; attempts to assassinate Fidel Castro were linked to other CIA assassination attempts, and so on. The revelation of one operation is likely to result in blown cover on others. Thus the White House calculates that its own involvement must be shielded at all costs. The protection of presidential legitimacy results in distancing, in loss of command and control, which results in the very failure the president was attempting to guard against in the first place.

One of the ways for a president to lower risks is to employ a "soft" prerogative strategy. When Reagan sent American troops to Lebanon in 1982, he agreed to sign a congressional resolution under the War Powers Act extending the commitment of U.S. forces for eighteen months; this seemed to indicate that Reagan was accepting the constitutionality of the law. But when he signed the Beirut Resolution, the president circulated a "signing statement" indicating that he had given away none of his constitutional powers to deploy U.S. armed forces. Similarly, just before commencing hostilities against Iraq in January 1991, Bush agreed to accept a congressional "authorization" for the use of force. Even so, Bush had already ordered U.S. special forces into Iraq and would have instituted hostilities against Iraq even had Congress not granted him authority; in effect he only agreed to the vote because congressional leaders had assured him the votes would be there. His son did likewise before the invasion of Iraq in 2003.

The assertion of prerogative power can lead to the complete collapse of a presidency, for part or all of a president's term, in an "overshoot and collapse" crisis of governance. The constitutional claim a president makes may be so sweeping, or his abuse of power so enormous, that Congress and the courts feel compelled to act. This is most likely to occur when the president seems to be infringing on core functions of coordinate institutions, such as Andrew Johnson's attempts to obstruct the postwar Reconstruction policy of the Republican Congress or Reagan's attempt to circumvent the congressional appropriations power in the Iran-Contra affair or when a president is engaged in obstruction of justice through a cover-up, such as Nixon's conspiracy to cover up the Watergate crimes. A president may be impeached or be subject to the impeachment process, and his administration may become so tied up in congressional investigations and legal proceedings that it becomes paralyzed.

Whether or not the president faces a threat of impeachment, his powers can be put in commission in a legitimacy crisis. In both the Watergate and Iran-Contra affairs, chiefs of staff were replaced: Former senator Howard Baker (R-TN), a leading inquisitor in the Watergate hearings, became Reagan's chief of staff in the midst of Iran-Contra. In both Watergate and Iran-Contra, the secretaries of state and defense held the government together in the aftermath of a presidential collapse because they had the confidence of Congress. "Super-K" as Henry Kissinger was called, dominated policymaking in the first year of the Ford administration and served as a symbol of continuity in American foreign policy; similarly George Shultz was considered at the time to have been insulated from the Iran-Contra affair and therefore was in a position to dominate American foreign policy for the remainder of the Reagan administration. A de facto "prime ministerial" system temporarily evolved, with power flowing to cabinet secretaries who enjoyed the confidence of Congress and the people.

There is a close connection between authority and legitimacy, and the president must guard both aspects of his relationship with the American people or suffer the consequences. A president must work at maintaining legitimacy: It is not a relationship that may be taken for granted. A president who decides to act unilaterally leaves himself open to two lines of attack once his fait accompli has become public: Critics will challenge his authority and claim he doesn't know what he's doing; they will also challenge his legitimacy by claiming that he lacks the constitutional powers he asserts, that he has usurped congressional powers, that he has gone beyond the constitutional powers of the government as a whole, or that he has taken actions that are unjust. A president who is managing issues successfully will benefit from a "frontlash" effect: Constitutional doubts will often be put aside, but when his policy fails his critics will have no such inhibitions—they will charge that he cut constitutional corners for no good reason. Prerogative politics becomes a high-risk gamble because it cuts against the grain of American democracy and limited constitutional government.

The American people have always been averse to the unchecked exercise of executive power, equating it with monarchs and dictators, so the president's critics will claim he was autocratic rather than democratic; second, the exercise of prerogative power, if it involved secrecy and a fait accompli, will be characterized by the president's critics as deceptive or evasive. Presidents respond by discrediting their critics as best they can. They argue that their actions were required in the national interest: Opponents of their policy either lack the facts to understand the national interest or do not have the national interest at heart. Why might their critics be misinformed or uninformed? Because in national security matters the president has intelligence sources that he cannot reveal (or else they might be compromised). He has information that must remain top secret. He knows things about the situation that his critics cannot know—and that the American people cannot know. The president argues that the critics should reserve judgment until he can brief them, and that the American people should trust him and other top officials to act in the national interest and prevent division and disunity—the claim of *arcana imperii*.

To members of his own party, the president will argue that those tempted to desert him are also sealing their own fate, because a party split will only help the opposition. To members of the opposition party the president will argue that his diplomatic prerogatives should be supported in a spirit of bipartisanship; that war-making prerogatives should be supported because to do otherwise is almost the same as giving "aid and comfort to the enemy" and that in covert operations the president's prerogatives should not be challenged because it might lead to embarrassing revelations that would damage the standing of the United States and its intelligence capabilities. For members of Congress partisan factors are more important than any consistent or principled constitutional position about presidential powers: Legislators usually support presidents of their own party, even if they have to give them the benefit of the doubt, while their partisan opponents will attack their exercise of prerogative. Franklin Roosevelt won support of most Northern Democrats but only a small percent of Republicans on votes involving presidential powers, a pattern similar for Truman and Kennedy. Only Johnson won majorities from both parties when issues involved his prerogatives. Republican presidents Nixon, Ford, and Reagan gained far more support from Republicans than Democrats in Congress on issues of presidential power, while only Eisenhower won bipartisan majorities.[53]

Politicians are prone to "situational constitutionalism." Democrats who supported expansive presidential diplomatic and military powers exercised by presidents from Franklin Roosevelt through Kennedy later shifted to criticize these powers when exercised by Nixon through Bush 43. A similar reversal occurred after the 1994 midterm elections, when Democrats defended Clinton's constitutional prerogatives in foreign affairs while the new Republican majority insisted that Congress play a greater role. We should not expect a principled position on constitutional issues from most politicians. A president who retains the support of his party will not suffer disaster, but he will have to work at it. And it is when his own partisans stop defending his prerogatives that he must begin to worry, as conservative commentator (and presidential candidate) Pat Buchanan did when he referred to Republican senators as "elephants running for the tall grass" in the midst of the Iran-Contra affair.

At the end of the day, what keeps his partisans in line, and what often saves a president who defends his use of prerogative power, is an appeal to shared American values. The president appeals to what the Greeks called *nomos*, the values of the community. Deep within the traditional political culture developed over two centuries is a pragmatic streak that pays less heed to legalities than to practicalities, that cares more about ends than about means, that is willing to bend the law or even break it to get things done, that cares more for keeping decisions consistent with values than with law. We distinguish between legal versus illegal and constitutional versus unconstitutional, but we also have separate criteria for right versus wrong. In guarding against presidential failure, cultivating this distinction is not a waste of time, for presidents or those who would presume to advise them.

Notes

1. Mark Bovens and Paul 't Hart, *Understanding Policy Fiascoes* (New Brunswick, NJ: Transaction Publishers, 1996).

2. Helmut K. Anheier, *When Things Go Wrong: Organizational Failures and Breakdowns* (Thousand Oaks, CA: Sage, 1999); Russ Marion, *The Edge of Organization:*

Chaos and Complexity Theories of Formal Social Systems (Thousand Oaks, CA: Sage, 1999).

3. Duncan J. Watts and Steven H. Strogatz, "The Collective Dynamics of 'Small World' Networks," *Nature* (June 1998): 440–42.

4. Scott Kirkpatrick et al., "Relation of Typical-Case Complexity to the Nature of the Phase Transition," *Random Structures Algorithms* vol. 15, nos. 3–4 (1999): 414–35.

5. Richard Neustadt, *Presidential Power and the Modern Presidents: The Politics of Leadership from FDR to Carter* (New York: Macmillan, 1986), 185.

6. Jonathan Fuerbringer, "A Science Truly Dismal at Prediction," *New York Times* (February 23, 1999): A10; John Dorfman, "Beware of Prophets Bearing Predictions," *Bloomberg Features* (1998).

7. Quoted in Tim Weiner, "Aging Shop of Horrors," *New York Times* (July 20, 1997): E-6.

8. Willis C. Armstrong et al., "The Hazards of Single-Outcome Forecasting," in H. Bradford Westerfield, ed., *Inside the CIA's Private World: Declassified Articles from the Agency's Internal Journal, 1955–1992* (New Haven, CT: Yale University Press, 1995), 238–54.

9. Richard Bernstein's "sell-side indicator" tracks changes in bullish and bearish attitudes of sixteen of the top stock market strategists to advise investors to do the *opposite* of what the majority recommends.

10. Kenneth Arrow, "I Know a Hawk from a Handsaw," in Michael Szenberg, ed., *Eminent Economists: Their Life Philosophies* (New York: Cambridge University Press, 1992), 46; Edward O. Wilson, *Consilience: The Unity of Knowledge* (New York: Vintage Books, 1998), 74.

11. Philip Tetlock, "Theory Driven Reasoning about Possible Pasts and Probable Futures in World Politics: Are We Prisoners of Our Preconceptions?" *American Journal of Political Science* vol 43, no. 2 (April 1999): 335–67.

12. M. Mitchell Waldrop, *Complexity: The Emerging Science at the Edge of Order and Chaos* (New York: Touchstone, 1992).

13. Alexander George, *Presidential Decisionmaking in Foreign Policy* (Boulder, CO: Westview Press, 1980).

14. Philip Mirowski, "When Games Grow Deadly Serious: The Military Influence on the Evolution of Game Theory," *History of Political Economy* vol. 23: 227–60.

15. Joe Klein, "Broken Contract," *New Yorker* (August 4, 1997): 28

16. H. W. J. Rittel and M. M. Webber, "Dilemmas in a General Theory of Planning," *Policy Sciences* vol. 4 (1973): 155–69; Yehezkel Dror, "Fateful Decisions as Fuzzy Gambles with History," *Jerusalem Journal of International Relations* vol. 12 (1990): 1–12.

17. Gerd Gigerenzer and Peter M. Todd, *Simple Heuristics That Make Us Smart* (New York: Oxford University Press, 1999); Jonathan Bendor, "A Model of Muddling Through," *American Political Science Review* vol. 89, no. 4 (December 1995): 819–40.

18. Richard Ned Lebow, *The Art of Bargaining* (Baltimore: Johns Hopkins Press, 1996), 55–134; Dean Pruitt, *Negotiation Behavior* (New York: Academic Press, 1981), 180–235.

19. George Gallup Jr., *The Gallup Poll: Public Opinion 1994* (Wilmington, DE: Scholarly Resources, Inc., 1995), 151–55.

20. Hart and Teeter poll, Council for Excellence in Government, released July 12, 1999.

21. John Hibbing and Elizabeth Theiss-Morse, *Congress as Public Enemy: Public Attitudes toward American Political Institutions* (New York: Cambridge University Press, 1995), 18.

22. Hibbing and Theiss-Morse, *Congress*, xii.

23. Marc J. Hetherington, "The Political Relevance of Political Trust," *American Political Science Review* vol. 92, no. 4 (December 1998): 791–808.

24. *New York Times* (July 23, 1997): A-15.

25. Jerry Gray, "House Speaker Takes Up a Political Cause in New Hampshire, But Whose?" *New York Times* (August 25, 1997): A10.

26. J. Patrick Dobel, *Compromise and Political Action: Public Morality in Liberal and Democratic Life* (Savage, MD: Rowman & Littlefield, 1990), 2–3; also Joseph Churba, *The Washington Compromise: How Government Betrays the National Interest* (Lanham, MD: University Press of America, 1995), x–xiii.

27. John R. Hibbing and Elizabeth Theiss-Morse, "The Media's Role in Fomenting Public Disgust with Congress," *Extensions* (Fall 1996): 15–18.

28. Dick Morris, *Behind the Oval Office: Getting Elected against All Odds* (New York: Random House, 1997), 209–25.

29. Jon Elster, *Ulysses and the Sirens: Studies in Rationality and Irrationality* (Cambridge, UK: Cambridge University Press, 1979), 132–33.

30. Richard Neustadt, *Presidential Power*, 183–85.

31. On the omission of strategic choice, preferences, and power stakes in rational choice theory, see Elster, *Ulysses and the Sirens*, 77.

32. Richard Neustadt, "Presidential Power: A Reflective View," *Presidential Studies Quarterly* vol. 4 (Fall 1980): 361–63.

33. Peter W. Sperlich, "Bargaining and Overload: An Essay on Presidential Power," in Aaron Wildavsky, ed., *Perspectives on the Presidency*, 2nd ed. (New York: Little, Brown and Co., 1980), 406–30; Harry A. Bailey Jr., "Neustadt's Thesis Revisited: Toward the Two Faces of Presidential Power," *Presidential Studies Quarterly* vol. 11 (Summer 1981): 351–63; Thomas E. Cronin, "Presidential Power Revisited and Reappraised," *Western Political Quarterly* vol. 32, no. 4 (December 1979): 381–95.

34. Fred I. Greenstein, "Eisenhower as an Activist President: A Look at New Evidence," *Political Science Quarterly* vol. 94, no. 4 (Winter 1979–1980): 575–600.

35. Bert A. Rockman, "Neustadt's Presidential Power: Some Residual Issues," *Presidential Studies Quarterly* vol. 11 (Summer 1981): 358–60.

36. Meg Greenfield, "Ringside at a Pillow Fight," *Newsweek* (October 29, 1990): 88.

37. Samuel Kernell, *Going Public: New Strategies of Presidential Leadership* (Washington, DC: Congressional Quarterly Press, 1986).

38. David Broder and Dan Balz, "Changing Directions Is Harder Than It Looks," *Washington Post National Weekly Edition* (May 24–30, 1993): 10.

39. Mary Stuckey, *The President as Interpreter-in-Chief* (Chatham, NJ: Chatham House Publishers, 1991).

40. Theodore Sorensen, "Presidents and the King's English," *New York Times Magazine* (August 19, 1979): 7–8.

Chapter 10

41. Quoted in *California Magazine* (May 1982): 10.

42. "Data from Figs. 4 and 5: The Declining Prime-Time Audience for Presidential Addresses, 1969–1996," in Kernell, *Going Public*, 132.

43. Thomas Patterson, "Bad News, Bad Governance," *Annals* vol. 546 (July 1996): 97–108.

44. Thomas Patterson, "Trust Politicians, Not the Press," *New York Times* (December 15, 1993): A-27.

45. Paul Leicester Ford, ed., *The Writings of Thomas Jefferson* vol. VIII (New York: G. P. Putnam's Sons, 1892–1899), 246.

46. Larry Arnhart, "'The God-Like Prince': John Locke, Executive Prerogative, and the American Presidency," *Presidential Studies Quarterly* vol. 9, no. 1 (Spring 1979): 121–30; for a contrary view see Thomas Langston and Michael Lind, "John Locke and the Limits of Presidential Prerogative," *Polity* vol. 24, no. 1 (Fall 1991): 49–68.

47. Roy P. Basler, ed., *Collected Works of Abraham Lincoln* vol. IV (New Brunswick, NJ: Rutgers University Press, 1953–1955): 429–30.

48. *In re Neagle*, 135 U.S. 1 (1880); *In re Debs*, 158 U.S. 564 (1895).

49. Harvey Mansfield Jr., *Taming the Prince: The Ambivalence of Modern Executive Power* (New York: Free Press, 1989).

50. Woodrow Wilson, *Constitutional Government in the United States* (New York: Columbia University Press, 1908), 30.

51. Concurring in *Youngstown Sheet and Tube v. Sawyer*, 343 U.S. 579 (1952) at 634–35.

52. *United States v. Nixon*, 418 U.S. 683 (1974); *Clinton v. Jones*, 520 U.S. 681 (1997); *Youngstown Sheet and Tube v. Sawyer*, 343 U.S. 579 (1952).

53. J. Richard Piper, "'Situational Constitutionalism' and Presidential Power," *Presidential Studies Quarterly* vol. 24, no. 3 (Summer 1994); "Table 1: Northern Democratic and Republican Support for Presidential Powers on Key Congressional Roll Calls, 1933–1989," 584.

11

Risk and Resilience

Toward a White House Learning Curve

PRESIDENTIAL FAILURE IS NO ORPHAN: Its parentage can be determined by backward mapping of presidential decision making. Foul-ups occur in tightly coupled operations demanding high performance because there is no margin of error and no way to recover when things go wrong.[1] There is either too much or too little White House command and control. Walking back the cat into the planning process, we see that presidents compound their risks by flawed approaches to gamesmanship, resulting in authorization of operations with constraints that increase operational risk. They think they can protect their power stakes by privatizing and permitting policy inversion, but that increases their risks. They rely on an advisory system that is top-heavy with the wrong kind of advisers using the wrong kind of data with the wrong kind of theories, and they get the wrong kind of advice.

Even when each unit of the institutionalized presidency performs accordingly to its standard operational procedures, their combined efforts result in "normal accidents." Flawed positioning and maneuvering in an antipolitical culture backfires on presidents: Their evasiveness or dissembling results in credibility gaps that compromise their authority. Their tendency to cut too many constitutional and legal corners by utilizing their prerogatives to establish parallel governance undermines their legitimacy, especially when their actions are not consonant with fundamental American values.

The distinguishing feature of presidential failure is not the march of folly but the limits of rational choice; not corrupt and base motivation or lack of character (Nixon's Watergate cover-up and Clinton's sex scandals excepted) but risk management gone awry. Presidents have tried to be too clever by half, too calculating by far. In each case what they saw as the right balance for themselves turned out to be disastrous for themselves—and for the country.

What is to be done? It is worth thinking about the observation of Anton Chekhov, a physician as well as playwright, who observed that when many remedies are recommended for the same disease, it is a sure sign that none will work. That was a fair point about nineteenth century medical practices, but twenty-first century medical protocols involve many different specialists, each intervening at the right time in the right way, each following the logic of a correct diagnosis (on a good day). So there may be many interventions we can recommend as presidential prophylaxis.

Until we have understood the epigenetic basis of political life (the emerging neuroscience of decision making will help in the next few decades), it is important for presidents to navigate cautiously.[2] It seems clear that more precision—and quantification—in the study of presidential decision making is required. But what techniques should be used? And how may students of the presidency and the White House distinguish consilient approaches from abstract model building lacking any empirical foundation, or theoretical approaches such as rational choice modeling or game theory, that are no more than pathological science?[3]

I would suggest that the emerging sciences of risk management, operations research, and information theory provide the best approaches for reducing the frequency of presidential failure and for creating robust decision making systems: those that will operate reliably even when component parts are unreliable and interact unpredictably.

New Thinking

Disasters in the White House repeat themselves in predictable patterns. The institutionalization of the modern presidency, designed to improve presidential performance, has increased rather than reduced the risks of failure, a phenomenon akin to the technological "revenge effect" in which new technologies (such as plastic packaging) create new problems (such as small particle ocean pollution).[4] Advances in command and control enable the White House to micromanage operations; the Executive Office agencies provide the president with more information, processed into more sophisticated theories, than ever before; the techniques of game theory and of spatial positioning have been advanced by academic analysis and media consultants; the Office of Communications has transformed the rhetoric of the presidency and merged religious and moral themes to strengthen presidential authority; the Office of Counsel is adept at deploying legal defenses to legitimize presidential prerogative. Yet each of these supposed capabilities of the institutionalized presidency has created more problems than it has solved: Excessive command and control reduces the initiative of operatives; aides sometimes cause more problems than they solve; reliance on unproven theories and weak data leads to bad advice; gamesmanship escalates crises; positioning becomes a liability outside the Beltway; inflated rhetoric is dissonant with the personal behavior of the incumbent and reduces authority; and the attempted legitimization of presidential decisions leads to overshoot and collapse.

Fail-Safe Mechanisms

What would the White House look like with more "fail-safe" controls in place? There is an analogy with vehicles equipped with safety features: These are not designed to improve performance and sometimes may even degrade it—but high performance is lowered in order to prevent catastrophe. When we strengthen what the Framers referred to as checks and balances, interior contrivances, and auxiliary precautions, we are engaged in the same trade-off that high-reliability engineers are engaged in when they try to ensure that performance of systems remain within a normal range.[5]

Yellow flags should go up when presidents are making decisions about matters in which they have poor track records. In domestic affairs these would include "global initiatives" in which economic or social theory is weak, data are poor, and trend extrapolation is problematic. In international affairs these would include privatization and inversion of covert operations, small-scale military interventions, and compellence diplomacy or wars of choice. Yellow flags also should fly when presidents substitute political judgment for more reasoned policy calculations on "hot button" issues: The danger is that they may risk their authority and legitimacy if they cannot maintain control of the values involved, as in the budget process.

Presidents and their aides need a better understanding of how uncertainty is transformed into risk and how organizations work to normalize risk. To the extent presidents engage in effective risk assessment (correctly estimating the odds of success), they can pay more attention to risk management (establishing policies and procedures to cut down on the likelihood of untoward events) through what systems engineers call "rituals of vigilance."

Presidents themselves must negotiate their risks to guard their power stakes, even though their natural tendency will be to assume that the odds and the gods are with them—after all, their ascent to the White House involved beating the odds. Once in office presidents must become alert for the normalization of risk: a pattern of discrepant events whose signals are overlooked, misinterpreted, or normalized by their advisers.[6] They need to recognize when officials bring proposals to them that are actually highly uncertain but that are couched in the language of manageable risk. Presidents must also guard against the possibility of "reverse risk homeostasis" in the institutionalized presidency: a situation in which better risk management leads to success but that success is later canceled by the disposition to engage in ever riskier operations. A White House that claims it is good at managing risk based on rational choice and game theory may wind up in the same place as the financial engineers who brought us the hedge fund and subprime mortgage fiascoes.

Presidents must reinvent their command and control procedures to guard against "normal accidents" and "rare events." They must *begin* with a complete grasp of the operation itself, and they must have an understanding of how risk has been negotiated at the lower levels before decisions have been presented to them. In tightly coupled operations in which the failure of any one component leads to a cascading series of failures down the line, the probabilities are Bayesian: Each percentage of possible failure, even if small, when multiplied by succeeding low percentages of failure in the next event, can soon result in a high probability of failure. On the other hand, when operations are arranged loosely, with redundancy, parallel processing of information, and separate problem solving by small autonomous units, each lateral unit's probability of success is not fully determined by the risks taken by other units, and small-unit flexibility and lateral coordination may enable units that are failing at one moment to recover in the next. They may get assistance from their colleagues, who can share their "local knowledge" of adverse conditions and their "user knowledge" of the resources at their disposal. So presidents must *design* operations that take advantage of the insights from theorists of complex interconnected networks, whether they involve transmission of goods, energy, information, or financial assets.[7] Recent research into complex adaptive systems has focused on the behavior of autonomous and adaptable local agents: Negative systemic efforts can be controlled, or the periphery and the system can stabilize and correct itself locally. The White House must encourage and not inhibit the development of adaptive systems.

Presidents and their aides must understand and cope with systemic effects. They must understand how tightly coupled or how forgiving operations will be. They must recognize cascade effects that might occur from degraded performance in the early stages. And they must be aware of the possibility of a "normal accident" occurring, creating failure even when all components of decision making seem to be functioning at peak performance.

Presidents should not authorize operations without bulkheads, firewalls, and circuit breakers, so that failure can be contained and minimized; or without backup and redundancy, so that even if one action fails the operation might succeed; or without feedback loops and horizontal coordination, in case command and control is inadequate. They should turn down operations without escape routes and exit strategies, with low retrievability and low tolerances for poor performance, particularly when an operation consists of interconnected systems that are tightly coupled.

The Risk of Eliminating Risk

The paradox is that these actions may themselves create new ways for presidents to fail. As the political scientist Aaron Wildavsky pointed out decades ago, there are trade-offs involved in the search for safety and downsides in attempts to eliminate all risky business. Attempts to create a completely fail-safe environment cannot work for several reasons. One is the "rule of sacrifice": In any complex system, one can have stability and safety in the parts at the expense of the stability of the whole, or in the whole at the expense of the parts, but one usually cannot have both. A supposedly safe environment resembles the *Titanic*: People will lower their guard and accept higher risks. The likelihood of "normal accidents" increases: Unexpected interactions of safety features may defeat some of them and leave people less safe than before.[8]

One can go too far in seeking to minimize risk. Seeking absolute safety may increase danger because it limits the resources available in the search for new opportunities. So what is needed is not a "search for safety," but rather new thinking about how to deploy presidential resources. The president must foster a "resilient" Oval Office and Executive Office: He must choose officials who can learn from adversity how to do better. His thinking must switch from attempts to anticipate every danger, lower political risk, and avoid entanglements to a strategy of accepting responsibility and then dealing with untoward events as they occur.

Reinventing the Presidency

It is said that when the Duke of Wellington was reviewing his troops in the Peninsular Campaign, his aide de camp asked him whether he thought they would frighten the French. "I do not know if they will frighten the French, sir," the Duke replied, "but by God they frighten me." And so it is with the aides in the White House Office, who sometimes seem to resemble a collection of bad habits: Their palace politics and internecine warfare are carried to extremes; their hyperactivity alternates with depression; their hustle and bustle amounting to little traction gained; their media spinning amounts to no more than spinning wheels.

How Much Help Does the President Need?

It is naive to assume, as the Brownlow Commission did in the 1930s, that the president in the future will be served by aides with "a passion for anonymity." The president must choose aides who are comfortable with media and effective in delivering his message. So much is obvious. What is less obvious is that the president needs to choose aides who know how to pose the conceptual questions necessary to evaluate risky and uncertain operations. What we need in the White House is a combination of "stand-up" men and women who can accept responsibility, yet who also are artful dodgers with the reflexes, the mother wit, and the stamina to know how to get out of jams, cut losses, extricate themselves, and avoid the next pitfall.

Within the White House the president needs help, and good help is hard to find. He or she needs a group of senior advisers, the "Oval Room" aides (named for their meetings with the president in the Oval Room in the family quarters) who are adept at integrating politics, imagery, and governance, and who are knowledgeable about the processes as well as the politics of presidential governance. He or she also needs a few unobtrusive men and women to carry on the work of the "invisible" presidency, as Harry Hopkins carried out missions abroad for Franklin Roosevelt during World War II. The president needs a chief of staff, to function as a coordinator and facilitator—a Howard Baker, Dick Cheney, James Baker, or Leon Panetta—political operators with prior political experience. He doesn't need a chief of staff functioning as "deputy president" and insulating him from debate, filtering opinions, serving as a buffer, and attempting to apply a corporate model in the White House. When he gets such an individual—a John Sununu, Donald Regan, or H. R. Haldeman—some of whom have little or no experience in government, the chief of staff becomes the problem and not the solution.[9]

"In multitude of counselors there is safety," it says in Proverbs 24:6, but perhaps a better maxim would be "subtraction is addition" as Brooklyn Dodger general manager Branch Rickey used to claim when he traded a problematic ballplayer. The president does need senior aides who are central to his thinking and activities and who will work on speeches with him. He or she does *not* need a large number of speechwriters, the lower ranks of whom are insulated from his or her thinking.[10] The president needs one or two wordsmiths who function as a Theodore Sorensen, as high-level alter egos, and a few deputies who can speak in his name when he lobbies Congress. He or she does *not* need a large congressional liaison office, whose staffers cannot deal for him because they lack the stature that personal contact with the president brings. Fewer aides would require presidents to become *personally* involved in the run-up to decisions: Whatever is presidential business should be important enough to involve the president directly from start to finish. Less staffing might translate into more clout, because the president would be forced to cut down on his agenda, and a smaller agenda would revalue upwards the value of presidential commitment to an issue.

All of this goes against the conventional wisdom of president and Congress watchers. Consider the views of savvy Beltway researcher and commentator Norman Ornstein about Clinton's first-year gaffes, which he blamed in part on an ill-considered pledge to cut the size of the staff:

> Coping with the forces inside the federal government, from the bureaucracy itself to Congress, and with the forces outside the government—including interest groups ranging from women and minorities to business and labor, along with the press, foreign governments, academic and governors, mayors and political parties—not to mention making and implementing all the decisions the president and his surrogates make, planning all the events over which a president presides, and juggling the commitments a president makes, takes a lot of people. Managing the people who do all of this requires yet more people.[11]

Ornstein is exactly right: To do what a president does requires a huge staff. But why take what the president does as a given? The president needs to do less and to make do with less. With decreased staff resources, the White House would have to consider more carefully what should be considered for rhetorical initiatives. The president would not remain a ubiquitous commentator on every event taking place each day, and this would revalue presidential rhetoric. With fewer liaison aides, the president would not be overscheduled, and this would revalue upward presidential "face time."

Real cuts, deep cuts, cuts that would drive a complete reorganization of how the White House Office conducts business are needed, and these are not to be confused with those Carter announced in 1977 (when he moved staff out of the White House Office but merely transferred them to the Executive Office of the President), nor cuts such as those Clinton announced in 1993—a supposed 25 percent cut from Bush's White House and Executive Office of the president staffing, which in reality was mostly symbolic, neither cutting personnel nor reducing costs, especially not in the White House Office.[12]

A smaller White House staff would mean less palace politics, less need for the sharp elbows needed to make it into the key meetings, less energy spent on becoming and maintaining status as an inside player. Fewer staffers would not only increase the proximity of each to the president but also would revalue their standing within the Washington community. As it now stands, too many aides meddle in too much departmental business, antagonize too many legislators, and provide fodder for too many reporters looking to add to their collection of White House scalps.

Participation by campaign aides in Oval Office business should be cut back. Of course presidential governance cannot be separated from campaign politics, and the president and his top aides must integrate both dimensions into his or her decision making. But the communications skills necessary for modern media campaigns put a premium on a political style that divides Americans and that exploits the divisions created by the campaign. The president is surrounded by aides who consider politics to be a form of warfare. To maneuver effectively in office, particularly in an antipolitics era, the president needs to bridge over divisions and create a governing coalition. These goals require a different skill set than those possessed by his campaigners. It is no accident that Reagan in the 1984 campaign was successful when he kept his campaign organization separate from his White House Office, and it is no accident that Bush's disorganized 1992 campaign, and the performance of his White House staff, both suffered from the lack of separation.[13]

Councils and Counsels

The Executive Office of the President (EOP) needs to be restructured, with fewer rather than more policy councils and counsels. As it stands each is a separate bailiwick, fiercely protective of its turf, so that activity in the West Wing and Old Executive Office Building resembles a rugby scrum. The president needs to reorganize these offices so that they employ more analysts of risk, who will take an adversarial rather than an entrepreneurial stance toward policy proposals. EOP agencies that deal with the processes of government—budgeting, management, personnel administration—need more continuity, more institutional memory, and more careerist staffing, especially at the highest levels.[14] Instead of layering these agencies with political executives to make them more politically responsive, these agencies should have more senior careerists at the top levels who should be expected to serve more than one administration and who could play a large role in the transition, providing the continuity, the institutional memory, and the operational competence that presidential transition staffs lack. There is no reason why they cannot combine expertise with the ability to serve the president's political interests, just as the Bureau of the Budget managed to do in the Truman presidency.[15]

Just about every group of advisers should be shadowed by at least one "team B" so the president is exposed to different viewpoints. There are advantages to redundant advisory systems: Political executives in the cabinet and subcabinet can be balanced against careerists within the departments, who in turn can be countered with outside consultants. What Franklin Roosevelt and Kennedy did on an ad hoc basis, presidents should now do routinely and systematically.

No organizational techniques to foster debate will work, however, unless the president avoids premature closure and makes the effort to force not only the options but also the reasoning behind the options, and the data analysis behind the reasoning, up to the top. The president must fully understand how risk is being negotiated within his administration. He must use that knowledge in making decisions about when to craft new legislative proposals "in house" and when, in the metaphor of political scientist Andrew Rudalevige, he should make the decision to outsource the manufacture of new programs to the departments.[16]

Learning Curves

Can presidents profit by their predecessors' mistakes? Presidents must be aware of the opportunities and the pitfalls that await them if they used advanced decision making "methodologies," especially mathematically sophisticated game theory. They must be aware when one game becomes linked to another and they must understand nested situations, in which a game is subordinated to one or more other games. Presidents must learn what some political scientists refer to as "heresthetic" leadership: The art of making the metadecisions that determine the rules and set up the processes for decision, which in turn structure the sequence of choices to be made so that outcomes can be influenced, if not predicted and controlled. They must be aware of the opportunities that may be exploited by changing the game at the correct moment. As Bill Tilden, the tennis great said, "Never change a winning game, always change a losing game."

A Feel for the Game

Presidents need a feel for decision making: not only knowing what to do when the choices are obvious and the risks can be calculated but also understanding what to do in the indeterminate situations. Like superstar athletes, they must have straight and peripheral vision, seeing angles that their lesser competitors do not. Like successful entrepreneurs in the marketplace, they must develop possibilities that no one has seen. Presidents can consciously try to develop the "pattern recognition" of recurring dicey situations. With street smarts about risk, presidents can gain the confidence to make the right move, the one that actually lowers operational risks or risks for presidential supporters and allies. Other politicians will recognize the "feel" that the president has for the issue and for their stakes in it, and they will respond to his or her lead.

Failures versus Failure

Failures are inevitable, because presidents are always feeling their way. But there is a difference between tolerating failure to develop a viable operational style and suffering defeat because the decisional style is flawed. Presidents will need all the "feel" they can muster. They must avoid the metaphorical illusions of seeking balance or of obtaining an equilibrium. There is no permanent equilibrium; no political system that achieves a stable state in which all interests have been properly balanced and a core solution (in the language of public choice economists) reached. The president cannot position himself to achieve a set equilibrium point; he can only navigate through one situation and into the next, generally not obtaining the most efficient solution. Maneuver in managing unfolding situations is a key trait of successful presidents, not attainment of illusory equilibrium and core solutions.

A presidential position on an issue has a history that the White House cannot easily jettison. It isn't simply where the White House locates itself *now* that counts: It is *where the president has been and where he or she is going* that defines the issue and creates power stakes. Any shift of position changes the odds of success: not because of the location on a single dimension, but because the change enables the president to slip a trap, or to lay a trap, or (when things go wrong) become enmeshed in a trap. When the president calibrates all the relevant spatial dimensions so that they are consonant with deeply held public values, then he or she will not only have achieved a viable political balance but also political momentum.

"Read the American Constitution," Clinton implored his critics. "It is about honorable compromise and that is not weakness if you are making progress."[17] But such compromises must now be practiced in an antipolitical culture, in which compromise itself seems to be a dirty word, in which traditional politicians have ceded place to true believers. To avoid failure in such a highly charged environment the president must avoid the appearance of maneuver just to enhance his power stakes and must remember that he cannot keep his options open forever. The president must be willing (and be seen to be willing) to expend his or her political capital, to sacrifice, and to put his or her presidency at risk. And to do so not merely for position and power, but for a national interest that is often distinct from a presidential interest.

There is no longer any political credit outside the Beltway for professionalism in playing politics: On the contrary, there is a considerable downside even when maneuvering is successful. The president must learn to play by the new rules: Sometimes positioning gets leveraged best through values politics, sometimes through ideological and "less versus more" politics. But almost never can presidential positioning and deal making be defended solely in pragmatic, "professional" terms. The president must be perceived as more than a player when he or she negotiates: He or she must be perceived by the public as the defender of core American values.

Toward Presidential Options Theory

Presidents need to be more precise in their analysis of power stakes. They must incorporate quantitative measurements of risk to their reputation, their influence with Congress, their electoral fortunes, even their place in history. It is possible to combine risk management techniques with power stakes analysis; this should improve presidential performance, although it will not necessarily do much to prevent presidential failure.

There are limits to how well risk management can work. There are too few cases in the White House to establish probabilities of the success of risky business. There is the problem of classifying cases, because of false analogies and ideologies, and even if correctly classified, it is difficult to determine the probability that the past will be a guide to the future because the situation for which odds have been calculated may have fundamentally changed.[18] Probability is usually estimated a posteriori: As more cases accumulate the odds change. But there is a tendency to overweight the most recent cases. Maynard Keynes got it right when he concluded that decisions result from "animal spirits" and "not as the outcome of a weighted average of quantitative benefits multiplied by quantitative probabilities."[19] Each president will value payoffs differently and have a different appetite for risk—even the same president may attach different values at different times in his term.

Intuitively presidency watchers have valued decisions today that keep options open tomorrow, that maintain a president's freedom to maneuver and the possibility of mastering the next situation. The insights of "real options theory" in corporate finance might help presidents do this more systematically. In financial analysis executives lay out all the options that flow from making a particular decision and then analyze the net present value of costs and benefits for each potential outcome. In "real options theory" one values each proposed course of action not merely by determining the costs and benefits of taking the decision but also by calculating the net present value of each of the various options it is likely to generate later on. Many, if not most, of these future opportunities would probably be aborted or would fail at an early stage, but the point is to have new possibilities after existing ones are exhausted. The generation of new options is itself a quantifiable value and therefore helps determine the valuations involved in the present decision to manage the current issue.

This approach (building on the conceptual breakthrough in financial options pricing by Myron Scholes, Robert Merton, and Fischer Black) is based on the insight that increased volatility in the valuation of an underlying enterprise increases the value of an option, because of the large range of possible successful or unsuccessful outcomes embedded within it. In the real world (as opposed to the world of financial instruments), organizations that make decisions that are likely to generate a large number of risky options must figure out how long to ride with a project that isn't earning its cost of capital or is running losses and when to shift to a new option that might do better. For the White House, the situation is analogous (although no precise quantification using net present value can be calculated): It makes no sense to tot up all the costs and benefits of a proposed course of action, since in all likelihood no single course of action will be carried to its end. Instead, most presidential decisions generate new possibilities, and subsequently the incumbent or his successor must pick and choose all over again. It makes more sense to choose the course of action that generates a larger and riskier range of options, with the possibilities of great success as well as failure, rather than take a "minimax" decision that narrows future choices or locks the president in to a narrow course of action with no chances for breakthrough successes. When all is said and done, risky business must be carried on, uncertainties will remain, and presidents must be willing to take risks and confront uncertainties. The only way for the president to succeed is to make decisions that might fail. But there are ways to minimize the likelihood that a decision will lead to a fiasco, or minimize the impact of a failed policy.

Regaining Authority and Legitimacy

How should the president manage failure? One trap is obvious: Any failure can be compounded into even larger failure; attempts to spin events may produce a credibility gap; plausible deniability may become implausible; lying may lead to charges of perjury and obstruction of justice; attempts to shift blame may lead to loss of authority; confrontations with Congress and courts may lead to a backlash and a loss of legitimacy. A dysfunctional president blames failure on outside forces over which the White House had no control; a resilient president assumes responsibility for error and figures out how to make the adjustments for the next situation—as Kennedy and Clinton were able to do.

Recapturing the Audience

The period from Nixon's Watergate through the second Bush presidency may well be known to future presidential historians as the era of the Diminished

Presidency. This is so primarily because presidents lost moral authority, and therefore governing authority, however many conflicts they sent the military to fight or bills they passed in Congress. The president must communicate to the American people an authentic vision about the potential and limits of government, a task that is increasingly difficult when an antipolitical mood in the country intersects with the increasing professionalism of Washington politics. In some respects, the better the president plays the game, the worse the country feels about him, so greater professionalism just compounds the problem.

When getting elected to office has become an advertising game, when voters have become consumers of media imagery, politics becomes confused with markets, and its practitioners lose their authority because a political market can never be as efficient in allocating preferences as a free economic market. We have another paradox: As the communications technology available to presidential candidates has advanced, the communicating authority of presidents in office has declined. If candidates are elected by using the techniques of used car salesmen, they will subsequently govern like used car salesmen. Their rhetoric becomes tinny when they call for microinitiatives, pinched when they proclaim the government lacks the "wallet" for large initiatives, and grandiloquent when they propose major programs without putting up the funds. If their primary audience is electoral constituencies rather than congressional colleagues, they will make unreasonable proposals while maintaining the pretense of reasonableness. Or they will successfully conclude closed-door negotiations while trying to maintain their base with unreasonable public rhetoric. Either way, the public will see that their positioning is out of sync with their rhetoric.

Presidents continue to go public, but the public has tuned out. Since the later years of the Carter presidency (with exceptions noted for crises), the White House has lost its audience. By 1997, Clinton was reduced to advancing his State of the Union address by one evening in order to avoid competing with the Miss U.S.A. pageant. In an information age, when it is easier than ever to be informed, there is yet another revenge effect against the communications capabilities of the White House. "It's like when we were kids, we'd drink near-beer," Clinton told reporters. "You've got all this information, and a lot of competition among news sources, and then you're competing with the near-news. And there is a danger that too much stuff cramming in on people's lives is just as bad for them as too little in terms of the ability to understand, to comprehend."[20]

How can presidents recapture their audience? They need a new kind of triangulation, not just spin that substitutes phony "values" for real ones. They have converted the "Bully Good Pulpit" of Theodore Roosevelt into a televangelical "feel good" pulpit, in which they tell people what they want to hear instead of what they need to know. Their rhetoric must once again engage the American people in substantive political issues: They need more Jeremiah and less Elmer Gantry. Their rhetoric should be more about risk and uncertainty and about the management of risk, and less about themselves, their emotions, and their willingness to feel our pain.

Adhering to Framework Laws

Both the restoration of authority and legitimacy can best be achieved by adhering to framework legislation mandating collaborative governance with Congress. A good-faith effort to adhere to the procedures in these laws would require presidents to make their case in advance to members of Congress. That in turn would force presidents to consider the rationale for proceeding, which would require them to question the premises of their advisers and their operational plans. Framework legislation not only puts presidents in a collaborative frame of mind but it also changes their risk assessments because they cannot escape responsibility for their actions and because they cannot order or implement actions until they have convinced (or at least consulted with) members of a coordinate branch of government.

Such consultation allows legislators to question high-level officials on their positions and to analyze *in advance* the game the president intends to play, the spatial positioning he intends to take, and the moves he intends to make. Because all of this occurs in advance, it provides an opportunity for a before-the-fact reconsideration of a proposed course of action, rather than the after-the-fact inquest into failure. Adherence to framework legislation designed to protect presidential legitimacy will also require the president to protect his political stakes by constantly reviewing his attempts to manage risk. Inter-branch codetermination should supplant Bush's discredited parallel governance mechanisms.

But how likely are such reforms? There is no indication that Congress itself wishes to strengthen its collaborative framework legislation. Congress has let laws such as the War Powers Resolution become dead letters in the run-up to the Iraq War and in its aftermath. It has done nothing to require the president to restrict himself to procedures required by the Foreign Intelligence Surveillance Act. Instead of eliminating military tribunals in the war on terrorism, Congress responded favorably to a Bush administration request to eliminate the habeas corpus jurisdiction of federal courts over them. If any change occurs, it is more likely to involve repeal or watering down of framework laws, such as Congress did with the independent counsel provision, rather than expansion of the collaborative model.

Those who want Congress to play a more important role in important presidential decisions recognize that at present Congress is neither institutionally nor intellectually equipped to do so and that it is too deferential to executive policymaking.[21] Congress could create a "core consultative group" of committee leaders with whom the president would meet and brief on national security matters.[22] But there is no indication that Congress wishes to reorganize itself and to take political responsibility for collaborative government. Congress suffers from an institutionalized "inferiority complex" when it comes to national security matters. It is more comfortable with traditional "after the fact" oversight because it can continue to pass the buck, avoid responsibility, and distance itself from potential fiascoes.

For their part, presidents have exhibited suspicion or outright disdain for framework laws, especially when these laws regulate what they believe to be their constitutional prerogatives. Whether they involve presidential war powers, budget mechanisms such as the deferral or rescission of funds, "report and wait" and legislative vetoes, or oversight mechanisms involving foreign covert intelligence operations, presidents and their subordinates sometimes refuse to comply with procedures established in these laws, or they exploit their loopholes.

A Congress that has shown itself unprepared to use the framework laws already in existence is hardly likely to pass an omnibus national security charter with real teeth in it requiring across-the-board interbranch collaboration. Even if it did, a national security charter that constrained presidential warmaking and intelligence operations would eventually lead to court challenges if a president disregarded them. The Supreme Court might well dismiss challenges to any presidential action (or inaction) disregarding the charter, or else render a decision striking down the framework. Certainly the composition of the court in the early twenty-first century gives us little reason to believe that constraints on presidential powers under a national security charter would be upheld.

Reformers concerned with keeping presidential power accountable have made a number of other suggestions, which strengthen the role of the courts. They have proposed that Congress pass laws making it easier for legislators or "private attorneys general" (i.e., lawyers for advocacy groups interested in public policy) to obtain standing to sue the president or other executive officials. They would have Congress limit by statute the immunity that a president may claim, stating specific exceptions to the general rules that protect a president from suit or damages if he or she takes actions within the scope of his or her official duties. They would have Congress go on record with a resolution that presidential violations of statutes requiring collaboration should not be treated by the courts as "political questions" between the two branches (and therefore dismissed), but should be treated as violations of law, subject to judicial remedies and penalties. They would have Congress pass laws that allow the courts to issue injunctions against national security officials, injunctions that might prevent national security decisions from being implemented.[23] There is no indication that Congress intends to do any of these things.

Presidents might find it useful to create their own internal safeguards that would ensure the legitimacy of prerogative power. The White House could unilaterally create some legal "circuit breakers": lawyers chosen from the Office of Presidential Counsel and the Justice Department inserted into decision making at an early stage, not as advocates for a course of action already decided on or as counselors standing ready to defend the president's decisions, but rather as "auditors" to review the legality of his or her proposed action. The president would not be required to take advice from this Team B, but its opinion would be on the record (and subject to congressional and judicial discovery), and the president would be on notice of the legal risks faced if he or she went ahead. Such a legal audit within the White House would complement the Government Accountability Office financial audits of covert operations now mandated to be done quarterly by the Senate Intelligence Committee.

Constraining Covert Actions

There is a special need for institutional reform of covert action. The National Security Planning Group of the NSC should review all covert operations. The president should encourage more oversight by the Intelligence Oversight Board, which already has the duty to "inform the President of intelligence activities that any member believes . . . are in violation of the Constitution or laws of the United States, Executive Orders, or presidential directives." The Intelligence Authorization Act of 1991 permits the president to opt out of notifying the intelligence committees about covert operations. It also has a loophole excluding "traditional diplomatic or military activities or routine support of such activities." These loopholes should be closed.[24] The Presidents Foreign Intelligence Advisory Board should conduct a review of *proposed* covert operations and intelligence collection in order to assess risk. Reagan's Executive Order 12,537 provided that the board "shall assess the quality, quantity, and adequacy of intelligence collection, of analysis and estimates, of counterintelligence, and other intelligence activities," but these reviews come after the fact: The president needs a review mechanism to deal with the logic and the technical issues in advance.[25] The need for these institutionalized reviews is even clearer after the 9/11 intelligence failures and the issues surrounding claims of Iraqi development of weapons of mass destruction before the war.

Finesse and Resilience

Presidents must reverse their order of decision. What they decide to undertake must be viable, legally and morally defensible, and consistent with American values. They should not make decisions based on power stakes or grossly simplified rational choice, then attempt to operationalize, explain, and justify them. These constraints should be taken as considerations helping the White House define its real stakes. The president serves himself best when he comes up with a decision that can work within these constraints.

"The Constitution is not a suicide pact," Justice Robert Jackson pointed out, and no sane person argues that the country must commit suicide so the president can stay within the bounds of the literal Constitution or follow all the procedures mandated in framework laws if the survival of the nation hangs in the balance. Jefferson acquired the Louisiana Territory although the Constitution is silent on acquisition of territory; Lincoln exercised war powers assigned to Congress; Franklin Roosevelt interpreted two congressional restrictions on arms sales out of existence to make his exchange of destroyers for naval bases with Great Britain during World War II. But national suicide was not at issue in fiascoes such as the Bay of Pigs, the *Mayaguez* rescue effort, or the Iran-Contra affair, and sacrificing adherence to international commitments or the rule of law at home was an excessive price to pay merely to lower a president's political risk.

In the final analysis the responsibility for presidential failures rests with presidents themselves. They must rethink the paradoxes of power, coming to a better understanding of what they can do as well as what they cannot and what they should not do. They need to do less, but do it smarter. The White House has a "Can Do" culture that oscillates between excessive risk-taking when an opportunity exists for political gain and excessive caution in the aftermath of a fiasco. To break the manic-depressive cycle of the Oval Office, presidents need *finesse*, meaning an appreciation for controlled technique. They can end their penchant for a frontal attack on all problems by lowering expectations of performance, by relying more on heresthetic metadecisions, by creating new decision frameworks, by using "soft-prerogative" rather than confronting Congress, and by combining values politics with pragmatic compromise.

Presidents can also operate with more precision and with more professionalism. They can quantify their power stakes to identify options and manage risk and analyze decisions for "satisfiability." They can use insights from operations research to develop better techniques to command and control operations. Presidents *can* succeed when their expertise is nonexistent, when their power to persuade is negligible, when their authority is ebbing, and when their prerogatives are under challenge. Truman did so with the Marshall Plan. Clinton did so with the Budget Summit of 1995. Resilient presidents who learn from their mistakes or from the successes of others *can* bootstrap their power even when it appears they are powerless, regaining their authority and legitimacy even when it appears they have squandered it.

The president's ability to avoid failure does not always come from the power to command nor from the power to persuade. It certainly does not come from the institutionalization of the presidency or the reliance on unbridled use of prerogative power. Over the long run presidents cannot avoid failure by relying on power stakes, positioning, and gamesmanship. Success comes to presidents *who avoid the avoidable failures*, who possess the skill and will to play politics and antipolitics simultaneously, who fuse substantive policy and epideictic rhetoric, and who complement their legitimate use of prerogative power with a willingness to abide by law and utilize framework legislation. Above all, it comes to presidents with the street smarts and learned skills of intelligent risk-takers, who can operate with finesse to avoid failure and who are resilient when (inevitably) they do fail. If presidents make decisions on the basis of what they perceive to be in the national interest, they might just find their own reputation is guarded and their power stakes preserved through their successes *and* their failures.

Notes

1. Charles Perrow, *Normal Accidents: Living with High-Risk Technologies* (New York: Basic Books, 1984).

2. Edward O. Wilson, *Consilience: The Unity of Knowledge* (New York: Vintage Books, 1998), 163–96.

3. Irving Langmuir (Robert N. Hall, ed.), "Pathological Science," *Physics Today* vol. 44 (October 1989); Nicholas J. Turro, "Toward a General Theory of Pathological Science," *21stC* issue 3.4 (Winter 1999): 9–10.

4. Edward Tenner, *Why Things Bite Back: Technology and the Revenge of Unintended Consequences* (New York: Alfred A. Knopf, 1996), 6.

5. Karlene H. Roberts, "New Challenges in Organizational Research: High Reliability Organizations," *Industrial Crisis Quarterly* vol. 3 (1989): 111–25.

6. Barry Turner and Nick F. Pidgeon, *Man-made Disasters*, 2nd ed. (Woburn, MA: Butterworth-Heinemann, 1997).

7. L. Troyansky, B. Selman, R. Zecchina, S. Kirkpatrick, and R. Monasson, "Relation of Typical-Case Complexity to the Nature of Phase Transition," *Random Structures and Algorithms* vol. 15, no. 3–4 (1999): 414–35.

8. Aaron Wildavsky, *Searching for Safety* (New Brunswick, NJ: Transaction Books, 1988), 5–18.

9. James P. Pfiffner, "The President's Chief of Staff: Lessons Learned," *Presidential Studies Quarterly* vol. 23, no. 1 (Winter 1993): 77–102.

10. Carol Gelderman, *All the Presidents' Words: The Bully Pulpit and the Creation of the Virtual Presidency* (New York: Walker and Co., 1997).

11. Norman Ornstein, "Blunders That Backfired," *Washington Post National Weekly Edition* (June 24–30, 1996): 27.

12. John Hart, "President Clinton and the Politics of Symbolism: Cutting the White House Staff," *Political Science Quarterly* vol. 110, no. 3 (Summer 1995): 385–403.

13. Kathryn Dunn Tenpas and Matthew Dickinson, "Governing, Campaigning, and Organizing the Presidency: An Electoral Connection?" *Political Science Quarterly* vol. 112, no. 1 (Winter 1997): 51–66.

14. Walter Williams, *Mismanaging America: The Rise of the Anti-Analytic Presidency* (Lawrence: University of Kansas Press, 1990).

15. Matthew Dickinson and Andrew Rudalevige, "Presidents, Responsiveness and Competence: Revisiting the 'Golden Age' at the Bureau of the Budget," *Political Science Quarterly* vol. 119, no. 4 (Winter 2004/5): 633–55.

16. Andrew Rudalevige, *Managing the President's Program: Presidential Leadership and Legislative Policy Formulation* (Princeton, NJ: Princeton University Press, 2002).

17. "Remarks in an Interview with Members of the Wisconsin Press," *Weekly Compilation of Presidential Documents* vol. 29 (July 26, 1993): 1390–91.

18. The metaodds problem is to determine the probability that the odds governing a situation have not changed because the possibility or confirmed existence of new factors.

19. John Maynard Keynes, *The General Theory of Employment, Interest and Money* (New York: Harcourt, Brace, 1936), 161.

20. *Weekly Compilation of Presidential Documents,* Monday, October 2, 1995, vol. 31, no. 39, 1681.

21. Stephen Weissman, *Culture of Deference: Congress's Failure of Leadership in Foreign Policy* (New York: Basic Books, 1996).

22. Harold Koh, *The National Security Constitution: Sharing Power after the Iran-Contra Affair* (New Haven, CT: Yale University Press, 1990), 192.

23. Koh, *National Security*, 182–83.

24. The Intelligence Oversight Act of 1991, S2834, defines covert action as "an activity or activities of the United States Government to influence political, economic or military conditions abroad where it is intended that the role of the United States Government will not be apparent or acknowledged publicly . . ." and does not include intelligence or counterintelligence collection, routine military or diplomatic activities, traditional law enforcement activities, or "activities to provide routine support to the overt activities" of U.S. government agencies abroad. See William H. Jackson Jr.,

"Congressional Oversight of Intelligence: Search for a Framework," *Intelligence and National Security* vol. 5, no. 3 (July 1990): 113–47.

25. W. Michael Reisman and James E. Baker, *Regulating Covert Action: Practices, Contexts, and Policies of Covert Coercion Abroad in International and American Law* (New Haven, CT: Yale University Press, 1992).

For Further Reading

Those wishing to pursue the study of the cases developed in this book will find the following sources (some of which I relied on heavily) to be invaluable for further reading.

The U-2 Shootdown

Stephen E. Ambrose, *Ike's Spies: Eisenhower and the Espionage Establishment* (Garden City, NY: Doubleday, 1981).

Michael R. Beschloss, *Mayday: Eisenhower, Khrushchev, and the U-2 Affair* (New York: Harper & Row, 1986).

Jef Verschueren, *International News Reporting: Metapragmatic Metaphors and the U-2* (Philadelphia: John Benjamins Publishing Company, 1985).

David Wise and Thomas B. Ross, *The U-2 Affair* (New York: Random House, 1962).

The Bay of Pigs Invasion

Luis Aguilar, ed. *Operation Zapata: The "Ultrasensitive" Report and Testimony of the Board of Inquiry on the Bay of Pigs* (Frederick, MD: University Publications of America, 1981).

James G. Blight and Peter Kornbluh, *Politics of Illusion: The Bay of Pigs Invasion Reexamined* (Boulder, CO: Lynne Rienner Publishers, 1998).

Trumbull Higgins, *The Perfect Failure: Kennedy, Eisenhower, and the CIA at the Bay of Pigs* (New York: W. W. Norton and Company, 1987).

Lyman B. Kirkpatrick, "Paramilitary Case Study: The Bay of Pigs," *Naval War College Review* vol. 2 (1972): 32–42.

Lucien S. Vandenbroucke, "Anatomy of a Failure: The Decision to Land at the Bay of Pigs," *Political Science Quarterly* vol. 99, no. 3 (Fall 1984): 471–91.

Peter Wyden, *The Bay of Pigs: The Untold Story* (New York: Simon & Schuster, 1979).

The *Mayaguez* Seizure

John F. Guilmartin Jr., *A Very Short War: The Mayaguez and the Battle of Koh Tang* (College Station: Texas A&M University Press, 1995).

Richard G. Head, Frisco W. Short, and Robert C. McFarlane, *Crisis Resolution: Presidential Decision Making in the Mayaguez and Korean Confrontations* (Boulder, CO: Westview Press, 1978).

Christopher Jon Lamb, *Belief Systems and Decision Making in the Mayaguez Crisis* (Gainesville: University of Florida Press, 1989).

Lucien S. Vandenbroucke, *Perilous Options: Special Operations as an Instrument of U.S. Foreign Policy* (New York: Oxford University Press, 1993).

The Vietnam Escalation

David M. Barrett, *Uncertain Warriors: Lyndon Johnson and His Vietnam Advisers* (Lawrence: University Press of Kansas, 1993).

David M. Barrett, *Lyndon B. Johnson's Vietnam Papers: A Documentary Collection* (College Station: Texas A&M Press, 1997).

Senator Gravel Edition, *The Pentagon Papers: The Defense Department History of United States Decisionmaking on Vietnam*, Vols. I–IV. (Boston: Beacon Press, 1971).

Larry Berman, *Planning a Tragedy: The Americanization of the War in Vietnam* (New York: W. W. Norton, 1982).

Brian VanDeMark, *Into the Quagmire: Lyndon Johnson and the Escalation of the Vietnam War* (New York: Oxford University Press, 1991).

William J. Duiker, *The Communist Road to Power in Vietnam*, 2nd ed. (Boulder, CO: Westview, 1996).

Daniel Ellsberg, *Papers on the War* (New York: Simon & Schuster, 1972).

William C. Gibbons, *The U.S. Government and the Vietnam War: Executive and Legislative Roles and Relationships*, Parts I–III. (Washington, DC: U.S. Government Printing Office, 1994).

Jeffrey Helsing, *Johnson's War/Johnson's Great Society: The Guns and Butter Trap* (New York: Columbia University Dissertation, 1991).

H. R. McMaster, *Dereliction of Duty: Lyndon Johnson, Robert McNamara, the Joint Chiefs of Staff, and the Lies That Led to Vietnam* (New York: Harper Collins, 1997).

Edwin E. Moïse, *Tonkin Gulf and the Escalation of the Vietnam War* (Chapel Hill: University of North Carolina Press, 1996).

Orrin Schwab, *Defending the Free World: John F. Kennedy, Lyndon Johnson, and the Vietnam War, 1961–1965* (Westport, CT: Praeger, 1998).

Ezra Y. Siff, *Why the Senate Slept: The Gulf of Tonkin Resolution and the Beginning of America's Vietnam War* (Westport, CT: Praeger, 1999).

The Energy Crisis

Marilu Hunt McCarty, "Economic Aspects of the Carter Energy Program," in Herbert D. Rosenbaum and Alexej Ugrinsky, eds., *The Presidency and Domestic Policies of Jimmy Carter* (Westport, CT: Greenwood Press, 1994).

Russell D. Motter, "Seeking Limits: The Passage of the National Energy Act as a Microcosm of the Carter Presidency," in Herbert D. Rosenbaum and Alexej Ugrinsky, eds., *The Presidency and Domestic Policies of Jimmy Carter* (Westport, CT: Greenwood Press, 1994).

The Iran-Contra Affair

Lou Cannon, *President Reagan: The Role of a Lifetime* (New York: Simon & Schuster, 1991).

Theodore Draper, *A Very Thin Line: The Iran-Contra Affairs* (New York: Hill and Wang, 1991).

Steven Emerson, *Secret Warriors: Inside the Covert Military Operations of the Reagan Era* (New York: Putnam, 1988).

Roy Gutman, *Banana Diplomacy: The Making of American Policy in Nicaragua, 1981–1987* (New York: Simon & Schuster, 1988).

Peter Kornbluh and Malcolm Byrne, eds., *The Iran-Contra Scandal: The Declassified History* (New York: New Press, 1993).

Joseph E. Persico, *Casey: From the OSS to the CIA* (New York: Viking, 1990).

President's Special Review Board, *Report of the Special Review Board* (Washington, DC: U.S. Government Printing Office, 1987).

Lawrence Walsh, *Iran-Contra: The Final Report* (New York: Times Books, 1994).

The Budget Summits

Richard Darman, *Who's in Control?: Polar Politics and the Sensible Center* (New York: Simon & Schuster, 1996).

Charles Kolb, *White House Daze: The Unmaking of Domestic Policy in the Bush Years* (New York: Free Press, 1994).

David Maraniss and Michael Weisskopf, *"Tell Newt to Shut Up!": Prize-Winning Washington Post Journalists Reveal How Reality Gagged the Gingrich Revolution* (New York: Simon & Schuster, 1996).

Elizabeth Drew, *Showdown: The Struggle between the Gingrich Congress and the Clinton White House* (New York: Simon & Schuster, 1996).

The Clinton Health Care Plan

Elizabeth Drew, *On the Edge: The Clinton Presidency* (New York: Simon & Schuster, 1994).

Bob Woodward, *The Agenda: Inside the Clinton White House* (New York: Simon & Schuster, 1994).

Jacob Hacker, *The Road to Nowhere: The Genesis of President Clinton's Plan for Health Security* (Princeton, NJ: Princeton University Press, 1997).

Haynes Johnson and David Broder, *The System: The American Way of Politics at the Breaking Point* (Boston: Little, Brown, 1996).

Theda Skocpol, *Boomerang: Clinton's Health Security Effort and the Turn against Government in U.S. Politics* (New York: W. W. Norton, 1996).

The Search for Weapons of Mass Destruction

Bob Drogin, *Curveball: Spies, Lies, and the Con Man Who Caused a War* (New York: Random House, 2007).

Richard A. Clarke, *Against All Enemies: Inside America's War on Terror* (New York: Free Press, 2004).

John Prados, *Hoodwinked: The Documents That Reveal How Bush Sold Us a War* (New York: New Press, 2004).

Ron Suskind, *The One Percent Doctrine: Deep Inside America's Pursuit of Its Enemies Since 9/11* (New York: Simon & Schuster, 2006).

Ron Suskind, *The Price of Loyalty: George W. Bush, the White House, and the Education of Paul O'Neill* (New York: Simon & Schuster, 2004).

George Tenet with Bill Harlow, *At the Center of the Storm: My Years at the CIA* (New York: HarperCollins, 2007).

Craig R. Whitney, ed., *The WMD Mirage: Iraq's Decade of Deception and America's False Premise for War* (New York: PublicAffairs, 2005).

Bob Woodward, *Plan of Attack* (New York: Simon & Schuster, 2004).

Index

Adams, Brock, firing/resignation of,
  105–6
Ad Hoc Energy Committee, by O'Neill,
  95–96
advisors, presidential: advantages to,
  286; Ball on, 58–59; choosing of,
  48–50; complexity of, 250–51;
  corruption of, 59–60; dysfunction of,
  56–57; exclusion of, 35; Ford's
  overruling of, 80; groupthink and, 32;
  hard problems and, 247–48; Johnson
  and, 48–49, 250; presidential fiascoes
  an, 6, 250–51; on Vietnam, 49–50
airline routing strategy,
  performance/failure of, 3–4
Alwan, Rafid Ahmed: aka Curveball,
  222; chemical/biological weapons lab
  and, 222
AMA. See American Medical Association
American arms sales: to Iran, 120–21;
  Weinberger/Smith on, 120
American Medical Association (AMA),
  186
antipolitical culture. See culture,
  antipolitical
Archer, Bill, 164, 165

Armey, Richard, 156, 160, 167, 175, 198,
  209
Arrow, Kenneth, 249
ARVN. See South Vietnamese Army

Ball, George, 49, 52, 54, 58–59, 64, 67;
  Johnson and, 50; predictions of, 51,
  60–61
Bay of Pigs invasion, 59, 87, 272; air
  support for, 42; Bissell and, 33, 36,
  37–38; Bundy on, 37; CIA and,
  30–44; contingency plans, lack of, 32;
  cost-benefit analysis of, 37; cover
  story for, 31; doubts regarding, 34;
  Dulles on, 36–37; failure of, 30–31,
  43–44; infiltration vs., 42; Kennedy,
  John, and, 1, 29–44; Khrushchev and,
  31; landing site of, 34, 36; logistical
  difficulties of, 30–31; media on, 43;
  mission cancelation and, 30–31;
  parameters of, 38; prediction
  regarding, 34–35; rationale of, 39–40;
  report of, 32; standard explanations
  for, 31–32; structuring of, 36; success
  probability of, 33–34
Bell, Griffin, firing/resignation of, 106

Bentsen, Lloyd, 154, 206

bin Laden, Osama, Hussein alliance with, 223

Bissell, Richard, 13; Bay of Pigs invasion and, 33, 36, 37–38

Blair, Tony: Bush, George W., and, 232–34; Iraq regime change supported by, 230, 232–33

Blumenthal, Michael, 94; firing/resignation of, 105–6

BND. *See* German Federal Intelligence Services

Boland amendment, 137, 139, 141; ambiguity of, 129; Contras and, 116; funding cutoffs violation and, 129

Boskin, Michael, 151, 153

Bowles, Chester, 34, 35

Brady, Nicholas, 154, 157

Broder, David, 1–2, 102, 183

Buchanan, Pat, 170, 275

Buckley, William, 118, 119

budget agreement: Bush's veto of, 161; character/promises/attitude and, 171–72; defining moments of, 167–72; Democrats accomplishment of, 166; division caused by, 159–62, 173–79; economy influenced by, 159, 169–70, 172; Gallup poll on, 161; House/Senate and, 161; income inequality and, 159–60; lobbying for, 160; Medicare/Medicaid influenced by, 166; poll on, 160; projected growth discussion and, 159; proposals for, 157–58; spending caps and, 165; stopgap spending resolutions and, 162; tax increases and, 159–60

budget politics: by Clinton, Bill, 173–79; conventional wisdom of, 149–50; Democrats and, 168–69

budget summit: at Andrews Air Force Base, 157–58; Bush, George H. W. and, 149–79; CBO numbers and, 173–74; Darman on, 153, 155; deadlines for, 154, 156–57; division caused by, 153–54, 156; Fitzwater/Sununu on, 152–53; gamesmanship and, 156–58; as high stakes gamble, 175; income inequality and, 155, 169; income taxes and, 158; media and, 152–53; negotiations and, 152–56, 171, 177; power stakes and, 172; spending cuts and, 154; Sununu on, 157–58; tax increases and, 153–55, 164–65

Buenos Aires Protocol of 1936, 40

Bundy, McGeorge, 31, 37, 52, 62, 64, 69; on operational risk, 41–42; on stalemate option, 53–54

Bundy, William, 48, 52, 64

Burke, Arleigh, 31, 34

Bush administration (George W.): denials of, 234–36; hypothetical reasoning limits and, 238; intelligence inversion by, 229–36; intelligence use by, 223–27; Iraq invasion and, 223–27; media on, 224; neoconservatives and, 237; parallel governance and, 240; petropolitics and, 237–38; political pressure and, 229; unitary executive prerogatives by, 217, 238

Bush, George H. W., 117, 132; budget agreement veto by, 161; budget compromise of, 149; budget summit and, 149–79; credibility of, 172; defining moments of, 168–72; detail attention, lack of, 163; economy under, 151–52; Gallup poll on, 161, 166–67, 171; gamesmanship and, 179; government shut down by, 161–62, 168, 176; Gulf War and, 236; indecision/flip-flops of, 163–67; leadership failure by, 170; media and, 163–64; negotiations impacting, 171; no tax increase promise by, 149; promises broken by, 172; Republican leaders excluded by, 162, 166, 171–72; Rollins on, 167; on tax increases, 168, 170; vulnerability of, 166, 167–68

Bush, George W., 2, 5, 273; Blair and, 232–34; credibility gap of, 264; on intelligence fixing, 234–35; prewar intelligence and, 220–23; WHIG and, 227; on WMD, 218

Caddell, Patrick, 92–93, 267; on malaise, 99–100; memo from, 99; on truth, 107
Califano, Joseph, 102; firing/resignation of, 105–6
Carter, Jimmy, 5, 193, 195, 217, 249–50; cabinet control by, 105–7; Caddell on, 92–93; Camp David meetings and, 99–100, 109–10; economic downfall caused by, 100, 106; Eizenstat on, 91; Emergency Natural Gas Act by, 93–94; energy policy and, 91, 110; failure of, 107–8, 111; Fallows on, 98; Gallup poll and, 92, 96, 99, 104–5, 107; gasoline rationing and, 98–99; government control of, 100; health care reform proposals of, 204–5; humility of, 110–11; Kennedy, Ted, vs., 92; leadership of, 97–98; malaise speech and, 91–111; McCarthy on, 101; natural gas crisis and, 93; 1977–1978 Energy Program of, 93–98; 1979 Energy Proposals by, 98–99; on oil companies, 96–97; political position of, 92; as practiced politician/outsider, 108–9; proposals of, 94–95; public opinion on, 91; rhetoric of, 94, 103; speaking tendencies of, 101; speech canceled by, 100; as storyteller, 267; successes/accomplishments of, 97, 109; thematic presidency of, 92
Carville, James, 184
Casey, William, 125, 128–29; congressional testimony of, 133–34; Iran-Contra affairs and, 137–38; Meese and, 137
Castro, Fidel, 30, 70; assassination plan for, 38; internal threat of, 33

CBO. *See* Congressional Budget Office
CEA. *See* Council of Economic Advisers
Central Intelligence Agency (CIA): Bay of Pigs invasion and, 30–44; Contras support of, 116; forecasting problems by, 249; Iranian arms transfer and, 119–20; Kennedy, John's, approval of, 37; misinformation by, 37; performance distortion of, 32; as rouge elephant, 136–38; U-2 flights and, 13–14; Vietnam escalation evaluation of, 52
Chafee, Lincoln, 196
chemical/biological weapons labs: Alwan and, 222; Powell on, 222; prewar intelligence and, 221–22
Cheney, Dick, 154, 156, 164, 219, 223, 225, 237, 284
CIA. *See* Central Intelligence Agency
CINCPAC. *See* Commander-in-Chief, Pacific Command
Civil Aeronautics Act of 1938, 22
Clarke, Richard, 223, 230
Clifford, Clark, 49, 57, 60, 62
Clinton, Bill, 3, 5, 254–55; approval of, 193, 195, 198; backlash against, 194–95; bill vetoed by, 173; budget politics by, 173–79; budget proposal by, 178; budget/tax compromise of, 149; on compromise, 288; congressional majorities lost by, 211; credibility issue against, 168; delegation by, 183; economic program by, 191; gamesmanship and, 179; on government shut down, 176; on health care reform, 207; health care reform decisions by, 186–87; health care reform proposal by, 184, 191–92; ill-timed interventions by, 211; improvising by, 183; initiative of, 197; Iraq plans of, 236–37; Kristol on, 195–96; media and, 202; national interests perceived by, 210; Ornstein on, 285; party government support belief by, 207; personality of, 4–5,

268; policy carts before party horses and, 206–7; political gains of, 211; political position of, 208; political security of, 174; political weakness of, 206; power stakes and, 190, 191, 263; pressure felt by, 175; programmatic/value politics of, 258; race relations of, 259; rhetoric of, 265; Schick on, 203; spatial positioning vs. valence politics and, 208–9; speech by, 192–93; Starr on, 204; strategic/tactical failures of, 209–12; tax increase and, 170, 190; testimonial approach of, 209; veto threat by, 198; vulnerability of, 191

Clinton, Hillary, 176; backlash against, 194–95; drug company bashing by, 194; health reform task force and, 183, 187; media and, 202; program innovation by, 187, 210

Commander-in-Chief, Pacific Command (CINCPAC), 80

Commander, U.S. Military Assistance Command, Vietnam (COMUSMACV), 59

compellence: national security managers and, 50–51; utility of, 70–71; Vietnam escalation as, 65–67

COMUSMACV. *See* Commander, U.S. Military Assistance Command, Vietnam

Congress: framework laws and, 293; health care reform fragments and, 195–203; inferiority complex of, 293

Congressional Budget Office (CBO), 173; budget numbers based on, 173–74; economic forecast of, 248–49; on Health Security Act numbers, 198

Contras: Boland amendment and, 116; CIA support of, 116; financial aid to, 116, 117, 129–30, 134; military assistance for, 118; resupply operation of, 131

Cooper, Chester, 55, 66

Cooper-Grandy bill: on health care reform, 197; support for, 197

cost-benefit analysis, 2, 6; of Bay of Pigs invasion, 37; Johnson and, 70; of lying, 11

Council of Economic Advisers (CEA), 151; economic forecast of, 248–49

councils/counsels, reorganization of, 286

covert action: institutional reform of, 294–95; logic/technical issues for, 204

crisis situations: decision making and, 43; lying in, 11–12

culture, antipolitical: bounded rationality and, 260; compromise and, 257, 258; positioning and, 256–58; president's failure and, 263; president's feeding into, 257–58; spatial compromise/valence issues and, 260; values and, 258–59

Darman, Richard, 151, 153, 156, 157, 164, 167

Daschle Budget, 177

decision making: crisis situations and, 43; dysfunctions in, 7; by Kennedy, John, 34; limits of, 8; political vs. rational, 6–7, 253; presidents and, 287, 290, 296

deficit crisis of 1990, 150–52; Democrats and, 151–52; House/Senate and, 151–52; proposals for, 150; tax increase and, 150–52

de Gaulle, Charles, 19–20

DeLay, Tom, 152, 156, 159, 171, 175

Democrats: budget agreement accomplishment by, 166; budget politics and, 168–69; deficit crisis of 1990 and, 151–52; Iraq invasion and, 236–37

Diminished Presidency, authority/legitimacy regaining from, 290–91

disqualification heuristic, of Kennedy, John, 35

Dole, Bob, 158, 161, 174, 177, 196, 198, 202, 209; Gingrich and, 175; on tax rates, 165

Downing Street Memos: facts/intelligence fixed and, 234; for Iraq invasion, 231–34; regime change decision before, 234; on UN inspection, 233

Dulles, Allen, 13, 36–37, 43

Earned Income Tax Credit, 166

Eastland, James, 88

Eisenhower, Dwight, 2, 5, 36, 38, 43, 87, 262; authority of, 266; crisis containment by, 15–19; dilemma of, 17; Johnson and, 68; Krushchev and, 15–16; lying by, 12–13, 21; media criticism of, 23–25; operational failure of, 12–13; Paris Summit and, 19–20; presummit calculations by, 14–15; rejection/humiliation of, 21–22; responsibility of, 18, 19; risk assessment by, 13–14; *Time* on, 24; U-2 flights and, 11–26; on Vietnam escalation, 68–69

Eizenstat, Stuart, 91, 98, 99, 100

Ellsberg, Daniel, 64, 69

Emergency Energy Conservation Act, 99

Emergency Natural Gas Act, by Carter, 93–94

íEnergy and National Goalsî (Stewart), 99

The Enterprise: arms bought by, 124; creation of, 116; hostages and, 130–31; Iran arms trading with, 118, 120–21; North and, 116–18; profits of, 117–18; resupply operation of, 117, 130–31, 246

EOP. *See* Executive Office of the President

Executive Office of the President (EOP), 286

Export Administration Act of 1979, 126

FACA. *See* Federal Advisory Committee Act

failure: of Bay of Pigs invasion, 30–31, 43–44; failures vs., 288–89; performance vs., 3; in presidential fiascoes, 2

Fallows, James, 98

Federal Advisory Committee Act (FACA), violation of, 188

Federalist No. 47 (Madison), 238–39

The Federalist Papers, 115

Feith, Douglas, 224–25

Fitzwater, Marlin, 152–53; media and, 163

Foley, Tom, 151, 153

Ford, Gerald, 6, 110, 195, 217; advisors overruled by, 80; authority/values of, 89; on casualties, 86–87; on CIA forecasting, 249; delayed orders of, 80, 85–86; *Mayaguez* rescue and, 77–89, 246; public opinion polls on, 79; WPR disregarded by, 84–85

Foreign Assistance Act of 1961, 126

Fulbright, James William, 24–25, 35, 50, 63

Gallup poll: on budget agreement, 161; on Bush, George H. W., 161, 166–67, 171; Carter and, 92, 96, 99, 104–5, 107; on health care reform, 184, 185–86, 205; *Mayaguez* rescue and, 88; Vietnam escalation and, 69

gamesmanship, 2; budget summit and, 156–58; Clinton, Bill/Bush, George H. W., and, 179; combinations/types of, 255; failure at, 251; feel for, 287; game theory vs., 253–54; inappropriate situations for, 255–56; Kennedy, John, and, 36–38; presidents and, 251–56; rational decision making/system complexity of, 252–53; rules/limits of, 254; single-/multiple-, 255; Vietnam escalation and, 253

GAO. *See* General Accounting Office

General Accounting Office (GAO), 88

German Federal Intelligence Services (BND), 222

Ghorbanifar, Manucher: negotiations of, 122–23; North and, 123

Gingrich, Newt, 152, 156, 160, 171, 201, 209, 254, 257; on budget proposal, 159; Dole and, 175; on public support numbers, 177

Goodpastor, Andrew, 13, 55, 69

Gore, Al, 174, 194

governance, parallel, 238–40; INC and, 240; justification for, 238–39; in War on Terrorism, 217–18

government shut down: by Bush, George H. W., 161–62, 168, 176; Clinton, Bill, on, 176; responsibility for, 176–77

Graham, Bob, 231, 235

Gramm, Phil, 157

Gramm-Rudman-Hollings Act (GRH), 150; deficit targets of, 157

Greenberg, Stanley, 185, 193

Greene, Wallace, 57, 61

Greenfield, Meg, 107, 172

Greenspan, Alan, 160, 237

GRH. *See* Gramm-Rudman-Hollings Act

groupthink: presidential advisors and, 32; Vietnam escalation as, 48

Guilmartin, John, 88

Hadley, Stephen, 221, 225, 226

Haggerty, Jim, 17, 19

Halberstam, David, 47

hard problems: experts/expertise and, 248–49; faulty data and, 248–50; presidential advisors and, 247–48; presidents and, 247–51; satisficing vs. satisfiability of, 247–48

health care: of Americans vs. other countries, 184; coverage lost for, 212; as issue, 184–86; major changes in, 204; as midterm election issue, 206

health care reform: backlash against, 194–95; bipartisan support needed for, 208; Carter's proposals for, 205; Chafee's proposal for, 196; Clinton, Bill, on, 207; Clinton, Bill's, proposal for, 184, 191–92; complexity of, 192–93; Congress fragments and, 195–203; Cooper-Grandy bill on, 197; death of, 203; division caused by, 205, 207; employers concerns for, 186; financing for, 205; Gallup poll on, 184, 185–86, 205; huge task of, 204; Kerrey's proposal for, 184; media on, 200–201; Michel's proposal for, 196; moderation of, 197; NFIB against, 194; power stakes and, 210; program planning for, 186–91; public opinion polls on, 209–10; reverse lobbying for, 195; by Roosevelt/Truman/Johnson, 204; single-payer, 185, 197; strategic/tactical failures and, 209–12; tax increase for, 185, 192; as three-tier system, 211–12; universal coverage, 185; what ifs regarding, 203–6; Wofford/Carville on, 184

Health Insurance Association of America (HIAA), 186

Health Security Act: abortion debate and, 201; benefits and, 201–2; CBO on, 198; complexity/understanding of, 200; division caused by, 193, 196–97; lobbying against, 199–200; public on, 200–201; support for, 196–97; tax savings from, 197

Herter, Christian, 18, 19, 21; testify of, 25

HIAA. *See* Health Insurance Association of America

Hilsman, Roger, 34, 51

Humphrey, Hubert, 49, 50, 60

Hussein, Saddam, 166; bin Laden alliance with, 223

ICBM. *See* intercontinental ballistic missile

INC. *See* Iraqi National Congress

Information Warriors, INC established by, 225–26

intelligence operations: congressional oversight bypass and, 127–28; laws regulating, 125–27

Intelligence Oversight Act of 1980, violation of, 127

Intelligence Oversight Act of 1991, 297n24–298n24

intercontinental ballistic missile (ICBM), 14–15

International Atomic Energy Agency (IAEA), Nigerian yellowcake dismissal of, 220–21

Iran-Contra affair: Becket scenario hypothesis of, 138–39; Casey and, 137–38; characteristics of, 115; covert operations of, 115; cover-up/presidential containment for, 131–32; disclosure of, 134; diversion document on, 141; funding for, 116; media and, 134; Nicaragua intervention and, 116–18; no direct orders for, 138–39; plausible deniability hypothesis of, 139–40; president' role hypothesis for, 135–42; Reagan and, 115–42; risk assessment and, 247; rogue elephant hypothesis of, 136–38; as smoking gun, 140–42; unraveling operations of, 130–34; Walsh on, 135. *See also* Iranian arms transfers

Iranian arms transfers, 118–25; from America, 120–21; approval of, 119; CIA and, 119–20; with The Enterprise, 118, 120–21; exposure of, 124; failed negotiations of, 122–25; funding for, 124; go-between negotiations for, 121–22; hostages and, 119–20, 121–25, 132; from Israel, 118–20; Meese inquiry of, 132–34; opposition to, 119; Poindexter on, 133; Reagan on, 132; Shultz on, 119; speculation of, 131–32

Iraq: aluminum centrifuges and, 221; chemical/biological weapons lab and, 221–22; Clinton, Bill's, plans for, 236–37; Nigerian yellowcake and, 220–21; al-Qaeda connection and, 222–23; regime change of, 230–31; WMD/terrorism and, 220

Iraqi National Congress (INC), 220; Information Warriors establishment of, 225–26; parallel governance and, 240

Iraq invasion, 293; administration denials and, 234–36; agency discretion and, 228–29; Bush administration and, 223–27; democratization/neocons and, 236–37; Downing Street Memos for, 231–34; early military planning for, 230–31; Greenspan on, 237; hypothetical reasoning limits and, 238; intelligence/policy failure and, 228–29; intentions and, 228; media and, 234–35; NSC and, 230–31; petropolitics and, 237–38; Pillar on, 235–36; political pressure for, 229; prewar intelligence for, 220–23; public opinion shaping and, 232–33; Rice on, 231; run-up to, 218–20; Senate Select Intelligence Committee against, 235; Straw on, 232; as war of choice, 236–38

Iraq Survey Group (ISG), 219

ISG. *See* Iraq Survey Group

Israel, Iranian arms transfer by, 118–20

Jackson, Andrew, 6, 264

Jackson, Robert, 271, 295

Jacobsen, David, 122, 131

JCS. *See* Joint Chiefs of Staff

Jefferson, Thomas, 6, 206, 269, 270

Johnson, Lyndon, 1, 5, 24, 104, 204, 249; Ball and, 50; conventional wisdom of, 67–68; credibility gap of, 264; deception of, 57–58; Eisenhower and, 68; media and, 63–64; military pressure from, 58; nation's status and, 64; political risk and, 68; power

stakes of, 67; presidential advisors
and, 48–49, 60–64, 250; risk
management by, 69–71; USS *Pueblo*
negotiations and, 78; Vietnam
escalation and, 47–71
Joint Chiefs of Staff (JCS), *Mayaguez*
rescue planned by, 79
Jordan, Hamilton, 106; authority of, 106

Kennedy, John F., 5, 65, 87, 101, 255,
272, 286; anti-Communist stance of,
42–43; authority restoration of, 266;
Bay of Pigs invasion and, 1, 29–44;
CIA approval of, 37; disqualification
heuristic of, 35; failure of, 43–44;
national security decision making of,
34; possible perception of, 43; power
stakes and, 42–44; presidential choice
of, 35; rational trade-offs by, 39–40;
risk assessment and, 41–42; risk
management/gamesmanship and,
36–38
Kennedy, Ted, Carter, Jimmy vs., 92
Kerrey, Bob, 202; health care reform
proposal by, 184
Khmer Rouge regime: casualties of, 84;
confrontation and, 78; *Mayaguez*
capture by, 78–79
Khrushchev, Nikita, 12, 255; apology
demanded by, 19–20; Bay of Pigs
invasion and, 31; Eisenhower and,
15–16; lying by, 19; Paris Summit
and, 19–20; political position of, 16
Kissinger, Henry, 77, 80, 273; on
Mayaguez rescue, 78, 86
Kistiakowski, George, 21–22
Kristol, William, 195–96, 209

leadership: Bush, George H. W.'s, failure
of, 170; of Carter, 97–98; ìhidden
handî style of, 38, 42, 262;
presidential fiascoes and, 4–6; Reagan
on, 264
learning curves: failures vs. failure,
288–89; *Mayaguez* rescue and, 88–89;

for presidency, 287–90; presidential
fiascoes and, 1–2; toward presidential
options theory, 289–90
Ledeen, Michael, 118, 119
Libby, Lewis ìScooter,î 225, 226, 236
al-Libi, Ibn al-Shaykh, Hussein/bin
Laden alliance claimed by, 223
Lincoln, Abraham, 6, 92, 103, 269, 270
Lippmann, Walter, 18, 24
Lott, Trent, 160, 173
lying: benefits/costs of, 11; cost-benefit
analysis of, 11; in crisis situations,
11–12; diplomatic view of, 11; by
Eisenhower, 12–13, 21; by
Khrushchev, 19

Madison, James, 238–39; partial
separation and, 239
Magaziner, Ira, 187, 191, 206, 207, 208,
251; program innovation by, 187,
210; secrecy imposed by, 188; tax
increase proposed by, 189
malaise speech: American democracy
threat identified by, 101; on
American spirit crisis, 102; blames
placed by, 103–4; Carter and, 91–111;
debate over, 99–100; on
faith/confidence, 102, 104; future
vision lack of, 101–2; media and, 100,
102–3, 104; poll after, 104–5;
proposals from, 102; rhetorical
contradictions of, 103; visual imagery
by, 104
Manning, David, on Rice, 231–32
Mann, Thomas, 34, 35
Mansfield, Mike, 49, 63, 85
Mayaguez rescue: accurate intelligence
for, 79; casualties during, 82–83, 84;
conflicting stories of, 82–83; crew
endangerment during, 80, 83, 89; as
crisis, 86; crisis prompting, 77–81;
delay for, 80, 85–86, 89; Eastland on,
88; Ford and, 77–89, 246; Gallup
polls and, 88; GAO on, 88;
Guilmartin on, 88; JCS plan for, 79;

Kissinger on, 78; learning curve and, 88–89; location for, 79; media on, 81–82; military force for, 79; military plans for, 80–81; Miller and, 77; note requesting release before, 79; O'Neill on, 87; regret expressed regarding, 87; Scowcroft on, 78, 86; Steele on, 77; success claims of, 81–84, 87; Thai government and, 87
McCarthy, Eugene, 101
McFarlane, Robert, 79, 117, 118, 119, 136–37, 139–40
McNamara, Robert, 2, 34, 49, 57, 60, 66; prediction of, 65; stalemate option and, 52–56, 63–64; Vietnam escalation and, 47–48
mechanism, fail safe, for presidents, 281–82
media: on Bay of Pigs invasion/Kennedy, John, 43; budget summit and, 152–53; on Bush administration, 224; Bush, George H. W., 163–64; on Carter's cabinet resignation, 106–7; Clinton, Bill/Hillary, and, 202; Fitzwater and, 163; on health care reform, 200–201; Iran-Contra affairs and, 134; Iraq invasion and, 234–35; Johnson/Vietnam escalation and, 63–64; malaise speech and, 100, 102–3, 104; on *Mayaguez* rescue, 81–82; National Health Care Campaign and, 197; personality and, 268; presidential authority and, 266; president's strategies of, 267, 291; on U-2 flights/Eisenhower, 23–25
Medicare/Medicaid: budget agreement influencing, 166; efficiencies of, 176; funding for, 178; overhaul proposal for, 212; spending cuts for, 190
Meese, Edwin A., 120, 121, 125, 132; Casey and, 137; Iranian arms transfer inquiry by, 132–34
MEOW. *See* moral equivalent of war
Meyer, Christopher, 230, 232
Michel, Robert, 192, 196, 209

micromanagement, 29, 89, 246
Miller, Charles T., 77
Mitchell, George, 152, 155, 159, 165
Mondale, Walter, 93, 100
Montevideo Convention of 1933, 40
moral equivalent of war (MEOW): Carter's rhetoric as, 94; 1977–1978 Energy Program as, 94
Moynihan, Patrick, 193, 201, 207
MRP. *See* Revolutionary Movement of the People

National Federation of Independent Businesses (NFIB), 186; against health care reform, 194
National Health Care Campaign, 197
National Intelligence Board, 62
National Intelligence Estimate (NIE): incorrect assessments of, 228; on WMD, 218
National Leadership Coalition for Health-Care Reform, 195
National Liberation Front (NLF), 56
National Security Council (NSC), 78; Boland amendment and, 130; Iraq invasion planning and, 230–31; national success model of, 237
national security managers: compellence and, 50–51; optimism of, 51
natural gas crisis: Carter and, 93; public's belief of, 97
Neustadt, Richard, 7, 248, 261–62
New Republic, 24, 43, 198
Newsweek, 24, 82, 102, 107, 164
New York Times, 16, 43, 81, 102
NFIB. *See* National Federation of Independent Businesses
Nguyen Cao Ky, 52, 55
NHOA. *See* Nicaraguan Humanitarian Assistance Office
Nicaragua, 116–18
Nicaraguan Humanitarian Assistance Office (NHOA), 117
NIE. *See* National Intelligence Estimate

Nigeria yellowcake: IAEA dismissal of, 220–21; uranium sell and, 220–21

1977–1978 Energy Program: by Carter, 93–98; complexity of, 95; conservation/tax credits and, 95; House/Senate reaction to, 95–97; as MEOW, 94; modification of, 97; O'Neill and, 95–96; proposals of, 94–95

1979 Energy Proposals: by Carter, 98–99; House/Senate reaction to, 98–99

Nixon, Richard, 4–5, 20, 43, 64, 110, 204, 262

NLF. *See* National Liberation Front

North, Oliver, 116–18, 121, 239; delusion of, 123–24; firing of, 140; Ghorbanifar and, 123; McFarlane on, 136–37; negotiations of, 122

NSC. *See* National Security Council

OAS Charter: Article 6 of, 41; Article 15 of, 41

ìOf Crisis and Opportunityî (Caddell), 92

Office of Independent Counsel (OIC), 135

Office of Management and Budget (OMB), 151; deficit predicted by, 155–56; economic forecast of, 248–49

Office of Special Plans (OSP), 224

OIC. *See* Office of Independent Counsel

OMB. *See* Office of Management and Budget

Omnibus Budget Reconciliation Act of 1990, deficit reduction/tax increase by, 165–66

Omnibus Diplomatic Security and Anti-Terrorism Act of 1986, 125–26

O'Neill, Tip, 87, 95–96

OPEC price cartel, 238; gas price hikes by, 98

Operation Desert Shield, budget process influenced by, 156

Ornstein, Norman, 285

Panetta, Leon, 206, 284; budget proposal of, 174

Paris Summit: conspiracy against, 20–21; Eisenhower/Khrushchev and, 19–20

partial separation: Madison and, 239; president's use of, 239

performance: failure vs., 3; in presidential fiascoes, 2; White House paradox for, 4, 283

personality: of Clinton, Bill, 4–5; media and, 268; of Nixon, 4–5; presidential fiascoes and, 4–6; Prussian General Staff classification of, 4

Pillar, Paul, 235–36

Poindexter, John, 120, 121, 126, 133, 139–40

Policy Counterterrorism Evaluation Group: Cheney on, 225; Feith's briefings of, 224–25

politics: petro-, 237–38; professionalism in, 288; solution vs. process, 93; spatial positioning vs. valence, 208–9, 258–59

positioning, 2; compromise and, 257; Gingrich on, 257; professional terms of, 288; public opinion on, 256; spatial, 208–9; as success/failure determinant, 256; valence, 260

Powell, Colin, 59, 99, 100, 121, 226; information challenged by, 226–27; on mobile chemical/biological weapons labs, 222

Powers, Francis Gary, 4n26, 12

power stakes, 2; budget summit and, 172; Clinton, Bill, and, 190, 191, 263; health care reform and, 210; of Johnson, 67; Kennedy, John, and, 42–44; miscalculation of, 70–71; national agenda and, 262–63; Neustadt on, 261–62; presidential fiascoes and, 7–8, 246, 260–63; protection of, 29, 86–88, 279, 281; understanding of, 261

prerogative power: assertion of, 273; congressional oversight bypassed and, 127–28; court legislation on, 271–72; decisions for, 271; Ford's use of, 84–86; framework laws regarding, 142; funding cutoff violation and, 129–30; gentleman's agreement violation and, 128–29; Hamiltonian concept of, 271; Jackson, Robert, on, 271; legitimacy of, 294; Madisonian concept of, 271; operation legality and, 125–27, 272; overshoot/collapse of, 142; Poindexter on, 126; Reagan and, 115; as ìsoftî strategy, 272–73; uses of, 270–71

presidency: equilibrium point and, 288; framework laws adherence and, 292–94; internal safeguards for, 294; learning curves for, 287–90; reinvention of, 283–87

president(s): accountability of, 246, 293; agenda control by, 259; amateurs vs. professional, 5, 263; American values and, 275; audiences for, 267–68, 291–92; behavior modification of, 262–63; command reinvention by, 282; communication and, 246, 291; compromise and, 258, 288–89; Constitutional violation of, 271; councils/counsels for, 286–87; critics and, 274; decision making and, 287, 290, 296; dispensing power of, 269–70; fail safe mechanisms for, 281–82; failure avoidance of, 296; failure of, 245–46; finesse/resilience of, 295–96; gamesmanship and, 251–56; game theory and, 255–56; hard problems and, 247–51; historical analogies and, 252; impeachment threat for, 273; intelligence sources for, 274; law versions superimposed by, 239; legislative/inherent/implied powers of, 270; maneuverability of, 289; media strategies by, 267, 291; micromanagement and, 29, 89, 246; operational understanding of,

282–83; opponents of, 265–66; partial separation used by, 239; personal involvement of, 284–85; polls/focus groups for, 265; problems compounded by, 263; professionalism/precision of, 295–96; public's trust for, 256, 265; public vs. political interest of, 5; quasi-rational approach of, 260; rallying for, 87; rational choice of, 253–54; risk assessments and, 245–47; risk management of, 281–82; risk normalization by, 252; staff balance for, 284–86; staff/help for, 284–86; strategic approach and, 7; valid information given to, 248; yellow flags for, 281

presidential advisors. *See* advisors, presidential

presidential authority: action justification and, 264; credibility gaps and, 279; Jackson, Andrew, and, 264; loss of, 250, 264–68; media and, 266; presidential legitimacy vs., 273–74; regaining of, 290–95; as relationship, 264; sustainability of, 266

presidential fiascoes: avoidance of, 296; failure machine and, 6–8; learning curves and, 1–2; limited rational choice and, 279; McNamara on, 2; ìnormal accidentsî as, 282, 283; performance vs. failure in, 2–4; personality/leadership and, 4–6; possible percentage for, 282; power stakes and, 7–8, 246, 260–63; presidential advisors and, 6, 250–51; regime creation and, 6; responsibility for, 295; risk management and, 280; transaction style of, 5–6

presidential legitimacy: determinant of, 269; loss of, 268–75; party split and, 274–75; presidential authority vs., 273–74; regaining of, 290–95

presidential options theory, learning curve toward, 289–90

President's Task Force on National
Health Care Reform: Clinton, Hillary,
as director of, 187; cluster groups
and, 187; financial scheme by,
189–90; lawsuit brought against,
188–89; recommendations proposed
by, 190; skeptics on, 187; support for,
188; working groups and, 187–88
prewar intelligence: aluminum
centrifuges and, 221; Bush, George
W., and, 220–23; chemical/biological
weapons lab and, 221–22; as
input/output, 229–36; Nigerian
yellowcake, 220–21; al-Qaeda
connection and, 222–23
program innovation: by Clinton,
Hillary/Magaziner, 187, 210; Jefferson
on, 205; before party horses, 206–7
Prussian General Staff, personality
classification by, 4

al-Qaeda, Iraq connection with,
222–23
Quayle, Dan, 164, 171

Rafsanjani, Hojatolislam Hashemi, 122,
131
Rafshoon, Gerald, 99, 100
rational choice, 2; irrationalities of,
38–40; limits of, 253–54, 279; nested
games and, 254
Reagan, Ronald, 103, 239, 264, 266, 272;
blackmail potential caused by, 124;
Boland amendments and, 129–30;
briefing of, 141–42; congressional
oversight bypass by, 127–28; covert
operations and, 115, 130; deception
of, 136–38; funding cutoff violation
by, 129–30; gentleman's agreement
violation by, 128–29; Iran-Contra
affair and, 115–42; on Iranian arms
transfers, 132; Nicaragua intervention
and, 116–18; North on, 140; plausible
deniability of, 139–40; prerogative
power and, 115; Shultz and, 132; tax

increase and, 170; testimony of, 135;
Tower Commission on, 135, 136
Regan, Donald, 119, 120, 132, 284
regime creation, presidential fiascoes
and, 6
Revolutionary Movement of the People
(MRP), 39
Rice, Condoleezza, 223, 226, 231
Rickey, Branch, 245, 284
risk assessment, 25–26; Arrow on, 249;
by Eisenhower, 13–14; Iran-Contra
affair and, 247; Kennedy, John, and,
41–42; presidents and, 245–47; of U-
2 flights, 13–14
risk management, 2; by Johnson, 69–71;
Kennedy, John, and, 36–38; limits to,
289; presidential fiascoes and, 280;
presidents and, 281–82
Rockefeller, Jay, 176, 225
Rollins, Ed, 153, 167
Roosevelt, Franklin, 5, 6, 93, 204, 270,
275, 286, 295
Rostenkowski, Dan, 164–65
Rumsfeld, Donald, 220, 225, 230
Rusk, Dean, 1, 30, 31, 34, 49, 57, 62, 64,
66
Russell, Richard, 63, 68

Schick, Allen, 203
Schlesinger, James, 80; energy proposals
of, 94; firing/resignation of, 105–6;
job security of, 99; oil prediction by,
249; task force organized by, 94
Scowcroft, Brent, 78, 79, 86
Secord, Richard, 116, 121
Senate Select Intelligence Committee,
against Iraq invasion, 235
September 11, 2001, terrorist attacks on,
219
Shalala, Donna, 186–87, 190
Shultz, George, 119, 120, 121, 125, 273;
Reagan and, 132
Smith, William French, 120, 126, 137
Sorensen, Theodore, 266–67, 284
South Vietnamese Army (ARVN), 55

Soviets: legitimate complaints of, 21; propaganda by, 21–22; U-2 flights and, 11–26
Starr, Paul, 189, 204
Steele, George P., 77
Stevenson, Adlai, 30, 35
Stewart, Gordon, 99, 100
Straw, Jack, 232, 233
Sununu, John, 151, 152–53, 157, 160, 163, 167, 172

tax increase: bipartisan commitment to, 152; Bush, George H. W., on, 168, 170; Clinton, Bill, and, 170, 190; for health care reform, 185, 192; as ideological principal issue, 169; Magaziner's proposal for, 189; poll on, 151, 169; Reagan and, 170; Republicans on, 152; by Rostenkowski, 164–65; spending cuts and, 167
Taylor, Maxwell, 48, 49, 51, 57
Taylor, Telford, 22, 24
Tenet, George, 221, 235
Thai government, *Mayaguez* rescue and, 87
ìThe Deuce,î flight of, 12–13
Thompson, Llewellyn, 18, 19
Time, 107, 163, 171; on U-2 flights/Eisenhower, 23–24
Tower Commission, 135, 136
Truman, Harry, 204, 210

U-2 flights, 87; airspace sovereignty and, 22–23; CIA and, 13–14; cover story for, 16; discovery of, 14; Eisenhower/Soviets and, 11–26; importance of, 15; justification for, 17, 23; legitimacy problem of, 22–23; media on, 19, 23–25; operational failure of, 12–13; questions regarding, 17; risk assessment of, 13–14; statements regarding, 18; suspension of, 19; *Time* on, 24; usefulness of, 2n26, 14; White on, 16, 17, 18

UN. *See* United Nations
United Nations (UN), WMD inspections by, 233–34
United Nations Charter: Article 4 of, 40; Article 5 of, 40
U.S. News and World Report, 102, 106, 164
USS *Pueblo*: capture of, 78; Johnson negotiations and, 78

Vance, Cyrus, 55, 105
Vietcong: political solution for, 52–53; Vietnam escalation and, 51; violence by, 53
Vietnam: Ball on, 49; Communist politics in, 70; deteriorating situation of, 48; game playing of, 65; knowledge, lack of, 49; presidential advisors on, 49–50; South's independence in, 53; stalemate option and, 52–56, 66, 70
Vietnam escalation, 59; American support of, 61, 64; Ball's objections to, 49–50, 52, 54, 60–61; Bundy, William, on, 48; CIA evaluation of, 52; Clifford on, 62; as compellence, 65–67; debates on, 60–64; decisions before escalation of, 48–52; destruction of, 66; Eisenhower on, 68–69; failure of, 61; favorable outcomes of, 56; Gallup poll and, 69; gamesmanship and, 253; game theory and, 74n95; as groupthink, 47; Halberstam on, 47; Humphrey on, 50; impact of, 65; Johnson and, 47–71; as limited war, 66; McNamara and, 47–48, 60; media and, 63–64; military role of, 57–58; moral/legal questions regarding, 57; National Intelligence Board on, 62; negotiations for, 54–56; policy for, 62–63, 66, 69–70; presidential advisors and, 48–50, 56–57; price tag for, 60, 63; as quagmire, 47; Taylor, Maxwell, on, 51; troop increase and,

51–52, 53, 55, 61, 63, 64; Vietcong
and, 51; Westmoreland on, 57;
withdrawal of, 61, 65

Walsh, Lawrence, 135
War on Terrorism: military phase of,
219; parallel governance in, 217–18,
240
War Powers Resolution of 1973 (WPR),
292; Ford's disregard for, 84–85;
procedures of, 84–85
Washington Post, 102, 198
Watergate break-in, 262
weapons of mass destruction (WMD):
Bush, George W., on, 219; intelligence
on, 235; NIE on, 218;
rationale/reason and, 236–38; UN
inspections for, 233–34; unknown
location of, 219, 238
Weinberger, Caspar, 119, 120
Westmoreland, William, 49, 53, 55, 57,
63

Wheeler, Earl, 51, 53, 62–63
WHIG. *See* White House Intelligence
Group
White House: on budget deficit
problem, 155; decision making of, 3;
new thinking regarding, 280–83;
performance paradox of, 4, 283;
predictable failure patterns of, 280
White House Intelligence Group
(WHIG), 226–27; Bush, George W.,
and, 227
White, Lincoln, 16, 17, 18
Whitewater stonewalling, Broder on, 1–2
Wilkerson, Lawrence, 226–27
Will, George, 103, 198
Wilson, Woodrow, 5, 92, 270
WMD. *See* weapons of mass destruction
Wofford, Harris, 206, 211; on health care
reform, 184
Wolfowitz, Paul, 232, 236
WPR. *See* War Powers Resolution of
1973

About the Author

Richard M. Pious holds the Adolph and Effie Ochs Chair in American Studies at Barnard College, where he has taught political science since 1973. He is also on the faculty of the Graduate School of Arts and Sciences at Columbia University, where he has taught since 1968.

His books include: *The American Presidency* (1979); *The President, Congress and the Constitution* (1984) coauthored with Christopher Pyle; *The Presidency* (1996); and *The War on Terrorism and the Rule of Law* (2006). He edited the centennial volume of the Academy of Political Science, *The Power to Govern* (1982) and its follow-up volume, *Presidents, Elections and Democracy* (1992). He has published articles in numerous journals, including *Political Science Quarterly, Presidential Studies Quarterly, Politics and Society, The Saint Louis University Law Journal, The Wisconsin Law Review, The Journal of International Affairs,* and *The Journal of Armed Forces and Society.* He has written articles in Russian for *Za Rubeshom* and *Pravda,* for *USA,* the journal of the Institute for the USA and Canada of the Russian Academy of Sciences, and in French for the *Journal des Elections* in Paris. He has been a consultant in several presidential election campaigns, an adviser to congressional committees dealing with presidential war powers, and a consultant to foreign governments on presidential powers. He has been on panels that rated the presidents for *New York Times Magazine* and *Chicago Sun-Times.* He served on the international advisory board of *Journal des Elections,* on the editorial board of *Political Science Quarterly,* and currently is a member of the editorial advisory board of *Presidential Studies Quarterly.*

Breinigsville, PA USA
15 March 2010
234154BV00001B/3/P